T0168160

THE FALL OF THE REPUBLIC
AND OTHER POLITICAL SATIRES

AMBROSE BIERCE

THE FALL OF THE REPUBLIC
AND OTHER POLITICAL SATIRES

EDITED BY S. T. JOSHI
AND DAVID E. SCHULTZ

THE UNIVERSITY OF TENNESSEE PRESS / KNOXVILLE

Copyright © 2000 by The University of Tennessee Press / Knoxville.
All Rights Reserved. Manufactured in the United States of America.
First Edition.

The paper used in this book meets the minimum requirements of ANSI/NISO Z39.48-
1992 (R 1997) (Permanence of Paper). The binding materials have been chosen for strength
and durability.

Library of Congress Cataloging-in-Publication Data

Bierce, Ambrose, 1842–1914?
The fall of the republic and other political satires / Ambrose Bierce; edited by S. T. Joshi
and David E. Schultz.— 1st ed.
        p. cm.
Includes bibliographical references.
ISBN 1-57233-095-3 (cl.: alk. paper)
ISBN 1-57233-096-1 (pbk.: alk. paper)
1. United States—Politics and government—Humor. 2. Political satire, American.
I. Joshi, S. T., 1958– II. Schultz, David E., 1952– III. Title.
PS1097 .A6 2000c   00-008439

CONTENTS

ESSAYS

INTRODUCTION

THIS VOLUME CONTAINS a variety of political writings spanning Ambrose Bierce's long career as a journalist, editorialist, and fiction writer. Some were included in his *Collected Works* (1909–12) but were not subsequently reprinted; others have never been reprinted since their appearance in newspapers and magazines from 1868 to 1910. Collectively, they represent some of the liveliest, wittiest, and most penetrating satires of the nineteenth century, establishing Bierce as America's Jonathan Swift and a mordant commentator on the political, social, legal, and intellectual failings of his countrymen.

Virtually the entire work of Ambrose Bierce (1842–1914?) is satirical in origin and function, not excluding his gripping tales of the Civil War and his stories of the supernatural. In his political satires he employs fantasy, comic exaggeration, parody, and deadpan humor to convey his criticism of a wide range of American social and political institutions. These satires are of two separate but related types: one, a series of sketches purportedly written by a historian of the distant future looking back upon the nineteenth and twentieth centuries; the other, a group of tales set in imaginary realms whose customs, laws, and traditions bear striking resemblances to (and differences from) those of America in Bierce's day. Bierce would not be entirely satisfied if his readers were merely to appreciate the cleverness and imaginative richness of his satires; as the essays and editorials (most of them not reprinted since their original appearances a century and more ago) included in the second part of this volume indicate, his criticisms were heartfelt and of long standing. And because they broach some of the most fundamental, sensitive, and still unresolved issues of American political thought, they continue to command interest and attention.

Bierce's satirical sketches began to appear at the very outset of his literary career. After serving in some of the bloodiest battles of the Civil War, he made his way to San Francisco and, in 1867, started publishing in some of the city's local publications. By 1868 he was an irregular contributor to the *San Francisco News Letter;* several sketches and articles that appeared at that time were later gathered in his early volumes, *The Fiend's Delight* (1873) and *Nuggets and Dust*

(1873). Many other items were never so collected, and only a careful study of Bierce's early stylistic mannerisms allows us to ascribe to him certain anonymous or pseudonymous works published in the *News Letter* prior to his assumption of that paper's editorship in December 1868. Six such items are contained herein: a series of four "Letters from a Hdkhoite" (April 1868), "The Aborigines of Oakland" (November 7, 1868), and "A Scientific Dream" (November 14, 1868). If these sketches are in fact by Bierce—both their style and their content seem unmistakably to be his—then the second item is the first of his future histories, while the "Letters" are the first of that group of tales set in a fantastic land. A seventh item—"Across the Continent" (*News Letter,* May 15, 1869)—appeared when Bierce was the editor of the paper and was signed with the pseudonym "Samboles." Although Bierce did not explicitly acknowledge the story as his, we believe that its attribution to him is secure.

It was not until Bierce migrated to England, where he lived from 1872 to 1875, that he resumed the writing of political satires. Amidst the enormous mass of journalism he produced during this period—including regular columns and contributions to the London papers *Figaro* and *Fun,* along with occasional appearances elsewhere—is a solitary item, "John Smith," appearing in *Fun* for May 10, 1873. Bierce included this future history, first published anonymously, in the first volume of his *Collected Works.*

Bierce returned to San Francisco in 1875. For two years he was literarily quiescent, but in March 1877 he resumed journalistic work. During his tenure with two weekly papers, the *Argonaut* (1877–79) and the *Wasp* (1881–86), he wrote only a single item that might be classed thematically among the other stories in this book: "'The Bubble Reputation,'" a brief futuristic whimsy appearing in the *Wasp* for May 8, 1886.[1] Bierce reprinted it among the "negligible tales" in the eighth volume (1911) of his *Collected Works.*

It was only when Bierce joined the *San Francisco Examiner* in 1887 as William Randolph Hearst's star editorial writer that both his political satires and his short fiction began appearing in great numbers. During his first five years with the *Examiner,* Bierce published the bulk of the stories he included in his two landmark collections, *Tales of Soldiers and Civilians* (1891) and *Can Such Things Be?* (1893). The former (later retitled *In the Midst of Life*) contained Civil War tales as well as tales of what is now termed *psychological horror,* whereas the latter consisted chiefly of stories of the supernatural. During this time a third body of fiction began to emerge—his political satires.

One week after he published the brief but amusing "For the Ahkoond" in the *Examiner* for March 18, 1888, the major satire "The Fall of the Republic: An Article from a 'Court Journal' of the Thirty-first Century" appeared, occupying four columns of that Sunday's feature section of the *Examiner.* Its appearance at that time was probably no accident. In January, Edward Bellamy's *Looking Backward: 2000–1887* was published, quickly reaching bestseller status and becoming one of the most widely discussed books of the later nineteenth century. This utopian novel, which proposed a radical redistribution of wealth to achieve social and economic equality, embodied political principles very different from those held by Bierce; and "The Fall of the Republic" may be among the earliest of the many responses to and imitations of Bellamy's novel that appeared over the next several decades.

Only a few weeks later Bierce published a lengthy sketch, "The Kingdom of Tortirra." It was the first of eleven pieces published between 1888 and 1907 that Bierce weaved together into the Swiftian satire "The Land Beyond the Blow," which at 21,000 words constitutes his longest work of fiction. The first four pieces appeared in 1888–89. After a hiatus of a full decade, three more appeared in 1898–99, and the remaining four were published sporadically in 1903–7. The result is somewhat of a hodgepodge, featuring a mixture of political satire, philosophical ruminations, and send-ups of current events such as the Spanish-American War. Nevertheless, as Bierce's most imaginative flight of fancy it deserves wider recognition.

The Future Historian began appearing with frequency as a narrator of Bierce's satires (along with such other characters as the Timorous Reporter, the Curmudgeon Philosopher, the Sentimental Bachelor, and the Bald Campaigner) in short pieces written shortly after Bierce moved to Washington, D.C., for health reasons in late 1899. At this time his work was being syndicated nearly simultaneously in Hearst's *New York Journal* (later *American*) and the *Examiner;* in some cases, his contributions appeared in only one paper or the other. Several of the Future Historian sketches were merely nested within such recurring columns of editorial commentary as "Prattle," "The Passing Show," or "The Views of One"; others were published as self-standing articles. Bierce gathered only three of these pieces—those that had appeared in Hearst's magazine *Cosmopolitan* in 1908–9—under the heading "The Future Historian" in the twelfth volume (1912) of his *Collected Works.*

As early as 1895 Bierce had assembled a collection of his political satires under the title *The Fall of the Republic and Other Satires.* For more than a decade he tirelessly shopped the book around to various publishers, but to no avail. The first we hear of the enterprise is in early January 1896,[2] when Bierce prods the Chicago publisher Stone & Kimball to make a decision on the book; the tone of Bierce's remarks suggests that the publisher had retained the manuscript for some time. In the absence of any specifications by Bierce, it is difficult to ascertain what items could have been included in this volume. "The Fall of the Republic" itself, in its original version, is only

6,250 words, while the first four segments of what later became "The Land Beyond the Blow" would only have added another 13,500 words. If "John Smith," "For the Ahkoond," and another brief futuristic story, "The Strike of 1899" (1895), were included, the total wordage of the book would have come to about 25,000 words. Such a small volume would not have been unheard of at the time. Stone & Kimball had in fact just published a very slim collection of the renowned architect Ralph Adam's Cram's ghost stories, *Black Spirits and White* (1895), comprising only 27,000 words.

In any event, Stone & Kimball declined the book, for at the end of 1897 Bierce had submitted his "satires—of the Lucian-Swift sort"[3] to another Chicago firm, Way & Williams. Bierce states that the publisher actually accepted the book along with *Fantastic Fables,* although he received no contract; but by May 1898 the two books were "coolly returned."[4] The book of fables appeared in 1899 from Putnam's, but the book of satires remained without a publisher.

We hear of no more attempts by Bierce to market his collection until early 1905. At this time we learn that the revised version of "The Fall of the Republic," "Ashes of the Beacon," having appeared in both the *Examiner* and the *New York American* in February, had been submitted the previous August or September to Robert Mackay, the editor of *Success* magazine and a sporadic correspondent of Bierce. Mackay had found the story "unsuitable" for his magazine,[5] but Bierce responded to the story's rejection with the following proposition: "Now, I have a whole book of satires in the manner of 'The Ashes of the Beacon'. I've always thought *that* could be made to go, but have long despaired of making anybody else think so. If you'd care to look at it you may. I could finish compiling it in a few days. Some of 'The Ashes' would fit into the leading satire (entitled 'The Downfall of the Republic') for it is written along the same line of thought." This suggests a number of interesting things. Firstly, it appears that "The Fall of the Republic" still existed as a viable work and had not been replaced by "Ashes of the Beacon." Secondly, the contemplated collection was now in a state of flux, since Bierce suggests reworking it somehow by incorporating portions of "Ashes of the Beacon" into "The Fall of the Republic." Possibly Bierce had further augmented the volume with the several additional episodes of "The Land Beyond the Blow" that had been written by this time.

Mackay did attempt to market the book for Bierce, but by September 1905 Bierce was asking for the return of the manuscript, since Mackay was manifestly unsuccessful. Bierce vowed "to make a try at all the firms in the country with it,"[6] but the degree to which he followed through on this ambitious plan is not clear. By June 1906 another literary colleague, John

O'Hara Cosgrave (editor of *Everybody's Magazine*)—who had been instrumental in persuading Doubleday, Page & Co. to issue Bierce's *Devil's Dictionary,* published later that year[7]—tried his hand at peddling *The Fall of the Republic.* But Cosgrave had as little success as Mackay and Bierce himself, and by November Bierce is again asking for the return of the manuscript.[8]

Bierce then thought of employing an agent to market the book, something he had rarely done on previous occasions. The agent in question was one Daniel Murphy. By August 1907 Murphy had collected four rejections of the book; Bierce acknowledges Murphy's industry by the wry comment: "That is lively work on his part."[9] Shortly thereafter Bierce's disciple Herman Scheffauer offered to market the book in London, as he was going on a tour of England and the Continent. Bierce stated, "I'd rather that it would come out there than here, but don't think it will find favor in either country."[10] Scheffauer had no luck, and by April 1908 the manuscript was back from England.[11]

By this time, Bierce's young friend Walter Neale had proposed the publication of Bierce's *Collected Works* in ten volumes (later expanded to twelve) with his fledgling firm, the Neale Publishing Company. By early June Bierce announced that he had finished compiling the first volume, which included "Ashes of the Beacon," "The Land Beyond the Blow," "For the Ahkoond," and "John Smith, Liberator," but not "The Fall of the Republic."[12] The rapidity with which Bierce assembled the volume suggests that much of the material had been assembled beforehand.[13] Indeed, it seems likely that the book marketed from 1905 onward by Mackay, Cosgrave, Murphy, and Scheffauer consisted of these four stories or some approximation of them, as they fill about 40,000 words. Two segments of "The Land Beyond the Blow"—"The Conflagration in Ghargaroo" (*Cosmopolitan,* February 1906) and "An Execution in Batrugia" (*Cosmopolitan,* May 1907)—had not yet been published, but all the others had, and it is likely that Bierce had assembled much of "The Land Beyond the Blow" well before 1905. "Ashes of the Beacon" was expanded by absorbing two articles published in *Cosmopolitan,* "The Jury in Ancient America" (August 1905) and "Insurance in Ancient America" (September 1906), so that it now stood at 14,000 words, thereby becoming Bierce's second-longest work of fiction.

The fact that Bierce included four political satires in the first volume of his *Collected Works* is of significance: it attested not only to his high regard for those works but also, perhaps, to a desire to lure readers with the prospect of material that had not been previously gathered in book form. (Half of the volume consists of the satires, the other half contains his stirring memoirs of the Civil War, "Bits of Autobiography." None of the items had previously appeared in Bierce's published books.) About a year after the publication of the volume, Bierce unqualifiedly deemed "Ashes of the Beacon" (although still referring to it under its old title, "The Fall of the Republic") his "most notable work."[14] The book of satires that he had marketed for so long had finally achieved print; and because he had complete editorial control over the contents, it presumably appeared much as he wished it.

The question of the literary influences that may have affected Bierce's political satires is not easily answered, since Bierce himself is virtually silent on the matter in both his letters and his published writings. One of the few hints we have on the matter is the fact that Bierce read Swift and Voltaire in 1868 at the instigation of James T. Watkins, departing editor of the *News Letter*. It is therefore not surprising that Bierce's earliest excursions into political satire date from this period.[15] It is worth noting that the parenthetical remark included below the title of "The Land Beyond the Blow"—"(After the method of Swift, who followed Lucian, and was himself followed by Voltaire and many others.)"—was added to the text only after the rest of the manuscript had been submitted to Neale for typesetting. Bierce explained: "My reason is that if I do not myself point out that the method (not the style) is as old as literature the contemporary critics will surely 'jump on' the stuff as 'plagiarism' from Swift. Of Lucian and Voltaire they know not."[16]

Bierce refers to the fact that Swift's *Gulliver's Travels*—of which "The Land Beyond the Blow" is quite obviously an imitation—itself had a dim predecessor in Lucian's *True Story (Alethōn diegēmatōn;* sometimes translated as *True History)*. In fact, there is little similarity between the two works, as Lucian's whimsical skit—a deliberately absurd account of a man who boards a vessel that travels to various fantastic realms, including the moon, the interior of a giant whale, and the Isles of the Blest—is a conscious parody of the "poets, historians and philosophers of old, who have written much that smacks of miracles and fables."[17] There is no political or social satire directed at the lands or people encountered by the narrator, as there is in Swift, Voltaire, and Bierce.

It may be of some interest to ascertain what edition of Lucian Bierce may have read. Not fluent in Greek, he was reliant on English translations, and there were few translations of Lucian in his day. Unless he read a four-volume collected edition,[18] it is likely that Bierce had at some point read *Trips to the Moon,* translated by Thomas Francklin (New York: Cassell, 1886). This volume contains only *A True Story, How to Write History (Pōs dei historian syngraphein),* and *Icaromenippus.* Bierce shows his familiarity with the second work when he advises a correspondent to read Lucian "on the writing of history,"[19] but does not exhibit knowledge of any other works by Lucian aside from the *True Story*.

The reference to Voltaire is similarly a bit of a stretch. It is true that Voltaire's *Micromégas* (1752) was itself inspired by *Gulliver,* but this account of the voyage to Earth by a native of the star Sirius, accompanied by a native of the planet Saturn, is chiefly a philosophical, not a political, satire. Perhaps to that degree it may have inspired the one segment of "The Land Beyond the Blow" ("An Interview with Gnarmag-Zote") that is purely philosophical, but the connections between the two works are not strong. Bierce may also have been thinking of such a work as Voltaire's *L'Ingénu* (1767), in which a Frenchman raised by the Huron tribe of Canada comes to France and makes observations on French society and religion; but this work is more in the tradition of Montesquieu's *Persian Letters* (1721)—the tradition of a foreigner, unaware of the patterns of European society, making *faux-naïf* comments that hint at a society's absurdities and artificialities unperceived by its own members. Both Swift and Bierce reverse the surface form of these works—a member of our own society travels to other realms and takes note of their customs, differing or similar as the case may be—although in the end the thrust of the satire is analogous.

"The Land Beyond the Blow" is no "plagiarism from Swift," but it does indeed owe a significant debt to *Gulliver.* As can be seen in our notes, Bierce borrowed or adapted many small particulars of Swift's satire for his own. One of the most striking of these is the use by both authors of a highly eccentric array of terms designating the languages of the various mythical regions entered by both narrators. (Bierce had initiated this practice as early as the "Letters from a Hdkhoite.") Like Swift (see *GT* 129), Bierce devises novel terms to denote measurements of height, distance, and the like. Bierce's use in "The Tamtonians" of reversed words (for example, *cilbuper* for "republic") may be a subtle imitation of the passage in *Gulliver* in which Swift invents the regions Tribnia and Langden (*GT* 227)—anagrams for Britain and England. The effect of these linguistic inventions in both Swift and Bierce is to render an impression of distance between the known world and his imaginary realms in the eyes of an unbiased observer while still knowingly implying that many similarities nevertheless exist between the two.

One of the most amusing facets of Bierce's narrative is the bland depiction of the bizarre social customs pertaining to his mythical realms ("the King . . . look[ed] over my head to signify that the interview was at an end; and I retired from the Presence on hands and feet, as is the etiquette in that country"). Swift does not make as much of this in *Gulliver,* but in one instance he does so:

> A messenger was dispatched half a day's journey before us, to give the King notice of my approach, and to desire that his Majesty would please to appoint a day and hour, when it would be his gracious pleasure that I might have the

honour to *lick the dust before his footstool*. That is the court style, and I found it to be more than matter of form. . . . Nay, sometimes the floor is strewed with dust on purpose, when the person to be admitted happens to have powerful enemies at court. . . . There is indeed another custom, which I cannot altogether approve of. When the King hath a mind to put any of his nobles to death in a gentle indulgent manner, he commands to have the floor strowed with a certain brown powder, of a deadly composition, which being licked up infallibly kills him in twenty-four hours. (*GT* 243)

Aside from glancing parallels of this sort, it is only in *Gulliver* that we find exhaustive discussions of the political, social, economic, legal, and cultural tendencies of the various regions visited by Gulliver, and these discussions—in both broad and minor particulars—are duplicated in "The Land Beyond the Blow."

Of course, differences between *Gulliver* and "The Land Beyond the Blow" abound. Swift is unusually precise in supplying the dates of Gulliver's various expeditions, and scarcely less precise in specifying the locations of his imaginary realms, complete with maps. Bierce provided dates in the original newspaper appearances of some stories but later removed them; and he never gave the remotest hint as to the locations of his invented regions. In the century and a half that had passed between Swift's and Bierce's heydays, the "unknown" parts of the world had largely been charted, so that Bierce could not plausibly follow Swift in topographical specificity—setting the floating island of Laputa off the coast of Japan, for example. Also, Bierce makes no attempt to suggest the genuineness of his narrator's voyage by the accumulation of realistic detail. Swift, however, is manifestly interested in effecting a kind of hoax with *Gulliver,* since his novel imitates the travelers' narratives of the period and was published as if Gulliver himself, not Swift, were the author. In a more general sense, however, Bierce's narrator clearly echoes Lemuel Gulliver's own hope that his account will lead to extensive moral, political, and aesthetic reformation:

> I desired you would let me know by a letter, when party and faction were extinguished; judges learned and upright; pleaders honest and modest, with some tincture of common sense; and Smithfield blazing with pyramids of law-books; the young nobility's education entirely changed; the physicians banished; the female Yahoos abounding in virtue, honour, truth and good sense; courts and levees of great ministers thoroughly weeded and swept; wit, merit and learning rewarded; all disgracers of the press in prose and verse condemned to eat nothing but their own cotton, and quench their thirst with their own ink. (*GT* 4–5)

Bierce makes no such explicit statement of purpose in "The Land Beyond the Blow," but he hardly need have done so: the above passage encapsulates in a remarkably complete way the overall moral thrust of Bierce's tale and, perhaps, of his entire career as a satirist. As Lawrence I. Berkove has emphasized,[20] Bierce's satire is almost always driven by moral concerns. Although Bierce himself habitually disclaimed any inclination toward the moral reformation of his contemporaries, his work should be read not as a misanthrope's indiscriminate abuse but as a pungent revelation of moral and intellectual failings; by implication, Bierce was recommending the exact opposite of the modes of behavior he was lampooning.

We have already remarked on the possibility that Bellamy's *Looking Backward: 2000–1887* may have been the immediate impetus for the writing of "The Fall of the Republic," published only two months after the appearance of Bellamy's work. In no sense can Bellamy be said to have been any real influence, literary or political, since Bierce had written several previous "future histories" long before he ever read Bellamy. It is true that an "Author's Preface" at the beginning of *Looking Backward* is purportedly written by an anonymous professor at the "Historical Section, Shawmut College, Boston, December 26, 2000," but otherwise Bellamy's novel is not a "future history" in the sense that Bierce's tales are, since most of the work consists merely of political discussions between Julian West—a man who had lapsed into a hypnotic trance in the year 1887—and the characters he finds upon waking in the year 2000. The political views of the two writers differ so radically that one might be inclined to think that Bierce published his work when he did as a direct response to Bellamy. The first known mention of Bellamy in Bierce's journalism appears in a passing, and rather derisive, mention in a "Prattle" column (*E,* May 27, 1888). Two years later he directed a particularly tart fable, "The Bellamy and the Members," at the author of *Looking Backward:*

> The Members of a body of Socialists rose in insurrection against their Bellamy.
>
> "Why," said they, "should we be all the time tucking you out with food when you do nothing to tuck us out?"
>
> So, resolving to take no further action, they went away and looking backward had the satisfaction to see the Bellamy compelled to sell his own book.[21]

Similarly, William Dean Howells's *A Traveler from Altruria* (1894) cannot be thought of as an influence upon Bierce, although some similarities exist between the two works, at least in regard to the social and political issues they treat. In contrast to Bierce's "The Land Beyond the Blow," Howells's Altrurian (whose countrymen seek to follow literally the original teachings of Christ by devoting themselves to altruism) spends much of the novel criticizing American social and political institutions, devoting particular attention to such issues as the conflict between labor and capital, class hatred, and suppression of women's political rights. Only toward the end does the Altrurian speak at length of the moral and political circumstances of his own land. Bierce lost little time in heaping abuse, not so much upon Howells's work itself (although no doubt he thought its precepts utterly unrealistic in light of the actual facts of human nature), as upon the array of "Altrurian colonies" that sprung up as a result. The following is only one instance among several: "Of the amiable asses who have founded the 'Altrurian' colony at Mark West it ought to be sufficient to explain that their scheme is based upon the intellectual diversions of such humorists as Plato, More, Fourier, Bellamy and Howells. That assures the ludicrous fizzle of the enterprise."[22] And yet the fact that Howells's sequel to his novel, *Through the Eye of the Needle,* appeared in 1907, at the very time when Bierce was making renewed attempts to market his own book of satires, may be of significance. In a letter Howells remarked: "There is now a revival of interest in such speculations, and the publishers think the book, with an interesting sequel, giving an account of life in Altruria, will succeed."[23] Possibly the appearance of Howells's sequel—and the belief that such accounts might prove popular with readers— had some slight influence in Bierce's decision to include his future histories in the first volume of his *Collected Works,* published two years later.

A purely literary evaluation of these satires, without regard to their political content, may be difficult, but the attempt is worth making: surely these works can be gauged in regard to their literary values whether or not they echo our own political and social predilections. Bierce was not primarily a political philosopher, but a satirist and wit; and he would have wished us to appreciate his tales on a literary level even if we disagreed with the political message he was conveying.

Each group of works—the future histories and the fantastic voyages— presents certain features not found in the other. The former tales gain some of their greatest piquancy from their suggestion that the facts of history may have been transmitted in a dim, fragmented way, resulting in comical errors, and that our own understanding of history may be similarly distorted. One wonders whether Bierce hints that there has been an actual collapse of our existing civilization and a period of primitivism or barbarism before the emergence of a new age: such is indeed the implication in "For the Ahkoond" (1888), where we learn that the entirety of the North American continent east of the Rockies has not merely been depopulated, but reinhabited by the beasts of prehistory, such as pterodactyls and mastodons. Similarly, in "John Smith, Liberator" the future era has suffered a collapse of technological knowledge (the telegraph, the steam locomotive, and printing are lost arts) and knowledge of pure science (the Copernican theory is regarded as false). Bierce's repeated suggestion that the people of the future will not understand our mode of reckoning time—specifically the use of the terms A.D. or *Christian era*—suggests that the Christian religion, like the myths of classical antiquity, will have no practical significance in the future.

A variant of this device tempers the criticism of the "ancient Americans" as found in "Ashes of the Beacon." The Future Historian's condemnation of such hallowed American principles as republican government and the rule of the majority might appear intolerably smug and high-handed if the historian himself did not reveal not merely his severely erroneous grasp of the facts of "ancient" history, but also his bland disbelief that his own "gracious Sovereign" could "by any possibility [be] wrong." Remarks of this kind do not necessarily subvert the historian's criticism of our own time, but qualify it by a covert suggestion that his own period is, in spite of his protestations, flawed in many particulars.

"Ashes of the Beacon" is far and away the finest of Bierce's future histories, and "For the Ahkoond" perhaps the most amusing. His later contributions of this kind seem to reveal somewhat of a falling off, largely because he was content to produce very short squibs—possibly written for a newspaper deadline—that did not allow his satirical skills their full play. Many of these (especially the items grouped here under the heading "Annals of the Future Historian") were inspired by relatively transient events ranging from serious but short-lived political crises (the Boxer Rebellion, disputes over the Panama Canal) to mere sporting events (Sir Thomas Lipton's attempt to win a yacht race). "The Maid of Podunk" (1901), a tart send-up of temperance advocate Carry Nation, is a meritorious exception; and several late sketches skewering Theodore Roosevelt's boasted prowess as a soldier and hunter are among the most delightful of the future histories.

Of the fantastic voyages, "The Land Beyond the Blow" is clearly the chief specimen. The nearly twenty-year gestation period and the seeming randomness of its assemblage compromise its unity, and in several particulars it is open to the charge of repetition: the criticism of Americans' fondness for accumulating wealth is elaborated upon in both "Sons of the Fair Star" and "A Conflagration in Ghargaroo," while "The Tamtonians" and "The Kingdom of Tortirra" partially duplicate each other in their suggestions of flaws in the American political system. "An Interview with Gnarmag-Zote," a purely philosophical discourse, seems out of place, and "The Dog in Ganegwag" is simply a flippant exhibition (one of many throughout Bierce's work) of his detestation of dogs. Despite its weaknesses, "The Land Beyond the Blow" remains compellingly readable on many counts: its imaginative scope in envisioning the anomalous customs and physical particulars of the imaginary realms; the exceptionally sharp satire directed at American politics (culminating, perhaps, in "The Tamtonians," where the presidential and vice presidential nominees consist of an idiot and a corpse); and, overall, a crispness of prose that propels the narrative dynamically and pungently.

An analysis of the full range of Bierce's political and social views is beyond the scope of this introduction, but those aspects bearing on the stories and essays included in this volume must necessarily be discussed. In so doing, care must be taken on several fronts. Firstly, we must guard against the tacit assumption that Bierce should be criticized for not reflecting our own opinions on the subjects in question; secondly, we should try to duplicate Bierce's own practice of ruthlessly cutting through the political rhetoric both of his day and of ours, so as to discern the fundamental issues at the core of the debate; and thirdly, we must be aware that the opinions expressed in his satires are exaggerated, distorted, or in other ways twisted for comic purposes, so that such remarks must be interpreted in the light of Bierce's actual views (so far as they can now be ascertained). It is for this reason that we have included the essays and editorials that make up the second part of this book.

Bierce's boldness in criticizing the fundamentals of the American political and social system is, for the most part, praiseworthy. Few American writers have had the courage to question such hallowed dogmas as the very principle of republican government and the efficacy of democracy, universal suffrage, and the legal system. On the whole, Bierce maintained a vigorous independence of thought, refusing to adhere to a party line and always seeking to probe to what he felt was the heart of a given issue. But to what degree can we accept Bierce's criticism of democracy? To what extent is a democracy merely a tyranny of the majority? If (as stated in "Ashes of the Beacon") selfishness is the "dominant characteristic and fundamental motive of human nature and human action respectively," and if the majority is "ignorant, restless and reckless," then people as a mass cannot possibly "govern themselves." Bierce's most compact expression of his skepticism of democracy occurs in a single sentence of "Ashes of the Beacon": "An inherent weakness in republican government was that it assumed the honesty and intelligence of the majority, 'the masses,' who were neither honest nor intelligent." In such a scenario, politicians can only be demagogues, and people will be swayed not by the soundest views but by the sweetest tongue. A generation later the writer H. P. Lovecraft came to very much the same conclusion:

> Democracy—as distinguished from universal opportunity and good treatment—is today a fallacy and impossibility so great that any serious attempt to

apply it cannot be considered other than a mockery and a jest. . . . Government "by popular vote" means merely the nomination of doubtfully qualified men by doubtfully authorised and seldom competent cliques of professional politicians representing hidden interests, followed by a sardonic farce of emotional persuasion in which the orators with the glibbest tongues and flashiest catch-words herd on their side a numerical majority of blindly impressionable dolts and gulls who have for the most part no idea of what the whole circus is about.[24]

An honest analysis of the last several presidential campaigns may convince us of the sad truth of this assertion.

What alternative did Bierce suggest? Did he have an alternative in mind? In his role as satirist Bierce repeatedly mocked the notion that he was merely "tearing down" without putting something in its place—that he was criticizing existing institutions without offering a viable replacement. Bierce was vehement in denouncing this attitude, as in the following (in the context of a critique of religion): "I fatigue and fall ill of this hoary, decrepit, and doddering protest of brainless imbecility; it is the first, last, intermediate and only argument of mental vacuity. . . . Truth is better than anything or all things; the next best thing to truth is absence of error. When you are in the dark, stand still; when you do not know what to do, do nothing."[25] On the issue in question, it does not seem likely that Bierce is seriously suggesting a return to monarchy: although in *The Devil's Dictionary* he defines "Monarchical Government" with the single word, "Government" (suggesting that monarchy is the only system that is, for good or ill, a government in a meaningful sense), and although a good many of his future histories clearly state that the world will indeed become monarchical again, it seems highly unlikely that Bierce ever conceived the United States as readopting this form of government. Nevertheless, it is evident that Bierce wished for some kind of higher political authority: if "self-government" is a paradox in that the people are incapable of governing themselves, then the only alternative would appear to be an aristocracy or an actual dictatorship. Bierce was not shy about embracing the latter; in remarking, as early as 1879, on some "rigorous measures" taken by the Czar of Russia and Chancellor Bismarck in suppressing Nihilists and Socialists, Bierce noted:

In the Czar of Russia and the Chancellor of the German Empire lie the hopes of civilization, for they are in all Christendom the only strong men— the one by virtue of great governmental powers which his predecessors had not the folly to fritter away, the other through similar, those lesser, powers and colossal brains. I firmly believe that if the despotic energies wielded by these two men fail of the purpose to which they are set the days of our civilization are numbered, and in the near future the continents of Europe and America will be devastated by barbarians from the Asian steppes, or infested with cut-throat savages sprung from our loins and wearing the skins of animals about their own.[26]

In the same column Bierce went on to say: "If government has any meaning or function it means the restraint of the many by the few—the subordination of numbers to brains. It means the determined denial to the masses of the right to cut their own throats." What this suggests is an aristocracy of "brains" in a paternalistic government that would, by the restriction of civil liberties (Bierce explicitly mentions "a vigilant censorship of the press, a firm hand upon the church," and other measures), protect the people from harming themselves. No doubt Bierce had a low view of both the intelligence and the morality of the masses; but he seems to have fallen into the fallacy that high intelligence must necessarily engender high moral standards. Indeed, he frequently repeated the view (extending back to Plato) that sin and crime are merely aspects of folly: "The criminal is merely a fool considered under another aspect—an idiot with an opportunity."[27]

It is manifest that many of Bierce's concerns on this issue were engendered by his scorn of anarchy and anarchists. The outrageous statement in "Ashes of the Beacon" that socialism and even reform are merely watered-down versions of anarchy is echoed in many of his newspaper columns. No doubt Bierce would have violently disagreed with the principles of philosophical anarchism—which stressed the elimination of all state authority and the organization of society purely on the basis of voluntary cooperation—but it is not likely that he even knew these principles, as expounded by such leading philosophical anarchists as Pierre Joseph Proudhon or, in the United States, Benjamin R. Tucker. Instead, Bierce looked only to the violence and death produced by anarchists following the theories of Mikhail Bakunin, who indeed advocated force in the overthrow of existing governments. The widespread public fear of anarchist violence in the last two decades of the nineteenth century is perhaps mirrored today by our fears of terrorists. Bierce's concerns may have reached their apex when President William McKinley was assassinated in 1901 by a professed anarchist, but his worries had emerged long before that. The Haymarket riots of 1886 (the subject of his editorial "Prevention vs. No Cure") were blamed upon anarchists, and (as we shall see presently) also fed Bierce's concerns about the dangers of labor unions.

Bierce's bland recommendation, in "Ashes of the Beacon," that suspected anarchists should simply be locked up and prevented from speaking or publishing is echoed by similar comments in his columns; but it does not appear that Bierce quite realizes the implications of his remarks. Who, exactly, are the "bad men" and "malcontents" who should be thus restrained? It may not be so easy to decide; and in some cases, or under certain regimes, comments such as those made by Bierce himself might be interdicted. Bierce repeatedly stated that Americans have an excessive reverence for "freedom of speech" as a sacred principle; but the United States has always had laws against explicit advocacy of violence or of the overthrow of the government. Perhaps Bierce was thinking of England, whose constitution, lacking an analogue to our First Amendment, makes it far easier for the government to suppress what it perceives to be "seditious" speech.

Bierce's observations on legal and judicial matters are similarly thought-provoking. Once again he seems to put his finger on a number of troublesome issues, but what recommendations for improvement he has to offer are unclear or even paradoxical. With Bierce's low view of the intelligence of the "masses," it is hardly surprising that he would scorn the mere possibility that a jury trial could produce a fair verdict, as he states in the extract titled "The Competence of Jurors": "Every human institution is a failure, but the jury system as a means of justice is the most lamentable failure of all. There is no way to get together twelve men of sufficient intelligence, honesty and skill in analysis of evidence to determine the simplest question of fact when the lawyers have done with it." Analogously, Bierce was incensed over the fact that lawyers are in some instances compelled to defend clients they know to be guilty, and to act in court as if they were innocent. The problem is a real one, and Bierce may well be right in declaring that the practice causes a serious corruption of some lawyers' moral standards. But again, what is the alternative? Does Bierce think guilty defendants should not receive legal defense?

Bierce similarly speaks frequently about the overturning of certain verdicts in criminal or civil cases, or even of statutes passed by the government, on appeal. He is right to point out the iniquity of confining a defendant in jail while his or her appeal is being decided: if the defendant is ultimately found innocent, then he or she will have served prison time unjustly. But the issue of the overturning of statutes is perhaps not so clear. Following Bierce's argument to its ultimate logical conclusion, we would be compelled to assume that all laws passed at any time in our history are and will be eternally valid. This posits a highly inelastic conception of history and would prevent different historical eras from determining their own legal and judicial fate. It would suggest, for instance, that such a decision as the Supreme Court's sanctioning of the "separate but equal" principle in race relations (*Plessy* v. *Ferguson,* 1896) could not, and should not, have been overturned by *Brown* v. *Board of Education* in 1954. Bierce's complaint seems to have been directed at what he perceived to be judges' overturning of statutes on whim or caprice, but his solution would appear to be worse than the problem.

One aspect of jurisprudence on which Bierce remained unwavering throughout his life was the issue of capital punishment. To be sure, as a vigorous proponent of it he could entertain himself cheaply by poking fun at the poor arguments advocated against it by theosophists (see "Blathering Blavatskians"), but his fundamental argument that capital punishment is indeed deterrent—an argument broached frequently by its proponents today—is not supported by any clear-cut evidence, then or now. Other of Bierce's arguments are scarcely worth addressing: his contention that the death penalty is a form of societal "self-defense" is pure sophistry; his opposition to the plea of innocence by reason of insanity, on the ground that the lunatic is better off dead anyway, is vicious and contemptible; and his assertion that it does not matter if an innocent man ("particularly the kind of innocent man that is likely to be accused and convicted of murder") is killed now and then might have been moderated if he himself had been one of those innocent men.

Where Bierce does put his finger directly on an issue of great sensitivity even today is the question of executing female criminals. Bierce is certainly correct in affirming that if a society is to have capital punishment at all, punishment should be exacted upon males and females alike. Bierce was resolutely facing an issue that many members of his society were squeamish to address; the residual chivalry, patronization, and chauvinism that held women to a higher moral standard, or perhaps tacitly regarded them as weak and therefore the objects of pity, continue to deprecate the execution of women—solely or largely because they are women—found guilty of crime, as the cases of Ethel Rosenberg in 1953 and Karla Faye Tucker in 1998 attest. Bierce's comments on this issue may have been inspired by two notorious instances. One of them, the so-called Nan Patterson case, involved a young actress in New York who was accused of killing a bookmaker, a married man named "Caesar" Young, while they were riding in a hansom cab on May 4, 1904. After two separate trials ended in hung juries, Patterson was freed in May 1905. Evidently Bierce regarded her as manifestly guilty, and her release outraged him.[28] At about this very time a second case was reaching its culmination, as Mary Mabel Rogers, clearly guilty of conspiring to kill her husband in 1902, was executed in December 1905 in Vermont, over the protests of many individuals across the country. It is the subject of Bierce's essay "Some Thoughts on the Hanging."

On the general question of women's rights—an issue that fuses political, economic, and social concerns—Bierce mercifully does not spend a great deal of space in his satires. Throughout his career he relentlessly opposed woman suffrage, expansion of economic opportunities for women, and virtually every other facet of women's liberation.[29] It appears that Bierce had an excessively narrow view of the "proper" sphere of woman's activity, and he regarded it as self-evident that women were physically, intellectually, and morally inferior to men. Although he counted numerous women among his acquaintances and correspondents, they were invariably the sort who accepted their limited social and political roles; the moment any of them sought to expand her horizons (such as the novelist Gertrude Atherton, who developed feminist tendencies from the 1890s onward), Bierce at once ceased association with her. It is typical that in "Ashes of the Beacon" his historian points out that the incursion of women into the workforce brought them no significant "material advantage": the historian (whose opinions here manifestly reflect Bierce's own, as found frequently in his journalism) cannot envision any other kind of advantage, such as the increase in self-esteem and self-sufficiency accruing from securing gainful employment and being free of economic subservience to men. And Bierce's simplistic argument that the entry of women into the workforce would displace men and produce widespread unemployment has proven fallacious: the world economy has shown itself to be sufficiently flexible to accommodate this increase in the workforce by the creation of new industries and services.

In other aspects of economics, Bierce similarly sought order and efficiency, even at the expense of individual rights and liberties. On an issue that exercised the attention of a great many politicians, economists, and businessmen of the period—"protection" vs. free trade—Bierce declared himself emphatically in the latter camp. In contrast to today's political alignments, protective tariffs were vigorously urged by the Republicans of Bierce's day (perhaps in an effort to curry favor with the wealthy businessmen throughout the country who would stand to gain by tariffs on foreign goods), whereas the Democrats were advocates of free trade. In a rare instance of an explicit avowal of his political faith, Bierce affirmed that he himself had been a mugwump (a Republican who had deserted his party in 1884 by refusing to vote for the party's presidential nominee, James G. Blaine) and had become a Democrat over the issue of free trade.[30] Bierce's remarks on the matter—exemplified in such editorials as "'Protection' vs. Fair Trade" (1887) and "Commercial Retaliation" (1898)—are cogent and perspicacious.

Where Bierce radically parted from his Democratic colleagues was over the complex issue of the dispute between labor and capital, summed up in the catchphrase of the period, "industrial discontent." Bierce was by no means alone in regarding the emergence of labor unions from the 1860s onward with alarm: hostility was directed toward them as potentially violent and anarchistic from many quarters in the business and political world. It should be remembered that such unions actually were outlawed in many European countries for centuries: England legalized trade unions only in 1871; France had done so in the 1860s, but the unions' radicalism caused a rapid shift of public opinion against them. Bierce had, as early as his *News Letter* period (1868–72), expressed opposition to such things as the campaign for an eight-hour working day, and his justifiable contempt for the Workingmen's party in California—led by the racist rabble-rouser Dennis Kearney—was of long standing. As mentioned, the Haymarket riots not only brought bad publicity to anarchists, but to labor unions as well: the Knights of Labor were held responsible for inciting the riots, although that group in fact had no involvement in them. From this point on, Bierce's opposition to unions was unremitting. It seems incredible that he could genuinely believe that the violence resulting from union strikes was solely the responsibility of the unions, but that indeed seems to have been his position. His harsh words in regard to the Homestead strike of 1892—in which hundreds of Pinkerton detectives hired by management attacked striking workers' pickets, killing ten of them—sums up his views: "At Homestead and Wardner the laborers committed robbery, pillage and murder, as striking workmen invariably do when they dare, and as coward newspapers and scoundrel politicians encourage them in doing. But what would you have? They conceive it to be to their interest to do these things." And he goes on to dismiss the arguments that the capitalists were doing violence of their own with the flippant remark: "This is the baldest nonsense."[31] Perhaps Bierce was merely seeking to counteract what he felt was the biased reporting of papers like his own union-supporting *Examiner;* but he rarely expressed the view that a strike is justified or that labor has any valid complaints against capitalist owners.

What Bierce refused to recognize is that unionization was the direct product of the "trusts" and monopolies that were dominating an increasing number of businesses. In "Ashes of the Beacon" the historian actually asserts that "combinations of labor entailed combinations of capital," when in fact the matter was exactly reversed. Bierce's bland assumption that a given worker, if unsatisfied with his pay or working conditions, should merely quit his job and seek better work elsewhere seems more suitable for the artisan worker phase of capitalism of a century earlier than the circumstances of his own day.

In some senses, however, his attitude toward trusts is ingenious: he asserts that it is in their own interest to sell products as cheaply as possible, so that society would benefit if all industries were in the hands of trusts. What he overlooks—except in the editorial "A Backslider" (1892)—is that, once a trust or monopoly has cornered the market on any given product or service, it can then raise the cost of that product or service at will; and, especially in big businesses such as oil, steel, or railroads, it would be difficult for other businesses to step in and begin competitive marketing of their own products or services, because of the immense expense involved in initiating such enterprises. One would think that someone who had spent the better part of his journalistic career fulminating against the monopolistic practices of the railroads would have known better. In "The Jumjum of Gokeetle-guk" Bierce rather startlingly suggests that the trusts should be rigidly supervised by the government—an anomalous instance of "socialism" from this die-hard free trader. In "Concerning Trusts" (1899) he goes so far as to say: "Governmental ownership and Governmental control [of trusts] are what we are coming to by leaps and bounds . . ."—a claim that would have floored even some of the more radical proponents of the New Deal two generations later.

And yet Bierce's assertion in a letter of 1902 that "I am something of a Socialist myself"[32] is no better exemplified than by his repeatedly expressed belief that all able-bodied persons who wish to work should be provided work—by the government, if necessary. In some senses Bierce's advocacy of this measure was part of his solution to rid the country of "tramps," but in the essay "Concerning Legislation 'To Solve the Tramp Problem'" (1900) he makes it abundantly clear that the "right to labor" is really a matter of human dignity.

On a broader economic issue—the attainment of wealth—Bierce similarly reveals certain quasi-socialistic beliefs. One of the most striking passages in "Ashes of the Beacon" is his condemnation of Americans' furious and single-minded quest for the acquisition of money. The "prosperity" of the country was purchased at a high price:

> By the neglect of all education except that crude, elementary sort which fits men for the coarse delights of business and affairs but confers no capacity of rational enjoyment; by exalting the worth of wealth and making it the test and touchstone of merit; by ignoring art, scorning literature and despising science, except as these might contribute to the glutting of the purse; by setting up and maintaining an artificial standard of morals which condoned all offenses against the property and peace of every one but the condoner; by pitilessly crushing out of their natures every sentiment and aspiration unconnected with accumulation of property, these civilized savages and commercial barbarians attained their sordid end.

Whether the essay "The Road to Wealth Is Open to All—Get Wealthy Ye Who Can" (1902) qualifies this searing condemnation is debatable: there Bierce merely asserts that opportunities for accumulating wealth are, in his day, abundant, and that it only takes brains and gumption to secure as much money as anyone wants.

One final aspect of Bierce's thought may be addressed here—his unremitting hostility to insurance. In some senses this may seem merely to be one of his crotchets, as with his dislike of dogs; but his attitude may seem less unusual if we realize the relative recency of the whole phenomenon of insurance. Although insurance of some sort can be traced as far back as ancient Babylonia, in reality it was chiefly a product of the later eighteenth and nineteenth centuries. In the United States, the first casualty policy was offered in 1832, while the Prudential Insurance Company, the pioneer of life insurance in America, was founded as recently as 1875. As such, insurance seemed to Bierce merely a new and alarming con game; in short, a form of gambling in which one could never beat "the man who kept the table." Bierce errs in some of his views—such as his assumption that the premiums paid on property over a lifetime would exceed the value of that property—but in other areas he seems on target. He shrewdly points out that insurers' boasts of the extent of their assets are an unwitting admission that they take in far more than they pay out. For Bierce, insurance was simply one more instance of the follies, hypocrisies, and inefficiencies infecting American society.

Ambrose Bierce never enunciated the entire range of his political, social, aesthetic, or philosophical opinions in a systematic way, and so his views must be collated or inferred by consultation of a vast aggregate of journalism. Perhaps he was better at pointing out what was wrong with the American political, legal, economic, and social system than at recommending viable solutions, but he saw this criticism as a legitimate exercise of his satirical, journalistic, and polemical talents. He also perceived that to couch his criticisms in the form of fiction, rather than essays or treatises, might be a far more potent and penetrating way of influencing his contemporaries.

What place do Bierce's satires occupy in his own work? Is he correct in thinking "Ashes of the Beacon" his most "notable" work? To be sure, such tales as "An Occurrence at Owl Creek Bridge," "Chickamauga," and "The Death of Halpin Frayser" allow the critic more latitude for analysis in regard to character development, dramatic irony, and the mingling of horror, pathos, and satire. But as flights of imagination, and certainly as fictionalized expressions of many facets of Bierce's political, social, and aesthetic thought, the satires rank supreme. Perhaps a comparison between the satires and his other tales is futile, given their radical difference in form, content, even style and tone; and perhaps it is best merely to appreciate both bodies of work for their own distinct virtues.

A Note on the Text

THE ITEMS IN THIS volume have been taken from Bierce's contributions to newspapers and magazines, and from his *Collected Works* (1909–12). Full bibliographical information on all items can be found at the rear of the volume. Although we present most of the fiction contained herein in chronological order, we have placed "Ashes of the Beacon" and "The Land Beyond the Blow" at the beginning, as they constitute Bierce's most significant political satires. They, along with "For the Ahkoond" and "John Smith, Liberator," have been taken from the first volume (1909) of the *Collected Works;* "'The Bubble Reputation'" from the eighth volume (1911); "The Great Strike of 1895," "Rise and Fall of the Aëroplane," "The Reversion to Barbarism," and "An Ancient Hunter" from the twelfth volume (1912). The last three were published under the heading "The Future Historian," but we have chosen to present them in their chronological sequence among the other related pieces. All other items have been reprinted directly from the newspapers and magazines in which they originally appeared. In cases where an item appeared in both the *San Francisco Examiner* and the *New York Journal/American,* we have generally followed the *Examiner* text, as it appears more in accordance with Bierce's customary usages. (Bierce complained frequently of editorial tampering with his work in the New York paper.) We have provided titles for the extracts of sketches that appear in his columns, "Prattle," "The Passing Show," and "The Views of One." They are: "Modern Penology," "The Fall of Christian Civilization," "On the Canal," "The Minister's Death," "The Republic of Panama," and "The Second American Invasion of China."

The essays in the second part of the volume are grouped in loose categories based on subject matter and exemplify Bierce's opinions on the political, social, legal, and other issues addressed in the satires. Many are unsigned editorials from the *San Francisco Examiner.* Bierce wrote many such pieces during his tenure with the *Examiner,* especially during the period 1887–95. He reprinted some in his *Collected Works,* but many of the items in this volume never were reprinted, so that there may be doubt as to their authorship. The editorials "Prevention vs. No Cure," "The Failure of 'Rotation,'" "'Protection' vs. Fair Trade," "A Backslider," "Infumiferous Tacitite," and "'Fly, Good Fleance, Fly!'" are contained in a scrapbook of Bierce's editorials at Stanford University. The scrapbook manifestly was assembled by Bierce himself, as it bears many notations in his hand, so that the attribution of these pieces to Bierce is secure. Other unsigned editorials contained herein were incorporated into various essays in his *Collected Works;*

see Sources for details. In these instances we have followed the original newspaper appearances rather than the texts in *Collected Works,* since the former are generally somewhat ampler. All other essays or columns included here are signed. In instances where we have presented excerpts from Bierce's columns, we have supplied titles of our own. These include the articles "Republican Government," "The Morality of Lawyers," "The Competence of Jurors," "The Insurance Folly," "Insurance and Crime," and "Prohibition."

In our headnotes and annotations to the stories and essays we seek to present background information on their composition; to elucidate political, literary, and other references in the text; and to cite passages in other works by Bierce that mirror the discussions in question. We have used the following abbreviations in the introduction, notes, and commentary:

A	*Argonaut* (San Francisco)
AB	Ambrose Bierce
BL	Bancroft Library, University of California
Co	*Cosmopolitan* (New York)
CW	*Collected Works* (1909–12; 12 vols.)
DD	*The Unabridged Devil's Dictionary,* ed. David E. Schultz and S. T. Joshi (Athens: University of Georgia Press, 2000)
E	*San Francisco Examiner*
FD	*The Fiend's Delight* (London: John Camden Hotten, 1873)
Fi	*Figaro* (London)
GT	Jonathan Swift, *Gulliver's Travels* (1726), in *Gulliver's Travels, A Tale of a Tub, The Battle of the Books, Etc.,* ed. William Alfred Eddy (New York: Oxford University Press, 1933)
HL	Huntington Library & Art Gallery (San Marino, Calif.)
NA	*New York American*
NJ	*New York Journal*
NL	*San Francisco News Letter and California Advertiser*
NP	New York Public Library
SS	*A Sole Survivor* (Knoxville: University of Tennessee Press, 1998)
VA	University of Virginia
W	*Wasp* (San Francisco)

FICTION

ASHES OF THE BEACON

An Historical Monograph Written in 4930

O F THE MANY CAUSES that conspired to bring about the lamentable failure of "self-government" in ancient America the most general and comprehensive was, of course, the impracticable nature of the system itself. In the light of modern culture, and instructed by history, we readily discern the folly of those crude ideas upon which the ancient Americans based what they knew as "republican institutions," and maintained, as long as maintenance was possible, with something of a religious fervor, even when the results were visibly disastrous.

To us of to-day it is clear that the word "self-government" involves a contradiction,[1] for government means control by something other than the thing to be controlled. When the thing governed is the same as the thing governing there is no government, though for a time there may be, as in the case under consideration there was, a considerable degree of forbearance, giving a misleading appearance of public order. This, however, soon must, as in fact it soon did, pass away with the delusion that gave it birth. The habit of obedience to written law, inculcated by generations of respect for actual government able to enforce its authority, will persist for a long time, with an ever lessening power upon the imagination of the people; but there comes a time when the tradition is forgotten and the delusion exhausted. When men perceive that nothing is restraining them but their consent to be restrained, then at last there is nothing to obstruct the free play of that selfishness which is the dominant characteristic and fundamental motive of human nature and human action respectively. Politics, which may have had something of the character of a contest of principles, becomes a struggle of interests, and its methods are frankly serviceable to personal and class advantage. Patriotism and respect for law pass like a tale that is told. Anarchy, no longer disguised as "government by consent," reveals his hidden hand, and in the words of our greatest living poet,

> lets the curtain fall,
> And universal darkness buries all![2]

The ancient Americans were a composite people; their blood was a blend of all the strains known in their time.[3] Their government, while they had one, being merely a loose and mutable expression of the desires and caprices of the majority—that is to say, of the ignorant, restless and reckless—gave the freest rein and play to all the primal instincts and elemental passions of the race. In so far and for so long as it had any restraining force, it was only the restraint of the present over the power of the past—that of a new habit over an old and insistent tendency ever seeking expression in large liberties and indulgences impatient of control. In the history of that unhappy people, therefore, we see unveiled the workings of the human will in its most lawless state, without fear of authority or care of consequence. Nothing could be more instructive.

Of the American form of government, although itself the greatest of evils afflicting the victims of those that it entailed, but little needs to be said here; it has perished from the earth,[4] a system discredited by an unbroken record of failure in all parts of the world, from the earliest historic times to its final extinction. Of living students of political history not one professes to see in it anything but a mischievous creation of theorists and visionaries—persons whom our gracious sovereign has deigned to brand for the world's contempt as "dupes of hope purveying to sons of greed."[5] The political philosopher of to-day is spared the trouble of pointing out the fallacies of republican government, as the mathematician is spared that of demonstrating the absurdity of the convergence of parallel lines; yet the ancient Americans not only clung to their error with a blind, unquestioning faith, even when groaning under its most insupportable burdens, but seem to have believed it of divine origin. It was thought by them to have been established by the god Woshington, whose worship, with that of such *dii minores* as Gufferson, Jaxon and Lincon (identical probably with the Hebru Abrem) runs like a shining thread through all the warp and woof of the stuff that garmented their moral nakedness. Some stones, very curiously inscribed in many tongues, were found by the explorer Droyhors in the wilderness bordering the river Bhitt (supposed by him to be the ancient Potomac) as lately as the reign of Barukam IV.[6] These stones appear to be fragments of a monument or temple erected to the glory of Woshington in his divine character of Founder and Preserver of republican institutions. If this tutelary deity of the ancient Americans really invented representative government they were not the first by many to whom he imparted the malign secret of its inauguration and denied that of its maintenance.

Although many of the causes which finally, in combination, brought about the downfall of the great American republic were in operation from the beginning—being, as has been said, inherent in the system—it was not until the year 1995 (as the ancients for some reason not now known reckoned time) that the collapse of the vast, formless fabric was complete. In that year the defeat and massacre of the last army of law and order in the lava beds of California extinguished the final fires of enlightened patriotism and quenched in blood the monarchical revival. Thenceforth armed opposition to anarchy was confined to desultory and insignificant warfare waged by small gangs of mercenaries in the service of wealthy individuals and equally feeble bands of proscripts fighting for their lives. In that year, too, "the Three Presidents"[7] were driven from their capitals, Cincinnati, New Orleans and Duluth, their armies dissolving by desertion and themselves meeting death at the hands of the populace.

The turbulent period between 1920 and 1995, with its incalculable waste of blood and treasure, its dreadful conflicts of armies and more dreadful massacres by passionate mobs, its kaleidoscopic changes of government and incessant effacement and redrawing of boundaries of states, its interminable tale of political assassinations and proscriptions—all the horrors incident to intestinal wars of a naturally lawless race—had so exhausted and dispirited the surviving protagonists of legitimate government that they could make no further head against the inevitable, and were glad indeed and most fortunate to accept life on any terms that they could obtain.

But the purpose of this sketch is not bald narration of historic fact, but examination of antecedent germinal conditions; not to recount calamitous events familiar to students of that faulty civilization, but to trace, as well as the meager record will permit, the genesis and development of the causes that brought them about. Historians in our time have left little undone in the matter of narration of political and military phenomena. In Golpek's "Decline and Fall of the American Republics," in Soseby's "History of Political Fallacies," in Holobom's[8] "Monarchical Renascence," and notably in Gunkux's immortal work, "The Rise, Progress, Failure and Extinction of The Connected States of America" the fruits of research have been garnered, a considerable harvest. The events are set forth with such conscientiousness and particularity as to have exhausted the possibilities of narration. It remains only to expound causes and point the awful moral.

To a delinquent observation it may seem needless to point out the inherent defects of a system of government which the logic of events has swept like political rubbish from the face of the earth, but we must not forget that ages before the inception of the American republics and that of France and Ireland[9] this form of government had been discredited by emphatic failures among the most enlightened and powerful nations of antiquity: the Greeks, the Romans, and long before them (as we now know) the Egyptians and the Chinese. To the lesson of these failures the founders of the eighteenth and nineteenth century republics were blind and deaf. Have we then reason to believe that our posterity will be wiser because instructed by a greater number of examples? And is the number of examples which they will have in memory really greater? Already the instances of China, Egypt, Greece and Rome are almost lost in the mists of antiquity; they are known, except by infrequent report, to the archæologist only, and but dimly and uncertainly to him. The brief and imperfect record of yesterdays which we call History is like that traveling vine of India which, taking new root as it advances, decays at one end while it grows at the other, and so is constantly perishing and finally lost in all the spaces which it has over-passed.

From the few and precious writings that have descended to us from the early period of the American republic we get a clear if fragmentary view of the disorders and lawlessness affecting that strange and unhappy nation. Leaving the historically famous "labor troubles" for more extended consideration, we may summarize here a few of the results of hardly more than a century and a quarter of "self-government" as it existed on this continent just previously to the awful end. At the beginning of the "twentieth century" a careful study by trustworthy contemporary statisticians of the public records and those apparently private ones known as "newspapers" showed that in a population of about 80,000,000[10] the annual number of homicides was not less than 10,000; and this continued year after year to increase, not only absolutely, but proportionately, until, in the words of Dumbleshaw, who is thought to have written his famous "Memoirs of a Survivor"[11] in the year 1908 of their era, "it would seem that the practice of suicide is a needless custom, for if a man but have patience his neighbor is sure to put him out of his misery." Of the 10,000 assassins less than three per cent. were punished, further than by incidental imprisonment if unable to give bail while awaiting trial. If the chief end of government is the citizen's security of life and his protection from aggression, what kind of government do these appalling figures disclose? Yet so infatuated with their imaginary "liberty"[12] were these singular people that the contemplation of all this crime abated nothing of the volume and persistence of their patriotic ululations, and affected not their faith in the perfection of their system. They were like a man standing on a rock already submerged by the rising tide, and calling to his neighbors on adjacent cliffs to observe his superior security.

When three men engage in an undertaking in which they have an equal interest, and in the direction of which they have equal power, it necessarily results that any action approved by two of them, with or without the assent of the third, will be taken. This is called—or was called when it was an accepted principle in political and other affairs—"the rule of the majority."[13]

Evidently, under the malign conditions supposed, it is the only practicable plan of getting anything done. A and B rule and overrule C, not because they ought, but because they can; not because they are wiser, but because they are stronger. In order to avoid a conflict in which he is sure to be worsted, C submits as soon as the vote is taken. C is as likely to be right as A and B; nay, that eminent ancient philosopher, Professor Richard A. Proctor[14] (or Proroctor, as the learned now spell the name), has clearly shown by the law of probabilities that any one of the three, all being of the same intelligence, is far likelier to be right than the other two.

It is thus that the "rule of the majority" as a political system is established. It is in essence nothing but the discredited and discreditable principle that "might makes right"; but early in the life of a republic this essential character of government by majority is not seen. The habit of submitting all questions of policy to the arbitrament of counting noses and assenting without question to the result invests the ordeal with a seeming sanctity, and what was at first obeyed as the command of power comes to be revered as the oracle of wisdom. The innumerable instances—such as the famous ones of Galileo and Keeley[15]—in which one man has been right and all the rest of the race wrong, are overlooked, or their significance missed, and "public opinion" is followed as a divine and infallible guide through every bog into which it blindly stumbles and over every precipice in its fortuitous path. Clearly, sooner or later will be encountered a bog that will smother or a precipice that will crush. Thoroughly to apprehend the absurdity of the ancient faith in the wisdom of majorities let the loyal reader try to fancy our gracious Sovereign by any possibility wrong, or his unanimous Ministry by any possibility right!

During the latter half of the "nineteenth century" there arose in the Connected States a political element opposed to all government, which frankly declared its object to be anarchy. This astonishing heresy was not of indigenous growth: its seeds were imported from Europe by the emigration or banishment thence of criminals congenitally incapable of understanding and valuing the blessings of monarchical institutions, and whose method of protest was murder. The governments against which they conspired in their native lands were too strong in authority and too enlightened in policy for them to overthrow. Hundreds of them were put to death, thousands imprisoned and sent into exile. But in America, whither those who escaped fled for safety, they found conditions entirely favorable to the prosecution of their designs.

A revered fetish of the Americans was "freedom of speech":[16] it was believed that if bad men were permitted to proclaim their evil wishes they would go no further in the direction of executing them—that if they might say what they would like to do they would not care to do it. The close relation between speech and action was not understood. Because the Americans themselves had long been accustomed, in their own political debates and discussions, to the use of unmeaning declamations and threats which they had no intention of executing, they reasoned that others were like them, and attributed to the menaces of these desperate and earnest outcasts no greater importance than to their own. They thought also that the foreign anarchists, having exchanged the tyranny of kings for that of majorities, would be content with their new and better lot and become in time good and law-abiding citizens.

The anarchist of that far day (thanks to the firm hands of our gracious sovereigns the species is now extinct) was a very different person from what our infatuated ancestors imagined him. He struck at government, not because it was bad, but because it was government. He hated authority, not for its tyranny, but for its power. And in order to make this plain to observation he frequently chose his victim from amongst those whose rule was most conspicuously benign.

Of the seven early Presidents of the American republic who perished by assassination no fewer than four were slain by anarchists with no personal wrongs to impel them to the deed—nothing but an implacable hostility to law and authority. The fifth victim, indeed, was a notorious demagogue who had pardoned the assassin of the fourth.[17]

The field of the anarchist's greatest activity was always a republic, not only to emphasize his impartial hatred of all government, but because of the inherent feebleness of that form of government, its inability to protect itself against any kind of aggression by any considerable number of its people having a common malevolent purpose. In a republic the crust that confined the fires of violence and sedition was thinnest.

No improvement in the fortunes of the original anarchists through immigration to what was then called the New World would have made them good citizens. From centuries of secret war against particular forms of authority in their own countries they had inherited a bitter antagonism to all authority, even the most beneficent. In their new home they were worse than in their old. In the sunshine of opportunity the rank and sickly growth of their perverted natures became hardy, vigorous, bore fruit. They surrounded themselves with proselytes from the ranks of the idle, the vicious, the unsuccessful. They stimulated and organized discontent. Every one of them became a center of moral and political contagion. To those as yet unprepared to accept anarchy was offered the milder dogma of Socialism, and to those even weaker in the faith something vaguely called Reform. Each was initiated into that degree to which the induration of his conscience and the character of his discontent made him eligible, and in which he could be most serviceable, the body of the people still cheating themselves with the false sense of security begotten of the belief that they were somehow exempt from the operation of all agencies inimical to their national welfare and integrity. Human nature, they thought, was different in the West from what it was in the East: in the New World the old causes would not have the old effects: a republic had some inherent vitality of its own, entirely independent of any action intended to keep it alive. They felt that words and phrases had some talismanic power, and charmed themselves asleep by repeating "liberty," "all men equal before the law," "dictates of conscience," "free speech" and all manner of such incantation to exorcise the spirits of the night. And when they could no longer close their eyes to the dangers environing them; when they saw at last that what they had mistaken for the magic power of their form of government and its assured security was really its radical weakness and subjective peril—they found their laws inadequate to repression of the enemy, the enemy too strong to permit the enactment of adequate laws. The belief that a malcontent armed with freedom of speech, a newspaper, a vote and a rifle less dangerous than a malcontent with a still tongue in his head, empty hands and under police surveillance was abandoned, but all too late. From its fatuous dream the nation was awakened by the noise of arms, the shrieks of women and the red glare of burning cities.

Beginning with the slaughter at St. Louis on a night in the year 1920, when no fewer than twenty-two thousand citizens were slain in the streets and half the city destroyed, massacre followed massacre with frightful rapidity. New York fell in the month following, many thousands of its inhabitants escaping fire and sword only to be driven into the bay and drowned, "the roaring of the water in their ears," says Bardeal, "augmented by the hoarse clamor of their red-handed pursuers, whose blood-thirst was unsated by the sea." A week later Washington was destroyed, with all its public buildings and archives; the President and his Ministry were slain, Congress was dispersed, and an unknown number of officials and private citizens perished. Of all the principal cities only Chicago and San Francisco escaped. The people of the former were all anarchists and the latter was valorously and successfully defended by the Chinese.[18]

The urban anarchists were eventually subdued and some semblance of order was restored, but greater woes and sharper shames awaited this unhappy nation, as we shall see.

In turning from this branch of our subject to consider the causes of the failure and bloody disruption of the great American republic other than those inherent in the form of government, it may not be altogether unprofitable to glance briefly at what seems to a superficial view the inconsistent phenomenon of great material prosperity. It is not to be denied that this unfortunate people was at one time singularly prosperous, in so far as national wealth is a measure and proof of prosperity. Among nations it was the richest nation. But at how great a sacrifice of better things was its wealth obtained! By the neglect of all education except that crude, elementary sort which fits men for the coarse delights of business and affairs but confers no capacity of rational enjoyment; by exalting the worth of wealth and making it the test and touchstone of merit; by ignoring art, scorning literature and despising science, except as these might contribute to the glutting of the purse; by setting up and maintaining an artificial standard of morals which condoned all offenses against the property and peace of every one but the condoner; by pitilessly crushing out of their natures every sentiment and aspiration unconnected with accumulation of property, these civilized savages and commercial barbarians attained their sordid end. Before they had rounded the first half-century of their existence as a nation they had sunk so low in the scale of morality that it was considered nothing discreditable to take the hand and even visit the house of a man who had grown rich by means notoriously corrupt and dishonorable; and Harley declares that even the editors and writers of newspapers, after fiercely assailing such men in their journals, would be seen "hobnobbing" with them in public places.[19] (The nature of the social ceremony named the "hobnob" is not now understood, but it is known that it was a sign of amity and favor.) When men or nations devote all the powers of their minds and bodies to the heaping up of wealth, wealth is heaped up. But what avails it? It may not be amiss to quote here the words of one of the greatest of the ancients whose works—fragmentary, alas—have come down to us.

"Wealth has accumulated itself into masses; and poverty, also in accumulation enough, lies impassably separated from it; opposed, uncommunicating, like forces in positive and negative poles. The gods of this lower world sit aloft on glittering thrones, less happy than Epicurus's gods, but as indolent, as impotent; while the boundless living chaos of ignorance and hunger welters, terrific in its dark fury, under their feet. How much among us might be likened to a whited sepulcher: outwardly all pomp and strength, but inwardly full of horror and despair and dead men's bones! Iron highways, with their wains fire-winged, are uniting all the ends of the land; quays and moles, with their innumerable stately fleets, tame the ocean into one pliant bearer of burdens; labor's thousand arms, of sinew and of metal, all-conquering everywhere, from the tops of the mount down to the depths of the mine and the caverns of the sea, ply unweariedly for the service of man; yet man remains unserved. He has subdued this planet, his habitation and inheritance, yet reaps no profit from the victory. Sad to look upon: in the highest stage of civilization nine-tenths of mankind have to struggle in the lowest battle of savage or even animal man—the battle against famine. Countries are rich, prosperous in all manner of increase, beyond example; but the men of these countries are poor, needier than ever of all sustenance, outward and inward; of belief, of knowledge, of money, of food."[20]

To this somber picture of American "prosperity" in the nineteenth century nothing of worth can be added by the most inspired artist. Let us simply inscribe upon the gloomy canvas the memorable words of an illustrious poet of the period:

> That country speeds to an untoward fate,
> Where men are trivial and gold is great.[21]

One of the most "sacred" rights of the ancient American was the trial of an accused person by "a jury of his peers."[22] This, in America, was a right secured to him by a written constitution. It was almost universally believed to have had its origin in Magna Carta, a famous document which certain rebellious noblemen of another country had compelled their sovereign to sign under a threat of death. That celebrated "bill of rights" has not all come down to us, but researches of the learned have made it certain that it contained no mention of trial by jury, which, indeed, was unknown to its authors. The words *judicium parium*[23] meant to them something entirely different—the judgment of the entire community of freemen. The words and the practice they represented antedated Magna Carta by many centuries and were common to the Franks and other Germanic nations, amongst whom a trial "jury" consisted of persons having a knowledge of the matter to be determined—persons who in later times were called "witnesses" and rigorously excluded from the seats of judgment.[24]

It is difficult to conceive a more clumsy and ineffective machinery for ascertaining truth and doing justice than a jury of twelve men of the average intelligence, even among ourselves. What, then, must this device have been among the half-civilized tribes of the Connected States of America! Nay, the case is worse than that, for it was the practice to prevent men of even the average intelligence from serving as jurors. Jurors had to be residents of the locality of the crime charged, and every crime was made a matter of public notoriety long before the accused was brought to trial; yet, as a rule, he who had read or talked about the trial was held disqualified to serve. This in a country where, when a man who could read was not reading about local crimes he was talking about them, or if doing neither was doing something worse!

To the twelve men so chosen the opposing lawyers addressed their disingenuous pleas and for their consideration the witnesses presented their carefully rehearsed testimony, most of it false. So unintelligent were these juries that a great part of the time in every trial was consumed in keeping from them certain kinds of evidence with which they could not be trusted; yet the lawyers were permitted to submit to them any kind of misleading argument that they pleased and fortify it with innuendoes without relevancy and logic without sense. Appeals to their passions, their sympathies, their prejudices, were regarded as legitimate influences and tolerated by the judges on the theory that each side's offenses would about offset those of the other. In a criminal case it was expected that the prosecutor would declare repeatedly and in the most solemn manner his belief in the guilt of the person accused, and that the attorney for the defense would affirm with equal gravity his conviction of his client's innocence. How could they impress the jury with a belief which they did not themselves venture to affirm? It is not recorded that any lawyer ever rebelled against the iron authority of these conditions and stood for truth and conscience. They were, indeed, the conditions of his existence as a lawyer, a fact which they easily persuaded themselves mitigated the baseness of their obedience to them, or justified it altogether.

The judges, as a rule, were no better, for before they could become judges they must have been advocates, with an advocate's fatal disabilities of judgment. Most of them depended for their office upon the favor of the people, which, also, was fatal to the independence, the dignity and the impartiality to which they laid so solemn claim. In their decisions they favored, so far as they dared, every interest, class or person powerful enough to help or hurt them in an election. Holding their high office by so precarious a tenure, they were under strong temptation to enrich themselves from the serviceable purses of wealthy litigants, and in disregard of justice to cultivate the favor of the attorneys practicing before them, and before whom they might soon be compelled themselves to practice.

In the higher courts of the land, where juries were unknown and appointed judges held their seats for life, these awful conditions did not obtain, and there Justice might have been content to dwell, and there she actually did sometimes set her foot. Unfortunately, the great judges had the consciences of their education. They had crept to place through the slime of the lower courts and their robes of office bore the damnatory evidence. Unfortunately, too, the attorneys, the jury habit strong upon them, brought into the superior tribunals the moral characteristics and professional methods acquired in the lower. Instead of assisting the judges to ascertain the truth and the law, they cheated in argument and took liberties with fact, deceiving the court whenever they deemed it to the interest of their cause to do so, and as willingly won by a technicality or a trick as by the justice of their contention and their ability in supporting it. Altogether, the entire judicial system of the Connected States of America was inefficient, disreputable, corrupt.

The result might easily have been foreseen and doubtless was predicted by patriots whose admonitions have not come down to us. Denied protection of the law, neither property nor life was safe. Greed filled his coffers from the meager hoards of Thrift, private vengeance took the place of legal redress, mad multitudes rioted and slew with virtual immunity from punishment or blame, and the land was red with crime.

A singular phenomenon of the time was the immunity of criminal women. Among the Americans woman held a place unique in the history of nations. If not actually worshiped as a deity, as some historians, among them the great Sagab-Joffoy, have affirmed, she was at least regarded with feelings of veneration which the modern mind has a difficulty in comprehending. Some degree of compassion for her mental inferiority, some degree of forbearance toward her infirmities of temper, some degree of immunity for the offenses which these peculiarities entail—these are common to all peoples above the grade of barbarians. In ancient America these chivalrous sentiments found open and lawful expression only in relieving woman of the burden of participation in political and military service; the laws gave her no express exemption from responsibility for crime. When she murdered, she was arrested; when arrested, brought to trial though the origin and meaning of those observances are not now known. Gunkux, whose researches into the jurisprudence of antiquity enable him to speak with commanding authority of many things, gives us here nothing better than the conjecture that the trial of women for murder, in the nineteenth century and a part of the twentieth, was the survival of an earlier custom of actually convicting and punishing them, but it seems extremely improbable that a people that once put its female assassins to death would ever have relinquished the obvious advantages of the practice while retaining with purposeless tenacity some of its costly preliminary forms. Whatever may have been the reason, the custom was observed with all the gravity of a serious intention. Gunkux professes knowledge of one or two instances (he does not name his authorities) where matters went so far as conviction and sentence, and adds that the mischievous sentimentalists who had always lent themselves to the solemn jest by protestations of great *vraisemblance* against "the judicial killing of women," became really alarmed and filled the land with their lamentations. Among the phenomena of brazen effrontery he classes the fact that some of these loud protagonists of the right of women to assassinate unpunished were themselves women! Howbeit, the sentences, if ever pronounced, were never executed, and during the first quarter of the twentieth century the meaningless custom of bringing female assassins to trial was abandoned. What the effect was of their exemption from this considerable inconvenience we have not the data to conjecture, unless we understand as an allusion to it some otherwise obscure words of the famous Edward Bok,[25] the only writer of the period whose work has survived. In his monumental essay on barbarous penology, entitled "Slapping the Wrist," he couples "woman's emancipation from the trammels of law" and "man's better prospect of death" in a way that some have construed as meaning that he regarded them as cause and effect. It must be said, however, that this interpretation finds no support in the general character of his writing, which is exceedingly humane, refined and womanly.

It has been said that the writings of this great man are the only surviving work of his period, but of that we are not altogether sure. There exists a fragment of an anonymous essay on woman's legal responsibility which many Americologists think belongs to the beginning of the twentieth century. Certainly it could not have been written later than the middle of it, for at that time woman had been definitely released from any responsibility to any law but that of her own will. The essay is an argument against even such imperfect exemption as she had in its author's time.

"It has been urged," the writer says, "that women, being less rational and more emotional than men, should not be held accountable in the same degree. To this it may be answered that punishment for crime is not intended to be retaliatory, but admonitory and deterrent. It is, therefore, peculiarly necessary to those not easily reached by other forms of warning and dissuasion. Control of the wayward is not to be sought in reduction of restraints, but in their multiplication. One who cannot be curbed by reason may be curbed by fear, a familiar truth which lies at the foundation of all penological systems. The argument for exemption of women is equally cogent for exemption of habitual criminals, for they too are abnormally inaccessible to reason, abnormally disposed to obedience to the suasion of their unregulated impulses and passions. To free them from the restraints of the fear of punishment would be a bold innovation which has as yet found no respectable proponent outside their own class.

"Very recently this dangerous enlargement of the meaning of the phrase 'emancipation of woman' has been fortified with a strange advocacy by the female 'champions of their sex.' Their argument runs this way: 'We are denied a voice in the making of the laws relating to infliction of the death penalty; it is unjust to hold us to an accountability to which we have not assented.' Of course this argument is as broad as the entire body of law; it amounts to nothing less than a demand for general immunity from all laws, for to none of them has woman's assent been asked or given. But let us consider this amazing claim with reference only to the proposal in the service and promotion of which it is now urged: exemption of women from the death penalty for murder. In the last analysis it is seen to be a simple demand for compensation. It says: 'You owe us a *solatium*.[26] Since you deny us the right to vote, you should give us the right to assassinate. We do not appraise it at so high a valuation as the other franchise, but we do value it.'

"Apparently they do: without legal, but with virtual, immunity from punishment, the women of this country take an average of one thousand lives annually, nine in ten being the lives of men. Juries of men, incited and sustained by public opinion, have actually deprived every adult male American of the right to live. If the death of any man is desired by any woman for any reason he is without protection. She has only to kill him and say that he wronged or insulted her. Certain almost incredible recent instances prove that no woman is too base for immunity, no crime against life sufficiently rich in all the elements of depravity to compel a conviction of the assassin, or, if she is convicted and sentenced, her punishment by the public executioner."[27]

In this interesting fragment, quoted by Bogul in his "History of an Extinct Civilization," we learn something of the shame and peril of American citizenship under institutions which, not having run their foreordained course to the unhappy end, were still in some degree supportable. What these institutions became afterward is a familiar story. It is true that the law of trial by jury was repealed. It had broken down, but not until it had sapped the whole nation's respect for all law, for all forms of authority, for order and private virtues. The people whose rude forefathers in another land it had served roughly to protect against their tyrants, it had lamentably failed to protect against themselves, and when in madness they swept it away, it was not as one renouncing an error, but as one impatient of the truth which the error is still believed to contain. They flung it away, not as an ineffectual restraint, but as a restraint; not because it was no longer an instrument of justice for the determination of truth, but because they feared that it might again become such. In brief, trial by jury was abolished only when it had provoked anarchy.

Before turning to another phase of this ancient civilization I cannot forbear to relate, after the learned and ingenious Gunkux, the only known instance of a public irony expressing itself in the sculptor's noble art. In the ancient city of Hohokus[28] once stood a monument of colossal size and impressive dignity. It was erected by public subscription to the memory of a man whose only distinction consisted in a single term of service as a juror in a famous murder trial, the details of which have not come down to us. This occupied the court and held public attention for many weeks, being bitterly contested by both prosecution and defense. When at last it was given to the jury by the judge in the most celebrated charge that had ever been delivered from the bench, a ballot was taken at once. The jury stood eleven for acquittal to one for conviction. And so it stood at every ballot of the more than fifty that were taken during the fortnight that the jury was locked up for deliberation. Moreover, the dissenting juror would not argue the matter; he would listen with patient attention while his eleven indignant opponents thundered their opinions into his ears, even when they supported them with threats of personal violence; but not a word would he say. At last a disagreement was formally entered, the jury discharged and the obstinate juror chased from the city by the maddened populace. Despairing of success in another trial and privately admitting his belief in the prisoner's innocence, the public prosecutor moved for his release, which the judge ordered with remarks plainly implying his own belief that the wrong man had been tried.

Years afterward the accused person died confessing his guilt, and a little later one of the jurors who had been sworn to try the case admitted that he had attended the trial on the first day only, having been personated during the rest of the proceedings by a twin brother, the obstinate member, who was a deaf-mute.

The monument to this eminent public servant was overthrown and destroyed by an earthquake in the year 2342.

One of the causes of that popular discontent which brought about the stupendous events resulting in the disruption of the great republic, historians and archæologists are agreed in reckoning "insurance."[29] Of the exact nature of that factor in the problem of the national life of that distant day we are imperfectly informed; many of its details have perished from the record, yet its outlines loom large through the mist of ages and can be traced with greater precision than is possible in many more important matters.

In the monumental work of Professor Golunk-Dorsto ("Some Account of the Insurance Delusion in Ancient America") we have its most considerable modern exposition; and Gakler's well-known volume, "The Follies of Antiquity," contains much interesting matter relating to it. From these and other sources the student of human unreason can reconstruct that astounding fallacy of insurance as, from three joints of its tail, the great naturalist Bogramus restored the ancient elephant, from hoof to horn.

The game of insurance, as practiced by the ancient Americans (and, as Gakler conjectures, by some of the tribesmen of Europe), was gambling, pure and simple, despite the sentimental character that its proponents sought to impress upon some forms of it for the greater prosperity of their dealings with its dupes. Essentially, it was a bet between the insurer and the insured.

The number of ways in which the wager was made—all devised by the insurer—was almost infinite, but in none of them was there a departure from the intrinsic nature of the transaction as seen in its simplest, frankest form, which we shall here expound.

To those unlearned in the economical institutions of antiquity it is necessary to explain that in ancient America, long prior to the disastrous Japanese war, individual ownership of property was unrestricted; every person was permitted to get as much as he was able, and to hold it as his own without regard to his needs, or whether he made any good use of it or not. By some plan of distribution not now understood even the habitable surface of the earth, with the minerals beneath, was parceled out among the favored few, and there was really no place except at sea where children of the others could lawfully be born. Upon a part of the dry land that he had been able to acquire, or had leased from another for the purpose, a man would build a house worth, say, ten thousand *drusoes*. (The ancient unit of value was the "dollar," but nothing is now known as to its actual worth.) Long before the building was complete the owner was beset by "touts" and "cappers"[30] of the insurance game, who poured into his ears the most ingenious expositions of the advantages of betting that it would burn down— for with incredible fatuity the people of that time continued, generation after generation, to build inflammable habitations. The persons whom the capper represented—they called themselves an "insurance company"—stood ready to accept the bet, a fact which seems to have generated no suspicion in the mind of the house-owner. Theoretically, of course, if the house did burn payment of the wager would partly or wholly recoup the winner of the bet for the loss of his house, but in fact the result of the transaction was commonly very different. For the privilege of betting that his property would be destroyed by fire the owner had to pay to the gentleman betting that it would not be, a certain percentage of its value every year, called a "premium." The amount of this was determined by the company, which employed statisticians and actuaries to fix it at such a sum that, according to the law of probabilities, long before the house was "due to burn," the company would have received more than the value of it in premiums. In other words, the owner of the house would himself supply the money to pay his bet, and a good deal more.

But how, it may be asked, could the company's actuary know that the man's house would last until he had paid in more than its insured value in premiums—more, that is to say, than the company would have to pay back? He could not, but from his statistics he could know how many houses in ten thousand of that kind burned in their first year, how many in their second, their third, and so on. That was all that he needed to know, the house-owners knowing nothing about it. He fixed his rates according to the facts,

and the occasional loss of a bet in an individual instance did not affect the
certainty of a general winning. Like other professional gamblers, the company expected to lose sometimes, yet knew that in the long run it *must* win;
which meant that in any special case it would *probably* win. With a thousand
gambling games open to him in which the chances were equal, the infatuated dupe chose to "sit into" one where they were against him! Deceived by
the cappers' fairy tales, dazed by the complex and incomprehensible "calculations" put forth for his undoing, and having ever in the ear of his imagination the crackle and roar of the impoverishing flames, he grasped at the hope
of beating—in an unwelcome way, it is true—"the man that kept the table."[31]
He must have known for a certainty that if the company could afford to
insure him he could not afford to let it. He must have known that the whole
body of the insured paid to the insurers more than the insurers paid to them;
otherwise the business could not have been conducted. This they cheerfully
admitted; indeed, they proudly affirmed it. In fact, insurance companies were
the only professional gamblers that had the incredible hardihood to parade
their enormous winnings as an inducement to play against their game. These
winnings ("assets," they called them) proved their ability, they said, to pay
when they lost; and that was indubitably true. What they did not prove,
unfortunately, was the *will* to pay, which from the imperfect court records of
the period that have come down to us, appears frequently to have been
lacking. Gakler relates that in the instance of the city of San Francisco (somewhat doubtfully identified by Macronus as the modern fishing-village of
Gharoo) the disinclination of the insurance companies to pay their bets had
the most momentous consequences.

In the year 1906 San Francisco was totally destroyed by fire. The
conflagration was caused by the friction of a pig scratching itself against an
angle of a wooden building. More than one hundred thousand persons perished, and the loss of property is estimated by Kobo-Dogarque at one and a
half million *drusoes*.[32] On more than two-thirds of this enormous sum the
insurance companies had laid bets, and the greater part of it they refused to
pay. In justification they pointed out that the deed performed by the pig was
"an act of God," who in the analogous instance of the express companies
had been specifically forbidden to take any action affecting the interests of
parties to a contract, or the result of an agreed undertaking.

In the ensuing litigation their attorneys cited two notable precedents. A
few years before the San Francisco disaster, another American city had experienced a similar one through the upsetting of a lamp by the kick of a cow.[33]
In that case, also, the insurance companies had successfully denied their liability on the ground that the cow, manifestly incited by some supernatural

power, had unlawfully influenced the result of a wager to which she was not a party. The companies defendant had contended that the recourse of the property-owners was against, not them, but the owner of the cow. In his decision sustaining that view and dismissing the case, a learned judge (afterward president of one of the defendant companies) had in the legal phraseology of the period pronounced the action of the cow an obvious and flagrant instance of unwarrantable intervention.[34] Kobo-Dogarque believes that this decision was afterward reversed by an appellate court of contrary political complexion and the companies were compelled to compromise, but of this there is no record. It is certain that in the San Francisco case the precedent was urged.[35]

Another precedent which the companies cited with particular emphasis related to an unfortunate occurrence at a famous millionaires' club in London, the capital of the renowned king, John Bul. A gentleman passing in the street fell in a fit and was carried into the club in convulsions. Two members promptly made a bet upon his life. A physician who chanced to be present set to work upon the patient, when one of the members who had laid the wager came forward and restrained him, saying: "Sir, I beg that you will attend to your own business. I have my money on that fit."

Doubtless these two notable precedents did not constitute the entire case of the defendants in the San Francisco insurance litigation, but the additional pleas are lost to us.

Of the many forms of gambling known as insurance that called life insurance appears to have been the most vicious. In essence it was the same as fire insurance, marine insurance, accident insurance and so forth, with an added offensiveness in that it was a betting on human lives—commonly by the policyholder on lives that should have been held most sacred and altogether immune from the taint of traffic.[36] In point of practical operation this ghastly business was characterized by a more fierce and flagrant dishonesty than any of its kindred pursuits. To such lengths of robbery did the managers go that at last the patience of the public was exhausted and a comparatively trivial occurrence fired the combustible elements of popular indignation to a white heat in which the entire insurance business of the country was burned out of existence, together with all the gamblers who had invented and conducted it. The president of one of the companies was walking one morning in a street of New York, when he had the bad luck to step on the tail of a dog and was bitten in retaliation. Frenzied by the pain of the wound, he gave the creature a savage kick and it ran howling toward a group of idlers in front of a grocery store. In ancient America the dog was a sacred animal, worshiped by all sorts and conditions of tribesmen. The idlers at once raised a great cry, and setting upon the offender beat him so that he died.

Their act was infectious: men, women and children trooped out of their dwellings by thousands to join them, brandishing whatever weapons they could snatch, and uttering wild cries of vengeance. This formidable mob overpowered the police, and marching from one insurance office to another, successively demolished them all, slew such officers as they could lay hands on, and chased the fugitive survivors into the sea, "where," says a quaint chronicle of the time, "they were eaten by their kindred, the sharks." This carnival of violence continued all the day, and at set of sun not one person connected with any form of insurance remained alive.

Ferocious and bloody as was the massacre, it was only the beginning. As the news of it went blazing and coruscating along the wires by which intelligence was then conveyed across the country, city after city caught the contagion. Everywhere, even in the small hamlets and the agricultural districts, the dupes rose against their dupers. The smoldering resentment of years burst into flame, and within a week all that was left of insurance in America was the record of a monstrous and cruel delusion written in the blood of its promoters.[37]

A remarkable feature of the crude and primitive civilization of the Americans was their religion. This was polytheistic, as is that of all backward peoples, and among their minor deities were their own women. This has been disputed by respectable authorities, among them Gunkux and the younger Kekler, but the weight of archæological testimony is against them, for, as Sagab-Joffoy ingeniously points out, none of less than divine rank would by even the lowest tribes be given unrestricted license to kill. Among the Americans woman, as already pointed out, indubitably had that freedom, and exercised it with terrible effect, a fact which makes the matter of their religion pertinent to the purpose of this monograph. If ever an American woman was punished by law for murder of a man no record of the fact is found; whereas, such American literature as we possess is full of the most enthusiastic adulation of the impossible virtues and imaginary graces of the human female. One writer even goes to the length of affirming that respect for the sex is the foundation of political stability, the cornerstone of civil and religious liberty![38] After the breakup of the republic and the savage intertribal wars that followed, Gyneolatry[39] was an exhausted cult and woman was relegated to her old state of benign subjection.

Unfortunately, we know little of the means of travel in ancient America, other than the names. It seems to have been done mainly by what were called "railroads," upon which wealthy associations of men transported their fellow-citizens in some kind of vehicle at a low speed, seldom exceeding fifty or sixty miles an hour, as distance and time were then reckoned—about equal to seven *kaltabs* a *grillog*. Notwithstanding this slow movement of the vehicles, the number and fatality of accidents were incredible. In the Zopetroq Museum of Archæology is preserved an official report (found in the excavations made by Droyhors on the supposed site of Washington) of a Government Commission of the Connected States. From that document we learn that in the year 1907 of their era the railroads of the country killed 5,000 persons and wounded 72,286—a mortality which is said by the commissioners to be twice that of the battle of Gettysburg, concerning which we know nothing but the name.[40] This was about the annual average of railroad casualties of the period, and if it provoked comment it at least led to no reform, for at a later period we find the mortality even greater. That it was preventable is shown by the fact that in the same year the railroads of Great Britain, where the speed was greater and the intervals between vehicles less, killed only one passenger. It was a difference of government: Great Britain had a government that governed; America had not. Happily for humanity, the kind of government that does not govern, self-government, "government of the people, by the people and for the people"[41] (to use a meaningless paradox of that time) has perished from the face of the earth.

An inherent weakness in republican government was that it assumed the honesty and intelligence of the majority, "the masses," who were neither honest nor intelligent. It would doubtless have been an excellent government for a people so good and wise as to need none. In a country having such a system the leaders, the politicians, must necessarily all be demagogues, for they can attain to place and power by no other method than flattery of the people and subserviency to the will of the majority. In all the ancient American political literature we look in vain for a single utterance of truth and reason regarding these matters. In none of it is a hint that the multitude was ignorant and vicious, as we know it to have been, and as it must necessarily be in any country, to whatever high average of intelligence and morality the people attain; for "intelligence" and "morality" are comparative terms, the standard of comparison being the intelligence and morality of the wisest and best, who must always be the few. Whatever general advance is made, those not at the head are behind—are ignorant and immoral according to the new standard, and unfit to control in the higher and broader policies demanded by the progress made. Where there is true and general progress the philosopher of yesterday would be the ignoramus of to-day, the honorable of one generation the vicious of another. The peasant of our time is incomparably superior to the statesman of ancient America, yet he is unfit to govern, for there are others more fit.

That a body of men can be wiser than its wisest member seems to the modern understanding so obvious and puerile an error that it is inconceivable that any people, even the most primitive, could ever have entertained it;[42] yet we know that in America it was a fixed and steadfast political faith. The people of that day did not, apparently, attempt to explain how the additional wisdom was acquired by merely assembling in council, as in their "legislatures"; they seem to have assumed that it was so, and to have based their entire governmental system upon that assumption, with never a suspicion of its fallacy. It is like assuming that a mountain range is higher than its highest peak. In the words of Golpek, "The early Americans believed that units of intelligence were addable quantities," or as Soseby more wittily puts it, "They thought that in a combination of idiocies they had the secret of sanity."

The Americans, as has been said, never learned that even among themselves majorities ruled, not because they ought, but because they could—not because they were wise, but because they were strong. The count of noses determined, not the better policy, but the more powerful party. The weaker submitted, as a rule, for it had to or risk a war in which it would be at a disadvantage. Yet in all the early years of the republic they seem honestly to have dignified their submission as "respect for the popular verdict." They even quoted from the Latin language the sentiment that "the voice of the people is the voice of God."[43] And this hideous blasphemy was as glib upon the lips of those who, without change of mind, were defeated at the polls year after year as upon those of the victors.

Of course, their government was powerless to restrain any aggression or encroachment upon the general welfare as soon as a considerable body of voters had banded together to undertake it. A notable instance has been recorded by Bamscot in his great work, "Some Evil Civilizations." After the first of America's great intestinal wars the surviving victors formed themselves into an organization which seems at first to have been purely social and benevolent, but afterward fell into the hands of rapacious politicians who in order to preserve their power corrupted their followers by distributing among them enormous sums of money exacted from the government by threats of overturning it. In less than a half century after the war in which they had served, so great was the fear which they inspired in whatever party controlled the national treasury that the total sum of their exactions was no less annually than seventeen million *prastams!* As Dumbleshaw naïvely puts it, "having saved their country, these gallant gentlemen naturally took it for themselves." The eventual massacre of the remnant of this hardy and impenitent organization by the labor unions more accustomed to the use of arms is beyond the province of this monograph to relate. The matter is mentioned at all only because it is a typical example of the open robbery that marked that period of the republic's brief and inglorious existence; the Grand

Army, as it called itself, was no worse and no better than scores of other organizations having no purpose but plunder and no method but menace. A little later
nearly all classes and callings became organized conspiracies, each seeking an
unfair advantage through laws which the party in power had not the firmness to
withhold, nor the party hoping for power the courage to oppose. The climax of
absurdity in this direction was reached in 1918, when an association of barbers,
known as Noblemen of the Razor, procured from the parliament of the country
a law giving it a representative in the President's Cabinet, and making it a misdemeanor to wear a beard.[44]

In Soseby's "History of Popular Government" he mentions "a monstrous political practice known as 'Protection to American Industries.'"
Modern research has not ascertained precisely what it was; it is known rather
from its effects than in its true character, but from what we can learn of it to-
day I am disposed to number it among those malefic agencies concerned in
the destruction of the American republics, particularly the Connected States,
although it appears not to have been peculiar to "popular government."
Some of the contemporary monarchies of Europe were afflicted with it, but
by the divine favor which ever guards a throne its disastrous effects were
averted. "Protection" consisted in a number of extraordinary expedients,
the purposes of which and their relations to one another cannot with certainty be determined in the present state of our knowledge. Debrethin and
others agree that one feature of it was the support, by general taxation, of a
few favored citizens in public palaces, where they passed their time in song
and dance and all kinds of revelry. They were not, however, altogether idle,
being required out of the sums bestowed upon them, to employ a certain
number of men each in erecting great piles of stone and pulling them down
again, digging holes in the ground and then filling them with earth, pouring
water into casks and then drawing it off, and so forth. The unhappy laborers
were subject to the most cruel oppressions, but the knowledge that their
wages came from the pockets of those whom their work nowise benefited
was so gratifying to them that nothing could induce them to leave the service of their heartless employers to engage in lighter and more useful labor.

Another characteristic of "Protection" was the maintenance at the principal seaports of "customs-houses," which were strong fortifications armed
with heavy guns for the purpose of destroying or driving away the trading
ships of foreign nations. It was this that caused the Connected States to be
known abroad as the "Hermit Republic," a name of which its infatuated
citizens were strangely proud, although they had themselves sent armed ships
to open the ports of Japan and other Oriental countries to their own commerce. In their own case, if a foreign ship came empty and succeeded in

evading the fire of the "customs-house," as sometimes occurred, she was permitted to take away a cargo.

It is obvious that such a system was distinctly evil, but it must be confessed our uncertainty regarding the whole matter of "Protection" does not justify us in assigning it a definite place among the causes of national decay. That in some way it produced an enormous revenue is certain, and that the method was dishonest is no less so; for this revenue—known as a "surplus"—was so abhorred while it lay in the treasury that all were agreed upon the expediency of getting rid of it, two great political parties existing for apparently no other purpose than the patriotic one of taking it out.

But how, it may be asked, could people so misgoverned get on, even as well as they did?

From the records that have come down to us it does not appear that they got on very well. They were preyed upon by all sorts of political adventurers, whose power in most instances was limited only by the contemporaneous power of other political adventurers equally unscrupulous. A full half of the taxes wrung from them was stolen. Their public lands, millions of square miles, were parceled out among banded conspirators. Their roads and the streets of their cities were nearly impassable. Their public buildings, conceived in abominable taste and representing enormous sums of money, which never were used in their construction, began to tumble about the ears of the workmen before they were completed. The most delicate and important functions of government were intrusted to men with neither knowledge, heart nor experience, who by their corruption imperiled the public interest and by their blundering disgraced the national name. In short, all the train of evils inseparable from government of any kind beset this unhappy people with tenfold power, together with hundreds of worse ones peculiar to their own faulty and unnatural system. It was thought that their institutions would give them peace, yet in the first three-quarters of a century of their existence they fought three important wars: one of revenge, one of aggression and one—the bloodiest and most wasteful known up to that time—among themselves.[45] And before a century and a half had passed they had the humiliation to see many of their seaport cities destroyed by the Emperor of Japan in a quarrel which they had themselves provoked by their greed of Oriental dominion.

By far the most important factor concerned in bringing about the dissolution of the republic and the incredible horrors that followed it was what was known as "the contest between capital and labor." This momentous struggle began in a rather singular way through an agitation set afoot by certain ambitious women who preached at first to inattentive and inhospitable ears, but with ever increasing acceptance, the doctrine of equality of the sexes, and demanded the "emancipation" of woman. True, woman was already an object of worship and had, as noted before, the right to kill. She was treated with profound and sincere deference, because of certain humble virtues, the product of her secluded life. Men of that time appear to have felt for women, in addition to religious reverence, a certain sentiment known as "love." The nature of this feeling is not clearly known to us, and has been for ages a matter of controversy evolving more heat than light. This much is plain: it was largely composed of good will, and had its root in woman's dependence. Perhaps it had something of the character of the benevolence with which we regard our slaves, our children and our domestic animals—everything, in fact, that is weak, helpless and inoffensive.

Woman was not satisfied; her superserviceable advocates taught her to demand the right to vote, to hold office, to own property, to enter into employment in competition with man. Whatever she demanded she eventually got. With the effect upon her we are not here concerned; the predicted gain to political purity did not ensue, nor did commercial integrity receive any stimulus from her participation in commercial pursuits. What indubitably did ensue was a more sharp and bitter competition in the industrial world through this increase of more than thirty per cent. in its wage-earning population. In no age nor country has there ever been sufficient employment for those requiring it. The effect of so enormously increasing the already disproportionate number of workers in a single generation could be no other than disastrous. Every woman employed displaced or excluded some man, who, compelled to seek a lower employment, displaced another, and so on, until the least capable or most unlucky of the series became a tramp—a nomadic mendicant criminal! The number of these dangerous vagrants in the beginning of the twentieth century of their era has been estimated by Holobom at no less than seven and a half *blukuks!* Of course, they were as tow to the fires of sedition, anarchy and insurrection. It does not very nearly relate to our present purpose, but it is impossible not to note in passing that this unhappy result, directly flowing from woman's invasion of the industrial field, was unaccompanied by any material advantage to herself. Individual women, here and there one, may themselves have earned the support that they would otherwise not have received, but the sex as a whole was not benefited. They provided for themselves no better than they had previously been provided for, and would still have been provided for, by the men whom they displaced. The whole somber incident is unrelieved by a single gleam of light.

Previously to this invasion of the industrial field by woman there had arisen conditions that were in themselves peculiarly menacing to the social fabric. Some of the philosophers of the period, rummaging amongst the dubious and misunderstood facts of commercial and industrial history, had discovered what they were pleased to term "the law of supply and demand"; and this they expounded with so ingenious a sophistry, and so copious a wealth of illustration and example that what is at best but a faulty and imperfectly applicable principle, limited and cut into by all manner of other considerations, came to be accepted as the sole explanation and basis of material prosperity and an infallible rule for the proper conduct of industrial affairs. In obedience to this "law"—for, interpreting it in its straitest sense they understood it to be mandatory—employers and employees alike regulated by its iron authority all their dealings with one another, throwing off the immemorial relations of mutual dependence and mutual esteem as tending to interfere with beneficent operation. The employer came to believe conscientiously that it was not only profitable and expedient, but under all circumstances his duty, to obtain his labor for as little money as possible, even as he sold its product for as much. Considerations of humanity were not banished from his heart, but most sternly excluded from his business. Many of these misguided men would give large sums to various charities; would found universities, hospitals, libraries; would even stop on their way to relieve beggars in the street; but for their own work-people they had no care. Straman relates in his "Memoirs" that a wealthy manufacturer once said to one of his mill-hands who had asked for an increase of his wages because unable to support his family on the pay that he was getting: "Your family is nothing to me. I cannot afford to mix benevolence with my business." Yet this man, the author adds, had just given a thousand *drusoes* to a "seaman's home." He could afford to care for other men's employees, but not for his own. He could not see that the act which he performed as truly, and to the same degree, cut down his margin of profit in his business as the act which he refused to perform would have done, and had not the advantage of securing him better service from a grateful workman.

On their part the laborers were no better. Their relations to their employers being "purely commercial," as it was called, they put no heart into their work, seeking ever to do as little as possible for their money, precisely as their employers sought to pay as little as possible for the work they got. The interests of the two classes being thus antagonized, they grew to distrust and hate each other, and each accession of ill feeling produced acts which tended to broaden the breach more and more. There was neither cheerful service on the one side nor ungrudging payment on the other.

The harder industrial conditions generated by woman's irruption into a new domain of activity produced among laboring men a feeling of blind discontent and concern. Like all men in apprehension, they drew together for mutual protection, they knew not clearly against what. They formed "labor unions," and believed them to be something new and effective in the betterment of their condition; whereas, from the earliest historical times, in Rome, in Greece, in Egypt, in Assyria, labor unions with their accepted methods of "striking" and rioting, had been discredited by an almost unbroken record of failure. One of the oldest manuscripts then in existence, preserved in a museum at Turin, but now lost, related how the workmen employed in the necropolis at Thebes, dissatisfied with their allowance of corn and oil, had refused to work, broken out of their quarters and, after much rioting, been subdued by the arrows of the military. And such, despite the sympathies and assistance of brutal mobs of the populace, was sometimes the end of the American "strike."

Originally organized for self-protection, and for a time partly successful, these leagues became great tyrannies, so reasonless in their demands and so unscrupulous in their methods of enforcing them that the laws were unable to deal with them, and frequently the military forces of the several States were ordered out for the protection of life and property; but in most cases the soldiers fraternized with the leagues, ran away, or were easily defeated. The cruel and mindless mobs had always the hypocritical sympathy and encouragement of the newspapers and the politicians, for both feared their power and courted their favor. The judges, dependent for their offices not only on "the labor vote," but, to obtain it, on the approval of the press and the politicians, boldly set aside the laws against conspiracy and strained to the utmost tension those relating to riot, arson and murder. To such a pass did all this come that in the year 1931 an innkeeper's denial of a half-holiday to an undercook resulted in the peremptory closing of half the factories in the country, the stoppage of all railroad travel and movement of freight by land and water and a general paralysis of the industries of the land. Many thousands of families, including those of the "strikers" and their friends, suffered from famine; armed conflicts occurred in every State; hundreds were slain and incalculable amounts of property wrecked and destroyed.

Failure, however, was inherent in the method, for success depended upon unanimity, and the greater the membership of the unions and the more serious their menace to the industries of the country, the higher was the premium for defection; and at last strike-breaking became a regular employment, organized, officered and equipped for the service required by the wealth and intelligence that directed it. From that moment the doom of labor unionism was decreed and inevitable. But labor unionism did not live long enough to die that way.

Naturally combinations of labor entailed combinations of capital. These were at first purely protective. They were brought into being by the necessity of resisting the aggressions of the others. But the trick of combination once learned, it was seen to have possibilities of profit in directions not dreamed of by its early promoters; its activities were not long confined to fighting the labor unions with their own weapons and with superior cunning and address. The shrewd and energetic men whose capacity and commercial experience had made them rich while the laborers remained poor were not slow to discern the advantages of coöperation over their own former method of competition among themselves. They continued to fight the labor unions, but ceased to fight one another. The result was that in the brief period of two generations almost the entire business of the country fell into the hands of a few gigantic corporations controlled by bold and unscrupulous men, who, by daring and ingenious methods, made the body of the people pay tribute to their greed.

In a country where money was all-powerful the power of money was used without stint and without scruple. Judges were bribed to do their duty, juries to convict, newspapers to support and legislators to betray their constituents and pass the most oppressive laws. By these corrupt means, and with the natural advantage of greater skill in affairs and larger experience in concerted action, the capitalists soon restored their ancient reign and the state of the laborer was worse than it had ever been before. Straman says that in his time two millions of unoffending workmen in the various industries were once discharged without warning and promptly arrested as vagrants and deprived of their ears because a sulking canal-boatman had kicked his captain's dog into the water. And the dog was a retriever.

Had the people been honest and intelligent, as the politicians affirmed them to be, the combination of capital could have worked no public injury—would, in truth, have been a great public benefit. It enormously reduced the expense of production and distribution, assured greater permanency of employment, opened better opportunities to general and special aptitude, gave an improved product, and at first supplied it at a reduced price. Its crowning merit was that the industries of the country, being controlled by a few men from a central source, could themselves be easily controlled by law if law had been honestly administered. Under the old order of scattered jurisdictions, requiring a multitude of actions at law, little could be done, and little was done, to put a check on commercial greed; under the new, much was possible, and at times something was accomplished. But not for long; the essential dishonesty of the American character enabled these capable and conscienceless managers—"captains of industry" and "kings of finance"—to buy with money advantages and immunities superior to those that the labor unions could obtain by menaces and the promise of votes. The legislatures, the courts, the executive officers, all the sources of authority and springs of control, were defiled and impested until right and justice fled affrighted from the land, and the name of the country became a stench in the nostrils of the world.

Let us pause in our narrative to say here that much of the abuse of the so-called "trusts" by their victims took no account of the folly, stupidity and greed of the victims themselves. A favorite method by which the great corporations crushed out the competition of the smaller ones and of the "individual dealers" was by underselling them—a method made possible by nothing but the selfishness of the purchasing consumers who loudly complained of it. These could have stood by their neighbor, the "small dealer," if they had wanted to, and no underselling could have been done. When the trust lowered the price of its product they eagerly took the advantage offered, then cursed the trust for ruining the small dealer. When it raised the price they cursed it for ruining themselves. It is not easy to see what the trust could have done that would have been acceptable, nor is it surprising that it soon learned to ignore their clamor altogether and impenitently plunder those whom it could not hope to appease.

Another of the many sins justly charged against the "kings of finance" was this: They would buy properties worth, say, ten millions of "dollars" (the value of the dollar is now unknown) and issue stock upon it to the face value of, say, fifty millions. This their clamorous critics called "creating" for themselves forty millions of dollars. They created nothing; the stock had no dishonest value unless sold, and even at the most corrupt period of the government nobody was compelled by law to buy. In nine cases in ten the person who bought did so in the hope and expectation of getting much for little and something for nothing. The buyer was no better than the seller. He was a gambler. He "played against the game of the man who kept the table" (as the phrase went), and naturally he lost. Naturally, too, he cried out, but his lamentations, though echoed shrilly by the demagogues, seem to have been unavailing. Even the rudimentary intelligence of that primitive people discerned the impracticability of laws forbidding the seller to set his own price on the thing he would sell and declare it worth that price. Then, as now, nobody had to believe him. Of the few who bought these "watered" stocks in good faith as an investment in the honest hope of dividends it seems sufficient to say, in the words of an ancient Roman, "Against stupidity the gods themselves are powerless."[46] Laws that would adequately protect the foolish from the consequence of their folly would put an end to all commerce. The sin of "over-capitalization" differed in magnitude only, not in kind, from the daily practice of every salesman in every shop. Nevertheless, the popular fury that it aroused must be reckoned among the main causes contributory to the savage insurrections that accomplished the downfall of the republic.

With the formation of powerful and unscrupulous trusts of both labor and capital to subdue each other the possibilities of combination were not exhausted; there remained the daring plan of combining the two belligerents! And this was actually effected. The laborer's demand for an increased wage was always based upon an increased cost of living, which was itself chiefly due to increased cost of production from reluctant concessions of his former demands. But in the first years of the twentieth century observers noticed on the part of capital a lessening reluctance. More frequent and more extortionate and reasonless demands encountered a less bitter and stubborn resistance; capital was apparently weakening just at the time when, with its strong organizations of trained and willing strike-breakers, it was most secure. Not so; an ingenious malefactor, whose name has perished from history, had thought out a plan for bringing the belligerent forces together to plunder the rest of the population. In the accounts that have come down to us details are wanting, but we know that, little by little, this amazing project was accomplished. Wages rose to incredible rates. The cost of living rose with them, for employers—their new allies wielding in their service the weapons previously used against them, intimidation, the boycott, and so forth— more than recouped themselves from the general public. Their employees got rebates on the prices of products, but for consumers who were neither laborers nor capitalists there was no mercy. Strikes were a thing of the past; strike-breakers threw themselves gratefully into the arms of the unions; "industrial discontent" vanished, in the words of a contemporary poet, "as by the stroke of an enchanter's wand."[47] All was peace, tranquillity and order! Then the storm broke.

A man in St. Louis purchased a sheep's kidney for seven-and-a-half dollars. In his rage at the price he exclaimed: "As a public man I have given twenty of the best years of my life to bringing about a friendly understanding between capital and labor. I have succeeded, and may God have mercy on my meddlesome soul!"

The remark was resented, a riot ensued, and when the sun went down that evening his last beams fell upon a city reeking with the blood of a hundred millionaires and twenty thousand citizens and sons of toil!

Students of the history of those troublous times need not to be told what other and more awful events followed that bloody reprisal. Within forty-eight hours the country was ablaze with insurrection, followed by intestinal wars which lasted three hundred and seventy years and were marked by such hideous barbarities as the modern historian can hardly bring himself to relate. The entire stupendous edifice of popular government, temple and citadel of fallacies and abuses, had crashed to ruin. For centuries its fallen columns and scattered stones sheltered an ever diminishing number of skulking anarchists, succeeded by hordes of skin-clad savages subsisting on offal and raw flesh—the race-remnant of an extinct civilization. All finally vanished from history into a darkness impenetrable to conjecture.

In concluding this hasty and imperfect sketch I cannot forbear to relate an episode of the destructive and unnatural contest between labor and capital, which I find recorded in the almost forgotten work of Antrolius, who was an eye-witness to the incident.

At a time when the passions of both parties were most inflamed and scenes of violence most frequent it was somehow noised about that at a certain hour of a certain day some one—none could say who—would stand upon the steps of the Capitol and speak to the people, expounding a plan for reconciliation of all conflicting interests and pacification of the quarrel. At the appointed hour thousands had assembled to hear—glowering capitalists attended by hireling body-guards with firearms, sullen laborers with dynamite bombs concealed in their clothing. All eyes were directed to the specified spot, where suddenly appeared (none saw whence—it seemed as if he had been there all the time, such his tranquillity) a tall, pale man clad in a long robe, bare-headed, his hair falling lightly upon his shoulders, his eyes full of compassion, and with such majesty of face and mien that all were awed to silence ere he spoke. Stepping slowly forward toward the throng and raising his right hand from the elbow, the index finger extended upward, he said, in a voice ineffably sweet and serious:

"Whatsoever ye would that men should do unto you, even so do ye also unto them."[48]

These strange words he repeated in the same solemn tones three times; then, as the expectant multitude waited breathless for his discourse, stepped quietly down into the midst of them, every one afterward declaring that he passed within a pace of where himself had stood. For a moment the crowd was speechless with surprise and disappointment, then broke into wild, fierce cries: "Lynch him, lynch him!" and some have testified that they heard the word "crucify." Struggling into looser order, the infuriated mob started in mad pursuit; but each man ran a different way and the stranger was seen again by none of them.

THE LAND BEYOND THE BLOW

*(After the method of Swift, who followed Lucian, and was himself
followed by Voltaire and many others.)*

Thither

A CROWD OF men were assisting at a dog-fight. The scene was one of
indescribable confusion. In the center of the tumult the dogs, obscure
in a cloud of dust, rolled over and over, howling, yarring, tearing each other
with sickening ferocity. About them the hardly less ferocious men shouted,
cursed and struck, encouraged the animals with sibilant utterances and threatened with awful forms of death and perdition all who tried to put an end to
the combat. Caught in the thick of this pitiless mob I endeavored to make
my way to a place of peace, when a burly blackguard, needlessly obstructing
me, said derisively:

"I guess you are working pockets."

"You are a liar!" I retorted hotly.

That is all the provocation that I remember to have given.

Sons of the Fair Star

WHEN CONSCIOUSNESS RETURNED the sun was high in the heavens, yet the light was dim, and had that indefinable ghastly quality that
is observed during a partial eclipse. The sun itself appeared singularly small,
as if it were at an immensely greater distance than usual. Rising with some
difficulty to my feet, I looked about me. I was in an open space among some
trees growing on the slope of a mountain range whose summit on the one
hand was obscured by a mist of a strange pinkish hue, and on the other rose
into peaks glittering with snow. Skirting the base at a distance of two or
three miles flowed a wide river, and beyond it a nearly level plain stretched
away to the horizon, dotted with villages and farmhouses and apparently in
a high state of cultivation. All was unfamiliar in its every aspect. The trees
were unlike any that I had ever seen or even imagined, the trunks being

mostly square and the foliage consisting of slender filaments resembling hair, in many instances long enough to reach the earth. It was of many colors, and I could not perceive that there was any prevailing one, as green is in the vegetation to which I was accustomed. As far as I could see there were no grass, no weeds, no flowers; the earth was covered with a kind of lichen, uniformly blue. Instead of rocks, great masses of metals protruded here and there, and above me on the mountain were high cliffs of what seemed to be bronze veined with brass. No animals were visible, but a few birds as uncommon in appearance as their surroundings glided through the air or perched upon the rocks. I say glided, for their motion was not true flight, their wings being mere membranes extended parallel to their sides, and having no movement independent of the body. The bird was, so to say, suspended between them and moved forward by quick strokes of a pair of enormously large webbed feet, precisely as a duck propels itself in water. All these things excited in me no surprise, nor even curiosity; they were merely unfamiliar. That which most interested me was what appeared to be a bridge several miles away, up the river, and to this I directed my steps, crossing over from the barren and desolate hills to the populous plain.

For a full history of my life and adventures in Mogon-Zwair,[1] and a detailed description of the country, its people, their manners and customs, I must ask the reader to await the publication of a book, now in the press, entitled *A Blackened Eye;* in this brief account I can give only a few of such particulars as seem instructive by contrast with our own civilization.[2]

The inhabitants of Mogon-Zwair call themselves Golampis,[3] a word signifying Sons of the Fair Star. Physically they closely resemble ourselves, being in all respects the equals of the highest Caucasian type. Their hair, however, has a broader scheme of color, hair of every hue known to us, and even of some imperceptible to my eyes but brilliant to theirs, being too common to excite remark. A Golampian assemblage with uncovered heads resembles, indeed, a garden of flowers, vivid and deep in color, no two alike. They wear no clothing of any kind, excepting for adornment and protection from the weather, resembling in this the ancient Greeks and the Japanese of yesterday;[4] nor was I ever able to make them comprehend that clothing could be worn for those reasons for which it is chiefly worn among ourselves. They are destitute of those feelings of delicacy and refinement which distinguish us from the lower animals, and which, in the opinion of our acutest and most pious thinkers, are evidences of our close relation to the Power that made us.

Among this people certain ideas which are current among ourselves as mere barren faiths expressed in disregarded platitudes receive a practical application to the affairs of life. For example, they hold, with the best, wisest and most experienced of our own race, and one other hereafter to be described, that wealth does not bring happiness and is a misfortune and an evil. None but the most ignorant and depraved, therefore, take the trouble to acquire or preserve it. A rich Golampi is naturally regarded with contempt and suspicion, is shunned by the good and respectable and subjected to police surveillance. Accustomed to a world where the rich man is profoundly and justly respected for his goodness and wisdom (manifested in part by his own deprecatory protests against the wealth of which, nevertheless, he is apparently unable to rid himself) I was at first greatly pained to observe the contumelious manner of the Golampis toward this class of men, carried in some instances to the length of personal violence; a popular amusement being the pelting them with coins. These the victims would carefully gather from the ground and carry away with them, thus increasing their hoard and making themselves all the more liable to popular indignities.

When the cultivated and intelligent Golampi finds himself growing too wealthy he proceeds to get rid of his surplus riches by some one of many easy expedients. One of these I have just described; another is to give his excess to those of his own class who have not sufficient to buy employment and so escape leisure, which is considered the greatest evil of all. "Idleness," says one of their famous authors, "is the child of poverty and the parent of discontent"; and another great writer says: "No one is without employment; the indolent man works for his enemies."

In conformity to these ideas the Golampis—all but the ignorant and vicious rich—look upon labor as the highest good, and the man who is so unfortunate as not to have enough money to purchase employment in some useful industry will rather engage in a useless one than not labor at all. It is not unusual to see hundreds of men carrying water from a river and pouring it into a natural ravine or artificial channel, through which it runs back into the stream. Frequently a man is seen conveying stones—or the masses of metal which there correspond to stones—from one pile to another. When all have been heaped in a single place he will convey them back again, or to a new place, and so proceed until darkness puts an end to the work. This kind of labor, however, does not confer the satisfaction derived from the consciousness of being useful, and is never performed by any person having the means to hire another to employ him in some beneficial industry. The wages usually paid to employers are from three to six *balukan* a day. This statement may seem incredible, but I solemnly assure the reader that I have known a bad workman or a feeble woman to pay as high as eight; and there have been instances of men whose incomes had outgrown their desires paying even more.

Labor being a luxury which only those in easy circumstances can afford, the poor are the more eager for it, not only because it is denied them, but because it is a sign of respectability. Many of them, therefore, indulge in it on credit and soon find themselves deprived of what little property they had to satisfy their hardfisted employers. A poor woman once complained to me that her husband spent every *rylat* that he could get in the purchase of the most expensive kinds of employment, while she and the children were compelled to content themselves with such cheap and coarse activity as dragging an old wagon round and round in a small field which a kind-hearted neighbor permitted them to use for the purpose. I afterward saw this improvident husband and unnatural father. He had just squandered all the money he had been able to beg or borrow in buying six tickets, which entitled the holder to that many days' employment in pitching hay into a barn. A week later I met him again. He was broken in health, his limbs trembled, his walk was an uncertain shuffle. Clearly he was suffering from overwork. As I paused by the wayside to speak to him a wagon loaded with hay was passing. He fixed his eyes upon it with a hungry, wolfish glare, clutched a pitchfork and leaned eagerly forward, watching the vanishing wagon with breathless attention and heedless of my salutation. That night he was arrested, streaming with perspiration, in the unlawful act of unloading that hay and putting it into its owner's barn. He was tried, convicted and sentenced to six months' detention in the House of Indolence.

The whole country is infested by a class of criminal vagrants known as *strambaltis,* or, as we should say, "tramps." These persons prowl about among the farms and villages begging for work in the name of charity. Sometimes they travel in groups, as many as a dozen together, and then the farmer dares not refuse them; and before he can notify the constabulary they will have performed a great deal of the most useful labor that they can find to do and escaped without paying a *rylat*. One trustworthy agriculturist assured me that his losses in one year from these depredations amounted to no less a sum than seven hundred *balukan!* On nearly all the larger and more isolated farms a strong force of guards is maintained during the greater part of the year to prevent these outrages, but they are frequently overpowered, and sometimes prove unfaithful to their trust by themselves working secretly by night.

The Golampi priesthood has always denounced overwork as a deadly sin, and declared useless and apparently harmless work, such as carrying water from the river and letting it flow in again, a distinct violation of the divine law, in which, however, I could never find any reference to the matter; but there has recently risen a sect which holds that all labor being pleasurable, each kind in its degree is immoral and wicked. This sect, which embraces many of the most holy and learned men, is rapidly spreading and becoming a power in the state. It has, of course, no churches, for these cannot be built without labor, and its members commonly dwell in caves and live upon such roots and berries as can be easily gathered, of which the country produces a great abundance though all are exceedingly unpalatable. These *Gropoppsu* (as the members of this sect call themselves) pass most of their waking hours sitting in the sunshine with folded hands, contemplating their navels; by the practice of which austerity they hope to obtain as reward an eternity of hard labor after death.

The Golampis are an essentially pious and religious race. There are few, indeed, who do not profess at least one religion. They are nearly all, in a certain sense, polytheists: they worship a supreme and beneficent deity by one name or another, but all believe in the existence of a subordinate and malevolent one, whom also, while solemnly execrating him in public rites, they hold at heart in such reverence that needlessly to mention his name or that of his dwelling is considered sin of a rank hardly inferior to blasphemy.[5] I am persuaded that this singular tenderness toward a being whom their theology represents as an abominable monster, the origin of all evil and the foe to souls, is a survival of an ancient propitiatory adoration. Doubtless this wicked deity was once so feared that his conciliation was one of the serious concerns of life. He is probably as greatly feared now as at any former time, but is apparently less hated, and is by some honestly admired.

It is interesting to observe the important place held in Golampian affairs by religious persecution.[6] The Government is a pure theocracy, all the Ministers of State and the principal functionaries in every department of control belonging to the priesthood of the dominant church. It is popularly believed in Mogon-Zwair that persecution, even to the extent of taking life, is in the long run beneficial to the cause enduring it. This belief has, indeed, been crystallized into a popular proverb, not capable of accurate translation into our tongue, but to the effect that martyrs fertilize religion by pouring out their blood about its roots. Acting upon this belief with their characteristically logical and conscientious directness, the sacerdotal rulers of the country mercilessly afflict the sect to which themselves belong. They arrest its leading members on false charges, throw them into loathsome and unwholesome dungeons, subject them to the cruelest tortures and sometimes put them to death. The provinces in which the state religion is especially strong are occasionally raided and pillaged by government soldiery, recruited for the purpose by conscription among the dissenting sects, and are sometimes actually devastated with fire and sword. The result is not altogether confirmatory of the popular belief and does not fulfil the pious hope of the governing powers who are cruel to be kind. The vitalizing efficacy of persecution is not to be doubted, but the persecuted of too feeble faith frequently thwart its beneficent intent and happy operation by apostasy.

Having in mind the horrible torments which a Golampian general had inflicted upon the population of a certain town I once ventured to protest to him that so dreadful a sum of suffering, seeing that it did not accomplish its purpose, was needless and unwise.

"Needless and unwise it may be," said he, "and I am disposed to admit that the result which I expected from it has not followed; but why do you speak of the *sum* of suffering? I tortured those people in but a single, simple way—by skinning their legs."

"Ah, that is very true," said I, "but you skinned the legs of one thousand."

"And what of that?" he asked. "Can one thousand, or ten thousand, or any number of persons suffer more agony than one? A man may have his leg broken, then his nails pulled out, then be seared with a hot iron. Here is suffering added to suffering, and the effect is really cumulative. In the true mathematical sense it is a *sum* of suffering. A single person can experience it. But consider, my dear sir. How can you add one man's agony to another's? They are not addable quantities. Each is an individual pain, unaffected by the other. The limit of anguish which ingenuity can inflict is that utmost pang which one man has the vitality to endure."

I was convinced but not silenced.

The Golampis all believe, singularly enough, that truth possesses some inherent vitality and power that give it an assured prevalence over falsehood; that a good name cannot be permanently defiled and irreparably ruined by detraction, but, like a star, shines all the brighter for the shadow through which it is seen; that justice cannot be stayed by injustice; that vice is powerless against virtue. I could quote from their great writers hundreds of utterances affirmative of these propositions. One of their poets, for example, has some striking and original lines, of which the following is a literal but unmetrical translation:[7]

> A man who is in the right has three arms,
> But he whose conscience is rotten with wrong
> Is stripped and confined in a metal cell.

Imbued with these beliefs, the Golampis think it hardly worth while to be truthful, to abstain from slander, to do justice and to avoid vicious actions. "The practice," they say, "of deceit, calumniation, oppression and immorality cannot have any sensible and lasting injurious effect, and it is most agreeable to the mind and heart. Why should there be personal self-denial without commensurate general advantage?"

In consequence of these false views, affirmed by those whom they regard as great and wise, the people of Mogon-Zwair are, as far as I have observed them, the most conscienceless liars, cheats, thieves, rakes and all-round, many-sided sinners that ever were created to be damned.[8] It was, therefore, with inexpressible joy that I received one day legal notification that I had been tried in the High Court of Conviction and sentenced to banishment to Lalugnan. My offense was that I had said that I regarded consistency as the most detestable of all vices.

An Interview with Gnarmag-Zote

MOGON-ZWAIR AND LALUGNAN, having the misfortune to lie on opposite sides of a line, naturally hate each other; so each country sends its dangerous political criminals into the other, where they usually enjoy high honors and are sometimes elevated to important office under the crown. I was therefore received in Lalugnan with hospitality and given every encouragement in prosecuting my researches into the history and intellectual life of the people. They are so extraordinary a people, inhabiting so marvelous a country, that everything which the traveler sees, hears or experiences makes a lively and lasting impression upon his mind, and the labor of a lifetime would be required to relate the observation of a single year. I shall notice here only one or two points of national character—those which differ most conspicuously from ours, and in which, consequently, they are least worthy.

With a fatuity hardly more credible than creditable, the Lalugwumps, as they call themselves, deny the immortality of the soul. In all my stay in their country I found only one person who believed in a life "beyond the grave," as we should say, though as the Lalugwumps are cannibals they would say "beyond the stomach." In testimony to the consolatory value of the doctrine of another life, I may say that this one true believer had in this life a comparatively unsatisfactory lot, for in early youth he had been struck by a flying stone from a volcano and had lost a considerable part of his brain.

I cannot better set forth the nature and extent of the Lalugwumpian error regarding this matter than by relating a conversation that occurred between me and one of the high officers of the King's household—a man whose proficiency in all the vices of antiquity, together with his service to the realm in determining the normal radius of curvature in cats' claws, had elevated him to the highest plane of political preferment. His name was Gnarmag-Zote.

"You tell me," said he, "that the soul is immaterial. Now, matter is that of which we can have knowledge through one or more of our senses. Of what is immaterial—not matter—we can gain no knowledge in that way. How, then, can we know anything about it?"[9]

Perceiving that he did not rightly apprehend my position I abandoned it and shifted the argument to another ground. "Consider," I said, "the analogous case of a thought. You will hardly call thought material, yet we know there are thoughts."

"I beg your pardon, but we do not know that. Thought is not a thing, therefore cannot *be* in any such sense, for example, as the hand *is*. We use the word 'thought' to designate the result of an action of the brain, precisely as we use the word 'speed' to designate the result of an action of a horse's legs. But can it be said that speed *exists* in the same way as the legs which produce it exist, or in any way? Is it a thing?"

I was about to disdain to reply, when I saw an old man approaching, with bowed head, apparently in deep distress. As he drew near he saluted my distinguished interlocutor in the manner of the country, by putting out his tongue to its full extent and moving it slowly from side to side. Gnarmag-Zote acknowledged the civility by courteously spitting, and the old man, advancing, seated himself at the great officer's feet, saying: "Exalted Sir, I have just lost my wife by death, and am in a most melancholy frame of mind. He who has mastered all the vices of the ancients and wrested from nature the secret of the normal curvature of cats' claws can surely spare from his wisdom a few rays of philosophy to cheer an old man's gloom. Pray tell me what I shall do to assuage my grief."

The reader can, perhaps, faintly conceive my astonishment when Gnarmag-Zote gravely replied: "Kill yourself."

"Surely," I cried, "you would not have this honest fellow procure oblivion (since you think that death is nothing else) by so rash an act!"

"An act that Gnarmag-Zote advises," he said, coldly, "is not rash."

"But death," I said, "death, whatever else it may be, is an end of life. This old man is now in sorrow almost insupportable. But a few days and it will be supportable; a few months and it will have become no more than a tender melancholy. At last it will disappear, and in the society of his friends, in the skill of his cook, the profits of avarice, the study of how to be querulous and in the pursuit of loquacity, he will again experience the joys of age. Why for a present grief should he deprive himself of all future happiness?"

Gnarmag-Zote looked upon me with something like compassion. "My friend," said he, "guest of my sovereign and my country, know that in any circumstances, even those upon which true happiness is based and conditioned, death is preferable to life. The sum of miseries in any life (here in Lalugnan at least) exceeds the sum of pleasures; but suppose that it did not.[10] Imagine an existence in which happiness, of whatever intensity, is the rule, and discomfort, of whatever moderation, the exception. Still there is some discomfort. There is none in death, for (as it is given to us to know) that is oblivion, annihilation.[11] True, by dying one loses his happiness as well as his sorrows, but he is not conscious of the loss. Surely, a loss of which one will never know, and which, if it operate to make him less happy, at the same time takes from him the desire and capacity and need of happiness, cannot be an evil. That is so intelligently understood among us here in Lalugnan that suicide is common, and our word for sufferer is the same as that for fool. If this good man had not been an idiot he would have taken his life as soon as he was bereaved."

"If what you say of the blessing of death is true," I said, smilingly, for I greatly prided myself on the ingenuity of my thought, "it is unnecessary to commit suicide through grief for the dead; for the more you love the more glad you should be that the object of your affection has passed into so desirable a state as death."

"So we are—those of us who have cultivated philosophy, history and logic; but this poor fellow is still under the domination of feelings inherited from a million ignorant and superstitious ancestors—for Lalugnan was once as barbarous a country as your own. The most grotesque and frightful conceptions of death, and life after death, were current; and now many of even those whose understandings are emancipated wear upon their feelings the heavy chain of heredity."

"But," said I, "granting for the sake of the argument which I am about to build upon the concession" (I could not bring myself to use the idiotic and meaningless phrase, "for the sake of argument") "that death, especially the death of a Lalugwump, is desirable, yet the act of dying, the transition state between living and being dead, may be accompanied by the most painful physical, and most terrifying mental phenomena. The moment of dissolution may seem to the exalted sensibilities of the moribund a century of horrors."

The great man smiled again, with a more intolerable benignity than before. "There is no such thing as dying," he said; "the 'transition state' is a creation of your fancy and an evidence of imperfect reason. One is at any time either alive or dead. The one condition cannot shade off into the other. There is no gradation like that between waking and sleeping.[12] By the way, do you recognize a certain resemblance between death and a dreamless sleep?"

"Yes—death as you conceive it to be."

"Well, does any one fear sleep? Do we not seek it, court it, wish that it may be sound—that is to say, dreamless? We desire occasional annihilation—wish to be dead for eight and ten hours at a time. True, we expect to awake, but that expectation, while it may account for our alacrity in embracing sleep, cannot alter the character of the state that we cheerfully go into. Suppose we did *not* wake in the morning, never did wake! Would our mental and spiritual condition be in any respect different through all eternity from what it was during the first few hours? After how many hours does oblivion begin to be an evil? The man who loves to sleep yet hates to die might justly be granted everlasting life with everlasting insomnia."

Gnarmag-Zote paused and appeared to be lost in the profundity of his thoughts, but I could easily enough see that he was only taking breath. The old man whose grief had given this turn to the conversation had fallen asleep and was roaring in the nose like a beast. The rush of a river near by, as it poured up a hill from the ocean, and the shrill singing of several kinds of brilliant quadrupeds were the only other sounds audible. I waited deferentially for the great antiquarian, scientist and courtier to resume, amusing myself meantime by turning over the leaves of an official report by the Minister of War on a new and improved process of making thunder from snail slime. Presently the oracle spoke.

"You have been born," he said, which was true. "There was, it follows, a time when you had not been born. As we reckon time, it was probably some millions of ages. Of this considerable period you are unable to remember one unhappy moment, and in point of fact there was none. To a Lalugwump that is entirely conclusive as to the relative values of consciousness and oblivion, existence and non-existence, life and death.[13] This old man lying here at my feet is now, if not dreaming, as if he had never been born. Would not it be cruel and inhuman to wake him back to grief? Is it, then, kind to permit him to wake by the natural action of his own physical energies? I have given him the advice for which he asked. Believing it good advice, and seeing him too irresolute to act, it seems my clear duty to assist him."

Before I could interfere, even had I dared take the liberty to do so, Gnarmag-Zote struck the old man a terrible blow upon the head with his mace of office. The victim turned upon his back, spread his fingers, shivered convulsively and was dead.

"You need not be shocked," said the distinguished assassin, coolly: "I have but performed a sacred duty and religious rite. The religion (established first in this realm by King Skanghutch, the sixty-second of that name) consists in the worship of Death. We have sacred books, some three thousand thick volumes, said to be written by inspiration of Death himself, whom no mortal has ever seen, but who is described by our priests as having the figure of a fat young man with a red face and wearing an affable smile. In art he is commonly represented in the costume of a husbandman sowing seeds.

"The priests and sacred books teach that death is the supreme and only good—that the chief duties of man are, therefore, assassination and suicide. Conviction of these cardinal truths is universal among us, but I am sorry to say that many do not honestly live up to the faith. Most of us are commendably zealous in assassination, but slack and lukewarm in suicide. Some justify themselves in this half-hearted observance of the Law and imperfect submission to the Spirit by arguing that if they destroy themselves their usefulness in destroying others will be greatly abridged. 'I find,' says one of our most illustrious writers, not without a certain force, it must be confessed, 'that I can slay many more of others than I can of myself.'

"There are still others, more distinguished for faith than works, who reason that if A kill B, B cannot kill C. So it happens that although many Lalugwumps die, mostly by the hands of others, though some by their own, the country is never wholly depopulated."

"In my own country," said I, "is a sect holding somewhat Lalugwumpian views of the evil of life; and among the members it is considered a sin to bestow it. The philosopher Schopenhauer taught the same doctrine,[14] and many of our rulers have shown strong sympathetic leanings toward it by procuring the destruction of many of their own people and those of other nations in what is called war."

"They are greatly to be commended," said Gnarmag-Zote, rising to intimate that the conversation was at an end. I respectfully protruded my tongue while he withdrew into his palace, spitting politely and with unusual copiousness in acknowledgment. A few minutes later, but before I had left the spot, two lackeys in livery emerged from the door by which he had entered, and while one shouldered the body of the old man and carried it into the palace kitchen the other informed me that his Highness was graciously pleased to desire my company at dinner that evening. With many expressions of regret I declined the invitation, unaware that to do so was treason. With the circumstances of my escape to the island of Tamtonia the newspapers have made the world already familiar.

The Tamtonians

IN ALL MY INTERCOURSE with the Tamtonians I was treated with the most distinguished consideration and no obstacles to a perfect understanding of their social and political life were thrown in my way. My enforced residence on the island was, however, too brief to enable me to master the whole subject as I should have liked to do.

The government of Tamtonia is what is known in the language of the island as a *cilbuper*. It differs radically from any form known in other parts of the world and is supposed to have been invented by an ancient chief of the race, named Natas, who was for many centuries after his death worshiped as a god, and whose memory is still held in veneration. The government is of infinite complexity, its various functions distributed among as many officers as possible, multiplication of places being regarded as of the greatest importance, and not so much a means as an end. The Tamtonians seem to think that the highest good to which a human being can attain is the possession of an office; and in order that as many as possible may enjoy that advantage they have as many offices as the country will support, and make the tenure brief and in no way dependent on good conduct and intelligent administration of official duty. In truth, it occurs usually that a man is turned out of his office (in favor of an incompetent successor) before he has acquired sufficient experience to perform his duties with credit to himself or profit to the country. Owing to this incredible folly, the affairs of the island are badly mismanaged. Complaints are the rule, even from those who have had their way in the choice of officers. Of course there can be no such thing as a knowledge of the science of government among such a people, for it is to nobody's interest to acquire it by study of political history. There is, indeed, a prevalent belief that nothing worth knowing is to be learned from the history of other nations—not even from the history of their errors—such is this extraordinary people's national vanity! One of the most notable consequences of this universal and voluntary ignorance is that Tamtonia is the home of all the discreditable political and fiscal heresies from which many other nations, and especially our own, emancipated themselves centuries ago. They are there in vigorous growth and full flower, and believed to be of purely Tamtonian origin.

It needs hardly to be stated that in their personal affairs these people pursue an entirely different course, for if they did not there could be no profitable industries and professions among them, and no property to tax for the support of their government. In his private business a Tamtonian has as high appreciation of fitness and experience as anybody, and having secured a good man keeps him in service as long as possible.

The ruler of the nation, whom they call a *Tnediserp,* is chosen every five years but may be rechosen for five more. He is supposed to be selected by the people themselves, but in reality they have nothing to do with his selection. The method of choosing a man for *Tnediserp* is so strange that I doubt my ability to make it clear.

The adult male population of the island divides itself into two or more *seitrap*.[15] Commonly there are three or four, but only two ever have any considerable numerical strength, and none is ever strong morally or intellectually. All the members of each *ytrap* profess the same political opinions, which are provided for them by their leaders every five years and written down on pieces of paper so that they will not be forgotten. The moment that any Tamtonian has read his piece of paper, or *mroftalp,* he unhesitatingly adopts all the opinions that he finds written on it, sometimes as many as forty or fifty, although these may be altogether different from, or even antagonistic to, those with which he was supplied five years before and has been advocating ever since.[16] It will be seen from this that the Tamtonian mind is a thing whose processes no American can hope to respect, or even understand. It is instantaneously convinced without either fact or argument, and when these are afterward presented they only confirm it in its miraculous conviction; those which make against that conviction having an even stronger confirmatory power than the others. I have said any Tamtonian, but that is an overstatement. A few usually persist in thinking as they did before; or in altering their convictions in obedience to reason instead of authority, as our own people do; but they are at once assailed with the most opprobrious names, accused of treason and all manner of crimes, pelted with mud and stones and in some instances deprived of their noses and ears by the public executioner. Yet in no country is independence of thought so vaunted as a virtue, and in none is freedom of speech considered so obvious a natural right or so necessary to good government.

At the same time that each *ytrap* is supplied with its political opinions for the next five years, its leaders—who, I am told, all pursue the vocation of sharpening axes—name a man whom they wish chosen for the office of *Tnediserp*. He is usually an idiot from birth, the Tamtonians having a great veneration for such, believing them to be divinely inspired. Although few members of the *ytrap* have ever heard of him before, they at once believe him to have been long the very greatest idiot in the country; and for the next few months they do little else than quote his words and point to his actions to prove that his idiocy is of entirely superior quality to that of his opponent—a view that he himself, instructed by his discoverers, does and says all that he can to confirm. His inarticulate mumblings are everywhere repeated as utterances of profound wisdom, and the slaver that drools from his chin is carefully collected and shown to the people, evoking the wildest enthusiasm of his supporters. His opponents all this time are trying to blacken his character by the foulest conceivable falsehoods, some even going so far as to assert that he is not an idiot at all! It is generally agreed among them that if he were chosen to office the most dreadful disasters would ensue, and that, *therefore,* he will not be chosen.

To this last mentioned conviction, namely that the opposing candidate *(rehtot lacsar)* cannot possibly be chosen, I wish to devote a few words here, for it seems to me one of the most extraordinary phenomena of the human mind. It implies, of course, a profound belief in the wisdom of majorities and the error of minorities. This belief can and does in some mysterious way co-exist, in the Tamtonian understanding, with the deepest disgust and most earnest disapproval of a decision which a majority has made.[17] It is of record, indeed, that one political *ytrap* sustained no fewer than six successive defeats without at all impairing its conviction that the right side must win.[18] In each recurring contest this *ytrap* was as sure that it would succeed as it had been in all the preceding ones—and sure *because* it believed itself in the right! It has been held by some native observers that this conviction is not actually entertained, but only professed for the purpose of influencing the action of others; but this is disproved by the fact that even after the contest is decided, though the result is unknown—when nobody's action can have effect—the leaders (ax-sharpeners) continue earnestly to "claim" this province and that, up to the very last moment of uncertainty, and the common people murder one another in the streets for the crime of doubting that the man is chosen whom the assassin was pleased to prefer. When the majority of a province has chosen one candidate and a majority of the nation another, the mental situation of the worthy Tamtonian is not over-easy of conception, but there can be no doubt that his faith in the wisdom of majorities remains unshaken.

One of the two antagonistic idiots having been chosen as ruler, it is customary to speak of him as "the choice of the people," whereas it is obvious that he is one of the few men, seldom exceeding two or three, whom it is certainly known that nearly one-half the people regard as unfit for the position.[19] He is less certainly "the people's choice" than any other man in the country excepting his unsuccessful opponents; for while it is known that a large body of his countrymen did not want him, it cannot be known how many of his supporters really preferred some other person, but had no opportunity to make their preference effective.

The Tamtonians are very proud of their form of government, which gives them so much power in selecting their rulers. This power consists in the privilege of choosing between two men whom but a few had a voice in selecting from among many millions, any one of whom the rest might have preferred to either. Yet every Tamtonian is as vain of possessing this incalculably small influence as if he were a Warwick in making kings and a Bismarck in using them.[20] He gives himself as many airs and graces as would be appropriate to the display of an honest pin-feather upon the pope's-nose of a mooley peacock.

Each congenital idiot whom the ax-grinders name for the office of *Tnediserp* has upon the "ticket" with him a dead man, who stands or falls with his leader. There is no way of voting for the idiot without voting for the corpse also, and *vice versa*. When one of these precious couples has been chosen the idiot in due time enters upon the duties of his office and the corpse is put into an ice-chest and carefully preserved from decay. If the idiot should himself become a corpse he is buried at once and the other body is then haled out of its ice to take his place. It is propped up in the seat of authority and duly instated in power. This is the signal for a general attack upon it. It is subjected to every kind of sacrilegious indignity, vituperated as a usurper and an "accident," struck with rotten eggs and dead cats, and undergoes the meanest misrepresentation.[21] Its attitude in the chair, its fallen jaw, glazed eyes and degree of decomposition are caricatured and exaggerated out of all reason. Yet such as it is it must be endured for the unexpired term for which its predecessor was chosen. To guard against a possible interregnum, however, a law has recently been passed providing that if it should tumble out of the chair and be too rotten to set up again its clerks *(seiraterces)* are eligible to its place in a stated order of succession. Here we have the amazing anomaly of the rulers of a "free" people actually appointing their potential successors!—a thing inexpressibly repugnant to all our ideas of popular government, but apparently regarded in Tamtonia as a matter of course.

During the few months intervening between the ax-men's selection of candidates and the people's choice between those selected (a period known as the *laitnediserp ngiapmac*) the Tamtonian character is seen at its worst. There is no infamy too great or too little for the partisans of the various candidates to commit and accuse their opponents of committing. While every one of them declares, and in his heart believes, that honest arguments have greater weight than dishonest; that falsehood reacts on the falsifier's cause; that appeals to passion and prejudice are as ineffectual as dishonorable, few have the strength and sense to deny themselves the luxury of all these methods and worse ones. The laws against bribery, made by themselves, are set at naught and those of civility and good breeding are forgotten. The best of friends quarrel and openly insult one another. The women, who know almost as little of the matters at issue as the men, take part in the abominable discussions; some even encouraging the general demoralization by showing themselves at the public meetings, sometimes actually putting themselves into uniform and marching in procession with banners, music and torchlights.[22]

I feel that this last statement will be hardly understood without explanation. Among the agencies employed by the Tamtonians to prove that one set of candidates is better than another, or to show that one political policy is more likely than another to promote the general prosperity, a high place is accorded to colored rags, flames of fire, noises made upon brass instruments, inarticulate shouts, explosions of gunpowder and lines of men walking and riding through the streets in cheap and tawdry costumes more or less alike. Vast sums of money are expended to procure these strange evidences of the personal worth of candidates and the political sanity of ideas. It is very much as if a man should paint his nose pea-green and stand on his head to convince his neighbors that his pigs are fed on acorns. Of course the money subscribed for these various controversial devices is not all wasted; the greater part of it is pocketed by the ax-grinders by whom it is solicited, and who have invented the system. That they have invented it for their own benefit seems not to have occurred to the dupes who pay for it. In the universal madness everybody believes whatever monstrous and obvious falsehood is told by the leaders of his own *ytrap,* and nobody listens for a moment to the exposures of their rascality. Reason has flown shrieking from the scene; Caution slumbers by the wayside with unbuttoned pocket. It is the opportunity of thieves!

With a view to abating somewhat the horrors of this recurring season of depravity, it has been proposed by several wise and decent Tamtonians to extend the term of office of the *Tnediserp* to six years instead of five, but the sharpeners of axes are too powerful to be overthrown. They have made the people believe that if the man whom the country chooses to rule it because it thinks him wise and good were permitted to rule it too long it would be impossible to displace him in punishment for his folly and wickedness. It is, indeed, far more likely that the term of office will be reduced to four years than extended to six. The effect can be no less than hideous!

In Tamtonia there is a current popular saying dating from many centuries back and running this way: *"Eht eciffo dluohs kees eht nam, ton eht nam eht eciffo"*— which may be translated thus: "No citizen ought to try to secure power for himself, but should be selected by others for his fitness to exercise it." The sentiment which this wise and decent phrase expresses has long ceased to have a place in the hearts of those who are everlastingly repeating it, but with regard to the office of *Tnediserp* it has still a remnant of the vitality of habit. This, however, is fast dying out, and a few years ago one of the congenital idiots who was a candidate for the highest dignity boldly broke the inhibition and made speeches to the people in advocacy of himself, all over the country. Even more recently another has uttered his preferences in much the same way, but with this difference: he did his speechmaking at his own home, the ax-grinders in his interest rounding up audiences for him and herding them before his door.[23] One of the two corpses, too, was galvanized into a kind of ghastly activity and became a talking automaton; but the other had been too long dead. In a few years more the decent tradition that a man should not blow his own horn will be obsolete in its application to the high office, as it is to all the others, but the popular saying will lose none of its currency for that.

To the American mind nothing can be more shocking than the Tamtonian practice of openly soliciting political preferment and even paying money to assist in securing it. With us such immodesty would be taken as proof of the offender's unfitness to exercise the power which he asks for, or bear the dignity which, in soliciting it, he belittles. Yet no Tamtonian ever refused to take the hand of a man guilty of such conduct, and there have been instances of fathers giving these greedy vulgarians the hands of their daughters in marriage and thereby assisting to perpetuate the species. The kind of government given by men who go about begging for the right to govern can be more easily imagined than endured.[24] In short, I cannot help thinking that when, unable longer to bear with patience the evils entailed by the vices and follies of its inhabitants, I sailed away from the accursed island of Tamtonia, I left behind me the most pestilent race of rascals and ignoramuses to be found anywhere in the universe; and I never can sufficiently thank the divine Power who spared me the disadvantage and shame of being one of them, and cast my lot in this favored land of goodness and right reason, the blessed abode of public morality and private worth—of liberty, conscience and common sense.

I was not, however, to reach it without further detention in barbarous countries. After being at sea four days I was seized by my mutinous crew, set ashore upon an island, and having been made insensible by a blow upon the head was basely abandoned.

Marooned on Ug

WHEN I REGAINED my senses I found myself lying on the strand a short remove from the margin of the sea. It was high noon and an insupportable itching pervaded my entire frame, that being the effect of sunshine in that country, as heat is in ours. Having observed that the discomfort was abated by the passing of a light cloud between me and the sun, I dragged myself with some difficulty to a clump of trees near by and found permanent relief in their shade. As soon as I was comfortable enough to examine my surroundings I saw that the trees were of metal, apparently copper, with leaves of what resembled pure silver, but may have contained alloy. Some of the trees bore burnished flowers shaped like bells, and in a breeze the tinkling as they clashed together was exceedingly sweet. The grass with which the open country was covered as far as I could see amongst the patches of forest was of a bright scarlet hue, excepting along the water-courses, where it was white. Lazily cropping it at some little distance away, or lying in it, indolently chewing the cud and attended by a man half-clad in skins and bearing a crook, was a flock of tigers. My travels in New Jersey[25] having made me proof against surprise, I contemplated these several visible phenomena without emotion, and with a merely expectant interest in what might be revealed by further observation.

The tigerherd having perceived me, now came striding forward, brandishing his crook and shaking his fists with great vehemence, gestures which I soon learned were, in that country, signs of amity and good-will. But before knowing that fact I had risen to my feet and thrown myself into a posture of defense, and as he approached I led for his head with my left, following with a stiff right upon his solar plexus, which sent him rolling on the grass in great pain. After learning something of the social customs of the country I felt extreme mortification in recollecting this breach of etiquette, and even to this day I cannot think upon it without a blush.

Such was my first meeting with Jogogle-Zadester, Pastor-King of Ug, the wisest and best of men. Later in our acquaintance, when I had for a long time been an honored guest at his court, where a thousand fists were ceremoniously shaken under my nose daily, he explained that my luke-warm reception of his hospitable advances gave him, for the moment, an unfavorable impression of my breeding and culture.

The island of Ug, upon which I had been marooned,[26] lies in the Southern Hemisphere, but has neither latitude nor longitude. It has an area of nearly seven hundred square *samtains* and is peculiar in shape, its width being considerably greater than its length. Politically it is a limited monarchy, the right of succession to the throne being vested in the sovereign's father, if he have one; if not in his grandfather, and so on upward in the line of ascent. (As a matter of fact there has not within historic times been a legitimate succession, even the great and good Jogogle-Zadester being a usurper chosen by popular vote.) To assist him in governing, the King is given a parliament, the Uggard word for which is *gabagab,* but its usefulness is greatly circumscribed by the *Blubosh,* or Constitution, which requires that every measure, in order to become a law, shall have an affirmative majority of the actual members, yet forbids any member to vote who has not a distinct pecuniary interest in the result. I was once greatly amused by a spirited contest over a matter of harbor improvement, each of two proposed harbors having its advocates. One of these gentlemen, a most eloquent patriot, held the floor for hours in advocacy of the port where he had an interest in a projected mill for making dead kittens into cauliflower pickles; while other members were being vigorously persuaded by one who at the other place had a clam ranch.[27] In a debate in the Uggard *gabagab* no one can have a "standing" except a party in interest; and as a consequence of this enlightened policy every bill that is passed is found to be most intelligently adapted to its purpose.

The original intent of this requirement was that members having no pecuniary interest in a proposed law at the time of its inception should not embarrass the proceedings and pervert the result; but the inhibition is now thought to be sufficiently observed by formal public acceptance of a nominal bribe to vote one way or the other. It is of course understood that behind the nominal bribe is commonly a more substantial one of which there is no record. To an American accustomed to the incorrupt methods of legislation in his own country the spectacle of every member of the Uggard *gabagab* qualifying himself to vote by marching up, each in his turn as his name is called, to the proponent of the bill, or to its leading antagonist, and solemnly receiving a *tonusi* (the smallest coin of the realm) is exceedingly novel. When I ventured to mention to the King my lack of faith in the principle upon which this custom is founded, he replied:

"Heart of my soul, if you and your compatriots distrust the honesty and intelligence of an interested motive why is it that in your own courts of law, as you describe them, no private citizen can institute a civil action to right the wrongs of anybody but himself?"

I had nothing to say and the King proceeded: "And why is it that your judges will listen to no argument from any one who has not acquired a selfish concern in the matter?"

"O, your Majesty," I answered with animation, "they listen to attorneys-general, district attorneys and salaried officers of the law generally, whose prosperity depends in no degree upon their success; who prosecute none but those whom they believe to be guilty; who are careful to present no false nor misleading testimony and argument; who are solicitous that even the humblest accused person shall be accorded every legal right and every advantage to which he is entitled; who, in brief, are animated by the most humane sentiments and actuated by the purest and most unselfish motives."

The King's discomfiture was pitiful: he retired at once from the capital and passed a whole year pasturing his flock of tigers in the solitudes beyond the River of Wine. Seeing that I would henceforth be *persona non grata* at the palace, I sought obscurity in the writing and publication of books. In this vocation I was greatly assisted by a few standard works that had been put ashore with me in my sea-chest.

The literature of Ug is copious and of high merit, but consists altogether of fiction—mainly history, biography, theology and novels. Authors of exceptional excellence receive from the state marks of signal esteem, being appointed to the positions of laborers in the Department of Highways and Cemeteries. Having been so fortunate as to win public favor and attract official attention by my locally famous works, "The Decline and Fall of the Roman Empire," "David Copperfield," "Pilgrim's Progress," and "Ben Hur,"[28] I was myself that way distinguished and my future assured. Unhappily, through ignorance of the duties and dignities of the position I had the mischance to accept a gratuity for sweeping a street crossing and was compelled to flee for my life.

Disguising myself as a sailor I took service on a ship that sailed due south into the Unknown Sea.

It is now many years since my marooning on Ug, but my recollection of the country, its inhabitants and their wonderful manners and customs is exceedingly vivid. Some small part of what most interested me I shall here set down.

The Uggards are, or fancy themselves, a warlike race: nowhere in those distant seas are there any islanders so vain of their military power, the consciousness of which they acquired chiefly by fighting one another. Many years ago, however, they had a war with the people of another island kingdom, called Wug. The Wuggards held dominion over a third island, Scamadumclitchclitch,[29] whose people had tried to throw off the yoke. In order to subdue them—at least to tears—it was decided to deprive them of garlic, the sole article of diet known to them and the Wuggards, and in that country dug out of the ground like coal. So the Wuggards in the rebellious island stopped up all the garlic mines, supplying their own needs by purchase from foreign trading proas. Having few cowrie shells, with which to purchase, the poor Scamadumclitchclitchians suffered a great distress, which so touched the hearts of the compassionate Uggards—a most humane and conscientious people—that they declared war against the Wuggards and sent a fleet of proas to the relief of the sufferers. The fleet established a strict blockade of every port in Scamadumclitchclitch, and not a clove of garlic could enter the island. That compelled the Wuggard army of occupation to reopen the mines for its own subsistence.[30]

All this was told to me by the great and good and wise Jogogle-Zadester, King of Ug.

"But, your Majesty," I said, "what became of the poor Scamadumclitchclitchians?"

"They all died," he answered with royal simplicity.

"Then your Majesty's humane intervention," I said, "was not entirely—well, fattening?"

"The fortune of war," said the King, gravely, looking over my head to signify that the interview was at an end; and I retired from the Presence on hands and feet, as is the etiquette in that country.

As soon as I was out of hearing I threw a stone in the direction of the palace and said: "I never in my life heard of such a cold-blooded scoundrel!"

In conversation with the King's Prime Minister, the famous Grumsquuztzy, I asked him how it was that Ug, being a great military power, was apparently without soldiers.

"Sir," he replied, courteously shaking his fist under my nose in sign of amity, "know that when Ug needs soldiers she enlists them. At the end of the war they are put to death."

"Visible embodiment of a great nation's wisdom," I said, "far be it from me to doubt the expediency of that military method; but merely as a matter of economy would it not be better to keep an army in time of peace than to be compelled to create one in time of war?"

"Ug is rich," he replied; "we do not have to consider matters of economy. There is among our people a strong and instinctive distrust of a standing army."

"What are they afraid of," I asked—"what do they fear that it will do?"

"It is not what the army may do," answered the great man, "but what it may prevent others from doing. You must know that we have in this land a thing known as Industrial Discontent."

"Ah, I see," I exclaimed, interrupting—"the industrial classes fear that the army may destroy, or at least subdue, their discontent."

The Prime Minister reflected profoundly, standing the while, in order that he might assist his faculties by scratching himself, even as we, when thinking, scratch our heads.

"No," he said presently; "I don't think that is quite what they apprehend—they and the writers and statesmen who speak for them. As I said before, what is feared in a case of industrial discontent is the army's preventive power. But I am myself uncertain what it is that these good souls dislike to have the army prevent. I shall take the customary means to learn."

Having occasion on the next day to enter the great audience hall of the palace I observed in gigantic letters running across the entire side opposite the entrance this surprising inscription:

"In a strike, what do you fear that the army will prevent which ought to be done?"

Facing the entrance sat Grumsquutzy, in his robes of office and surrounded by an armed guard. At a little distance stood two great black slaves,
each bearing a scourge of thongs. All about them the floor was slippery with
blood. While I wondered at all this two policemen entered, having between
them one whom I recognized as a professional Friend of the People, a great
orator, keenly concerned for the interests of Labor. Shown the inscription
and unable or unwilling to answer, he was given over to the two blacks and,
being stripped to the skin, was beaten with the whips until he bled copiously
and his cries resounded through the palace. His ears were then shorn away
and he was thrown into the street. Another Friend of the People was brought
in, and treated in the same way; and the inquiry was continued, day after
day, until all had been interrogated. But Grumsquutzy got no answer.

A most extraordinary and interesting custom of the Uggards is called the
Naganag and has existed, I was told, for centuries. Immediately after every war,
and before the returned army is put to death, the chieftains who have held high
command and their official head, the Minister of National Displeasure, are conducted with much pomp to the public square of Nabootka, the capital. Here all
are stripped naked, deprived of their sight with a hot iron and armed with a club
each. They are then locked in the square, which has an enclosing wall thirty
clowgebs high. A signal is given and they begin to fight. At the end of three days
the place is entered and searched. If any of the dead bodies has an unbroken
bone in it the survivors are boiled in wine; if not they are smothered in butter.

Upon the advantages of this custom—which surely has not its like in the
whole world—I could get little light. One public official told me its purpose was
"peace among the victorious"; another said it was "for gratification of the military instinct in high places," though if that is so one is disposed to ask "What was
the war for?" The Prime Minister, profoundly learned in all things else, could
not enlighten me, and the commander-in-chief in the Wuggard war could only
tell me, while on his way to the public square, that it was "to vindicate the truth
of history."

In all the wars in which Ug has engaged in historic times that with Wug was
the most destructive of life. Excepting among the comparatively few troops that
had the hygienic and preservative advantage of personal collusion with the enemy, the mortality was appalling. Regiments exposed to the fatal conditions of
camp life in their own country died like flies in a frost.[31] So pathetic were the
pleas of the sufferers to be led against the enemy and have a chance to live that
none hearing them could forbear to weep. Finally a considerable number of
them went to the seat of war, where they began an immediate attack upon a
fortified city, for their health; but the enemy's resistance was too brief materially
to reduce the death rate and the men were again in the hands of their officers.

On their return to Ug they were so few that the public executioners charged with the duty of reducing the army to a peace footing were themselves made ill by inactivity.

As to the navy, the war with Wug having shown the Uggard sailors to be immortal, their government knows not how to get rid of them, and remains a great sea power in spite of itself. I ventured to suggest mustering out, but neither the King nor any Minister of State was able to form a conception of any method of reduction and retrenchment but that of the public headsman.

It is said—I do not know with how much truth—that the defeat of Wug was made easy by a certain malicious prevision of the Wuggards themselves: something of the nature of heroic self-sacrifice, the surrender of a present advantage for a terrible revenge in the future. As an instance, the commander of the fortified city already mentioned is reported to have ordered his garrison to kill as few of their assailants as possible.

"It is true," he explained to his subordinates, who favored a defense to the death—"it is true this will lose us the place, but there are other places; you have not thought of that."

They had not thought of that.

"It is true, too, that we shall be taken prisoners, but"—and he smiled grimly—"we have fairly good appetites, and we must be fed. That will cost something, I take it. But that is not the best of it. Look at that vast host of our enemies—each one of them a future pensioner on a fool people. If there is among us one man who would willingly deprive the Uggard treasury of a single dependent—who would spare the Uggard pigs one *gukwam* of expense, let the traitor stand forth."

No traitor stood forth, and in the ensuing battles the garrison, it is said, fired only blank cartridges, and such of the assailants as were killed incurred that mischance by falling over their own feet.

It is estimated by Wuggard statisticians that in twenty years from the close of the war the annual appropriation for pensions in Ug will amount to no less than one hundred and sixty *gumdums* to every enlisted man in the kingdom. But they know not the Uggard customs of exterminating the army.

The Dog in Ganegwag

A T ABOUT THE END of the thirty-seventh month of our voyage due south from Ug we sighted land, and although the coast appeared wild and inhospitable, the captain decided to send a boat ashore in search of fresh water and provisions, of which we were in sore need. I was of the boat's crew and thought myself fortunate in being able to set foot again upon the earth. There were seven others in the landing party, including the mate, who commanded.

Selecting a sheltered cove, which appeared to be at the mouth of a small creek, we beached the boat, and leaving two men to guard it started inland toward a grove of trees. Before we reached it an animal came out of it and advanced confidently toward us, showing no signs of either fear or hostility. It was a hideous creature, not altogether like anything that we had ever seen, but on its close approach we recognized it as a dog, of an unimaginably loathsome breed. As we were nearly famished one of the sailors shot it for food. Instantly a great crowd of persons, who had doubtless been watching us from among the trees, rushed upon us with fierce exclamations and surrounded us, making the most threatening gestures and brandishing unfamiliar weapons. Unable to resist such odds we were seized, bound with cords and dragged into the forest almost before we knew what had happened to us. Observing the nature of our reception the ship's crew hastily weighed anchor and sailed away. We never again saw them.[32]

Beyond the trees concealing it from the sea was a great city, and thither we were taken. It was Gumammam, the capital of Ganegwag, whose people are dog-worshipers. The fate of my companions I never learned, for although I remained in the country for seven years, much of the time as a prisoner, and learned to speak its language, no answer was ever given to my many inquiries about my unfortunate friends.

The Ganegwagians are an ancient race with a history covering a period of ten thousand *supintroes*. In stature they are large, in color blue, with crimson hair and yellow eyes. They live to a great age, sometimes as much as twenty *supintroes,* their climate being so wholesome that even the aged have to sail to a distant island in order to die. Whenever a sufficient number of them reach what they call "the age of going away" they embark on a government ship and in the midst of impressive public rites and ceremonies set sail for "the Isle of the Happy Change." Of their strange civilization, their laws, manners and customs, their copper clothing and liquid houses I have written—at perhaps too great length—in my famous book, "Ganegwag the Incredible." Here I shall confine myself to their religion, certainly the most amazing form of superstition in the world.

Nowhere, it is believed, but in Ganegwag has so vile a creature as the dog obtained general recognition as a deity.[33] There this filthy beast is considered so divine that it is freely admitted to the domestic circle and cherished as an honored guest. Scarcely a family that is able to support a dog is without one, and some have as many as a half-dozen. Indeed, the dog is the special deity of the poor, those families having most that are least able to maintain them. In some sections of the country, particularly the southern and southwestern provinces, the number of dogs is estimated to be greater than that of the children, as is the cost of their maintenance. In families of the rich they are fewer in number, but more sacredly cherished, especially by the female members, who lavish upon them a wealth of affection not always granted to the husband and children, and distinguish them with indescribable attentions and endearments.

Nowhere is the dog compelled to make any other return for all this honor and benefaction than a fawning and sycophantic demeanor toward those who bestow them and an insulting and injurious attitude toward strangers who have dogs of their own, and toward other dogs. In any considerable town of the realm not a day passes but the public newsman relates in the most matter-of-fact and unsympathetic way to his circle of listless auditors painful instances of human beings, mostly women and children, bitten and mangled by these ferocious animals without provocation.

In addition to these ravages of the dog in his normal state are a vastly greater number of outrages committed by the sacred animal in the fury of insanity, for he has an hereditary tendency to madness, and in that state his bite is incurable, the victim awaiting in the most horrible agony the sailing of the next ship to the Isle of the Happy Change, his suffering imperfectly medicined by expressions of public sympathy for the dog.

A cynical citizen of Gumammam said to the writer of this narrative: "My countrymen have three hundred kinds of dogs, and only one way to hang a thief." Yet all the dogs are alike in this, that none is respectable.

Withal, it must be said of this extraordinary people that their horrible religion is free from the hollow forms and meaningless ceremonies in which so many superstitions of the lower races find expression. It is a religion of love, practical, undemonstrative, knowing nothing of pageantry and spectacle. It is hidden in the lives and hearts of the people; a stranger would hardly know of its existence as a distinct faith. Indeed, other faiths and better ones (one of them having some resemblance to a debased form of Christianity) co-exist with it, sometimes in the same mind. Cynolatry[34] is tolerant so long as the dog is not denied an equal divinity with the deities of other faiths. Nevertheless, I could not think of the people of Ganegwag without contempt and loathing; so it was with no small joy that I sailed for the contiguous island of Ghargaroo to consult, according to my custom, the renowned statesman and philosopher, Juptka-Getch, who was accounted the wisest man in all the world, and held in so high esteem that no one dared speak to him without the sovereign's permission, countersigned by the Minister of Morals and Manners.

A Conflagration in Ghargaroo

THROUGH THE HAPPY accident of having a mole on the left side of my nose, as had also a cousin of the Prime Minister, I obtained a royal rescript permitting me to speak to the great Juptka-Getch, and went humbly to his dwelling, which, to my astonishment, I found to be an unfurnished cave in the side of a mountain. Inexpressibly surprised to observe that a favorite of the sovereign and the people was so meanly housed, I ventured, after my salutation, to ask how this could be so. Regarding me with an indulgent smile, the venerable man, who was about two hundred and fifty years old and entirely bald, explained.

"In one of our Sacred Books, of which we have three thousand," said he, "it is written, '*Golooloo ek wakwah betenka,*' and in another, '*Jebeb uq seedroy im aboltraqu ocrux ti smelkit.*'"[35]

Translated, these mean, respectively, "The poor are blessed," and, "Heaven is not easily entered by those who are rich."

I asked Juptka-Getch if his countrymen really gave to these texts a practical application in the affairs of life.

"Why, surely," he replied, "you cannot think us such fools as to disregard the teachings of our gods! That would be madness. I cannot imagine a people so mentally and morally depraved as that! Can you?"[36]

Observing me blushing and stammering, he inquired the cause of my embarrassment. "The thought of so incredible a thing confuses me," I managed to reply. "But tell me if in your piety and wisdom you really stripped yourself of all your property in order to obey the gods and get the benefit of indigence."

"I did not have to do so," he replied with a smile; "my King attended to that. When he wishes to distinguish one of his subjects by a mark of his favor, he impoverishes him to such a degree as will attest the exact measure of the royal approbation. I am proud to say that he took from me all that I had."

"But, pardon me," I said; "how does it occur that among a people which regards poverty as the greatest earthly good all are not poor? I observe here as much wealth and 'prosperity' as in my own country."

Juptka-Getch smiled and after a few moments answered: "The only person in this country that owns anything is the King; in the service of his people he afflicts himself with that burden. All property, of whatsoever kind, is his, to do with as he will. He divides it among his subjects in the ratio of their demerit, as determined by the *waguks*—local officers—whose duty it is to know personally every one in their jurisdiction. To the most desperate and irreclaimable criminals is allotted the greatest wealth, which is taken from them, little by little, as they show signs of reformation."

"But what," said I, "is to prevent the wicked from becoming poor at any time? How can the King and his officers keep the unworthy, suffering the punishment and peril of wealth, from giving it away?"

"To whom, for example?" replied the illustrious man, taking the forefinger of his right hand into his mouth, as is the fashion in Ghargaroo when awaiting an important communication. The respectful formality of the posture imperfectly concealed the irony of the question, but I was not of the kind to be easily silenced.

"One might convert one's property into money," I persisted, "and throw the money into the sea."

Juptka-Getch released the finger and gravely answered: "Every person in Ghargaroo is compelled by law to keep minute accounts of his income and expenditures, and must swear to them. There is an annual appraisement by the *waguk,* and any needless decrease in the value of an estate is punished by breaking the offender's legs. Expenditures for luxuries and high living are, of course, approved, for it is universally known among us, and attested by many popular proverbs, that the pleasures of the rich are vain and disappointing. So they are considered a part of the punishment, and not only allowed but required. A man sentenced to wealth who lives frugally, indulging in only rational and inexpensive delights, has his ears cut off for the first offense, and for the second is compelled to pass six months at court, participating in all the gaieties, extravagances and pleasures of the capital, and—"

"Most illustrious of mortals," I said, turning a somersault—the Ghargarese manner of interrupting a discourse without offense—"I am as the dust upon your beard, but in my own country I am esteemed no fool, and right humbly do I perceive that you are *ecxroptug nemk puttog peleemy*."

This expression translates, literally, "giving me a fill," a phrase without meaning in our tongue, but in Ghargarese it appears to imply incredulity.

"The gaieties of the King's court," I continued, "must be expensive. The courtiers of the sovereign's entourage, the great officers of the realm—surely they are not condemned to wealth, like common criminals!"

"My son," said Juptka-Getch, tearing out a handful of his beard to signify his tranquillity under accusation, "your doubt of my veracity is noted with satisfaction, but it is not permitted to you to impeach my sovereign's infallible knowledge of character. His courtiers, the great officers of the realm, as you truly name them, are the richest men in the country because he knows them to be the greatest rascals. After each annual reapportionment of the national wealth he settles upon them the unallotted surplus."

Prostrating myself before the eminent philosopher, I craved his pardon for my doubt of his sovereign's wisdom and consistency, and begged him to cut off my head.

"Nay," he said, "you have committed the unpardonable sin and I cannot consent to bestow upon you the advantages of death. You shall continue to live the thing that you are."

"What!" I cried, remembering the Lalugwumps and Gnarmag-Zote, "is it thought in Ghargaroo that death is an advantage, a blessing?"

"Our Sacred Books," he said, "are full of texts affirming the vanity of life."[37]

"Then," I said, "I infer that the death penalty is unknown to your laws!"

"We have the life penalty instead.[38] Convicted criminals are not only enriched, as already explained, but by medical attendance kept alive as long as possible. On the contrary, the very righteous, who have been rewarded with poverty, are permitted to die whenever it pleases them.

"Do not the Sacred Books of your country teach the vanity of life, the blessedness of poverty and the wickedness of wealth?"

"They do, O Most Illustrious, they do."

"And your countrymen believe?"

"Surely—none but the foolish and depraved entertain a doubt."

"Then I waste my breath in expounding laws and customs already known to you. You have, of course, the same."

At this I averted my face and blushed so furiously that the walls of the cave were illuminated with a wavering crimson like the light of a great conflagration! Thinking that the capital city was ablaze, Juptka-Getch ran from the cave's mouth, crying, "Fire, fire!" and I saw him no more.

An Execution in Batrugia

MY NEXT VOYAGE was not so prosperous.[39] By violent storms lasting seven weeks, during which we saw neither the sun nor the stars, our ship was driven so far out of its course that the captain had no knowledge of where we were. At the end of that period we were blown ashore and wrecked on a coast so wild and desolate that I had never seen anything so terrifying. Through a manifest interposition of Divine Providence I was spared, though all my companions perished miserably in the waves that had crushed the ship among the rocks.

As soon as I was sufficiently recovered from my fatigue and bruises, and had rendered thanks to merciful Heaven for my deliverance, I set out for the interior of the country, taking with me a cutlass for protection against wild beasts and a bag of sea-biscuit for sustenance. I walked vigorously, for the weather was then cool and pleasant, and after I had gone a few miles from the inhospitable coast I found the country open and level. The earth was covered with a thick growth of crimson grass, and at wide intervals were groups of trees. These were very tall, their tops in many instances invisible in a kind of golden mist, or haze, which proved to be, not a transient phenomenon, but a permanent one, for never in that country has the sun been seen, nor is there any night. The haze seems to be self-luminous, giving a soft, yellow light, so diffused that shadows are unknown. The land is abundantly supplied with pools and rivulets, whose water is of a beautiful orange color and has a pleasing perfume somewhat like attar of rose. I observed all this without surprise and with little apprehension, and went forward, feeling that anything, however novel and mysterious, was better than the familiar terrors of the sea and the coast.

After traveling a long time, though how long I had not the means to determine, I arrived at the city of Momgamwo, the capital of the kingdom of Batrugia, on the mainland of the Hidden Continent, where it is always twelve o'clock.

The Batrugians are of gigantic stature, but mild and friendly disposition. They offered me no violence, seeming rather amused by my small stature. One of them, who appeared to be a person of note and consequence, took me to his house (their houses are but a single story in height and built of brass blocks), set food before me, and by signs manifested the utmost good will. A long time afterward, when I had learned the language of the country, he explained that he had recognized me as an American pigmy, a race of which he had some little knowledge through a letter from a brother, who had been in my country. He showed me the letter, of which the chief part is here presented in translation:[40]

"You ask me, my dear Tgnagogu, to relate my adventures among the Americans, as they call themselves. My adventures were very brief, lasting altogether not more than three *gumkas,* and most of the time was passed in taking measures for my own safety.

"My skyship, which had been driven for six moons before an irresistible gale, passed over a great city just at daylight one morning, and rather than continue the voyage with a lost reckoning I demanded that I be permitted to disembark. My wish was respected, and my companions soared away without me. Before night I had escaped from the city, by what means you know, and with my remarkable experiences in returning to civilization all Batrugia is familiar. The description of the strange city I have reserved for you, by whom only could I hope to be believed. Nyork, as its inhabitants call it, is a city of inconceivable extent—not less, I should judge, than seven square *glepkeps!* Of the number of its inhabitants I can only say that they are as the sands of the desert. They wear clothing—of a hideous kind, 'tis true— speak an apparently copious though harsh language, and seem to have a certain limited intelligence. They are puny in stature, the tallest of them being hardly higher than my breast.

"Nevertheless, Nyork is a city of giants. The magnitude of all things artificial there is astounding! My dear Tgnagogu, words can give you no conception of it. Many of the buildings, I assure you, are as many as fifty *sprugas* in height, and shelter five thousand persons each. And these stupendous structures are so crowded together that to the spectator in the narrow streets below they seem utterly devoid of design and symmetry—mere monstrous aggregations of brick, stone and metal—mountains of masonry, cliffs and crags of architecture hanging in the sky!

"A city of giants inhabited by pigmies! For you must know, oh friend of my liver, that the rearing of these mighty structures could not be the work of the puny folk that swarm in ceaseless activity about their bases. These fierce little savages invaded the island in numbers so overwhelming that the giant builders had to flee before them. Some escaped across great bridges which, with the help of their gods, they had suspended in the air from bank to bank of a wide river parting the island from the mainland, but many could do no better than mount some of the buildings that they had reared, and there, in these inaccessible altitudes, they dwell to-day, still piling stone upon stone. Whether they do this in obedience to their instinct as builders, or in hope to escape by way of the heavens, I had not the means to learn, being ignorant of the pigmy tongue and in continual fear of the crowds that followed me.

"You can see the giants toiling away up there in the sky, laying in place the enormous beams and stones which none but they could handle. They look no bigger than beetles, but you know that they are many *sprugas* in stature, and you shudder to think what would ensue if one should lose his footing. Fancy that great bulk whirling down to earth from so dizzy an altitude! . . . .

"May birds ever sing above your grave.

                                    "JOQUOLK WAK MGAPY."

By my new friend, Tgnagogu, I was presented to the King, a most enlightened monarch, who not only reigned over, but ruled absolutely, the most highly civilized people in the world. He received me with gracious hospitality, quartered me in the palace of his Prime Minister, gave me for wives the three daughters of his Lord Chamberlain, and provided me with an ample income from the public revenues. Within a year I had made a fair acquaintance with the Batrugian language, and was appointed royal interpreter, with a princely salary, although no one speaking any other tongue, myself and two native professors of rhetoric excepted, had ever been seen in the kingdom.

One day I heard a great tumult in the street, and going to a window saw, in a public square opposite, a crowd of persons surrounding some high officials who were engaged in cutting off a man's head. Just before the executioner delivered the fatal stroke, the victim was asked if he had anything to say. He explained with earnestness that the deed for which he was about to suffer had been inspired and commanded by a brass-headed cow and four bushels of nightingales' eggs!

"Hold! hold!" I shouted in Batrugian, leaping from the window and forcing a way through the throng; "the man is obviously insane!"

"Friend," said a man in a long blue robe, gently restraining me, "it is not proper for you to interrupt these high proceedings with irrelevant remarks. The luckless gentleman who, in accordance with my will as Lord Chief Justice, has just had the happiness to part with his head was so inconsiderate as to take the life of a fellow-subject."

"But he was insane," I persisted, "clearly and indisputably *ptig nupy uggydug!*"—a phrase imperfectly translatable, meaning, as near as may be, having flitter-mice in his campanile.

"Am I to infer," said the Lord Chief Justice, "that in your own honorable country a person accused of murder is permitted to plead insanity as a reason why he should not be put to death?"

"Yes, illustrious one," I replied, respectfully, "we regard that as a good defense."

"Well," said he slowly, but with extreme emphasis, "I'll be *Gook swottled!*"

(*"Gook,"* I may explain, is the name of the Batrugian chief deity; but for the verb "to swottle" the English tongue has no equivalent. It seems to signify the deepest disapproval, and by a promise to be *"swottled"* a Batrugian denotes acute astonishment.)

"Surely," I said, "so wise and learned person as you cannot think it just to punish with death one who does not know right from wrong. The gentleman who has just now renounced his future believed himself to have been commanded to do what he did by a brass-headed cow and four bushels of nightingales' eggs—powers to which he acknowledged spiritual allegiance.

To have disobeyed would have been, from his point of view, an infraction of a law higher than that of man."

"Honorable but erring stranger," replied the famous jurist, "if we permitted the prisoner in a murder trial to urge such a consideration as that—if our laws recognized any other justification than that he believed himself in peril of immediate death or great bodily injury—nearly all assassins would make some such defense. They would plead insanity of some kind and degree, and it would be almost impossible to establish their guilt. Murder trials would be expensive and almost interminable, defiled with perjury and sentiment. Juries would be deluded and confused, justice baffled, and red-handed man-killers turned loose to repeat their crimes and laugh at the law. Even as the law is, in a population of only one hundred million we have had no fewer than three homicides in less than twenty years! With such statutes and customs as yours we should have had at least twice as many. Believe me, I know my people; they have not the American respect for human life."

As blushing is deemed in Batrugia a sign of pride, I turned my back upon the speaker—an act which, fortunately, signifies a desire to hear more.

"Law," he continued, "is for the good of the greatest number. Execution of an actual lunatic now and then is not an evil to the community, nor, when rightly considered, to the lunatic himself. He is better off when dead, and society is profited by his removal. We are spared the cost of exposing imposture, the humiliation of acquitting the guilty, the peril of their freedom, the contagion of their evil example."

"In my country," I said, "we have a saying to the effect that it is better that ninety-nine guilty escape than that one innocent be punished."

"It is better," said he, "for the ninety-nine guilty, but distinctly worse for everybody else.[41] Sir," he concluded with chilling austerity, "I infer from their proverb that your countrymen are the most offensive blockheads in existence."

By way of refutation I mentioned the English, indignantly withdrew from the country and set sail for Gokeetle-guk, or, as we should translate the name, Trustland.

The Jumjum of Gokeetle-guk

ARRIVING AT THE CAPITAL of the country after many incredible adventures, I was promptly arrested by the police and taken before the Jumjum. He was an exceedingly affable person,[42] and held office by appointment, "for life or fitness," as their laws express it. With one necessary exception all offices are appointive and the tenure of all except that is the same. The Panjandrum, or, as we should call him, King, is elected for a term of ten years,[43] at the expiration of which he is shot. It is held that any man who has been so long in high authority will have committed enough sins and blunders to deserve death, even if none can be specifically proved.

Brought into the presence of the Jumjum, who graciously saluted me,[44] I was seated on a beautiful rug and told in broken English by an interpreter who had escaped from Kansas that I was at liberty to ask any questions that I chose.

"Your Highness," I said, addressing the Jumjum through the interpreting Populist,[45] "I fear that I do not understand; I expected, not to ask questions, but to have to answer them. I am ready to give such an account of myself as will satisfy you that I am an honest man—neither a criminal nor a spy."

"The gentleman seems to regard himself with a considerable interest," said the Jumjum, aside to an officer of his suite—a remark which the interpreter, with characteristic intelligence, duly repeated to me. Then addressing me the Jumjum said:

"Doubtless your personal character is an alluring topic, but it is relevant to nothing in any proceedings that can be taken here. When a foreigner arrives in our capital he is brought before me to be instructed in whatever he may think it expedient for him to know of the manners, customs, laws, and so forth, of the country that he honors with his presence. It matters nothing to us what he is, but much to him what we are. You are at liberty to inquire."

I was for a moment overcome with emotion by so noble an example of official civility and thoughtfulness, then, after a little reflection, I said: "May it please your Highness, I should greatly like to be informed of the origin of the name of your esteemed country."

"Our country," said the Jumjum, acknowledging the compliment by a movement of his ears, "is called Trustland because all its industries, trades and professions are conducted by great aggregations of capital known as 'trusts.' They do the entire business of the country."

"Good God!" I exclaimed; "what a terrible state of affairs that is! I know about trusts. Why do your people not rise and throw off the yoke?"

"You are pleased to be unintelligible," said the great man, with a smile. "Would you mind explaining what you mean by 'the yoke'?"

"I mean," said I, surprised by his ignorance of metaphor, but reflecting that possibly the figures of rhetoric were not used in that country—"I mean the oppression, the slavery under which your people groan, their bondage to the tyrannical trusts, entailing poverty, unrequited toil and loss of self-respect."

"Why, as to that," he replied, "our people are prosperous and happy.

There is very little poverty and what there is is obviously the result of vice or improvidence. Our labor is light and all the necessaries of life, many of the comforts and some of the luxuries are abundant and cheap. I hardly know what you mean by the tyranny of the trusts; they do not seem to care to be tyrannous, for each having the entire market for what it produces, its prosperity is assured and there is none of the strife and competition which, as I can imagine, might breed hardness and cruelty. Moreover, we should not let them be tyrannous. Why should we?"

"But, your Highness, suppose, for example, the trust that manufactures safety pins should decide to double the price of its product. What is to prevent great injury to the consumer?"

"The courts. Having but one man—the responsible manager—to deal with, protective legislation and its enforcement would be a very simple matter. If there were a thousand manufacturers of safety pins, scattered all over the country in as many jurisdictions, there would be no controlling them at all. They would cheat, not only one another but the consumers, with virtual immunity. But there is no disposition among our trusts to do any such thing. Each has the whole market, as I said, and each has learned by experience what the manager of a large business soon must learn, and what the manager of a small one probably would not learn and could not afford to apply if he knew it—namely, that low prices bring disproportionately large sales and therefore profits. Prices in this country are never put up except when some kind of scarcity increases the cost of production. Besides, nearly all the consumers are a part of the trusts, the stock of which is about the best kind of property for investment."

"What!" I cried,—"do not the managers so manipulate the stock by 'watering' it and otherwise as to fool and cheat the small investors?"

"We should not permit them. That would be dishonest."

"So it is in my country," I replied, rather tartly, for I believed his apparent *naïveté* assumed for my confusion, "but we are unable to prevent it."

He looked at me somewhat compassionately, I thought. "Perhaps," he said, "not enough of you really wish to prevent it. Perhaps your people are—well, different from mine—not worse, you understand—just different."

I felt the blood go into my cheeks and hot words were upon my tongue's end, but I restrained them; the conditions for a quarrel were not favorable to my side of it. When I had mastered my chagrin and resentment I said:

"In my country when trusts are formed a great number of persons suffer, whether the general consumer does or not—many small dealers, middle men, drummers and general employees. The small dealer is driven out of the business by underselling. The middle man is frequently ignored, the trust dealing directly, or nearly so, with the consumer. The drummer is discharged because, competition having disappeared, custom must come without solicitation. Consolidation lets out swarms of employees of the individual concerns consolidated, for it is nearly as easy to conduct one large concern as a dozen smaller ones. These people get great sympathy from the public and the newspapers and their case is obviously pitiable. Was it not so in this country during the transition stage, and did not these poor gentlemen have to"—the right words would not come; I hardly knew how to finish. "Were they not compelled to go to work?" I finally asked, rather humbly.

The great official was silent for several minutes. Then he spoke.

"I am not sure that I understand you about our transition state. So far as our history goes matters with us have always been as they are to-day. To suppose them to have been otherwise would be to impugn the common sense of our ancestors. Nor do I quite know what you mean by 'small dealers,' 'middle men,' 'drummers,' and so forth."

He paused and fell into meditation, when suddenly his face was suffused with the light of a happy thought. It so elated him that he sprang to his feet and with his staff of office broke the heads of his Chief Admonisher of the Inimical and his Second Assistant Audible Sycophant. Then he said:

"I think I comprehend. Some eighty-five years ago, soon after my induction into office, there came to the court of the Panjandrum a man of this city who had been cast upon the island of Chicago (which I believe belongs to the American archipelago) and had passed many years there in business with the natives. Having learned all their customs and business methods he returned to his own country and laid before the Panjandrum a comprehensive scheme of commercial reform. He and his scheme were referred to me, the Panjandrum being graciously pleased to be unable to make head or tail of it. I may best explain it in its application to a single industry—the manufacture and sale of gootles."

"What is a gootle?" I asked.

"A metal weight for attachment to the tail of a donkey to keep him from braying,"[46] was the answer. "It is known in this country that a donkey cannot utter a note unless he can lift his tail. Then, as now, gootles were made by a single concern having a great capital invested and an immense plant, and employing an army of workmen. It dealt, as it does today, directly with consumers. Afflicted with a sonant donkey a man would write to the trust and receive his gootle by return mail, or go personally to the factory and carry his purchase home on his shoulder—according to where he lived. The reformer said this was primitive, crude and injurious to the interests of the public and especially the poor. He proposed that the members of the gootle trust divide their capital and each member go into the business of making gootles for himself—I do not mean for his personal use—in different parts of the country. But none of them was to sell to consumers, but to other men, who would sell in quantity to still other men, who would sell single gootles for domestic use. Each manufacturer would of course require a full complement of officers, clerks and so forth, as would the other men—everybody but the consumer—and each would have to support them and make a profit himself. Competition would be so sharp that solicitors would have to be employed to make sales; and they too must have a living out of the business. Honored stranger, am I right in my inference that the proposed system has something in common with the one which obtains in your own happy, enlightened and prosperous country, and which you would approve?"

I did not care to reply.

"Of course," the Jumjum continued, "all this would greatly have enhanced the cost of gootles, thereby lessening the sales, thereby reducing the output, thereby throwing a number of workmen out of employment. You see this, do you not, O guest of my country?"

"Pray tell me," I said, "what became of the reformer who proposed all this change?"

"All this change? Why, sir, the one-thousandth part is not told: he proposed that his system should be general: not only in the gootle trust, but every trust in the country was to be broken up in the same way! When I had him before me, and had stated my objections to the plan, I asked him what were its advantages.

"'Sir,' he replied, 'I speak for millions of gentlemen in uncongenial employments, mostly manual and fatiguing. This would give them the kind of activity that they would like—such as their class enjoys in other countries where my system is in full flower, and where it is deemed so sacred that any proposal for its abolition or simplification by trusts is regarded with horror, especially by the working men.'

"Having reported to the Panjandrum (whose vermiform appendix may good angels have in charge) and received his orders, I called the reformer before me and addressed him thus:

"'Illustrious economist, I have the honor to inform you that in the royal judgment your proposal is the most absurd, impudent and audacious ever made; that the system which you propose to set up is revolutionary and mischievous beyond the dreams of treason; that only in a nation of rogues and idiots could it have a moment's toleration.'

"He was about to reply, but cutting his throat to intimate that the hearing was at an end, I withdrew from the Hall of Audience, as under similar circumstances I am about to do now."

I withdrew first by way of a window, and after a terrible journey of six years in the Dolorous Mountains and on the Desert of Despair came to the western coast. Here I built a ship and after a long voyage landed on one of the islands constituting the Kingdom of Tortirra.

The Kingdom of Tortirra

O F THIS UNKNOWN country and its inhabitants I have written a large volume which nothing but the obstinacy of publishers has kept from the world, and which I trust will yet see the light. Naturally, I do not wish to publish at this time anything that will sate public curiosity, and this brief sketch will consist of such parts only of the work as I think can best be presented in advance without abating interest in what is to follow when Heaven shall have put it into the hearts of publishers to square their conduct with their interests. I must, however, frankly confess that my choice has been partly determined by other considerations. I offer here those parts of my narrative which I conceive to be the least credible—those which deal with the most monstrous and astounding follies of a strange people. Their ceremony of marriage by decapitation; their custom of facing to the rear when riding on horseback; their practice of walking on their hands in all ceremonial processions; their selection of the blind for military command; their pig-worship—these and many other comparatively natural particulars of their religious, political, intellectual and social life I reserve for treatment in the great work for which I shall soon ask public favor and acceptance.[47]

In Tortirran politics, as in Tamtonian, the population is always divided into two, and sometimes three or four "parties," each having a "policy" and each conscientiously believing the policy of the other, or others, erroneous and destructive. In so far as these various and varying policies can be seen to have any relation whatever to practical affairs they can be seen also to be the result of purely selfish considerations. The self-deluded people flatter themselves that their elections are contests of principles, whereas they are only struggles of interests. They are very fond of the word *slagthrit,* "principle"; and when they believe themselves acting from some high moral motive they are capable of almost any monstrous injustice or stupid folly. This insane devotion to principle is craftily fostered by their political leaders who invent captivating phrases intended to confirm them in it; and these deluding aphorisms are diligently repeated until all the people have them in memory, with no knowledge of the fallacies which they conceal. One of these phrases is "Principles, not men." In the last analysis this is seen to mean that it is better to be governed by scoundrels professing one set of principles than by good men holding another. That a scoundrel will govern badly, regardless of the principles which he is supposed somehow to "represent," is a truth which, however obvious to our own enlightened intelligence, has never penetrated the dark understandings of the Tortirrans. It is chiefly through the dominance of the heresy fostered by this popular phrase that the political leaders are able to put base men into office to serve their own nefarious ends.[48]

I have called the political contests of Tortirra struggles of interests. In nothing is this more clear (to the looker-on at the game) than in the endless disputes concerning restrictions on commerce. It must be understood that lying many leagues to the southeast of Tortirra are other groups of islands, also wholly unknown to people of our race. They are known by the general name of *Gropilla-Stron* (a term signifying "the Land of the Day-dawn"), though it is impossible to ascertain why, and are inhabited by a powerful and hardy race, many of whom I have met in the capital of Tanga. The Stronagu, as they are called, are bold navigators and traders, their proas making long and hazardous voyages in all the adjacent seas to exchange commodities with other tribes. For many years they were welcomed in Tortirra with great hospitality and their goods eagerly purchased. They took back with them all manner of Tortirran products and nobody thought of questioning the mutual advantages of the exchange. But early in the present century a powerful Tortirran demagogue named Pragam began to persuade the people that commerce was piracy—that true prosperity consisted in consumption of domestic products and abstention from foreign.[49] This extraordinary heresy soon gathered such head that Pragam was appointed Regent and invested with almost dictatorial powers. He at once distributed nearly the whole army among the seaport cities, and whenever a Stronagu trading proa attempted to land, the soldiery, assisted by the populace, rushed down to the beach, and with a terrible din of gongs and an insupportable discharge of stink-pots—the only offensive weapon known to Tortirran warfare—drove the laden vessels to sea, or if they persisted in anchoring destroyed them and smothered their crews in mud. The Tortirrans themselves not being a sea-going people, all communication between them and the rest of their little world soon ceased. But with it ceased the prosperity of Tortirra. Deprived of a market for their surplus products and compelled to forego the comforts and luxuries which they had obtained from abroad, the people began to murmur at the effect of their own folly. A reaction set in, a powerful opposition to Pragam and his policy was organized, and he was driven from power.

But the noxious tree that Pragam had planted in the fair garden of his country's prosperity had struck root too deeply to be altogether eradicated. It threw up shoots everywhere, and no sooner was one cut down than from roots underrunning the whole domain of political thought others sprang up with a vigorous and baleful growth. While the dictum that trade is piracy no longer commands universal acceptance, a majority of the populace still hold a modified form of it, and that "importation is theft" is to-day a cardinal political "principle" of a vast body of Tortirra's people. The chief expounders and protagonists of this doctrine are all directly or indirectly engaged in making or growing such articles as were formerly got by exchange with the Stronagu traders. The articles are generally inferior in quality, but consumers, not having the benefit of foreign competition, are compelled to pay extortionate prices for them, thus maintaining the unscrupulous producers in needless industries and a pernicious existence. But these active and intelligent rogues are too powerful to be driven out. They persuade their followers, among whom are many ignorant consumers, that this vestigial remnant of the old Pragam policy is all that keeps the nation from being desolated by small-pox and an epidemic of broken legs.[50]

It is impossible within these limits to give a full history of the strange delusion whose origin I have related. It has undergone many modifications and changes, as it is the nature of error to do, but the present situation is about this. The trading proas of the Stronagu are permitted to enter certain ports, but when one arrives she must anchor at a little distance from shore. Here she is boarded by an officer of the government, who ascertains the thickness of her keel, the number of souls on board and the amount and character of the merchandise she brings. From these data—the last being the main factor in the problem—the officer computes her unworthiness and adjudges a suitable penalty. The next day a scow manned by a certain number of soldiers pushes out and anchors within easy throw of her, and there is a frightful beating of gongs. When this has reached its lawful limit as to time it is hushed and the soldiers throw a stated number of stink-pots on board the offending craft. These, exploding as they strike, stifle the captain and crew with an intolerable odor. In the case of a large proa having a cargo of such commodities as the Tortirrans particularly need, this bombardment is continued for hours. At its conclusion the vessel is permitted to land and discharge her cargo without further molestation. Under these hard conditions importers find it impossible to do much business, the exorbitant wages demanded by seamen consuming most of the profit. No restrictions are now placed on the export trade, and vessels arriving empty are subjected to no penalties; but the Stronagu having other markets, in which they can sell as well as buy, cannot afford to go empty handed to Tortirra.

It will be obvious to the reader that in all this no question of "principle" is involved. A well-informed Tortirran's mental attitude with regard to the matter may be calculated with unfailing accuracy from a knowledge of his interests. If he produces anything which his countrymen want, and which in the absence of all restriction they could get more cheaply from the Stronagu than they can from him, he is in politics a *Gakphew,* or "Stinkpotter"; if not he is what that party derisively calls a *Shokerbom,* which signifies "Righteous Man"—for there is nothing which the Gakphews hold in so holy detestation as righteousness.

Nominally, Tortirra is an hereditary monarchy; virtually it is a democracy, for under a peculiar law of succession there is seldom an occupant of the throne, and all public affairs are conducted by a Supreme Legislature sitting at Felduchia, the capital of Tanga, to which body each island of the archipelago, twenty-nine in number, elects representatives in proportion to its population, the total membership being nineteen hundred and seventeen. Each island has a Subordinate Council for the management of local affairs and a Head Chief charged with execution of the laws. There is also a Great Court at Felduchia, whose function it is to interpret the general laws of the Kingdom, passed by the Supreme Council, and a Minor Great Court at the capital of each island, with corresponding duties and powers.[51] These powers are very loosely and vaguely defined, and are the subject of endless controversy everywhere, and nowhere more than in the courts themselves—such is the multiplicity of laws and so many are the contradictory decisions upon them, every decision constituting what is called a *lantrag,* or, as we might say, "precedent." The peculiarity of a *lantrag,* or previous decision, is that it is, or is not, binding, at the will of the honorable judge making a later one on a similar point. If he wishes to decide in the same way he quotes the previous decision with all the gravity that he would give to an exposition of the law itself; if not, he either ignores it altogether, shows that it is not applicable to the case under consideration (which, as the circumstances are never exactly the same, he can always do), or substitutes a contradictory *lantrag* and fortifies himself with that. There is a precedent for any decision that a judge may wish to make, but sometimes he is too indolent to search it out and cite it. Frequently, when the letter and intent of the law under which an action is brought are plainly hostile to the decision which it pleases him to render, the judge finds it easier to look up an older law, with which it is compatible, and which the later one, he says, does not repeal, and to base his decision on that; and there is a law for everything, just as there is a precedent. Failing to find, or not caring to look for, either precedent or statute to sustain him, he can readily show that any other decision than the one he has in will would be *tokoli impelly;* that is to say, contrary to public morals, and this, too, is considered a legitimate consideration, though on another occasion he may say, with public assent and approval, that it is his duty, not to make the law conform to justice, but to expound and enforce it as he finds it.[52] In short, such is the confusion of the law and the public conscience that the courts of Tortirra do whatever they please, subject only to overruling by higher courts in the exercise of *their* pleasure; for great as is the number of minor and major tribunals, a case originating in the lowest is never really settled until it has gone through all the intermediate ones and been passed upon by the highest, to which it might just as well have been submitted at first. The evils of this astonishing system could not be even baldly catalogued in a lifetime. They are infinite in number and prodigious in magnitude. To the trained intelligence of the American observer it is incomprehensible how any, even the most barbarous, nation can endure them.

An important function of the Great Court and the Minor Great Court is passing upon the validity of all laws enacted by the Supreme Council and the Subordinate Councils, respectively. The nation as a whole, as well as each separate island, has a fundamental law called the *Trogodal,* or, as we should say, the Constitution; and no law whatever that may be passed by the Council is final and determinate until the appropriate court has declared that it conforms to the Trogodal. Nevertheless every law is put in force the moment it is perfected and before it is submitted to the court. Indeed, not one in a thousand ever is submitted at all, that depending upon the possibility of some individual objecting to its action upon his personal interests, which few, indeed, can afford to do. It not infrequently occurs that some law which has for years been rigorously enforced, even by fines and imprisonment, and to which the whole commercial and social life of the nation has adjusted itself with all its vast property interests, is brought before the tribunal having final jurisdiction in the matter and coolly declared no law at all. The pernicious effect may be more easily imagined than related, but those who by loyal obedience to the statute all those years have been injured in property, those who are ruined by its erasure and those who may have suffered the severest penalties for its violation are alike without redress. It seems not to have occurred to the Tortirrans to require the court to inspect the law and determine its validity before it is put in force. It is, indeed, the traditional practice of these strange tribunals, when a case is forced upon them, to decide, not as many points of law as they can, but as few as they may; and this dishonest inaction is not only tolerated but commended as the highest wisdom. The consequence is that only those who make a profession of the law and live by it and find their account in having it as little understood by others as is possible can know which acts and parts of acts are in force and which are not. The higher courts, too, have arrogated to themselves the power of declaring unconstitutional even parts of the Constitution, frequently annulling most important provisions of the very instrument creating them!

A popular folly in Tortirra is the selection of representatives in the Councils from among that class of men who live by the law, whose sole income is derived from its uncertainties and perplexities. Obviously, it is to the interest of these men to make laws which shall be uncertain and perplexing—to confuse and

darken legislation as much as they can. Yet in nearly all the Councils these men
are the most influential and active element, and it is not uncommon to find
them in a numerical majority. It is evident that the only check upon their ill-
doing lies in the certainty of their disagreement as to the particular kind of
confusion which they may think it expedient to create. Some will wish to accomplish their common object by one kind of verbal ambiguity, some by another; some by laws clearly enough (to them) unconstitutional, others by contradictory statutes, or statutes secretly repealing wholesome ones already existing.
A clear, simple and just code would deprive them of their means of livelihood
and compel them to seek some honest employment.

So great are the uncertainties of the law in Tortirra that an eminent
judge once confessed to me that it was his conscientious belief that if all
cases were decided by the impartial arbitrament of the *do-tusis* (a process
similar to our "throw of the dice") substantial justice would be done far
more frequently than under the present system; and there is reason to believe that in many instances cases at law are so decided—but only at the
close of tedious and costly trials which have impoverished the litigants and
correspondingly enriched the lawyers.[53]

Of the interminable train of shames and brutalities entailed by this pernicious
system, I shall mention here only a single one—the sentencing and punishment
of an accused person in the midst of the proceedings against him, and while his
guilt is not finally and definitively established. It frequently occurs that a man
convicted of crime in one of the lower courts is at once hurried off to prison
while he has still the right of appeal to a higher tribunal, and while that appeal is
pending. After months and sometimes years of punishment his case is reached in
the appellate court, his appeal found valid and a new trial granted, resulting in his
acquittal. He has been imprisoned for a crime of which he is eventually declared
not to have been properly convicted. But he has no redress; he is simply set free
to bear through all his after life the stain of dishonor and nourish an ineffectual
resentment. Imagine the storm of popular indignation that would be evoked in
America by an instance of so foul injustice![54]

In the great public square of Itsami, the capital of Tortirra, stands a golden
statue of Estari-Kumpro, a famous judge of the Civil Court.[55] This great man
was celebrated throughout the kingdom for the wisdom and justice of his decisions and the virtues of his private life. So profound were the veneration in
which he was held and the awe that his presence inspired, that none of the
advocates in his court ever ventured to address him except in formal pleas: all
motions, objections, and so forth, were addressed to the clerk and by him disposed of without dissent: the silence of the judge, who never was heard to utter

a word, was understood as sanctioning the acts of his subordinate. For thirty years, promptly at sunrise, the great hall of justice was thrown open, disclosing the judge seated on a loftly dais beneath a black canopy, partly in shadow, and quite inaccessible. At sunset all proceedings for the day terminated, everyone left the hall and the portal closed. The decisions of this august and learned jurist were always read aloud by the clerk, and a copy supplied to the counsel on each side. They were brief, clear and remarkable, not only for their unimpeachable justice, but for their conformity to the fundamental principles of law. Not one of them was ever set aside, and during the last fifteen years of the great judge's service no litigant ever took an appeal, although none ever ventured before that infallible tribunal unless conscientiously persuaded that his cause was just.

One day it happened during the progress of an important trial that a sharp shock of earthquake occurred, throwing the whole assembly into confusion. When order had been restored a cry of horror and dismay burst from the multitude—the judge's head lay flattened upon the floor, a dozen feet below the bench, and from the neck of the rapidly collapsing body, which had pitched forward upon his desk, poured a thick stream of sawdust! For thirty years that great and good man had been represented by a stuffed manikin. For thirty years he had not entered his own court, nor heard a word of evidence or argument. At the moment of the accident to his simulacrum he was in his library at his home, writing his decision of the case on trial, and was killed by a falling chandeller. It was afterward learned that his clerk, twenty-five years dead, had all the time been personated by a twin brother, who was an idiot from birth and knew no law.

Hither

L ISTENING TO THE HISTORY of the golden statue in the great square, as related by a Tortirran storyteller, I fell asleep. On waking I found myself lying in a cot-bed amidst unfamiliar surroundings. A bandage was fastened obliquely about my head, covering my left eye, in which was a dull throbbing pain. Seeing an attendant near by I beckoned him to my bedside and asked: "Where am I?"

"Hospital," he replied, tersely but not unkindly. He added: "You have a bad eye."

"Yes," I said, "I always had; but I could name more than one Tortirran who has a bad heart."

"What is a Tortirran?" he asked.

LETTERS FROM A HDKHOITE

EDITOR NEWS LETTER:—Having now been some time in your country, and being the only person who for many centuries has left my own, I esteem it a duty to let your people know how they and their manners and customs impress the inhabitants of other lands. I believe there have several foreigners visited your shores, and some of them have penetrated some distance into the interior; but as none of them have ever written anything about you, I hope my letters may prove novel as well as interesting. As I have never heard the name of my country mentioned since leaving it, and upon alluding to it myself have invariably been regarded as insane, I am forced to the conclusion that the Americans are ignorant even of its existence. I will begin, therefore, with some account of my native land and its claims to consideration. Its manners, customs, and internal policy will best be shown by comparing and contrasting them with yours as occasion shall offer in the course of my remarks.

The Kingdom of Hdkho is situated in the exact geographical centre of the universe, which is in Asia, beyond what you call the Himalaya Mountains. The precise spot I cannot point out to you, because your maps are totally wrong, and upon my departure I left mine behind, thinking that I could purchase one anywhere. Suffice it that Hdkho is the birth place of the human race, the fountainhead of mankind. The Garden of Hadeen, of which I find you possess some imperfect traditions, is located in the very heart of this great country. From long disuse, however, the garden has degenerated into a crab-orchard, much overgrown with brambles and nettles. The angel who, after the ejection of the delinquent tenant, Mr. Adamaneve, guarded this delightful spot with a blazing sword, was long ago removed from his sinecure and succeeded in this office by a Scotch gardener at a reduced salary. His—the gardener's—habits of dissipation have done much to hasten the decay of the place. The government of Hdkho is what you call an absolute monarchy;[1] which I understand to mean, a state in which the king may do as he thinks fit, so long as his ministers and army think fit also. The reigning king is a great and good ruler. All reigning kings are; though after they have been some time dead, some of them seem little enough. His name is Khobal Khodam Piltot Youhym Ge Se Wham, which means "refulgent." His titles are too numerous to be given here. They fill four large volumes of royal octavo, and bear strong testimony to the king's virtues and power.[2] Your wretched language is incapable of expressing a millionth part of their grandeur and magnificence. We have no Congress, Parliament, or anything of that kind. Nor does the king usually trouble himself to make or execute the laws. He has quite enough to do hunting, gaming and listening to the petitions of his nobles. Those of the common people are carefully packed away, to be acted upon by the next monarch.

The laws are made by the press. There are persons called Wampoos, whose business it is to carefully read all the newspapers, and, cutting out every suggestion, paste them into large blank books. These books, after an interval of one hundred years, become the code of the kingdom. As it is said to be proof of the divine nature of your Scriptures that such vast amounts of intellect have been expended in explaining, reconciling, upholding and refuting them, so in like manner the wisdom of our code is more clearly evident from the fact that one million of the wisest Hdkhoites are employed to explain them, than from any other circumstance, even the working of the laws themselves. I would warmly recommend the adoption of this plan in your country. It seems wonderful that the obvious benefits of it can so long have escaped the notice of your rulers. I am sure it must have suggested itself to some of them, but they prefer to oppress you with arbitrary laws of their own. See what a reform it would work in your country press and city weeklies. As for your city dailies, I cannot see that any reform is possible; they seem admirably adapted to the purpose for which they were designed, whatever that may be. Under the system proposed, the editors, being deprived of any influence whatever upon cotemporary[3] legislation, could be actuated only by a desire to benefit posterity; and as only good and wise men take any interest in measures which do not immediately concern either themselves or their party, it is clear that legislation would be placed in the hands of such men.

Consider for a moment what vast amounts of editorial dullness in relation to the proposed Tide-Land grant to the Pacific Railroad[4] would never have been perpetrated by the *Bulletin* under my policy. What long breaths of relief would be drawn by its readers at the total disappearance from its columns of all allusion to a Public Park. The very paper upon which the *Alta* is printed would rattle for joy at being relieved from the incubus of the Montgomery street extension and the impeachment of the President. The little *Call's* daily editorial paragraph would incontinently die out, and we should have only those delightful *Letters from the People,* which, as they usually contain no intelligible allusion to any interest of the present day, may fairly be set down as affecting posterity only. The *Times* would make no suggestions at all, for it is indisputable that not one man a hundred years hence could understand a word of what it says. It requires some study even now.[5]

These are but a few illustrations of the benefits of the system. I shall probably recur to this part of my subject again. I have occupied too much space in explaining what relates to my own country, but this seemed absolutely unavoidable for a correct understanding. In my next I shall more particularly notice some customs of your country as seen from the stand-point of a Hdkhoite.

EDITOR NEWS LETTER:—Upon his arrival in your country, the first thing that strikes the intelligent Hdkhoite—myself—is your wonderful religion. I am confident that in no other quarter of the globe is there a system so worthy of deep study; and I understand that a great number of your learned men are well paid to study it. It is a pity that they are not required to give an intelligible explanation of it. Just think; your religion has now been openly professed and written upon for near twenty centuries, and yet I am told there are still several points in it about which your churches differ—and some persons among you, whose opinions seem entitled to great respect, claim that these differences are growing wider and more numerous each year. In Hdkho, when there is any ambiguity, contradiction, or absurdity noticed in the national creed—a thing which, I reluctantly admit, sometimes does occur—one dozen of the wise men, alluded to in my former letter, are immediately selected by the king to explain the matter in question. This assembly is termed the Council of the *Assizz,* whence is derived your word "Assizes." Each member receives, as daily compensation, one *kapec,* about three bits, United States gold coin. If, at the end of ten minutes, they differ as to what is clearly the truth in the case, they are hanged, and their property reverts either to the Church or to the poor, at the option of the former. I am happy to say, that for three thousand years the wretched mendicants have received no benefit from this custom. I have the honor to recommend the immediate appointment, by Governor Haight, of a Council of *Assizz,* at the usual salary, composed of the following named persons: Father Gallagher, Horatio Stebbins, Dr. Scudder, the Rev. Mr. Fitzgerald, Dr. Eels, Dr. Wadsworth, the Rev. Mr. B. T. Martin, U. S. Branch Mint, Elder Knapp, Peter Job, Michael Reese, Wemyss Jobson, and the Emperor Norton.[6] To these let all questions of theology be referred for final settlement. Let them distinctly understand, that unless their duty is promptly performed and their decisions are unanimously arrived at, they are to forfeit not only the emoluments of their office, but the distinguished esteem in which they are held by your citizens. The Hdkhoian penalty, although it might be beneficial to society, would hardly be necessary. I give you the word of a Hdkhoite you would be surprised at the congruity and reasonableness of those parts of your religion which, but for this learned council, must always have seemed contradictory and absurd. It matters little whether their decisions would be right or wrong. I learn that, in matters of faith, your people are not fatiguingly critical, though in pecuniary and mercantile affairs, the dictates of what you call common sense are esteemed of much importance. The main things in religion are the having a good leader to follow, and the following him without question. The tendency to do the latter is so strongly marked a trait in your national character, that even some of your domestic animals have acquired it from you. Probably the most splendid piece of sarcasm on record is the sentence in which the ingenious founder of your religion alludes to this trait in his followers: "Feed my sheep."[7] The stigma has never been removed, and they are called lambs to this day.

EDITOR NEWS LETTER:—Since my last letter there has come to my knowledge a most extraordinary transaction. One of your citizens has been arrested for a violation of what you call the Sunday Law. He gave a theatrical exhibition and neglected to send the officers of the law complimentary tickets; a great blunder, and one likely to entail upon him considerable annoyance. However, the *rdustraldibs*—by which name in Hdkho we designate those who enforce the laws, in order to distinguish them from the *fdustraldibs* or thieves—magnanimously allowed the show to proceed, by which it does not appear that anybody was hurt. I learn, however, that several pious persons who were at church hardly three miles distant, were so annoyed by what they termed the "noisy and barbarous amusement," that they quite forgot to be sincere in praying for their enemies. I am told that the Sunday Law was framed expressly to prevent so deplorable a catastrophe, and, I can well believe it, for there seems to be no other valid reason for retaining it in your law-books. These pious persons—the Rev. Horatio Stebbins was not one of them, himself being guilty of the like practice—united in a petition for the immediate punishment of the offender, as an enemy to religion. This at first seemed strange to me, as I have always heard that pious people pray for mercy and forgiveness to their enemies. But a kind gentleman has since explained to me that these prayers, being addressed only to God, are not intended to influence their fellow men in dealing out justice to the enemies of the Church. This seems to me like asking a faithful dog to spare the child which has been torn from his keeping by a hungry wolf. But I have not yet been long enough among you to fully understand your ways. A longer familiarity with your customs will doubtless increase my respect for them. But as I was saying, these holy persons soon convinced an eminent *rdustlraldib*, whose name I will not hand down to posterity, that what you call Christian

Civilization was much in danger of immediate extinction, and furthermore, that such a result would be an evil; two truths of equal clearness. The worthy gentleman at once wrote out a warrant and dispatched one Michael Feeney to *serve* it. For my part I would have served it differently from what Mr. Feeney did. I would have burnt it. The upshot of it was that Mr. Charles Fitsch was arrested and tried for fracturing the Sabbath and disturbing the placid meditations of all holy Christians. Judge Provines, before whom the unhappy criminal was tried, has reserved his decision until the 20th inst. Meanwhile, however, I shall see him and direct him to discharge the prisoner, for to convict him would be unjust, and therefore, contrary to law, and unconstitutional, for of course, in a great country like yours, "constitutional" and "just" mean exactly the same thing.

In Hdkho, we believe like you in a Supreme Being, though never having seen him we are not very positive when we assert his existence. Still we worship him when we have nothing else to do, and read very attentively the laws which are attributed to him—though I must confess that none of these are authenticated by his signature, and the names of those who compiled them are not certainly known. Many of these laws require us to abstain from certain actions whose performance would injure no one, nor be a sin except for the laws themselves forbidding them.

When any person violates one of these, we say that inasmuch as it hurts no man, no man has the right to punish the offender. We think that as only God has suffered by the offence, only he can judge of the proper punishment. We make no laws except for our own protection, and leave God to take care of Himself. I assure you it would be esteemed quite absurd in Hdkho, and quite presumptious too, to attempt to strengthen the laws of God by the laws of man; and he who should attempt to punish one who had in no way injured his fellow creatures, would himself be put to death. We would not even presume to punish those who injure their fellow men, except that we find God never does it for us.

EDITOR NEWS LETTER:—I went on last Saturday to witness a ceremony peculiar, I believe, to your people; at least, I have never observed any such custom among other polite nations, and I have traveled extensively among the Cossacks, Calmucks, and the various Indian tribes of your Continent. It was the laying of the corner stone of the building to be erected by the Young Men's Christian Association—though what they need a building for is not quite clear. After an address by Mr. Barstow, the stone was fixed in its place by the Rev. Mr. Lathrop. I am told he is an eminent divine, but to me he looked little more than human. He proclaimed the stone "duly laid in the name of the Father, Son, and Holy Spirit, and to the glory of Christ and the Lord; than whom no other Corner Stone is known."[8] The solemnity with which he made this profound and original remark was very impressive—probably because I did not understand it. Now I wish to ask a few questions, which I hope some kind gentleman will answer, and so instruct a foreigner in some of the mysteries of your religion. First, what *is* the name of the Father, Son and Holy Spirit; and how can a stone be laid in it? In Hdkho we lay them in mortar. I have heard something about taking the name of the Lord in vain, but this, surely, is not what is meant. Second, if Christ is the only corner stone known, are there four of him? if not, what supports the other corners of the edifice erected upon him? I asked this question of a gentleman present, and here is his reply, of which I do not comprehend a word: "My friend," said he, "it is wicked to inquire into holy things, but as you seem to be a stranger, I will tell you this much, which you can verify at your leisure. The other three corners of the edifice to which you refer, *are* supported by corner stones, but these are so unsightly that they are kept constantly covered by a kind of mastic called Cant, which has been so unsparingly laid on that it now covers nearly the whole edifice. Several inquisitive persons, however, have at various times dug through this mastic, and revealed the nature of the stones. The first of these is a kind of rock quarried from the lowest stratum of what is termed the Social Formation, where it is found in vast quantities. Several distinguished geologists have asserted that it is the original 'bed rock' of humanity. It is said to take the name from *ignis,* fire, for its warmth is such as to nourish into life a great many varieties of pebbles and noxious weeds, besides warping and killing numerous fair plants which grow above its bed. The second corner is supported by a sort of rotten stone, called by two different names, according as it is seen from the inside or the outside of the building. It is found in all countries, but most abundantly in the immediate vicinity of the rock just described, of which it is an offshoot, if I may use so unscientific a term, and, as its name implies, *stands* immediately *above* it.[9] The third corner stone is hewn from a rock found in every country but this. It is used principally in the construction of prisons for heretics and the benefactors of mankind; and in San Francisco, small pieces of it, imported from Japan, are in great demand for pelting Chinamen. It was deposited at the time of the flood from a solution of the other two rocks which I have mentioned. It is often mentioned in our Scriptures—in fact, they are full of it. It is alluded to in the passage: 'Thou art Peter, and upon this rock I will build my Church;'[10] but it was afterwards decided to use the other stones also." I confess I was much perplexed at this profound geological discourse, and shall apply to Professor

Whitney and the Academy of Natural Sciences to explain it.[11] It will be observed that my informer did not mention the name of any one of these rocks. Perhaps some of my readers may be able to guess them. It's all Greek to me.

I was much gratified at the kindness of the young men in erecting a building to the glory of the Father—or the Son—or the Holy Spirit, which is it? I do not fully understand the sublime doctrine of the Trinity[12]—do you? I am sure that God (or Christ—or the Holy Spirit) must be very grateful for this attempt to enhance his fame at the expense of $54,000. The Architect of the Universe cannot but be extremely edified to see a handsome brick building going up, to his glory. I finally left the ground, quite as wise as I came there, but a man has since told me that many others were not so fortunate.

To the Public.—I have just been notified by the Editor, that he will now graciously permit me to discontinue these letters. I therefore hasten to improve this last opportunity to tell you, that after mature deliberation, I am forced to conclude, from all I have seen in this wonderful country, that the inhabitants are a set of savages, totally unworthy of any further instruction from me, and I shall no longer waste words upon them; and as for the Editor of the News Letter, he's—another

[We deemed it due to the public to put a stop to the unprovoked abuse which our degraded foreign correspondent seemed determined to heap upon them, and shall publish nothing more from his slanderous pen. He is evidently a wolf in sheep's clothing. It is hardly necessary to state that we have brought suit against him for libel. We expect to recover $1,000,000.—Ed. N. L.]

The Aborigines of Oakland

THE ABORIGINES WHO once inhabited the spot upon which now stands the great city of Oakland and of whose history only a few vague accounts have descended to us, seem to have been a singular race. We learn from the pages of that old chronicler, the renowned Jokot Bumfustian,[1] who devoted a more than ordinarily long life to the study of this ancient people, that they were descended from the Chinese, who were driven from the Flowery Kingdom some time in the first century of our era, by an anti-Coolie movement[2] which originated in the heart of China and extended to the most remote provinces—to the very fingers and toes of the country, as it were. Compelled to take to their junks, they were driven to this continent, landing at Victoria, then a flourishing village of Chinooks.[3] Being unable to show the proper papers, they were accused of attempting to defraud the revenue, confiscated, and their ships sold to the junk dealers. After several centuries of servitude their task-masters became tired of them, and drove them southward, after imparting to them much of their own language and complexion, and a great many of their customs. We next hear of them in the mountain fastnesses of Oregon, or, as it was then called, Boo-bum-pum-kin, then a cold and inhospitable region, covered with glaciers eleven months in the year. Here they tarried long enough to cover every available spot of ground with female seminaries, and then were driven out by the powerful and warlike Blatherskites, who killed all the males and made free with the women. The next generation consequently differed somewhat from the original type, presenting, in the quaint words of the old chronicler, "a mottled uncomeliness of face, exceeding unpleasant to look upon, and a great overfluency of speech, so that no one could hear their vaporings but he straightway stopped his ears and ran away."

We next find this wandering people laying out town lots in what is now Yolo county, then a vast marsh inhabited only by the Megatherium, Behemoth, Castilian, Democrat and other obsolete forms.[4] The lots advanced so rapidly in value that there was not money enough in the community to pay the taxes upon them, and this unfortunate people were compelled again to emigrate. They quarreled about the location of a city hall and separated, one party going directly southward, to Stockton, and passing west through the Diablo range to San Leandro, another southwest to the present site of Vallejo, across the straits of Carquinez, and so along the bay, until they arrived opposite Goat Island.[5] They distributed tracts along these routes, setting forth the advantages of a collegiate education and investments in real estate. By these means the Yahoos,[6] through whose domains they passed, were converted to Polytheism, and built churches innumerable and several State universities,[7] the ruins of which are still shown. In the course of a few years the tribes were all united upon the spot now called Oakland, and had attained a high degree of civilization. Religious ceremonies, commencements, real estate auctions and alumni meetings were frequent. Forty-seven railroads were projected, each having both termini in their city. Some of their singular customs have been recorded with minute fidelity by the learned Bumfustian, among others the religious rite called in their elegant tongue "kfchqtlxjompootizzery," which may be translated into English by the words "anathema maranatha."[8] This consisted of a weekly display by the entire community, of the most extreme contempt for a barren peninsula lying to westward of their town, and which they believed to be the abode of pestilent spirits inimical to the prosperity of their city. The ceremony was too revoltingly indecent for the chaste and sober pen of the venerable Bumfustian, and we are left in ignorance as to how it was performed. Space will not allow further description of this singular people. Suffice it to say that in the year 1349 their city was entirely destroyed by an earthquake, and only one family of the entire nation escaped. From them are descended the present inhabitants, and many speculative writers have traced in them a fanciful resemblance to the ancient and powerful nation whose history we have briefly outlined.

A Scientific Dream

ONE DAY LAST WEEK, while sitting in a little canvas booth on the side-walk, having my Benkerts preternaturally polished, I picked up an old dogs-eared volume, which some one had carelessly left upon the seat, and began to read. It proved to be Darwin's great work on the Origin of Species.[1] Mr. Darwin's theory, as is tolerably well known, supposes a constant advance in man and animals toward perfection, or rather a constant adaptation of a race to the cir-cumstances of its surroundings. The great naturalist holds that whatever pecu-liarity in our physical conformation enables us to resist the destroying forces of Nature, will be inherited by our descendants, until the cumulative accession of such protective peculiarities shall confer upon our race immunity from the ills which now afflict us. The destroying agencies continue, but the race becomes better able to resist them. I wondered whether in the course of time Man might not become so changed that lightning, fire, flood and earthquakes would no longer be fatal, and cause no more annoyance than we now suffer from fleas, mothers-in-law and the *Alta California* newspaper. Overcome by these specula-tions and the pleasant titillation of my corns by the bootblack's brush, I fell asleep. When I awoke I found myself in a strange city, and a singular-looking new building in front of me bore the astounding inscription, "Erected 4868." I had slept thirty centuries. A crowd of wonderful and astonishingly dressed people surrounded me, eying me with great curiosity, and from them I learned that I was still in San Francisco. I was about to make further inquiries, when there was a rumbling noise beneath my feet, and a swaying motion of the ground warned me that an earthquake was upon us. The buildings rocked violently to and fro, and in mortal terror I sprang screaming into the middle of the street. The throng of idlers stood chatting gaily and laughing at me. Just then a massive stone cor-nice fell from an adjoining twelve story building amongst a bevy of school girls. I shrieked with horror, expecting to see them crushed to the consistency of Yarmouth bloater paste. Imagine my surprise when they stood unshaken, and burst into a loud laugh as the enormous stones glanced off their heads and were smashed into fragments on the pave. A great hotel, covering five or six squares and sixteen stories high, next came to the ground, and when the dust had settled, I saw the thousands of inmates covering the unsightly ruins like ants upon a mole-hill, dragging the fragments of their baggage from the debris. I then saw it all. Man had become adapted to his conditions. The frequent earthquakes had killed off the tender and soft-headed, and those whose physical conformation had enabled them to resist falling walls had lived and left offsprings inheriting their protective peculiarities. The shock and my nervousness having subsided, I turned to a man who stood near me, calmly smoking, and asked him why it was that man's mind had not kept pace with his body—why, when he was able to resist falling walls, he had not progressed so far as to be able to build walls which could not fall? "The fact is," said he, "we should now have been able to do so but for one reason. Our remote ancestors, in 1868 had a little quake one day,[2] and their wise men, as soon as they got partially over the scare, all rushed into the public prints with plans for building earthquake-proof houses. With that reverence for antiquated notions so characteristic of our race, we have ever since been, to some extent, following their suggestions, and the city has in consequence been completely overturned by shocks nine hundred and sixty-three thousand times. We are now just learning to discard their theories and use our own common-sense. In the course of twenty or thirty centuries more we shall build houses capable of resisting any shock." Fifty centuries to get rid of ancient stupidity and precedent! Yes, these fellows were certainly human. As I passed down the street I met the most singular object my eyes ever beheld. It walked upright, on two legs, and had a human head, excepting that the ears had developed into gills. In place of arms, its sides were adorned with two pendant fins, and a long dragon-like tail, similar to that of a mermaid, wriggled in the dust behind. "Surely," thought I, "this must be an inhabitant of Sacramento on a visit to this city. The floods up there have made him what he is. He seems uneasy as a fish out of water." I afterwards discovered he was a Front street merchant. At every shock a tidal wave engulphed all the lower part of the city, and Nature had adapted the residents to their condition of life. This fellow had been thrown inland by the last shock, and was now going up on Russian Hill to take dinner with a cousin whom he saw soaring on airy pinions above the city. The constant winds prevailing in the latter's elevated ward frequently carried folks off their feet, and so had tended to develop wings. Smitten with wonder to see my favorite theory so incontestably proved, I cried aloud, "Great is Darwin and his theory of"—just then a brick, which had been thrown sky-high by the falling hotel, descended upon my head. Fire shot in sparkles from my eyes, and as I closed them for the last time the bootblack hit me another one aside the head with his brush, and bellowed in my ear, "Get out o' this, old snorer, and give the other coves a show. Fifteen cents if yer please. Next!"

ACROSS THE CONTINENT

IN THE YEAR 3973 I had the hardihood to make a vow that I would cross the continent from the extreme eastern limit of New York city to the Pacific coast. It was with many misgivings that I left upon a journey which few men of the present century have dared attempt. My way lay directly through the inhospitable deserts peopled by the wandering tribe of "White Indians." By the by, I have somewhere met with a doubtful statement that these savages are descended from a singular ancient race, known as the Moormen, who inhabited a large city somewhere near a great lake, the dry bed of which is said to be still known to explorers. Here they lived and grew rich, until the early merchants of Chicago got after them, despoiled them of their worldly goods, outraged their women, assassinated their leaders, and drove them forth into the deserts to starve.[1] How much, if any, of this is true we shall never know, but it is certain that these Indians are the most abject and degraded of the human race. Some of their customs are very singular. Among other eccentricities, their marital relation is deserving of mention. Each woman insists upon having at least twenty husbands, and they fight terrible battles for their rights in this regard, in which many of the males are slain. They subsist principally upon snakes and grasshoppers. I will not recount my terrible adventures among these savages—how they destroyed my air ship, ate my provisions, and murdered my slaves. Thank God, I left the most valuable of my niggers upon the plantation in Massachusetts! After nine months of hard walking and precarious subsistence, I arrived at the almost unknown region of New Vaddah—probably so called from its recent discovery.[2] In crossing a frightful range of mountains beyond, I found a singular cave, open at both ends, but choked up with rubbish within. In digging near its mouth for water, I came upon a curiously shaped broken bar of iron about three feet long. It was attached by spikes to a piece of petrified wood. It is impossible to describe the feelings with which I gazed upon this interesting relic. There could be no doubt of it—it was a piece of the ancient iron road to the Pacific. There are, I believe, several of these relics in the possession of antiquarians. How strange was the infatuation of our ancestors, how blind their devotion to iron roads! They built them, and built them, until the wealthy companies who controlled them combined together, and, under their united oppression, civilization withered like a tender flower in the focus of a burning-glass. Had it not been for the purely accidental discovery of aerial navigation by the Hottentots, the entire Anglo-Saxon race in America would have died out under the monopolies of their own creation. Probably the strangest chapter in the annals of antiquity relates to our present subject. Archæologists tell us of the ancient Californians, that when their iron road was completed, their merchants, bankers, land-owners and other chieftains, joined in a great rejoicing over the event; fondly imagining that the tide of population and wealth would flow toward them from the more civilized States.[3] They were doomed to a bitter disappointment. Their population was composed mainly of vagabonds from all parts of the world, who had been lured thither by false representations, and who, being unable to return, had assisted in keeping up the deception. But no sooner was the last rail laid, and pegged down with what is known in the catalogue of the British Museum as the NOOS LETTAH SPIKE,[4] than these chafing thousands arose *en masse,* took possession of the entire road and compelled the company to run their trains night and day, until not a soul was left in the sterile valleys, and upon the arid plains of California. So horrible were their accounts of the country from which they had emancipated themselves, that for three hundred years not a man crossed the Rocky Mountains. To this day a blight and a curse seem to rest upon the country. In flying over it birds are said to fall down dead. Not a green thing grows within its borders. Where are said to have stood the populous cities of Sham Sanfrisco, Shakermantoe, Mud String and Yoobee Dan, are now nothing but clean level wastes of white sand, or stagnant pools of black water, travelers disagree which. But I digress.

John Smith, Liberator

(FROM A NEWSPAPER OF THE FAR FUTURE)

AT THE QUIET little village of Smithcester, which certain archæologists have professed to "identify" as the ancient London, will be celebrated to-day the thirtieth centennial anniversary of the birth of this remarkable man, the foremost figure of antiquity. The recurrence of what no more than six centuries ago was a popular *fête* day and even now is seldom permitted to pass without recognition by those to whom liberty means something more precious than opportunity for gain, excites a peculiar emotion. It matters little whether or no tradition has correctly fixed the time and place of Smith's birth. That he was born; that being born he wrought nobly at the work that his hand found to do; that by the mere force of his powerful intellect he established and perfected our present benign form of government, under which civilization has attained its highest and ripest development—these are facts beside which mere questions of chronology and geography are trivial and without significance.

That this extraordinary man originated the Smithocratic form of government is, perhaps, open to intelligent doubt; possibly it had a *de facto* existence in crude and uncertain shapes as early as the time of Edward XVII,—an existence local, unorganized and intermittent. But that he cleared it of its overlying errors and superstitions, gave it definite form and shaped it into a coherent and practical scheme there is unquestionable evidence in fragments of ancestral literature that have come down to us, disfigured though they are with amazingly contradictory statements regarding his birth, parentage and manner of life before he strode out upon the political stage as the Liberator of Mankind. It is said that Shakspar, a poet whose works had in their day a considerable vogue, though it is difficult to say why, alludes to him as "the noblest Roman of them all,"[1] our forefathers of the period being known as Romans or Englishmen, indifferently. In the only authentic fragment of Shakspar extant, however, this passage is not included.

Smith's military power is amply attested in an ancient manuscript of un-doubted authenticity which has recently been translated from the Siamese. It is an account of the water battle of Loo, by an eye-witness whose name, unfortunately, has not reached us. It is stated that in this famous engagement Smith overthrew the great Neapolitan general, whom he captured and con-veyed in chains to the island of Chickenhurst.[2]

In his "Political History of Europe" the late Professor Mimble has this luminous sentence: "With the single exception of Ecuador there was no European government that the Liberator did not transform into a pure Smithocracy, and although some of them relapsed transiently into the primitive forms, and others grew into extravagant and fanciful systems begotten of the intellectual activity to which he had stirred the whole world, yet so firmly did he establish the principle that in the thirty-second century the civilized world had become, and has remained, virtually Smithocratic."

It may be noted here as a singular coincidence that the year which is believed to have seen the birth of him who founded rational government witnessed the death of him who perfected literature: Martin Farquhar Tupper (after Smith the most noted name in history) starved to death in the streets of London.[3] Like that of Smith his origin is wrapped in obscurity. No fewer than seven British cities claim the honor of his nativity.[4] Meager indeed is our knowledge of this only British bard whose works have endured through thirty centuries. All that is certain is that he was once arrested for deer-stealing;[5] that, although blind, he fought a duel with a person named Salmasius,[6] for which he was thrown into Bedford gaol, whence he escaped to the Tower of London; that the manuscript of his "Proverbial Philosophy"[7] was for many years hidden in a hollow oak tree, where it was found by his grandmother, Ella Wheeler Tupper,[8] who fled with it to America and published many brilliant passages from it over her own name. Had Smith and Tupper been contemporaries the iron deeds of the former would doubtless have been recorded in the golden pages of the latter, to the incalculable enrichment of Roman history.

Strangely unimpressible indeed must be the mind which, looking backward through the mists of the centuries upon the primitive race from which we are believed to have sprung, can repress a feeling of sympathetic interest. The names of John Smith and Martin Farquhar Tupper, blazoned upon the page of that dim past and surrounded by the lesser names of Shakspar, the first Neapolitan, Oliver Cornwell, that Mynheer Baloon who was known as the Flying Dutchman, Julia Cæsar, commonly known as the Serpent of the Nile—all these are richly suggestive. They call to mind the odd custom of wearing "clothes"; the incredible error of Copernicus and other wide and wild guesses of ancient "science"; the lost arts of telegramy, steam locomotion, printing, and the tempering of iron. They set us thinking of the zealous idolatry that led men on pious pilgrimages to the accessible regions about the north pole and into the then savage interior of Africa in search of the fountain of youth. They conjure up visions of bloodthirsty "Emperors," tyrannical "Kings," vampire "Presidents," and robber "Parliaments"—grotesque and horrible shapes in terrible contrast with the serene and benign figures and features of our modern Smithocracy.

Let us to-day rejoice and give thanks to Bungoot[9] that the old order of things has passed forever away. Let us praise Him that our lot has been cast in more wholesome days than those in which Smith wrought and Tupper sang. And yet let us not forget whatever there was of good, if any, in the pre-Smithian period, when men cherished quaint superstitions and rode on the backs of beasts—when they settled questions of right and expediency by counting noses—when cows were enslaved and women free—when science had not dawned to chase away the shadows of imagination and the fear of immortality—and when the cabalistic letters "A.D.," which from habit we still affix to numerals designating the date, had perhaps a known signification. It is indeed well to live in this golden age, under the benign sway of that supreme and culminating product of Smithocracy, our gracious sovereign, his Majesty John CLXXVIII.

"THE BUBBLE REPUTATION"

How Another Man's Was Sought and Pricked

IT WAS A STORMY night in the autumn of 1930. The hour was about eleven. San Francisco lay in darkness, for the laborers at the gas works had struck and destroyed the company's property because a newspaper to which a cousin of the manager was a subscriber had censured the course of a potato merchant related by marriage to a member of the Knights of Leisure.[1] Electric lights had not at that period been reinvented. The sky was filled with great masses of black cloud which, driven rapidly across the star-fields by winds unfelt on the earth and momentarily altering their fantastic forms, seemed instinct with a life and activity of their own and endowed with awful powers of evil, to the exercise of which they might at any time set their malignant will.

An observer standing, at this time, at the corner of Paradise avenue and Great White Throne walk in Sorrel Hill cemetery[2] would have seen a human figure moving among the graves toward the Superintendent's residence. Dimly and fitfully visible in the intervals of thinner gloom, this figure had a most uncanny and disquieting aspect. A long black cloak shrouded it from neck to heel. Upon its head was a slouch hat, pulled down across the forehead and almost concealing the face, which was further hidden by a half-mask, only the beard being occasionally visible as the head was lifted partly above the collar of the cloak. The man wore upon his feet jack-boots whose wide, funnel-shaped legs had settled down in many a fold and crease about his ankles, as could be seen whenever accident parted the bottom of the cloak. His arms were concealed, but sometimes he stretched out the right to steady himself by a headstone as he crept stealthily but blindly over the uneven ground. At such times a close scrutiny of the hand would have disclosed in the palm the hilt of a poniard, the blade of which lay along the wrist, hidden in the sleeve. In short, the man's garb, his movements, the hour—everything proclaimed him a reporter.

But what did he there?

On the morning of that day the editor of the *Daily Malefactor* had touched the button of a bell numbered 216 and in response to the summons Mr. Longbo Spittleworth, reporter, had been shot into the room out of an inclined tube.

"I understand," said the editor, "that you are 216—am I right?"

"That," said the reporter, catching his breath and adjusting his clothing, both somewhat disordered by the celerity of his flight through the tube,—"that is my number."

"Information has reached us," continued the editor, "that the Superintendent of the Sorrel Hill cemetery—one Inhumio, whose very name suggests inhumanity[3]—is guilty of the grossest outrages in the administration of the great trust confided to his hands by the sovereign people."

"The cemetery is private property," faintly suggested 216.

"It is alleged," continued the great man, disdaining to notice the interruption, "that in violation of popular rights he refuses to permit his accounts to be inspected by representatives of the press."

"Under the law, you know, he is responsible to the directors of the cemetery company," the reporter ventured to interject.

"They say," pursued the editor, heedless, "that the inmates are in many cases badly lodged and insufficiently clad, and that in consequence they are usually cold. It is asserted that they are never fed—except to the worms. Statements have been made to the effect that males and females are permitted to occupy the same quarters, to the incalculable detriment of public morality. Many clandestine villainies are alleged of this fiend in human shape, and it is desirable that his underground methods be unearthed in the *Malefactor*. If he resists we will drag his family skeleton from the privacy of his domestic closet. There is money in it for the paper, fame for you—are you ambitious, 216?"

"I am—bitious."

"Go, then," cried the editor, rising and waving his hand imperiously—"go and 'seek the bubble reputation'."

"The bubble shall be sought," the young man replied, and leaping into a man-hole in the floor, disappeared. A moment later the editor, who after dismissing his subordinate, had stood motionless, as if lost in thought, sprang suddenly to the man-hole and shouted down it: "Hello, 216?"

"Aye, aye, sir," came up a faint and far reply.

"About that 'bubble reputation'—you understand, I suppose, that the reputation which you are to seek is that of the other man."

In the execution of his duty, in the hope of his employer's approval, in the costume of his profession, Mr. Longbo Spittleworth, otherwise known as 216, has already occupied a place in the mind's eye of the intelligent reader. Alas for poor Mr. Inhumio!

A few days after these events that fearless, independent and enterprising guardian and guide of the public, the San Francisco *Daily Malefactor*, contained a whole-page article whose headlines are here presented with some necessary typographical mitigation:

"Hell Upon Earth! Corruption Rampant in the Management of the Sorrel Hill Cemetery. The Sacred City of the Dead in the Leprous Clutches of a Demon in Human Form. Fiendish Atrocities Committed in 'God's Acre.' The Holy Dead Thrown around Loose. Fragments of Mothers. Segregation of a Beautiful Young Lady Who in Life Was the Light of a Happy Household. A Superintendent Who Is an Ex-Convict. How He Murdered His Neighbor to Start the Cemetery. He Buries His Own Dead Elsewhere. Extraordinary Insolence to a Representative of the Public Press. Little Eliza's Last Words: 'Mamma, Feed Me to the Pigs.' A Moonshiner Who Runs an Illicit Bone-Button Factory in One Corner of the Grounds. Buried Head Downward. Revolting Mausoleistic Orgies. Dancing on the Dead. Devilish Mutilation—a Pile of Late Lamented Noses and Sainted Ears. No Separation of the Sexes; Petitions for Chaperons Unheeded. 'Veal' as Supplied to the Superintendent's Employees. A Miscreant's Record from His Birth. Disgusting Subserviency of Our Contemporaries and Strong Indications of Collusion. Nameless Abnormalities. 'Doubled Up Like a Nut-Cracker.' 'Wasn't Planted White.' Horribly Significant Reduction in the Price of Lard. The Question of the Hour: Whom Do You Fry Your Doughnuts In?"

FOR THE AHKOOND

IN THE YEAR 4591 I accepted from his gracious Majesty the Ahkoond of Citrusia[1] a commission to explore the unknown region lying to the eastward of the Ultimate Hills, the range which that learned archæologist, Simeon Tucker, affirms to be identical with the "Rocky Mountains" of the ancients. For this proof of his Majesty's favor I was indebted, doubtless, to a certain distinction that I had been fortunate enough to acquire by explorations in the heart of Darkest Europe. His Majesty kindly offered to raise and equip a large expeditionary force to accompany me, and I was given the widest discretion in the matter of outfit; I could draw upon the royal treasury for any sum that I might require, and upon the royal university for all the scientific apparatus and assistance necessary to my purpose. Declining these encumbrances, I took my electric rifle and a portable waterproof case containing a few simple instruments and writing materials and set out. Among the instruments was, of course, an aerial isochronophone which I set by the one in the Ahkoond's private dining-room at the palace. His Majesty invariably dined alone at 18 o'clock, and sat at table six hours: it was my intention to send him all my reports at the hour of 23, just as dessert would be served, and he would be in a proper frame of mind to appreciate my discoveries and my services to the crown.

At 9 o'clock on the 13th of Meijh I left Sanf Rachisco and after a tedious journey of nearly fifty minutes arrived at Bolosson, the eastern terminus of the magnetic tube, on the summit of the Ultimate Hills. According to Tucker this was anciently a station on the Central Peaceful Railway,[2] and was called "German," in honor of an illustrious dancing master. Prof. Nupper, however, says it was the ancient Nevraska, the capital of Kikago, and geographers generally have accepted that view.

Finding nothing at Bolosson to interest me except a fine view of the volcano Carlema, then in active eruption, I shouldered my electric rifle and with my case of instruments strapped upon my back plunged at once into the wilderness, down the eastern slope. As I descended the character of the vegetation altered. The pines of the higher altitudes gave place to oaks, these to ash, beech and maple. To these succeeded the tamarack and such trees as affect a moist and marshy habitat; and finally, when for four months I had been steadily descending, I found myself in a primeval flora consisting mainly of giant ferns, some of them as much as twenty *surindas* in diameter. They grew upon the margins of vast stagnant lakes which I was compelled to navigate by means of rude rafts made from their trunks lashed together with vines.

In the fauna of the region that I had traversed I had noted changes corresponding to those in the flora. On the upper slope there was nothing but the mountain sheep, but I passed successively through the habitats of the bear, the deer and the horse. This last mentioned creature, which our naturalists have believed long extinct, and which Dorbley declares our ancestors domesticated, I found in vast numbers on high table lands covered with grass upon which it feeds. The animal answers the current description of the horse very nearly, but all that I saw were destitute of the horns, and none had the characteristic forked tail. This member, on the contrary, is a tassel of straight wiry hair, reaching nearly to the ground—a surprising sight. Lower still I came upon the mastodon, the lion, the tiger, hippopotamus and alligator, all differing very little from those infesting Central Europe, as described in my "Travels in the Forgotten Continent."

In the lake region where I now found myself, the waters abounded with ichthyosauri, and along the margins the iguanodon dragged his obscene bulk in indolent immunity. Great flocks of pterodactyls, their bodies as large as those of oxen and their necks enormously long, clamored and fought in the air, the broad membranes of their wings making a singular musical humming, unlike anything that I had ever heard. Between them and the ichthyosauri there was incessant battle, and I was constantly reminded of the ancient poet's splendid and original comparison of man to

> dragons of the prime
> That tare each other in their slime.[3]

When brought down with my electric rifle and properly roasted, the pterodactyl proved very good eating, particularly the pads of the toes.

In urging my raft along the shore line of one of the stagnant lagoons one day I was surprised to find a broad rock jutting out from the shore, its upper surface some ten *coprets* above the water. Disembarking, I ascended it, and on examination recognized it as the remnant of an immense mountain which at one time must have been 5,000 *coprets* in height and doubtless the dominating peak of a long range. From the striations all over it I discovered that it had been worn away to its present trivial size by glacial action. Opening my case of instruments, I took out my petrochronologue and applied it to the worn and scratched surface of the rock. The indicator at once pointed to K 59 xpc $^1/_2$! At this astonishing result I was nearly overcome by excitement: the last erosions of the ice-masses upon this vestige of a stupendous mountain range which they had worn away, had been made as recently as the year 1945! Hastily applying my nymograph, I found that the name of this particular mountain at the time when it began to be enveloped in the mass of ice moving down upon it from the north, was "Pike's Peak."[4] Other observations with other instruments showed that at that time the country circumjacent to it had been inhabited by a partly civilized race of people known as Galoots,[5] the name of their capital city being Denver.

That evening at the hour of 23 I set up my aerial isochronophone[6] and reported to his gracious Majesty the Ahkoond as follows:

> "*Sire:* I have the honor to report that I have made a startling discovery. The primeval region into which I have penetrated, as I informed you yesterday—the ichthyosaurus belt—was peopled by tribes considerably advanced in some of the arts almost within historic times: in 1920. They were exterminated by a glacial period not exceeding one hundred and twenty-five years in duration. Your Majesty can conceive the magnitude and violence of the natural forces which overwhelmed their country with moving sheets of ice not less than 5,000 *coprets* in thickness, grinding down every eminence, destroying (of course) all animal and vegetable life and leaving the region a fathomless bog of detritus. Out of this vast sea of mud Nature has had to evolve another creation, beginning *de novo,* with her lowest forms. It has long been known, your Majesty, that the region east of the Ultimate Hills, between them and the Wintry Sea, was once the seat of an ancient civilization, some scraps and shreds of whose history, arts and literature have been wafted to us across the gulf of time; but it was reserved for your gracious Majesty, through me, your humble and unworthy instrument, to ascertain the astonishing fact that these were a pre-glacial people—that between them and us stands, as it were, a wall of impenetrable ice. That all local records of this unfortunate race have perished your Majesty needs not to be told: we can supplement our present imperfect knowledge of them by instrumental observation only."

To this message I received the following extraordinary reply:

> "All right—another bottle of—ice goes: push on—this cheese is too— spare no effort to—hand me those nuts—learn all you can—damn you!"

His most gracious Majesty was being served with dessert, and served badly.

I now resolved to go directly north toward the source of the ice-flow and investigate its cause, but examining my barometer found that I was more than 8,000 *coprets* below the sea-level; the moving ice had not only ground down the face of the country, planing off the eminences and filling the depressions, but its enormous weight had caused the earth's crust to sag, and with the lessening of the weight from evaporation it had not recovered.

I had no desire to continue in this depression, as I should in going north, for I should find nothing but lakes, marshes and ferneries, infested with the same primitive and monstrous forms of life. So I continued my course eastward and soon had the satisfaction to find myself meeting the sluggish current of such streams as I encountered in my way. By vigorous use of the new double-distance telepode, which enables the wearer to step eighty *surindas* instead of forty, as with the instrument in popular use, I was soon again at a considerable elevation above the sea-level and nearly 200 *prastams* from "Pike's Peak." A little farther along the water courses began to flow to the eastward. The flora and fauna had again altered in character, and now began to grow sparse; the soil was thin and arid, and in a week I found myself in a region absolutely destitute of organic life and without a vestige of soil. All was barren rock. The surface for hundreds of *prastams,* as I continued my advance, was nearly level, with a slight dip to the eastward. The rock was singularly striated, the scratches arranged concentrically and in helicoidal curves. This circumstance puzzled me and I resolved to take some more instrumental observations, bitterly regretting my improvidence in not availing myself of the Ahkoond's permission to bring with me such apparatus and assistants as would have given me knowledge vastly more copious and accurate than I could acquire with my simple pocket appliances.

I need not here go into the details of my observations with such instruments as I had, nor into the calculations of which these observations were the basic data. Suffice it that after two months' labor I reported the results to his Majesty in Sanf Rachisco in the words following:

"*Sire:* It is my high privilege to apprise you of my arrival on the western slope of a mighty depression running through the center of the continent north and south, formerly known as the Mississippi Valley. It was once the seat of a thriving and prosperous population known as the Pukes,[7] but is now a vast expanse of bare rock, from which every particle of soil and everything movable, including people, animals and vegetation, have been lifted by terrific cyclones and scattered afar, falling in other lands and at sea in the form of what was called meteoric dust! I find that these terrible phenomena began to occur about the year 1860, and lasted, with increasing frequency and power, through a century, culminating about the middle of that glacial period which saw the extinction of the Galoots and their neighboring tribes. There was, of course, a close connection between the two malefic phenomena, both, doubtless, being due to the same cause, which I have been unable to trace. A cyclone, I venture to remind your gracious Majesty, is a mighty whirlwind, accompanied by the most startling meteorological phenomena, such as electrical disturbances, floods of falling water, darkness and so forth. It moves with great speed, sucking up everything and reducing it to powder. In many days' journey I have not found a square *copret* of the country that did not suffer a visitation. If any human being escaped he must speedily have perished from starvation. For some twenty centuries the Pukes have been an extinct race, and their country a desolation in which no living thing can dwell, unless, like me, it is supplied with Dr. Blobob's Condensed Life-pills."

The Ahkoond replied that he was pleased to feel the most poignant grief for the fate of the unfortunate Pukes, and if I should by chance find the ancient king of the country I was to do my best to revive him with the patent resuscitator and present him the assurances of his Majesty's distinguished consideration; but as the politoscope showed that the nation had been a republic I gave myself no trouble in the matter.

My next report was made six months later and was in substance this:

"*Sire:* I address your Majesty from a point 430 *coprets* vertically above the site of the famous ancient city of Buffalo, once the capital of a powerful nation called the Smugwumps.[8] I can approach no nearer because of the hardness of the snow, which is very firmly packed. For hundreds of *prastams* in every direction, and for thousands to the north and west, the land is covered with this substance, which, as your Majesty is doubtless aware, is extremely cold to the touch, but by application of sufficient heat can be turned into water. It falls from the heavens, and is believed by the learned among your Majesty's subjects to have a sidereal origin.

"The Smugwumps were a hardy and intelligent race, but they entertained the vain delusion that they could subdue Nature. Their year was divided into two seasons—summer and winter, the former warm, the latter cold. About the beginning of the nineteenth century according to my archæthermograph, the summers began to grow shorter and hotter, the winters longer and colder. At every point in their country, and every day in the year, when they had not the hottest weather ever known in that place, they had the coldest. When they were not dying by hundreds from sunstroke they were dying by thousands from frost. But these heroic and devoted people struggled on, believing that they were becoming acclimated faster than the climate was becoming insupportable. Those called away on business were even afflicted with nostalgia, and with a fatal infatuation returned to grill or freeze, according to the season of their arrival. Finally there was no summer at all, though the last flash of heat slew several millions and set most of their cities afire, and winter reigned eternal.

"The Smugwumps were now keenly sensible of the perils environing them, and, abandoning their homes, endeavored to reach their kindred, the Californians, on the western side of the continent in what is now your Majesty's ever-blessed realm. But it was too late: the snow growing deeper and deeper day by day, besieged them in their towns and dwellings, and they were unable to escape. The last one of them perished about the year 1943, and may God have mercy on his fool soul!"

To this dispatch the Ahkoond replied that it was the royal opinion that the Smugwumps were served very well right.

Some weeks later I reported thus:

"*Sire:* The country which your Majesty's munificence is enabling your devoted servant to explore extends southward and southwestward from Smugwumpia many hundreds of *prastams,* its eastern and southern borders being the Wintry Sea and the Fiery Gulf, respectively. The population in ancient times was composed of Whites and Blacks in about equal numbers and of about equal moral worth—at least that is the record on the dial of my ethnograph when set for the twentieth century and given a southern exposure. The Whites were called Crackers and the Blacks known as Coons.

"I find here none of the barrenness and desolation characterizing the land of the ancient Pukes, and the climate is not so rigorous and thrilling as that of the country of the late Smugwumps. It is, indeed, rather agreeable in point of temperature, and the soil being fertile exceedingly, the whole land is covered with a dense and rank vegetation. I have yet to find a square *smig* of it that is open ground, or one that is not the lair of some savage beast, the haunt of some venomous reptile, or the roost of some offensive bird. Crackers and Coons alike are long extinct, and these are their successors.

"Nothing could be more forbiding and unwholesome than these interminable jungles, with their horrible wealth of organic life in its most objectionable forms. By repeated observations with the necrohistoriograph I find that the inhabitants of this country, who had always been more or less dead, were wholly extirpated contemporaneously with the disastrous events which swept away the Galoots, the Pukes and the Smugwumps. The agency of their effacement was an endemic disorder known as yellow fever. The ravages of this frightful disease were of frequent recurrence, every point of the country being a center of infection; but in some seasons it was worse than in others. Once in every half century at first, and afterward every year[9] it broke out somewhere and swept over wide areas with such fatal effect that there were not enough of the living to plunder the dead; but at the first frost it would subside. During the ensuing two or three months of immunity the stupid survivors returned to the infected homes from which they had fled and were ready for the next outbreak. Emigration would have saved them all, but although the Californians (over whose happy and prosperous descendants your Majesty has the goodness to reign) invited them again and again to their beautiful land, where sickness and death were hardly known, they would not go, and by the year 1946 the last one of them, may it please your gracious Majesty, was dead and damned."

Having spoken this into the transmitter of the aerial isochronophone at the usual hour of 23 o'clock I applied the receiver to my ear, confidently expecting the customary commendation. Imagine my astonishment and dismay when my master's well-remembered voice was heard in utterance of the most awful imprecations on me and my work, followed by appalling threats against my life!

The Ahkoond had changed his dinner-time to five hours later and I had been speaking into the ears of an empty stomach!

THE FALL OF THE REPUBLIC

An Article from a "Court Journal" of the Thirty-first Century

ALTHOUGH MANY OF THE causes which finally, in combination, brought about the downfall of the great American republic were in operation from the very beginning of its political life—being inherent in the system—it was not until the year 1950 that the collapse of the vast fabric was complete. In that year the defeat of the last republican army near Smithville, in the lava beds of Northern California, extinguished the last fires of insurrection against the monarchical revival, and thenceforth armed opposition was confined to desultory and insignificant guerrilla warfare, whose object was pillage and whose method murder. In that year, too, Field Marshal Sir Henry Burnell, whose astonishing military genius had subdued all the republican forces west of the Sierra Nevada, turned his victorious arms against his royal master, Leonard "the Chicken-Hearted," tore him from the throne of California, suppressed his Legislature, and with it the last remnant of legislative government on the American continent and established himself in absolute power as Emperor of the Occident. His dynasty, it is needless to say, endured without a break in its continuity almost to our own times, when, in the year 2781, John XI was compelled to abdicate and the scepter passed to the hand of our present gracious sovereign, William of Pescadero.[1] For ten years before the usurpation of Henry I peace had prevailed in all the country east of the Sierra Nevada to the Atlantic, and the reign of "the Three Kings" was undisputed. The turbulent period between 1895 and 1940, with its incalculable waste of blood and treasure, its dreadful conflicts of armies and more dreadful massacres of the people, its kaleidoscopic changes of government and incessant effacement of boundaries, its succession of political assassinations, popular insurrections pitilessly subdued—all the horrors incident to the extirpation of a system rooted in the hearts and traditions of a mighty race—had so exhausted and dispirited the surviving protagonists of the republican regime that they made no further head against the inevitable, and were, indeed, glad enough to accept life on any terms, justifying their submission, and at the same time condemning their former obstinacy by quoting the words of the great poet:

> For forms of government let fools contest—
> What e'er is best administered is best.[2]

When at the battle of Smithville the last spark of what had been absurdly known as "civil and religious liberty" was quenched in blood and the Pacific Coast brought under the light and beneficent yoke of Absolute Monarchy, the three kingdoms east of the Sierra Nevada had for a whole decade enjoyed in peace and with increasing satisfaction the advantage of those natural and now universal institutions which their valiant but shortsighted and misguided forefathers had madly flung away. The name of George Washington had already begun to sink into the infamy which now covers it, and that of the illustrious sovereign against whom he raised his impious hand and traitor sword shone with a brightening splendor.

But the purpose of this treatise is not historical, but philosophic; not to recount events familiar to all students of history, but to trace the genesis and development of a few of the causes which produced them. The historians have left nothing undone to give a true account of these events. In Mancher's *Decline and Fall of the American Republics,* in Lenwith's *History of Popular Government,* in Bardeal's *Monarchical Renascence* and in Staley's immortal work, *The Rise, Progress and Extinction of the United States,* the facts are set forth with such copiousness and particularity as to have exhausted all attainable stores of information, and it remains for investigators of this later time only to expound the causes and point the moral.

It may seem needless at this time to point out the inherent defects of a system of government which the logic of events has swept like political rubbish from the face of the earth, but we must not forget that ages before the inception of the American republics and of that of France and Ireland this form of government had been discredited by emphatic failures among the most enlightened and powerful nations of antiquity: the Greeks, the Romans and long before them (as we now know) the Egyptians and the Chinese. To the lesson of these failures the founders of the eighteenth and nineteenth century republics were blind and deaf. Have we then reason to believe that our posterity will be wiser because instructed by a greater number of examples? And is the number of examples which they will have in memory really greater? Already the instances of China, Egypt, Greece and Rome are almost lost in the mists of antiquity; they are known, except by infrequent report, only to the archæologist, and but dimly and uncertainly to him. The brief and imperfect record of yesterdays which we call History is like that traveling vine of India, which, taking new root as it advances, decays at one end while it grows at the other, and so is constantly perishing and finally lost in all the spaces which it has over-passed.

Our republican ancestors, with an ignorance of the meaning of words which now seems hardly credible, called theirs a "government of the people, for the people, by the people"—which was to say, that in so far as this catching phrase described it, it was no government at all. Government means control; it means limitation of the will of the governed by some power superior to himself. But if the will of A is limited only by the will of A it is unlimited. We still speak of self-control, but it means now, as it always meant, just nothing at all; for where the will to be controlled and the controlling will are one there can be no limitation: whatever is done is done as much by the will that we figure to ourselves as restrained as by the will that we figure to ourselves as restraining it. Yet our republican ancestors tickled their own ears with this senseless phrase during the whole brief period of their national existence, and all the political literature of the time is full of it, used with ludicrous gravity and doubtless with telling effect upon the popular intelligence. But how, it may be asked, could they go on even so long as they did with no government, properly so called? From the records that have come down to us it does not appear that they went on very well. They were preyed upon by all sorts of political adventurers, whose power in most instances was limited only by the contemporaneous power of other political adventurers equally unscrupulous and mischievous. A full half of the taxes wrung from them were stolen. Their public lands, millions of square miles, were parceled out among banded conspirators. Their roads and the streets of their cities were nearly impassable. Their public buildings, conceived in abominable taste and representing enormous sums of money which never were used in their construction, began to tumble about the ears of the workmen before they were completed. The most delicate and important functions of government were intrusted to men with neither knowledge, heart nor experience, who by their corruption imperiled the public interest and by their blundering disgraced the national name. In short, all the train of evils inseparable from government of any kind beset this unhappy people with tenfold power, together with hundreds of worse ones peculiar to their own faulty and unnatural system. It was thought that their institutions would give them peace, yet in the first three-quarters of a century of their existence they fought three important wars: one of revenge, one of aggression and one—the bloodiest and most wasteful known up to that time—among themselves. And before the full century had passed they had the humiliation to see all their seaport cities destroyed by the Emperor of China in a quarrel which they had themselves provoked, the enormous sums of money taken indirectly from the pockets of the people by a monstrous process known as "Protection to American Industries" having been suffered to lie idle in the treasury instead of being intelligently applied to the defense of their harbors.

In illustration of the means by which their public men climbed to power, and as one of the causes of the final collapse, the learned Professor Dunkle relates this almost incredible instance. At the close of their great civil war—brought about by lack of foresight, political animosity and sheer incapacity on the part of their "public servants," as their tyrants loved to call themselves—there were nearly two millions of mostly young men who had borne arms on the victorious side. These men had been true patriots: they had enlisted from a simple sense of duty, with no desire for, nor thought of, other reward than the nominal pay of the private soldier or the considerable salary of the officer. At the conclusion of hostilities the survivors returned to their homes, happy and proud to have saved their country, as they believed, and wholly content to have escaped with their lives. They were praised and honored by all, even the vanquished. Their service and sufferings constituted them a distinct class, and unhappily, with the best of intentions, they broadened the line which marked them off from their fellow-citizens by forming an association so organized that it was capable, through its officers, of direction as one man. The members all had "votes"; that is, each one was permitted, under the vicious system of republican government, to help select the country's rulers. Here were present all the conditions of political mischief and the demagogues of the time were swift to avail themselves of the opportunity. By the basest sycophancy and the most shameless appeals to the sordid side of the soldiers' nature, these scheming men soon obtained control of the whole organization and used it to elevate themselves to power. When in power they had to retain their places against the efforts of others equally ambitious and equally unscrupulous by distributing the people's money to those who had advanced them. At first the money was given—rightly enough, according to the practice of nations—to those whose wounds in battle had made them wholly or partly unable to support themselves. Afterward, to those who had been wounded at all. Later, to all who were said to have contracted diseases in the service which had become chronic, and still later, to all who for any reason were unable or indisposed to work. Dazzled and corrupted by these successive concessions, the old soldiers, who had been patriots, became perjurers and plunderers; and at last, throwing off all pretense to decency, those whom shame had not compelled to withdraw from the organization demanded as a right that they and all their relatives be supported in comfort and even luxury by the rest of the people; and their demand was granted. In the mean time their numbers, instead of decreasing by death, had doubled and trebled by fraud; and thirty years after the close of the war, during the Presidency of General Ingalls,[3] the annual pension charge, computed in our money, amounted to the prodigious sum of 9,500,000,000 drusoes! Soon afterward the people rose against the Grand Army—as the members called themselves—and being more accustomed to the use of arms, though greatly outnumbered, put them all to death.

I have mentioned "a monstrous practice known as 'Protection to American Industries.'" Modern research has not ascertained precisely what it was: it is known rather from its effects than in its true character, but from what we can learn of it to-day from the fragmentary records that have come down to us, I am disposed to number it among those malefic agencies concerned in the destruction of the American republics, particularly the United States, although it appears not to have been peculiar to "popular government." Some of the contemporary monarchies of Europe were afflicted with it, but by the Divine favor which ever guards a throne its disastrous effects were averted. "Protection" consisted in a number of extraordinary expedients, the purposes of which, and their relations to one another, cannot with certainty be determined in the present state of our knowledge. Barclay, Debrethin, Henley, Villemassant and Schleibach agree that one feature of it was the support, by general taxation, of a few favored citizens in public palaces, where they passed their time in song and dance and all kinds of revelry. They were not, however, altogether idle, being required, out of the sums bestowed upon them, to employ a certain number of men each in erecting great piles of stone and pulling them down again, digging holes in the ground and then filling them up, pouring water into casks and then drawing it off, and so forth. These unhappy laborers were subject to the most cruel oppressions, but the knowledge that their wages came from the pockets of those whom their work nowise benefited was so gratifying to them that nothing could induce them to leave the service of their heartless employers to engage in lighter and more useful labor.

Another characteristic of "Protection" was the maintenance at the principal seaports of "custom-houses," which were strong fortifications, armed with heavy guns, for the purpose of destroying or driving away the trading ships of foreign nations. It was this that caused the United States to be known abroad as the "Hermit Republic," a name of which its infatuated citizens were strangely proud, although they had themselves sent armed ships to open the ports of Japan and other Oriental countries to their own commerce. In their own case, if a foreign ship came empty and succeeded in evading the fire of the "custom-house," as sometimes occurred, she was permitted to take away a cargo. It is obvious that such a system was distinctly mischievous, but it must be confessed our uncertainty regarding the whole matter of "Protection" does not justify us in assigning it a definitive place among the causes of national decay. That in some way it produced an enormous revenue is certain, and that the method was dishonest is no less so; for this revenue—known as a "surplus"—was so abhorred while it lay in the treasury that all were agreed upon the expediency of getting it out again, one great political party existing for apparently no other purpose than the patriotic one of taking it themselves, with all the evils which its possession would entail.

The fundamental fallacy of republican or popular government is now seen to be the extraordinary delusion that two or more follies make one wisdom—the greater the number of added idiocies, the higher the resulting intelligence. It is easy now to trace the origin of this error. When three men engage in any undertaking in which they have an equal interest and in the direction of which they have equal power, it necessarily results that any action approved by two of them, with or without the assent of the third, will be taken. This is called—or was called when it was an accepted principle in political and other affairs—"the rule of the majority." Evidently, under the mischievous conditions supposed it is the only practicable plan of getting anything done. A and B rule and overrule C, not because they ought, but because they can; not because they are wiser, but because they are stronger. In order to avoid a conflict in which he is sure to be worsted, C submits as soon as the vote is taken. C is as likely to be right as A and B; nay, that eminent ancient philosopher, Professor Richard A. Proctor (or Proroctor as the learned now spell the name), has clearly shown by the law of probabilities that any one of the three, all being of the same intelligence, is far likelier to be right than the other two; but submits because he must.

It is thus that the "rule of the majority" as a political system is established. It is in essence nothing but the discredited and discreditable principle that "might makes right"; but early in the life of a republic this essential character of government by majority is lost sight of. The habit of submitting all questions of policy to the arbitrament of counting noses and assenting without question to the result invests the ordeal with a seeming sanctity, and what was at first obeyed as the mandate of power comes to be revered as the oracle of wisdom. Hence originated that ancient blasphemy, adopted and held in high favor in every republic: *Vox populi vox Dei.* The innumerable instances—such as the famous ones of Galileo and Keeley—in which one man has been right and all the rest of the race wrong, are overlooked, or their significance missed and "public opinion" is followed as a divine and infallible guide through every bog into which it blindly stumbles and over every precipice in its fortuitous path. Clearly, there will sooner or later be encountered a bog that will smother, or a precipice that will crush. Thoroughly to apprehend the absurdity of the ancient faith in the wisdom of majorities let the loyal reader try to fancy our gracious Sovereign by any possibility wrong, or his unanimous Ministry by any possibility right!

During the latter half of the nineteenth century there arose in the United States a political element opposed to all government, which frankly declared its object to be Anarchy. This astonishing heresy was not of indigenous growth: its seeds were imported from Europe by the emigration or banishment thence of criminals congenitally incapable of understanding and appreciating the blessings of monarchical institutions, and whose method of protest was murder. The governments against which they conspired in their native lands were too strong in authority and too enlightened in policy for them to succeed in their wicked attempts. Hundreds of them were put to death, thousands imprisoned and sent into exile. But in America, whither those who escaped fled for safety, they found conditions entirely favorable to the prosecution of their designs.

A revered fetish of the Americans was "freedom of speech": it was foolishly believed that if bad men were permitted to proclaim their evil wishes they would go no further in the direction of executing them—that if they might say what they would like to do they would not try to do it. The close relation between speech and action was not understood. Because the Americans themselves had long been accustomed, in their own political debates and discussions, to the use of unmeaning declamation and threats which they had no intention of executing, they reasoned that others were like them, and attributed to the menaces of these desperate and earnest outcasts no greater importance than to their own. They thought also that the foreign Anarchists, having exchanged the tyranny of kings for the tyranny of majorities, would be content with their new and better lot and become in time good and law-abiding citizens. Had their lot been really better this could never have happened; from secretly warring for generations against the particular forms of authority in their native lands they had inherited a bitter antagonism against all authority, even the most beneficent. In their new home they were worse than in their old. In the sunshine of opportunity the rank and sickly growth of their perverted natures became hardy, vigorous, bore fruit. They surrounded themselves with proselytes from the ranks of the idle, the vicious, the unsuccessful. They stimulated and organized discontent. Every one of them became a center of contagion. To those as yet unprepared to accept Anarchy was offered the milder dogma of Socialism, and to those even weaker in the faith something vaguely called Reform. Each was initiated into that degree to which the induration of his conscience and the character of his discontent made him eligible, and in which he could be most useful; the body of the people still cheating themselves with a false sense of security begotten of the belief that they were somehow exempt from the operation of all agencies inimical to their national welfare and integrity. Human nature, they thought, was different in the West from what it was in the East: in the New World the old causes would not have the old effects: a republic had some inherent vitality of its own, entirely independent of any action intended to keep it alive. They felt that words and phrases had some talismanic power, and charmed themselves asleep by repeating "liberty," "all men equal before the law," "dictates of conscience," "free speech," and all manner of such shibboleth to exorcise the evil spirits of the night. And when they could no longer close their eyes to the dangers environing them—when they saw at last that what they had mistaken for the magic power of their form of government and its assured security was really its radical weakness and subjective peril—they found their laws inadequate to repression of the enemy, the enemy too strong to permit the enactment of adequate laws. The belief that a malcontent armed with freedom of speech, a newspaper, a vote and a rifle is less dangerous than a malcontent with a still tongue in his head, empty hands and under police surveillance was abandoned, but all too late. From its fatuous dream the nation was awakened by the noise of arms, the shrieks of women and the glare of burning cities.

Beginning with the slaughter at St. Louis on the night of Christmas in the year 1897, when no fewer than twenty-two thousand citizens were slain in their beds and half of the city destroyed, massacre followed massacre with frightful rapidity. New York fell in the month following, many thousands of its inhabitants escaping fire and sword only to be driven into the bay and drowned, "the roaring of the water in their ears," says Bardeal, "augmented by the hoarse clamor of their red-handed pursuers whose blood-thirst was unsated by the sea." A week later Washington was destroyed, with all its public buildings and archives; the President and his Ministry were slain, the Parliament was dispersed and an unknown number of officials and private citizens perished. Of all the principal cities, Chicago and San Francisco alone escaped. The people of the former were all Anarchists and the latter was valorously and successfully defended by the Chinese.

In turning from this branch of our inquiry to consider the causes of the failure and bloody disruption of the great American republic other than those inherent in the form of government, it may not be altogether unprofitable to glance briefly at what seems to a superficial view the inconsistent phenomenon of great material prosperity. It is not to be denied that this unfortunate people was singularly prosperous, in so far as national wealth is a measure and proof of prosperity. It was the richest nation among nations. But at how great a sacrifice of better things was its wealth obtained! By the neglect of all education except that crude elementary sort which fit men for the coarse delights of business and affairs, but confers no capacity of rational enjoyment; by exalting the worth of wealth and making it the test and touchstone of merit; by ignoring art, scorning literature and despising science, except as these might contribute to the glutting of the purse; by setting up and maintaining an artificial standard of morals which condoned all offenses against the property and peace of every one but the condoner; by pitilessly crushing out of their natures every sentiment and aspiration unconnected with accumulation of property, these civilized savages and commercial robbers attained their sordid end. Before they had rounded the first half-century of their existence as a nation they had sunk so low in the scale of true morality that it was considered nothing discreditable to take the hand and even visit the house of a man who had grown rich by means notoriously corrupt and dishonorable; and Harley declares that even the editors and writers of newspapers, after fiercely assailing such men in their journals, would be seen "hobnobbing" with them in public places. (The nature of the social ceremony named the "hobnob" is not now understood, but it is known that it was a mark of amity and favor.) When men or nations devote all the powers of their minds and bodies to the heaping up of wealth, wealth is heaped up. But what avails it? It may not be amiss to quote here the words of one of the greatest of the ancient Americans whose works—fragmentary, alas—have come down to us.

> Wealth has accumulated itself into masses; and poverty, also in accumulation enough, lies impassably separated from it; opposed, uncommunicating, like forces in positive and negative poles. The gods of this lower world sit aloft on glittering thrones, less happy than Epicurus's gods, but as indolent, as impotent; while the boundless living chaos of ignorance and hunger welters, terrific in its dark fury, under their feet. How much among us might be likened to a whited sepulcher: outwardly all pomp and strength, but inwardly full of horror and despair and dead men's bones! Iron highways, with their wains fire-winged, are uniting all the ends of the land; quays and moles, with their innumerable stately fleets, tame the ocean into one pliant bearer of burdens; labor's thousand arms, of sinew and of metal, all-conquering everywhere, from the tops of the mount down to the depths of the mine and the caverns of the sea, ply unweariedly for the service of man; yet man remains unserved. He has subdued this planet, his habitation and inheritance, yet reaps no profit from the victory. Sad to look upon: in the highest stage of civilization nine-tenths of mankind have to struggle in the lowest battle of savage or even animal man—the battle against famine. Countries are rich, prosperous in all manner of increase, beyond example; but the men of these countries are poor, needier than ever of all sustenance, outward and inward; of belief, of knowledge, of money, of food.

To this somber picture of American "prosperity" in the Nineteenth century nothing of worth can be added by the most inspired artist. Let us simply inscribe upon the gloomy canvas the memorable words of our greatest and wisest living poet:

> Ill fares the land, to hastening ills a prey,
> Where wealth accumulates and men decay.[4]

In the space allotted to me in the royal journal by his most gracious Majesty I have room to consider but a single one of the many additional causes that effected the downfall of republican government in the United States. This was the strange and unnatural antagonism known in that far

time as the "contest between Capital and Labor." It was the direct result and
legitimate sequence of the abolition of that beneficent and advantageous
system of slavery (now happily restored) but it was as needless as inhuman
and disastrous. Even in that day it was by many seen to be so, but their
deprecation was unheeded and their admonition scorned. Some of the philosophers of the period, rummaging amongst the dubious and misunderstood facts of commercial and industrial history, had discovered what they
were pleased to term "the law of supply and demand"; and this they expounded with so ingenious sophistry and so copious a wealth of illustration
and example that what is at best but a faulty and imperfectly applicable
principle, limited and cut into by all manner of other considerations, came
to be accepted as the sole explanation and basis of material prosperity and an
infallible rule for the proper conduct of affairs. In obedience to its mandate,
as they understood it—interpreting it in its narrowest and straitest sense—
employers and employees alike regulated by its iron authority all their dealings with one another, throwing off the immemorial relations of mutual
dependence and mutual esteem as tending to interfere with the beneficent
operation of the new Law. The employer came to believe conscientiously
that it was not only profitable and expedient, but under all circumstances his
duty to obtain his labor for as little money as possible, even as he sold its
product for as much. Considerations of humanity were not banished from
his heart, but most sternly excluded from his business. Many of these misguided men would give large sums to various charities; would found universities, hospitals, libraries; would even stop on their way to relieve beggars
in the street; but for their own work-people they had no care. Strahan
relates in his *Memoirs* that a wealthy manufacturer once said to one of his
mill-hands who had asked for an increase of his wages because unable to
support his family on the pay that he was receiving: "Your family is nothing
to me. I cannot afford to mix benevolence with my business." Yet this man,
the author adds, had just given a thousand gold pieces to a "seaman's home."
He could afford to care for other men's employees, but not his own. He
could not see that the act which he performed as truly, and to the same
degree, cut down his margin of profit in his business as the act which he
refused to perform would have done, and had not the advantage of securing
him better service from a grateful workman.

On their part, the laborers were no better. Their relations to their employers being "purely commercial," as it was called, they put no heart into
their work, seeking ever to do as little as possible for their money, precisely
as their employers sought to pay as little as possible for the work they got.
The interests of the two classes being thus antagonized, they grew to distrust

and hate one another, and each accession of ill feeling produced acts which tended to broaden the breach more and more. There was neither cheerful service on the one side, nor ungrudging payment on the other.

The laborers at last thought they had discovered a plan of power which would give them control of the situation: they began to combine in vast leagues, agreeing that the grievance of one should be the grievance of all. Originally organized for self-protection, and for a while partly successful, these leagues became in the course of time great tyrannies, so reasonless in their demands and so unscrupulous in their methods of enforcing them that the laws were unable to deal with them, and frequently the military forces of the several States were ordered out for the protection of life and property; but in every case the soldiers either fraternized with the leagues, ran away or were easily defeated. The "strikers," as these cruel and mindless mobs were called, had always the hypocritical sympathy and encouragement of the press and the politician, for both feared their power and courted their favor. The judges, dependent for their offices not only on their votes, but on the approval of the press and the politicians, boldly set aside the laws against conspiracy, and strained to the utmost tension those against riot, arson and murder. To such a pass did all this come that in the year 1891 an inn-keeper's denial of a half-holiday to an under cook resulted in the peremptory closing of half the factories in the country, the stoppage of all the railroad travel and the movement of all freight by land and water and a general paralysis of all the industries in the land. Many thousands of families, including those of the "strikers" and their friends, suffered from famine; armed conflicts occurred in every State; hundreds were slain and incalculable amounts of property wrecked and destroyed.

In the mean time capital had not been idle. As it had at first taught labor the law of supply and demand and the mischievous advantages of the "purely commercial relation," so now it learned from labor the malevolent lesson of protective and aggressive leagues. "Strikes" were met by "lockouts," the "boycott" begot the "blacklist," force was repelled by force. The assistance denied by the police and the military was secured by armies of hirelings armed with the most deadly weapons known at the time. In a country where money was all-powerful the power of money was used without stint and without scruple. The judges were bribed to do their duty, juries to convict, newspapers to support, and legislators to betray their constituents and pass the most oppressive laws. By these corrupt means, and with the natural advantage of greater skill in affairs and larger experience in concerted action (gained in corporations, syndicates and that form of piracy known as "trusts") the capitalists soon restored their ancient reign and the state of the laborer was worse than it ever had been before. Strahan says that in his time two millions of unoffending workmen in the various industries were once discharged without warning and promptly arrested as vagrants and deprived of their ears because a sulking canal-boatman had kicked his captain's dog into the water. And the dog was a retriever.

Even without these monstrous measures, except for the lawless wrecking of property, capital must eventually have triumphed, and in point of fact commonly did. Cheered and consoled by the knowledge that the whole country suffered with him, the man whose workmen had struck or been locked out could with tranquillity forego his profits; but however sustained by spiritual satisfaction the workmen could not forego their dinners. Their leagues, moreover, were at a peculiar and remediless disadvantage in this: the more nearly they succeeded in making their membership universal and their strikes general and ruinous, the stronger was the temptation to treason in and defection from their own ranks. When capital, most imperiled, most needed trusty labor the trade of being a non-union man was most lucrative, and became at last one of the "overcrowded professions." The labor leagues had made the fatal mistake of allowing too little for human cupidity.

The leagues were finally broken up, the laborer, reduced to the condition of a serf, became an Anarchist and his subsequent deeds in that character, briefly glanced at elsewhere in this treatise, are recorded in blood upon his page of the awful annals of that "fierce democracy" of which he was ever the central figure and for long the controlling power.

In reviewing the history of those turbulent times one cannot help thinking how different it all might have been if the "law of supply and demand" and the "purely commercial relation" had remained undiscovered, or had perished unexpounded with their discoverer when he was hanged; if in ancient America, as under the benign sway of our most gracious and ever-blessed sovereign, the employer had studied, not how little he could get his labor for, but how much he could afford to give for it, and if the employee, instead of calculating how badly he could do his work and keep his place, had considered how well he could do it and keep his health.

In concluding this hasty and imperfect sketch I cannot forbear to relate an episode of the bloody and unnatural contest between labor and capital, which I find recorded in the almost forgotten work of Antrolius, who was an eye-witness to the incident. At a time when the passions of both parties were most inflamed and scenes of violence most frequent, it was somehow noised about in Washington that at a certain hour of a certain day some one—none knew who—would stand upon the steps of the Capitol and speak to the people, expounding a plan for the reconciliation of all conflicting interests and the pacification of the quarrel. At the specified hour, there being a general strike and lockout in the city, thousands of idlers had assembled to hear—glowering capitalists attended by hireling body-guards with repeating rifles, sullen laborers with dynamite bombs concealed beneath their coats. All eyes were directed to the appointed spot, where suddenly appeared (none could say whence—it seemed as if he had been standing there all the time, such were his immobility and composure) a tall, pale man clad in a long robe, bare-headed, his hair falling lightly upon his shoulders, his eyes full of compassion, and with such majesty of face and mien that all were awed to silence ere he spoke. Slightly raising his right hand from the elbow, the index finger extended upward, he said in a voice ineffably sweet and serious: "As ye would that others should do unto you, do ye even so unto them." These words he repeated in the same solemn and thrilling tones three times; then, as the expectant multitude waited breathless for him to begin his discourse, stepped quietly down among them into their very midst, every one afterward averring that he passed within a pace of where himself stood. For an instant the crowd was speechless with surprise and disappointment, then broke into wild, fierce cries of "Lynch him! Lynch him!" and struggling into looser order started in mad pursuit. But each man ran a different way and the stranger was seen again by none of them.

THE WIZARD OF BUMBASSA

M R. GEORGE WESTINGHOUSE, the air-brake man, did a cruel and need-less thing in going out of his way to try to destroy humanity's hope of being shot along the ground at a speed of one hundred miles an hour. There is no trouble, it appears, in building locomotives able to snatch a small village of us through space at the required speed; the difficulty lies in making, with sufficient promptness, those unschedulary stops necessitated by open switches, missing bridges, and various obstacles that industrial discontent is wont to grace the track withal. Even on a straight line—what the civil engineers find a pleasure in call-ing a tangent—the prosperous industrian at the throttle-valve cannot reasonably be expected to discern these hindrances at a greater distance than one thousand feet; and Mr. Westinghouse sadly confessed that in that distance his most effec-tive appliance could not do more than reduce the rate from one hundred miles an hour to fifty—an obviously inadequate reduction. He held out no hope of being able to evolve from his inner consciousness either a brake of superior effectiveness or a pair of spectacles that would enable the engine driver to dis-cover a more distant danger on a tangent, or to see round a curve.

All this begets an intelligent dejection. If we must renounce our golden dream of cannonading ourselves from place to place with a celerity suitable to our rank in the world's *fauna*—comprising the shark, the hummingbird, the hornet and the jackass rabbit—civilization is indeed a failure. But it is forbidden to the wicked pessimist to rejoice, for there is a greater than Mr. Westinghouse and he has demonstrated his ability to bring to a dead stop within its own length any railway train, however short and whatever its rate of speed. It were unwise, though, to indulge too high a hope in this matter, even if the gloomy vaticinations of the Westinghouse person are fallacious. Approaching an evidence of social unrest at a speed of one and two-thirds mile a minute on a down grade, even in a train equipped by a greater than Mr. Westinghouse, may not be an altogether pleasing performance.

This possibility can be best illustrated by recalling to the reader's memory the history of the Ghargaroo and Gallywest Railway in Bumbassa. As is well known, the trains on that road attained a speed that had not theretofore been dreamed of except by the illustrious projector of the road. But the King of Bumbassa was not content: with an indifference to the laws of dynamics which in the retro-spect seems almost imperial, he insisted upon instantaneous stoppage. To the royal demand the clever and prudent gentleman who had devised and carried out the enterprise responded with an invention which he assured his Majesty would accomplish the desired end. A trial was made in the sovereign's presence, the coaches being loaded with his chief officers of state and other courtiers, and it was eminently successful. The train, going at a speed of ninety miles an hour, was brought to a dead stop within the length of the rhinoceros-catcher and directly in front of the blue cotton umbrella beneath which his Majesty sat to observe the result of the test. The passengers, unfortunately, did not stop so promptly, and were afterward scraped off the woodwork at the forward ends of the cars and decently interred. The train-hands had all escaped by the ingenious plan of absenting themselves from the proceedings, with the exception of the engineer, who had thoughtfully been selected for the occasion from among the relatives of the projector's wife, and instructed how to shut off the steam and apply the brake. When hosed off the several parts of the engine he was found to have incurred a serious dispersal of the viscera.

The King's delight at the success of the experiment was somewhat mitigated by the reflection that if the train had been freighted with *bona fide* travelers instead of dignitaries whom he could replace by appointment the military resources of the state would have suffered a considerable loss; so he commanded the projector to invent a method of stopping the passengers and the trains simultaneously. This, after much experiment, was done by fixing the passengers to the seats by clamps extending across the abdomen and chest; but no provision being made for the head, a general decapitation ensued at each stop; and people who valued their heads preferred thereafter to travel afoot or ostrichback, as before. It was found, moreover, that, as arrested motion is converted into heat, the royal requirement frequently resulted in igniting and consuming the trains— which was expensive.

These various hard conditions of railroading in Bumbassa eventually subdued the spirits of the stockholders, drove the projector to drink and led at last to withdrawal of the concession—whereby one of the most promising projects for civilizing the Dark Continent was, in the words of the Ghargaroo *Palladium,* "knocked perfectly cold."

I have thought it well to recall this melancholy incident here for its general usefulness in pointing a moral, and for its particular application to the fascinating enterprise of a one-hundred-miles-an-hour electric road from New York to Chicago—a road whose trains, intending passengers are assured, will be under absolute control of the engineers and "can be stopped at a moment's notice." If I have said anything to discourage the enterprise I am sorry, but really it is not easy to understand why anybody should wish to go from New York to Chicago.

MODERN PENOLOGY

AFTER LYING FOR more than a century dead I was revived, given a new body, and restored to society. This was in the year 2015. The first thing of interest that I observed was an enormous building, covering a square mile of ground. It was surrounded on all sides by a high, strong wall of hewn stone upon which armed sentinels paced to and fro. In each face of the wall was a single gate of massive iron, strongly guarded. While admiring the cyclopean architecture of this "reverend pile"[1] I was accosted by Colonel Andrews, with a cheerful salutation.

"Colonel," I said, pressing his hand, "it gives me pleasure to find some one that I know and can believe. Pray tell me what is this building."

"That," said the colonel, "is the new State penitentiary. It is one of twelve, all alike."

"You surprise me," I replied. "Surely the criminal element must have increased enormously."

"Yes, indeed," he assented; "under the Reform *regime,* which began about 1895, it became so powerful, bold and fierce that arrests were no longer possible and the prisons then in existence were soon overcrowded. The State was compelled to erect others of greater capacity."

"But, Colonel," I protested, "if the criminals were too bold and powerful to be taken into custody, of what use are the prisons? And how are they crowded?"

My friend fixed upon me a look that I could not fail to interpret as expressing a doubt of my sanity. "What!" he said, "is it possible that the modern Penology is unknown to you? Do you suppose we practice the antiquated and ineffective method of shutting up the rascals? Sir, the growth of the criminal element has, as I said, compelled the erection of more and larger prisons. We have now enough to hold comfortably all the honest men and women of the State. Within these protecting walls they carry on all the necessary vocations of life excepting commerce. That is necessarily in the hands of the rogues, as before."

"Venerated vestige of the past," I exclaimed, wringing his hand with effusion, "you are Knowledge, you are History, you are the Higher Education! We must talk further. Come, let us enter this benign edifice; you shall show me your apartment and instruct me in the rules. You shall propose me as an inmate."

I walked rapidly to the nearest gate. When challenged by the sentinel I turned to summon my instructor and friend. He was nowhere visible: desolate and forbidding, as about the broken statue of Ozymandias,

The lone and level sands stretched far away.[2]

The Great Strike of 1895

NEW YORK, July 2, 1895.—The strike of the American Authors' Guild continues to hold public attention. No event in the history of trades-unionism since the great railroad strike of last year has equaled it in interest. Nothing else is talked of here. In some parts of the city all business is suspended and the excitement grows more intense hourly.

At about 10 o'clock this morning a non-union author attempting to enter the premises of D. Appleton & Co. with a roll of manuscript was set upon by a mob of strikers and beaten into insensibility. The strikers were driven from their victim by the police, but only after a fight in which both sides suffered severely.

NEW YORK, July 3.—Rioting was renewed last night in front of the boycotted publishing house of Charles Scribner's Sons, 153–157 Fifth avenue. Though frequently driven back by charges of the police, who used their clubs freely, the striking authors succeeded in demolishing all the front windows by stone-throwing. One shot was fired into the interior, narrowly missing a young lady typewriter. Mr. William D. Howells,[1] a member of the Guild's board of managers, declares that he has irrefragable proof that this outrage was committed by some one connected with the Publishers' Protective League for the purpose of creating public sympathy.

It has been learned that the non-union author so severely beaten yesterday died of his injuries last night. His name is said to have been Richard Henry (or Hengist) Stoddard,[2] formerly a member of the Guild, but expelled for denouncing the action of President Brander Matthews[3] in ordering the strike.

LATER.—Matters look more and more threatening. A crowd of ten thousand authors, headed by Col. Thomas Wentworth Higginson,[4] is reported to be marching upon the Astor Library,[5] which is strongly guarded by police, heavily armed. Many book-stores have been wrecked and their contents destroyed.

Mrs. Julia Ward Howe, who was shot last night while setting fire to the establishment of Harper & Bros., cannot recover. She is delerious, and lies on her cot in the Bellevue Hospital singing "The Battle Hymn of the Republic."[6]

BOSTON, July 3.—Industrial discontent has broken out here. The members of the local branch of the American Authors' Guild threw down their pens this morning and declared that until satisfactory settlement of novelists' percentages should be arrived at not a hero and heroine should live happily ever afterward in Boston. The publishing house of Houghton, Mifflin & Co. is guarded by a detachment of Pinkerton men[7] armed with Winchester rifles and a Gatling gun. The publishers say that they are getting all the manuscripts that they are able to reject, and profess to have no apprehension as to the future. Mr. Joaquin Miller, a non-union poet from Nevada, visiting some Indian relatives here, was terribly beaten by a mob of strikers to-day. Mr. Miller was the aggressor; he was calling them "sea-doves"—by which he is said to have meant "gulls."[8]

CHICAGO, July 3.—The authors' strike is assuming alarming dimensions and is almost beyond control by the police. The Mayor is strongly urged to ask for assistance from the militia, but the strikers profess to have no fear of his doing so. They say that he was once an author himself, and is in sympathy with them. He wrote "The Beautiful Snow."[9] In the mean time a mob of strikers numbering not fewer than one thousand men, women and children, headed by such determined labor leaders as Percival Pollard and Hamlin Garland,[10] are parading the streets and defying the authorities. A striker named Opie Reed,[11] arrested yesterday for complicity in the assassination of Mr. Stone, of the publishing firm of Stone & Kimball,[12] was released by this mob from the officers that had in him custody. Mr. Pollard publishes a letter in the *Herald* this morning saying that Mr. Stone was assassinated by an emissary of the Publishers' Protective League to create public sympathy, and strongly hints that the assassin is the head of the house of McClurg & Co.

NEW YORK, July 4.—All arrangements for celebrating the birthday of American independence are "off." The city is fearfully excited, and scenes of violence occur hourly. Macmillan & Co.'s establishment was burned last night, and four lives were lost in the flames. The loss of property is variously estimated. All the publishing houses are guarded by the militia, and it is said that Government troops will land this afternoon to protect the United States mails carrying the manuscripts of strike-breaking authors, in transit to publishers. The destruction of the Astor Library and the Cooper Union[13] and the closing of all the book-stores that escaped demolition in yesterday's rioting have caused sharp public distress. No similar book-famine has ever been known in this city. Novel-readers particularly, their needs being so imperative, are suffering severely, and unless relieved soon will leave the metropolis. While beating a noisy person named E. W. Townsend[14] last night, one Richard Harding Davis[15] had the misfortune to break two of his fingers. He said Townsend was a strike-breaker and had given information to the police, but it turns out that he is a zealous striker, and was haranguing the mob at the time of the assault. His audience of rioting authors, all of whom belonged to the War Story branch of the Guild, mistook Mr. Davis for an officer of the peace and ran away. Mr. Townsend, who cannot recover and apparently does not wish to, is said to be the author of a popular book called *The Chimney Fadder*. Advices from Boston relate the death of a Pinkerton spy named T. B. Aldrich,[16] who attempted to run the gauntlet of union pickets and enter the premises of The Arena Publishing Company, escorting Walter Blackburn Harte.[17] Mr. Harte was rescued by the police and sailed at once for England.

Philadelphia, July 5.—A mob of striking authors attacked the publishing house of J. B. Lippincott & Co. this morning and were fired on by the militia. Twenty are known to have been killed outright—the largest number of writers ever immortalized at one time.

New York, July 5.—In an interview yesterday Mrs. Louise Chandler Moulton,[18] treasurer of the Guild, said that notwithstanding the heavy expense of maintaining needy strikers with dependent families, there would be no lack of funds to carry on the fight. Contributions are received daily from sympathetic trades. Sixty dollars have been sent in by the Confederated Undertakers and forty-five by the Association of Opium-Workers. President Brander Matthews has telegraphed to all the Guild's branches in other cities that they can beat the game if they will stand pat.

NEW YORK, July 6.—Sympathy strikes are the order of the day, and "risings" are reported everywhere. In this city the entire East Side is up and out. Shantytown, Ballyspalpeen, Goatville and Niggernest are in line. Among those killed in yesterday's conflict with the United States troops at Madison-square was Mark Twain,[19] who fell while cheering on a large force of women of the town. He was shot all to rags, so as to be hardly distinguishable from a human being.

CHICAGO, July 7.—John Vance Cheney[20] was arrested at 3 o'clock this morning while placing a dynamite bomb on the Clark-street bridge. He is believed to have entertained the design, also, of setting the river on fire. Two publishers were shot this morning by General Lew Wallace,[21] who escaped in the confusion of the incident. The victims were employed as accountants in the Methodist Book Concern.

NEW YORK, July 8.—The authors' strike has collapsed, and the strikers are seeking employment as waiters in the places made vacant by the lockout of the Restaurant Trust. The Publishers' Protective League declares that no author concerned in the strike will ever again see his name upon a title-page. The American Authors' Guild is a thing of the past. Arrests are being made every hour. As soon as he can procure bail, President Brander Matthews will go upon the vaudeville stage.

ANNALS OF THE FUTURE HISTORIAN

The Fall of Christian Civilization

"IT IS INTERESTING to observe," wrote the Future Historian, his toes flying rapidly across his paper, "what an apparently trivial cause brought about the downfall of what is commonly known as the "Christian civilization"—in reality its essential and characteristic feature was not Christianity, but the Pink Shirt. Many pious persons have professed to see in the extinction of the blood-thirsty heathens of that ancient regime a signal instance of divine justice. Certain it is that in their zeal to destroy one another they evolved a malefic agency which, directly and indirectly, destroyed them all; but whether or not that beneficent result was due to the will of Buddha it is not given to mortals to know. At a time shortly anterior to the reign of the first American Kings all the great pink-shirted nations began to experiment with smokeless and noiseless gunpowder. (Gunpowder was a liquid explosive which the ancients used in tubes to kill one another, as we, to destroy the irritating nightingale, use crystallized thunder.) In about three jowyows after they began their experiments they succeeded in making a gunpowder whose explosion was absolutely silent and invisible, and used it in "war" with great satisfaction. But they very soon learned that it could be used in private assassination, and with almost perfect immunity from detection. Men and women began to fall dead in the streets, slain from behind window shutters, along highways bordered with bushes, in theatres and churches and all manner of public assemblies. Statesmen addressing Senates and demagogues haranguing the people would pitch forward and give up the ghost, the only thing they had ever been known to give up. By use of a short tube a villain could mingle in a crowd and slaughter a half-dozen victims without removing his hand from his pocket. Everywhere was sudden death; no one who had an enemy was safe, and the passion for killing wantonly so infected all classes, particularly the women, that eventually nobody dared go out of doors until necessity compelled. The courts were powerless. Not only could they seldom procure evidence to convict, but few judges lived to finish a trial. Finally all took to the woods, no one daring to meet another. Civilization is gregarious; isolation is barbarism. In two or three generations the world was a wilderness sparsely infested by naked savages, mostly cannibals and Republicans. And such was the state of affairs when our hardy forefathers alighted at Topeka."

On the Canal

TAKING A NEW PEN and placing it between the fifth and sixth toes of his left foot, according to the fashion of his time, the Future Historian wrote as follows:

> During what were known as the "nineteenth" and "twentieth" centuries (for what reason is not now even conjectured) the middle part of our continent was inhabited by a people calling themselves Amorigans. They appear to have consisted of four great tribes: In the East the Smugwumps, in the North the Pewks, in the South the Coons, and in the West the Galoots.[1] The seat of government (Throne) was at Laundryton,[2] which is believed to have been situated at the confluence of the Jojuk and Gwap Rivers—then known as the Potstomach and Mishashippy. Here their national parliament met and for more than fifty years discussed nothing but the making of a canal through the Republic of Niggerawgua, which lay to the southward. Many parties of surveyors, engineers and statesmen were sent at enormous expense to select a route, survey it and estimate the cost of the canal. Several treaties were made with other nations that lived on the other side of the world and having no rights in the matter would make any treaty desired if it cost them nothing and gave them some share in the ownership. Dumbleshaw, an historian of the period, quoted in one of the sacred books of the prophet Mark Twain, says that a new treaty was negotiated every full moon and amended every foggy morning. At one time the disputes about the canal caused a great civil war in which the Coons were beaten by the Smugwumps and the Pewks, and which resulted incidentally in emancipation of all the mules in the country. Finally, during the early part of the "Twentieth" Century, while in both houses of the Potstomach parliament the dispute was at its hottest and no fewer than four commissions were in Niggerawgua re-examining the route, the French, who had long been working at a better place near by, completed their own canal, which was promptly seized by the British, who never permitted a competing one to be made nor an Amorigan to pass through that one. The site of it is not now known.

The Minister's Death

THE FUTURE HISTORIAN had been out all night dallying unwisely with the gin rickey of his period and was indisposed. He sat a long time at his work, evolving nothing worthy of his genius; then as the electrical whistle in a neighboring church pealed the hour of forty-nine his dead faculties revived and he wrote rapidly as follows:

> It was a solemn and painful scene. The unhappy Minister had asked that he might die in his robes of state, and he was led to execution clad in the barbarous magnificence of his time, his country and his office. His appearance was in strong contrast with that of the President, who wore what one of the poets of the period has graphically if not now altogether intelligibly described as "a long-tailed coat all buttoned down before." As commander-in-chief of the American army he was attended by a glittering retinue, led by a dashing young officer of uncertain rank named Miles or Mills.[3] As the doomed Chinaman had committed no crime but that of incessant garrulity he was spared other indignity than the necessary binding of his hands, though the obvious suggestion had been made by a mean-spirited writer that a more appropriate and needful precaution would be the tying of his tongue. In his character of hostage the illustrious diplomat was accorded every immunity and mark of respect that was consistent with the right of the populace to pelt him with stones and the duty of the soldiers to shoot him.

At this point the narrative inaccountably merged into a subtle dissertation on what was once known as "international law", but is now ascertained to have been the fantastic invention of a lunatic, the discredit of whose birth is now disclaimed by seven cities. This dissertation now fills seven octavo volumes. The narrative of the execution was then resumed in too horrible detail to be repeated here. It concluded as follows:

> As the troops and people marked past the mangled body they seem to have experienced a revulsion of feeling. Many who had known the unfortunate man in life and had won money from him at a game of chance called poker, even some of those who had thrown stones at him as he went to his death turned away their heads and sighed heavily. The President himself was visibly affected. His retinue glittered sympathetically and the dashing young officer mentioned as its commander stood gloomily apart, silently dashing, in profound dejection. Thus perished, in atonement for the crimes of his government and people, an illustrious man and beloved servant of the Daughter of Heaven. The City of Washington is no more. Its site is unknown. The people of whose ancestors it was the capital are naked savages without a

tribal designation. But history has forever embalmed the name and fame of Wu Ting Fang, inventor and expounder of the State of Peace attended with Appalling Casualties.

The Maid of Podunk

O F THE GIRLHOOD of Mrs. Nation (wrote the Historian of the Future) little that is authentic is known. She is commonly believed to have been born at Podunk,[4] where as lately as the year 2730 a monument stood inscribed with her name, her virtues and her deeds. In that year it was destroyed by the great earthquake that overthrew that famous city, which was then the national capital.[5]

It is known that she was of humble origin and was brought up (her mother having died in giving birth to her) "on the bottle."[6] The meaning of that phrase, much in use among her contemporaries, is not now accurately understood, for it is obvious that unless the ardent spirits of that day were materially different from those of our time they would not have served as the sole diet of infants. To the deleterious effects of "the bottle" on the child's health we perhaps can trace that passionate antagonism to strong drink which was the keynote to her character and career.

When little Carrie was eleven years old, say about 1830, her father removed to Whitchita, or Whickity, a frontier town in Kansas, or Mormont— authorities disagree.[7] It was here that she began to hear the mysterious "voices" that moved her to take up arms against the "joints."[8] These, it appears, were places in which strong drinks were made by daring criminals and forced down the throats of persons who had been seized on the highways and carried into them.

The evolution of the word "joint," as given by the learned and ingenious Potwin Dumbleshaw, in his great work on the philology of the ancients, is interesting. A man who had been carried into one of these terrible places and made to swallow the noxious liquid there produced was singularly affected by it: he was so limber as to be unable either to stand or sit—it was as if he had joints all over him. Hence he was known as a "jointer." Now, in the ancient Americanese tongue a "horser" was one who rode the now extinct animal called a "horse," a "schooner" was one who sailed in a ship called a "schoon," and so forth, the termination "er" implying always a certain relation to a place or thing.[9] So, by an odd forward-and-back analogy, the word "joint," meaning originally a point of flection in a limb, came to mean also, through its own derivative, a place where the "jointer" was jointed. "I know not," says Prof. Dumbleshaw, "a more curious instance of the perversion and shifting of words from thing to thing."

It is only fair to explain that Dr. Nubler, Professor of Extinct Languages at the Seacaucus University, holds a different view, to the effect that Prof. Dumbleshaw is an ass.

For many centuries there has been much controversy regarding the "voices" said to have been heard by the young Carrie Slupsky[10] (that was her maiden name), and many duels are said to have resulted from the conflicting opinions.

The chief protagonists of Miss Slupsky—the men most solemnly convinced of her veracity and good faith in affirming her guidance by the "voices"—are Bastien Lapage, a famous author of the nineteenth century, and Mark Twain (or Duane), a painter of great renown.[11] Both these worthies, each in his way, have put upon record their profound persuasion of the maiden's actual inspiration by audible voices in the air, and both were her contemporaries and compatriots. Not much of the work of either has come down to us—a few leaves from the book of Lapage, a fragment of a painting by Twain—or Duane.

An odd circumstance is that in one of the former, Mrs. Nation's birthplace and home of her girlhood is mentioned as "Domremy."[12] The name occurs in several fragments of European literature of an even earlier date, and these facts have given rise to much discussion, evolving more heat than light.

Prof. Clambuck, writing in the year 2641, explains this apparent discrepancy somewhat as follows: In the Pottawottomy dialect, which in the nineteenth century prevailed over the greater part of America among the illiterate, "po" and "dom" meant the same thing—a cow. Now, "dunk" meant a place of refreshment, or entertainment, and "remy" is an old Algonquin word for salt. Having these meanings in mind, it is easy, says the learned professor, to see that the names "Podunk" and "Domremy" are virtually the same: they signify a place of refreshment for cows, a place where those animals go for salt—a "cow-lick."[13]

It is not, generally speaking, within the province of the historian to utter dogmatic judgment in such matters, but this seems to be a pretty flagrant instance of ingenuity. I mention it only to show to what lengths the learned will sometimes go in explaining what is obviously a grammatical error (like the "ablative absolute" in Latin)[14] or a mere slip of the pen, as when it was said that Edwin Markham was born in Bethlehem.[15]

There can be no reasonable doubt that Mrs. Nation was born in Podunk, nor that the writer who first used the name Domremy did so in a moment of abstraction. As to the cows coming to Podunk to lick salt, the acute reader will not fail to observe the similarity in sound between "lick" and "liquor," the ancient Americanese word for strong drink—a significant circumstance, though it is not the business of history to inquire what it signifies.

At about thirteen years of age, Miss Slupsky said that the "voices" directed her to go to a certain place where she would find a hatchet—a small axe, sometimes called a "sword"—suitable for smashing joints. She did so, and, finding the implement, tried its edge on a cherry tree. Asked by her father if she knew who had felled the tree she replied: "I cannot tell a lie, father, you know I cannot tell a lie; I don't know a thing about it."[16]

The reception accorded to that statement is believed by Geezer ("The Ministry of Pain," iv., 327) to have had a stupendous effect upon the course of history. It gave the beautiful Maid of Podunk a distaste for a sedentary occupation and urged her forth to the tented field. From that day the demon Drink trembled in his frail glass armor, and when, in 1904, the lady was caught and burned as a witch there was not in all Topeka (says the Future Historian, in conclusion) enough wine to christen a canal boat.

The Extinction of the Smugwumps

ALTHOUGH (WROTE THE FUTURE HISTORIAN) the American climate, since the continent's discovery by the Swedish Admiral, Galumphus,[17] had never been what we Saharans of to-day would call supportable, yet for several centuries a considerable population did manage to withstand its horrors, and even multiplied. Indeed, so great was the fecundity of the mongrel races inhabiting that continent that at one time the people of the United States alone are believed to have numbered nearly twenty millions.

This estimate is based on an extant report of the United States Pension Bureau for the year 1915, from which it appears that the whole number of pensioners on the rolls was then 17,534,196. It is known that, as the learned Jupileter points out, "the entire body of the people drew pensions, the only persons debarred from that civic privilege being those who had served honorably in the wars and been sufficiently rewarded by the gratitude and respect of their countrymen."

Professor Smiitthh, of the University of Timbuctoo, presents some reasons for his belief that the astonishing multiplication of the ancient Americans was assisted by a process called "immigration," the nature of which is not now understood. The word is perhaps a medical term.

In their long battle with Nature the Americans were of course defeated.[18] With their crude and fragmentary knowledge of natural laws and their inaptitude in the arts and sciences they were unable to protect themselves against the increasing rigors of their murderous climate, and paid with their lives the penalty of ignorance. In all that vast territory lying east of the Mountain of Rocks the winters grew successively colder, the summers successively warmer. Every year, in nearly all places in that region, the temperature was officially reported both lower in the one season and higher in the other than it had ever been before and with a correspondingly unprecedented death rate.

During the Presidency of Samuel Gompers,[19] in 1908, no fewer than 16,042 persons perished in one summer's heat in New York City alone; and although in the annual report of the Bureau of Vital Statistics this total is reduced to 7,993 by deducting the number that had perished of cold in the preceding winter, the figures were sufficiently alarming to cause a general exodus from the place.

Other places, however, were no better off; the only persons who improved their condition were the comparatively few who could reach the Pacific Coast or cross to the Old World before all ships had been withdrawn from the transatlantic trade.

After the year 1908 no records of the mortality appear to have been made; none, at least, have come down to us. It was not, however, until nearly a generation later that in the mad struggle against these malign and terrible conditions all Government ceased, and with it every form of human activity except for the immediate preservation of individual life. Out of that vast welter of death and the peril of death nothing could have come but cries and lamentations, and these the perished arts did not record.

Not climate only—another dread, implacable agency of doom was concerned in this unexampled tragedy! As early as 1870, in the Presidency of General Linkon, scientists had observed that the eastern littoral of North America was slowly sinking into the sea, while the western was rising at the same rate. Year by year, while the Bay San Francisco, now an inland village, but then a flourishing seaport, grew shallow the Atlantic made greater and greater inroads upon the land. The continent, as Dumbleshaw has graphically expressed it, "was turning over like a man in bed."

The Eastern pleasure resorts, with their "bathing-beaches," were first to be engulfed by the winter storms; then the rising tides invaded the great commercial cities of New York, Pittsburg,[20] Podunk and many others, whose names are lost in the mists of antiquity. By the end of the Twentieth century, as the ancients for some unknown reason reckoned time, the entire vast region east of the Mountain of Rocks had disappeared. Yet not a living thing

was drowned, for none had survived the terrible vicissitudes of that insupportable climate!

To the modern understanding it seems hardly credible that in order to
reach the ruins of Honolulu the ancient archæologist had to traverse three
hundred and ten *surindas* of sea that rolled between them and the Califuranian
coast! The journey is now made, through the populous kingdom of Citrusia,[21]
in two days.

Industrial Discontent in Ancient America

LIGHTING A FRESH CIGAR of tea leaves and putting on an electro-mag-
netic thinking-cap the Future Historian wrote as follows:

The capital weakness of the "Labor Movement" in ancient America—a
fundamental disability which nothing could cure—was its reliance on moral
qualities which are not universal; with which, indeed, human nature is but
sparingly endowed.

Man then, as now, was a selfish animal, fond of high and noble sentiments when without occasion for their exercise, but in all practical affairs
guided by short and narrow views of self-interest and incapable of general
actions in furtherance of the general welfare.

Then, as now, it was easy to kindle a bright flame of enthusiasm for some
great "cause" requiring concerted action and heroic devotion, but impossible to enlist in its service those who could see a personal advantage in
standing aloof.

For "organized labor" to succeed, it was necessary that all laborers belong
to the organizations; yet this was obviously impossible to bring about. Nor
were matters much mended by a close approach to it.

The fewer that remained outside, with freedom of individual action, the
greater was the demand for their labor during "strikes," and the higher were
the wages that they could command; the result, as might have been foreseen,
being greater defections from the unions. So the conditions that the unions
strove to create were the very conditions most fatal to their success.

"Unionism" bore in its bosom the seeds of its own dissolution. At every
step toward attainment of its end, it offered an added premium to desertion;
its success was father to failure.

So paralyzing, so incurable and at last so universally obvious was this inherent disability that, as early as 1912, during the Presidency of General Gompers,[22] the Administration tried to force through Congress an amendment to the Constitution making labor unions unlawful and strikes felonious.

The measure failed, because, as Senator Debs[23] explained, it was needless: the common sense of the country was a "sufficient protection against the scheming of ambitious demagogues and the mischievous incitements of self-seeking agitators."

In Dumbleshaw's "History of Human Delusions," that ingenious investigator relates that, owing to the prevalence of "unionism," non-union workingmen so prospered through high wages and steady employment that they became one of the overcrowded professions, and they finally formed a league, the National Federation of Scabs, the chief purposes of which were to limit its own membership and secure by strikes and other appropriate means a monopoly of employment.

The immediate provocation to this action on their part is found in the fact that, yielding to the suasion of avarice, one J. P. Morgan,[24] a man unskilled in the use of his hands, threw up a very good position in a steel trust and went to work in a non-union coal mine.

"That," says a quaint chronicler of the period, rather obscurely, "was the limit and called for the kibosh." (The meaning of "kibosh" is not now understood. The word has a suggestive resemblance to "Bigosh," the name of a popular deity of the time, frequently invoked, particularly in agricultural affairs. "Kibosh" may have been the title of an officer of the constabulary.)[25]

As a practical working organization the National Federation of Scabs appears to have had but a brief existence and a rather stormy one. Of all labor leagues it was by far the most tyrannical and intolerant.

In 1907, during its famous strike against the employment of union men as nurse maids in the Podunk Asylum for Female Foundlings, it committed so many offences against life and property that the entire military force of the State of Buffalo was called out for its suppression, but was defeated with great slaughter.

It was then attacked by the Grand Army of the Republic and the Army of Government Pensioners, but, as neither of these forces had ever been accustomed to the use of arms, they shared the fate of their more experienced allies.

Finally the Federation was subdued by the Quakers, a powerful tribe in Pennsylvania, led by Matthew Quay;[26] its chiefs were banished to Nebraska and a general boycott declared against all its surviving members.

It went out of existence in the year 1915, during the Presidency of John Smith, known in his time as "the Dark Horse."[27]

After 1918 there were no more "labor troubles" in America. In that year, at a great Congress of all the industries, it was almost unanimously resolved that the wage system was a failure, Government ownership a delusion, co-operation impossible and combination disgusting.

The congress urged a return to the ancient and beneficent system of slavery. The advice was eagerly taken by all, and thenceforth until the submersion of the continent the term "industrial discontent" was heard no more in the speech of a happy, happy people.

The Future Historian and His Fatigue

"AT LAST, in the year 1903, as, for some reason now unknown, time was then reckoned," wrote the Future Historian, "the Cup was won by Sir Thomas the Lifter, with the Shamyacht III. He had made twelve previous attempts, but had been foiled every time by some trick of construction or sailing. It was during these contests that the term 'Yan Kee trick' came into use, and we still have it. Yan Kee was the name of the Chinese mariner who always sailed the American boat, our knowledge of which fact we owe to that distinguished philologist, Dr. Joch Ooblebubber, who with Um Licomemsel, the archaeologist, discovered the ruins of Minnesota

"Sir Thomas escaped the vengeance of the mob, but was drowned with all his crew on the voyage back to England, and the celebrated Cup was forever lost. His last words were 'Don't give up the ship!'—one of the most memorable sayings of antiquity.

"Ten years later another cup was presented by the Irish Parliament, and the contests were renewed, continuing with varying fortunes for a quarter of a century, when they were forbidden by both governments under pressure of the Allied Powers.

"In reviewing the history of this extraordinary craze one cannot fail to be struck by its incredible unreason, in which it was unmatched even in those barbarous times. Compared with it the famous conflict between Science and Religion seems almost an intelligent contention, a manly sport.

"As a means of gambling these yacht races were distinctly inferior to flipping a coin, to running the 'horse,' whatever that animal may have been, or to the game (what we know of it) called draw-the-poker.

"It developed no useful qualities in either the men who built the boats or those who sailed them, for the boats were so absurdly unlike anything else afloat that both construction and handling were particular arts, without utility in the shipyard or on the sea. In fact, the vessels never were used for any purpose but racing, and in only the one race for which they were made did anybody take the faintest interest. The sole superiority of one over another consisted in a deeper draught—a lengthening downward and weighing of the 'fin keel' so as to make it possible to carry more sail without upsetting. The knowing ones talked and wrote very learnedly of a thousand other features of construction, but that was all moonshine; the yacht that could safely carry the greatest spread of sail always beat the other. With this controlling advantage any 'model' was good enough. True, it took these primitive reasoners many years to learn so simple a truth. Philosophers (who did not take the trouble to point it out) knew it as early as 1903, but the persons most interested did not perceive it until fifteen years later, when a remodelled old mudscow, with a fin keel fifty feet deep, met the cup winner of that year off the Irish coast and beat her out of sight.

"After this revelation there could be but one end of it all—keels grew deeper and deeper and more and more heavily weighted, masts taller, booms longer and sails bigger. Accidents and wrecks from trying to achieve both lightness and strength were even more frequent than they had been at the beginning of the century, and in the final race (before the interdiction) both yachts grounded in the middle of the Atlantic and were beaten to pieces in a half hour, whereby both the King of New York and the Panjandrum of Great Britain and the Isle of Man, who were guests on board, had the bad luck to lose their lives.

"It is doubtful," concluded the Future Historian, smiling as the toes holding his pen flew rapidly across his sheet of prepared sky, "if the annals of folly contain anything so distressing to human pride as this yacht-racing episode in the history of the ancient inhabitants of Great Britain and her transatlantic dependency. In the words of our greatest and most original humorist, 'it makes me tired.'"

A Chronicle of the Time To Be

THE FUTURE HISTORIAN sat paring his nails before his telepathic type writer, which merrily clicked off his thoughts. "By the year 1907," it wrote, "the Japanese had so consolidated their power in Manchuria that Russia appears to have despaired of further success against them and to have relinquished all hopes of recovering the province. The Czar's death in the terrible battle of Harbin,[28] the destruction of the Baltic fleet in its desperate attempt to retake Port Arthur, the frightful famine caused by the Chinese General Ma's possession of the Siberian railroad—all these untoward events had so subdued the spirit of the people of the Russian Empire that further war was impossible. 'The Colossus of the North' lay bleeding and helpless on the field of his ambition, while his hereditary enemy, Great Britain, restrained only by fear of Germany and France, rectified her Indian frontier almost as it pleased her.

"Germany, indeed, was almost a negligible quantity in the problem, her mountebank Emperor having troubles of his own. With the Socialist rebellion of 1906 he had barely been able to cope, and his hard-earned victory had left him with no stomach for fighting in the interest of his allies. France, still suffering from her brief but bloody contest with the United States of America over complications arising from the sale of the Panama Canal concession,[29] was equally averse to war, and had perfidiously repudiated her treaty obligations and turned a deaf ear to the demands of her ally. So it was that Russia as an Asiatic power was virtually effaced, while in Europe she had declined to the third rank among military nations.

"Matters stood in this unhappy plight when, as related in a former chapter of this history, the usurper Kuropatkin[30] seized the reins of power, overturning the Romanoff dynasty and either putting to death or banishing all its considerable adherents. This able, ambitious and unscrupulous man seemed for a time content with the glory of his achievement and the subjection of his own country to his will. He made an inglorious peace with Japan, satisfied Great Britain with shameful concessions and even consented to the permanent occupation of Trans-Balkal Siberia by China. But behind all these apparently cowardly surrenders the fierce, indomitable will of the ancient Huns burned with an inextinguishable flame. In the apathy of a hopeless people were still some vestiges of the same persistent spirit that had survived even the defeat at Chalons fifteen centuries before.[31] For two decades the new Czar devoted himself to a patient reorganization of the civil and military administration, to the promotion of the empire's industries and commerce, to creation of a powerful navy. So effectually, yet so secretly withal, was this gigantic task accomplished that in the year 1928 Russia was again a menace to the peace of Europe without having alarmed even the most suspicious of the Great Powers. Now and again, it is true, some voice in the wilderness of politics or journalism cried an unheeded warning, but these prophets of evil lacked the facts to verify their dismal predictions, for the Russian press was under a strict censorship, and the Imperial Government pursued a policy of silence. Statistics were among the secret archives of the Government, accessible to none but its own officials.

"Meantime, China was undergoing something of the same regeneration which for nearly a century had made Japan the paradox and marvel of the world. The entire form and texture of her civilization had begun to change, and—incredible fatuity!—the change was assisted and acclaimed by all the Caucasian nations of the world, which vied with one another to maintaining the one condition under which it was possible—'the integrity of China.'³² The imperial army had increased to vast though unknown numbers, and was trained by European mercenaries of all nationalities, without a protest from Russia, whom it seemed most to menace. Great arsenals manufactured and stored against a future need immense quantities of destructive modern weapons, and under the fostering care of European intelligence the Chinese navy grew to formidable proportions and efficiency. The new Emperor, Chon Lu, an enlightened but cunning and ambitious ruler, pursued during this period a policy of apparent hostility to Russia, resulting in frequent but trivial and fruitless disputes, in which neither side obtained an important advantage.

"Such was the situation when, on the ever-memorable fourth of September, 1928, the world was startled by an identical rescript from Pekin and St. Petersburg announcing an offensive alliance between the Russian and Chinese empires! Of the stupendous consequences that ensued, entailing nothing less than the effacement of the ancient European civilization, it is impossible to write even at this distant day without the profoundest emotion."

The Republic of Panama

"IN THE MONTH of February of the year 1904, as for some reason not now understood the Americans reckoned time," wrote the Future Historian, "the Senate passed the last of a series of resolutions commanding the President to transmit to that august body forthwith all the information remaining in his possession relating to the rise of the new republic of Panama and his recognition of it as a treaty-making power. It was commonly believed that the secession of this Colombian province and its erection into an independent State had been brought about by an unlawful conspiracy in which he was deeply involved, if not the actual instigator. The resolution, drawn in the most peremptory terms, passed with only three dissenting votes—those of Senators Hoar, Morgan and Gorman³³—and was at once sent by a special messenger to the White Palace, the Senate refusing to adjourn until a reply should be received. After a wait of two hours, during which the excited populace poured into the galleries, thronged the corridors of the entire Capitol and swarmed in immeasurable multitudes about the statue of Adam, near the east front, the messenger returned and delivered the President's reply. The seals were broken in profound silence and the message read. To the amazement of both Senate and people it was found to consist of only three words— 'I will not!' Of the momentous events that ensu. . . . . . ." Here the Future Historian, overcome by the magnitude of his subject, broke off and took to his bed. Alas, that so brilliant a narrative must remain forever incomplete— that so stupendous events must belong eternally to the realm of conjecture!

The Second American Invasion of China

FOLLOWING IS AN EXTRACT from "The Second American Invasion of China," by the Future Historian:

"To what extent the disasters to the American arms in the bloody campaign of 1907 were justly attributable to the general staff of the army may never accurately be known. The severest critic of the general staff was Senator Hale of Maine, who at all times and with considerable eloquence bitterly averred a criminal lack of foresight and preparation. Hostilities, he declared, had been obviously inevitable for many months before the dispatch of the army of invasion of its punitive mission, yet no proper study of the theatre of war had been made and no systematic and coherent plan of operation devised. So violent were this great statesman's denunciations of the general staff for apathy and procrastination, that he was put in irons and removed from the Senate chamber to an asylum for the insane, where he rose to great eminence."

Rise and Fall of the Aëroplane

THE CRAZE FOR FLYING appears to have culminated in the year 369 Before Smith. In that year the aëroplane (a word of unknown derivation) was almost the sole means of travel. These flying-machines were so simple and cheap that one who had not a spare half-hour in which to make one could afford to purchase. The price for a one-man machine was about two dollars—one-tenth of a gooble. Double-seated ones were of course a little more costly. No other kinds were allowed by law, for, as was quaintly explained by a chronicle of the period, "a man has a right to break his own neck, and that of his wife, but not those of his children and friends." It had been learned by experiment that for transportation of goods and for use in war the aëroplane was without utility. (Of balloons, dirigible and indirigible, we hear nothing after 348 B.S.; the price of gas, controlled by a single corporation, made them impossible.)

From extant fragments of Jobblecopper's *History of Invention* it appears that in America alone there were at one time no fewer then ten million aëroplanes in use. In and about the great cities the air was so crowded with them and collisions resulting in falls were so frequent that prudent persons neither ventured to use them nor dared to go out of cover. As a poet of the time expressed it:

> With falling fools so thick the sky is filled
> That wise men walk abroad but to be killed.
> Small comfort that the fool, too, dies in falling,
> For he'd have starved betimes in any calling.
> The earth is spattered red with their remains:
> Blood, flesh, bone, gristle—everything but brains.[34]

The reaction from this disagreeable state of affairs seems to have been brought about by a combination of causes.

First, the fierce animosities engendered by the perils to pedestrians and "motorists"—a word of disputed meaning. So savage did this hostility become that firing at aëroplanes in flight, with the newly invented silent rifle, grew to the character of a national custom. Dimshouck has found authority for the statement that in a single day thirty-one aëronauts fell from the heavens into the streets of Nebraska, the capital of Chocago, victims of popular disfavor; and a writer of that time relates, not altogether lucidly, the finding in a park in Ohio of the bodies of "the Wright brothers, each pierced with bullets from hip to shoulder, the ears cut off, and without other marks of identification."

Second in importance of these adverse conditions was the natural disposition of the ancients to tire of whatever had engaged their enthusiasm—the fickleness that had led to abandonment of the bicycle, of republican government, of baseball, and of respect for women. In the instance of the aëroplane this reaction was probably somewhat hastened by the rifle practice mentioned.

Third, invention of the electric leg. As a means of going from place to place the ancients had from the earliest ages of history relied largely on the wheel. Just how they applied it, not in stationary machinery, as we do ourselves, but as an aid to locomotion, we cannot now hope to know, for all the literature of the subject has perished; but it was evidently a crude and clumsy device, giving a speed of less than two hundred miles (four and a half sikliks)[35] an hour, even on roadways specially provided with rails for its rapid revolution. We know, too, that wheels produced an intolerable jolting of the body, whereby many died of a disease known as "therapeutics." Indeed, a certain class of persons who probably traveled faster than others came to be called "rough riders,"[36] and for their sufferings were compensated by appointment to the most lucrative offices in the gift of the sovereign. Small wonder that the men of that day hailed the aëroplane with intemperate enthusiasm and used it with insupportable immoderation!

But when the younger Eddy invented that supreme space-conquering device, the electric leg, and within six months perfected it to virtually what it is to-day, the necessity for flight no longer existed. The aëroplane, ending its brief and bloody reign a discredited and discarded toy, was "sent to the scrap-heap," as one of our brightest and most original modern wits has expressed it.[37] The wheel followed it into oblivion, whither the horse had preceded it, and Civilization lifted her virgin fires as a dawn in Eden, and like Cytherea leading her moonrise troop of nymphs and graces, literally legged it o'er the land!

The Dispersal

SO SOMBRE A PHENOMENON as the effacement of an ancient and brilliant civilization within the lifetime of a single generation is, fortunately, known to have occurred only once in the history of the world. The catastrophe is not only unique in history, but all the more notable for having befallen, not a single state overrun by powerful barbarians, but half of the world; and for having been effected by a seemingly trivial agency that sprang from the civilization itself. Indeed, it was the work of one man.

Hiram Perry (or Percy) Maximus was born in the latter part of the nineteenth century of "the Christian Era," in Podunk, the capital of America. Little is known of his ancestry, although Dumbleshaw affirms on evidence not cited by him that he came of a family of pirates that infested the waters of Lake Erie (now the desert of Gobol) as early as "1813"—whenever that may have been.

The precise nature of Hiram Perry's invention, with its successive improvements, is not known—probably could not now be understood. It was called "the silent firearm"—so much we learn from fragmentary chronicles of the period; also that it was of so small size that it could be put into the "pocket." (In his *Dictionary of Antiquities* the learned Pantin-Gwocx defines "pocket" as, first, "the main temple of the American deity"; second, a "a small receptacle worn on the person." The latter definition is the one, doubtless, that concerns us if the two things are not the same.) Regarding the work of "the silent firearm" we have light in abundance. Indeed, the entire history of the brief but bloody period between its invention and the extinction of the Christian civilization is an unbroken record of its fateful employment.

Of course the immense armies of the time were at once supplied with the new weapon, with results that none had foreseen. Soldiers were thenceforth as formidable to their officers as to their enemies. It was no longer possible to maintain discipline, for no officer dared offend, by punishment or reprimand, one who could fatally retaliate as secretly and securely, in the repose of camp as in the tumult of battle. In civic affairs the deadly device was malignly active. Statesmen in disfavor (and all were hateful to men of contrary politics) fell dead in the forum by means invisible and inaudible. Anarchy, discarding her noisy and imperfectly effective methods, gladly embraced the new and safe one.

In other walks of life matters were no better. Armed with the sinister power of life and death, any evil-minded person (and most of the ancient Caucasians appear to have been evil-minded) could gratify a private revenge or wanton malevolence by slaying whom he would, and nothing cried aloud the lamentable deed.

So horrible was the mortality, so futile all preventive legislation, that society was stricken with a universal panic. Cities were plundered and abandoned; villages without villagers fell to decay; homes were given up to bats and owls, and farms became jungles infested with wild beasts. The people fled to the mountains, the forests, the marshes, concealing themselves from one another in caves and thickets, and dying from privation and exposure and diseases more dreadful than the perils from which they had fled. When every human being distrusted and feared every other human being solitude was esteemed the only good; and solitude spells death. In one generation Americans and Europeans had slunk back into the night of barbarism.

An Ancient Hunter

IN THE NINETEENTH CENTURY of what, in honor of Christopher Columbum, a mythical hero, the ancients called the "Christian era," Africa was an unknown land of deserts, jungles, fierce wild beasts, and degraded savages. It is believed that no white man had ever penetrated it to a distance of one league from the coast. All the literature of that time relating to African exploration, conquest, and settlement is now known to be purely imaginative—what the ancients admired as "fiction" and we punish as felony.

Authentic African history begins in the early years of the twentieth century of the "era" mentioned, and its most stupendous events are the first recorded, the record being made, chiefly, by the hand that wrought the work—that of Tudor Rosenfelt, the most illustrious figure of antiquity. Of this astonishing man's parentage and early life nothing is certainly known: legend is loquacious, but history is silent. There are traditions affirming his connection with a disastrous explosion at Bronco, a city of the Chinese province of Wyo Ming,[38] his subjugation of the usurper Tammano[39] in the American city of N'yorx (now known to have had no existence outside the imagination of the poets) and his conquest of the island of Cubebs;[40] but from all this bushel of fable we get no grain of authenticated fact. The tales appear to be merely hero-myths, such as belong to the legendary age of every people of the ancient world except the Greeks and Romans. Further than that he was a American Indian nothing can be positively affirmed of Tudor Rosenfelt before the year "1909" of the "Christian [Columbian] era." In that year we glimpse him disembarking from two ships on the African coast near Bumbassa,[41] and, with one foot in the sea and the other on dry land, swearing through clenched teeth that other forms of life than Man shall be no more. He then strides, unarmed and unattended, into the jungle, and is lost to view for ten years!

Legend and myth now reassert their ancient reign. In that memorable decade, as we know from the ancient author of "Who's Whoest in Africa," the most incredible tales were told and believed by those who, knowing the man and his mission, suffered insupportable alternations of hope and despair. It was said that the Dark Continent into which he had vanished was frequently shaken from coast to coast as by the trampling and wrestling of titanic energies in combat and the fall of colossal bulks on the yielding crust of the earth; that mariners in adjacent waters heard recurrent growls and roars of rage and shouts of triumph—an enormous uproar that smote their ships like a gale from the land and swept them affrighted out to sea; that so loud were these terrible sounds as to be simultaneously audible in the Indian and Atlantic oceans, as was proved by comparing the logs of vessels arriving from both seas at the port of Berlin. As is quaintly related in one of these marine diaries, "The noise was so strenuous that our ears was nigh to busting with the wolume of the sound." Through all this monstrous opulence of the primitive rhetorical figure known as the Lie we easily discern a nucleus of truth: something uncommon was going on in Africa.

At the close of the memorable decade (*circa* "1919") authentic history again appears in the fragmentary work of Antrolius:[42] Rosenfelt walks out of the jungle at Mbongwa on the side of the continent opposite Bumbassa. He is now attended by a caravan of twenty thousand camels and ten thousand native porters, all bearing trophies of the chase. A complete list of these would require more pages than Homer Wheeler Wilcox's catalogue of ships,[43] but among them were heads of elephants with antlers attached; pelts of the checkered lion and the spiny hippopotentot, respectively the most ferocious and the most venomous of their species; a skeleton of the missing lynx (*Pithecanthropos erectus compilatus*);[44] entire bodies of pterodactyls and broncosauruses; a slithy tove[45] mounted on a fine specimen of the weeping wanderoo; the downy electrical whacknasty (*Ananias flabbergastor*);[46] the carnivorous mastodon; ten specimens of the skinless tiger (*Felis decorticata*);[47] a saber-toothed python, whose bite produced the weeping sickness; three ribnosed gazzadoodles; a pair of blood-sweating bandicoots; a night-blooming jeewhillikins;[48] three and a half varieties of the crested skynoceros; a purring crocodile, or buzz-saurian; two Stymphalian[49] linnets; a skeleton of the three footed swammigolsis—afterwards catalogued at the Podunk Museum of Defective Types as *Talpa unopede noninvento;*[50] a hydra from Lerna;[51] the ring-tale mollycoddle and the fawning polecat (*Civis nondesiderabilis*).[52]

These terrible monsters, which from the dawning of time had ravaged all Africa, baffling every attempt at exploration and settlement, the Exterminator, as he came to be called, had strangled or captured with his bare hands; and the few remaining were so cowed that they gave milk. Indeed, such was their terror of his red right arm that all forsook their evil ways, offered themselves as beasts of burden to the whites that came afterward, and in domestication and servitude sought the security that he denied to their ferocity and power. Within a single generation prosperous colonies of Caucasians sprang up all along the coasts, and the silk hat and pink shirt, immemorial pioneers and promoters of civilization, penetrated the remotest fastnesses, spreading peace and plenty o'er a smiling land!

The later history of this remarkable man is clouded in obscurity. Much of his own account of his exploits, curiously intertangled with those of an earlier hero named Hercules, is extant, but it closes with his re-embarkation for America. Some hold that on returning to his native land he was assailed with opprobrium, loaded with chains, and cast into Chicago; others contend that he was enriched by gifts from the sovereigns of the world, received with acclamation by his grateful countrymen, and even mentioned for the presidency to succeed Samuel Gompers[53]—an honor that he modestly declined on the ground of inexperience and unfitness. Whatever may be the truth of these matters, he doubtless did not long suffer affliction nor enjoy prosperity, for in the great catastrophe of the year 254 B.S. the entire continent of North America and the contiguous island of Omaha were swallowed up by the sea. Fortunately his narrative is preserved in the Royal Library of Timbuktu, in which capital of civilization stands his colossal statue of ivory and gold. In the shadow of that renowned memorial I write this imperfect tribute to his worth.

A Leaf Blown In from Days To Be

THE FUTURE HISTORIAN set his psychograph on the table before him, clasped the band of the transmitting wire about his head, lay back in his easy-chair and closed his eyes. The record, of which ten thousand copies were automatically delivered, follows.

"In the year 1909, as the ancient Americans reckoned time, President Thaddeus Rosenfelt was for some offense not now known banished from his country and sent under heavy guard to Kalamazoo, an African penal colony noted for the number and ferocity of its tigers. To these he was thrown by his keepers, as was secretly commanded by Congress, sitting as a high court of impeachment and conviction. But from a contemporaneous chronicle by Wee Chandler (whose works are now in the imperial library of Timbuctoo) it appears that the tigers would not eat him. On the contrary, he ate them, 'a marked instance,' says another writer of the period, 'of interposition by an overruling Providence.'[54]

"Awed by this obvious miracle, the fallen President's keepers renounced the faith of their fathers and worshiped him as a deity. Not only so, but by force and arms they set up for him a temporal sovereignty which he administered from an ancient palace known as the Bleak House. He bore the title of It, a word signifying Me. The meaning of Me is unknown.

"In subduing the natives, who, according to Herodotus the Tetrarch, were known as Gringos, Rosenfelt came into conflict with many powerful kings, chief of whom was Rhi Nosey Rose,[55] who could summon fifty thousand warriors by a blast upon his horn. Allied with this potentate was the scarcely less powerful High Potamus,[56] of Riparia.[57] (Riparia was a Theocracy; the word potamus appears to have meant priest, and probably alluded to the 'pot' in which hierarchs of another faith were purged of their error by boiling.)

"Contemporary accounts of military operations incident to the conquest have not come down to us. It is known, however, that Rosenfelt, armed with a big sticker, penetrated to the interior of Kankakee and fought the fierce battle of Waterloo, in which the Gringo power was disastrously overthrown by the leader's lone charge up the hill of San Juan Smith. With that memorable feat African independence cease to exist: the entire continent came under the sway of Bueno Gumbo, 'the man who ate tigers.'

"Among the spoils of war was an almost incalculable number of domestic animals: the gorilla (*Lignifer docilis*),[58] the elephantom, the long-necked graft (*Latro circumspector*),[59] the hobby horse, the teddibear,[60] the skunk (*Curio flabbergastor*),[61] the three-legged ophecleide, the gargoyle, the lion (*Leo arator*),[62] used by the natives in plowing corn, the aeroplane, and many other species now long extinct. So great was the multitude of these animals that the task of slaughtering them in order to sell their bones to Smith's Onion Institution for fertilizing was one of extreme difficulty.[63] It was proposed by Nairoba (or Niobe),[64] a friendly chief, that they be shot, but no one would undertake the work but Rosenfelt himself, and he was unacquainted with the use of firearms, having always in his native land hunted with his bare hands, making his kills by a cruel process known as the Presidential massage. The animals were finally chloroformed and shipped to the port of Hohokus, where they were admitted duty free as works of fiction.

"Weeping freely because there were no more worlds to conquer (it was not then known that Arkansas had not been brought under the sway of the Whites) the victor resolved to invade his own country and carry away the Presidential Chair which he had once occupied, and which was then considered the most precious object existing since the Golden Fleece and the Holy Grail.

"Placing his son Kismet[65] on the throne, he gathered a great army of Blacks, and traveling incognito under the name of 'Stanley,' reached the western boundary of his new realm amid the acclamation of his troops, who shouted, 'Thalassa, thalassa!' that being their name for the river Rubicon, separating Africa from America.[66] There at the island of Elba he crossed on a secret bridge and was received with effusion by the populace, by whose spokesmen, Lord Gifford of Pinchot, he was thrice offered a kingly crown, which, according to Shakesporr, an obscure chronicler of the time, he did thrice refuse.[67] This occurred in the reign of William the Fat, whom as an afterthought he deposed and bastinadoed.[68]

"Firmly seated in the Presidential Chair (which had itself been firmly reseated for William) Rosenfelt resolved to remain in the land that loved him for the ructions he had made. By way of assuring the peace, he proceeded to destroy a colony of Ananiasites[69] who had fortified themselves in the fastnesses of the Rocky Mountains, and then he marched against the Nacherfaquers,[70] a formidable tribe of the Bostonese hinterland. Afterwards he subdued and sold into slavery a troublesome people known as Democrats, who were taken to Lincoln, Nebraska, loaded with chains. The name of the purchaser is unknown.

"From this time on, the career of this remarkable personality is lost in the mists of antiquity. Some say that the earth opened and swallowed him; others that he wrote a book; and in an extant fragment of an ancient poem he is represented as chained to a rock in a caucus, with 'vultures' (epicures) eating his liver.[71] Whatever may have been the manner of his second removal from office, he is now, doubtless, as dead as the vivacity of his disposition permits."

ESSAYS

GOVERNMENT VS. ANARCHY

Prevention vs. No Cure

A RUSSIAN PHYSICIAN, an avowed Nihilist, now in Chicago, is reported to have said: "It is only in this free country and under the stars and stripes that we are at liberty to conspire with a view to the ultimate liberation of our country"—he meant Russia. It must be confessed that a free country is the conspirator's opportunity. It is here that he finds his highest and ripest development. And it matters nothing whether he is a conspirator against some foreign country from which he may have been kicked across the sea, or against the country in which he conspires; his opportunity is pretty much the same. That conspiracies against the lives, liberties and property of our own citizens may be hatched with impunity and matured without check is sufficiently attested by recent events in the very city which this frank rascal has chosen as an advantageous place to plot his mischief and utter its intent. Free speech and a free press are indubitably excellent things; rather, we should say freedom of speech and freedom of the press, for the speeches and the newspapers themselves, which this freedom has fostered, are not invariably admirable. But liberty is not an end; it is a means; and, as Mr. Fitz-James Stephen neatly put it, is desirable or not according to the use that is made of it.[1] That use which consists in the utterance of seditious and criminal sentiments and the perfecting of conspiracies to kill is a perversion of a free country's advantages which ought to work a forfeiture of them, and must, in simple common sense, be reckoned among the demerits of the system.

It is in the nature of republican institutions to be peculiarly open to the perils of conspiracy and sedition; that is their weak side. A country

> Where, girt about by friends nor foes,
> A man may speak the thing he will,[2]

is obviously well adapted to dissemination of "views," good and bad. Obviously, too, it is the paradise of cranks and crooks—a promised land toward which every enemy of his race will turn his toes as his welcome cools in lands less free. We are beginning dimly to discern the fact that there are more of these irreclaimables than we had thought, and that by letting them speak the thing they will, we aid and abet them in doing the thing they ought not. Chicago has a half-dozen of them in the County Jail under sentence of death and is afraid to hang them. There is hardly a policeman in the State of Illinois who would not breathe more freely if all would dig out and escape. If they had not been weakly permitted to perfect their conspiracy under the very noses of those at whose lives it was aimed, the statesmen of that afflicted commonwealth would not now be suffering this present embarrassment. Moreover, several very worthy policemen lately deceased would still be in the line of duty and promotion.

The Failure of "Rotation"

THE REPORT THAT Mr. Warner Miller has declined to go into the Cabinet as Secretary of War, on the ground that he would not have patronage enough to "go round" among his expectants, is suggestive.[3] It serves to remind us of a similar deficiency with reference to the larger matter of office-holding in general. There are not enough offices to "go round." Many worthy citizens are doomed to lives of hopeless political disappointment. The entire body of officers—Federal, State, County, Township and Municipal—probably does not comprise a million souls. This in a population of more than sixty millions is a pitiful showing. By adopting the principle of "rotation in office" and reducing the tenure to its lowest term we have done as much as we safely can to give every adult male patriot a chance at political preferment, but the country's population grows at a rate unforeseen by the founders of the Republic and with which by multiplication of places we are unable to cope. By the ingenious device of "Commissions" charged with duties properly devolving upon elective officers we have done something in this State to mitigate the hardship of the situation, but the plan has pretty strait limitations which inhere in the nature of it, and affords inadequate relief. With all our efforts we are unable to assure to every male citizen even the briefest season of honor and authority and a lifelong title having a basis of fact. Thousands are born to blush unseen in the "halls of legislation" and the "seats of power," and many indeed are the immigrants landing upon our shores from a "far countree,"[4] with high hopes of rank and station, who must go down to the grave with an unsated ambition and all their music in them, as it were. There are not enough offices to "go round," and in despite of accomplishing civic distinction multitudes embrace the profession of Colonel and drag out a miserable existence in hateful obscurity, detested by all who know them.

They are the old maids of political life; vessels of wrath; living monuments attesting the imperfection of our system, the fallibility of its founders and the vanity of human life.

Such being the hard and unalterable facts of the situation, it is pertinent and wise to inquire what should be done about it. Since the great majority of the American people are predestined to arrested political development and must pine on the stem of private station, it is prudent to encourage them longer in pursuit of the unattainable by practically declaring public office a private right? Would it not be wiser to confess that the scheme of "rotation" has failed in the most lamentable way to accomplish the only conceivable purpose that it could ever have had, and throw it over? Would it not be well to admit that knowledge, experience and tested fidelity have the same value in the business of government as in any other business, and since there are not offices enough to "go round" endeavor to secure an intelligent and decent administration of such offices as there are? In order to secure this practicable if lesser advantage, no constitutional changes are necessary; the political system needs undergo no heroic treatment. If frequent elections are deemed desirable and wholesome the tenure of civic office may retain the beautiful brevity that now distinguishes it from that which we find advantageous in military, commercial and industrial affairs. It is only necessary to cultivate a reasonable sentiment favorable to re-election of good servants, not only as a reward for faithful services in the past but as an assurance of intelligent service in the future. Instead of retiring an official before he has fairly learned the duties of his position, thus surely denying ourselves the advantage of skill, experience and zeal in the conduct of public affairs and making provision for successive relays of ignorance and intrigue with all their hideous host of evils, why not apply to these graver and more delicate matters the same common sense that we use in our private business? Let us no longer recognize any other "claim" to public office than honest and intelligent service already performed in positions of trust and profit. It is time that "rotation," having had its turn and, like its creatures, made a mess of it, were itself deposed and succeeded by another system. When this is done activity in politics will cease to be deemed a proper subject for contrition at the confessional.

Republican Government

SINCE PUBLICATION OF my remarks, two weeks ago, on Anarchists and Anarchism friendly readers have done me the honor to solicit my views on so many phases of "modern discontent" that full compliance is impossible. But some of my correspondents will, I trust, find their doubts of my position resolved in the course of what I shall venture to advance concerning matters not in all instances identical with those about which they inquire. Naturally, dissenters from the comfortable creed that "whatever is is right";[5] persons content with "the established order of things" are not commonly hot to provoke a discussion of it. The landowner, for example, does not feel himself "called upon" to write letters to the newspapers, affirming the right divine to monopolize as much as he can of that upon which all must live who do not live at sea. The person who is sudden and quick in controversy on that point is the malcontent whose birth was a trespass, and who finds immunity from daily prosecution in the safe seclusion of the public highway, or pickles his personal bacon in the spindrift of the indivisible sea—one of Nature's commodores.

As to that—the right of private ownership in land—the sons of dissent are a trifle needy of argument: Herbert Spencer has left them nothing to say.[6] True, Henry George has "supplied an omission" by demanding the robbery of those in present possession, who, if not blameless, are no more guilty than the rest of us, by whose assent, formulated in laws as old as civilization, they hold.[7] Mr. George has an eye for omissions, both malign and benign, both actual and potential. In the commandment "Thou shalt not steal," he would make one by elision of the negative. He has a fine sense of humor, too, and can relieve a tedious discussion of its gravity as nimbly as a slender hand unloads an alien pocket. It is difficult to conceive of Mr. George dissociated from a congenial environment of pockets, and without a circumspective confederate.

I am sorry to observe that most of my correspondents who dissent (with more heat than light) from "the established order of things" manifest an imperfect acquaintance with the causes and methods of its establishment, and a surprising ignorance as to who is "responsible." Most of them, indeed, appear to think that it was set up yesterday by its present beneficiaries, or those whom they think such. They forget, if they ever took the trouble to know, that the conditions of modern life, industrial, social, political and what not, have been the slow and imperceptible growth of more centuries than one can count; that not a man living to-day has done as much in their genesis and development as has been accomplished by a single coral-insect in building the most stupendous reef in the Pacific. Not from this infinitesimal blame is any person exempt. The Socialist, the Communist, the Anarchist—the protagonist of every kind of dissent, the proponent of every variety of reform—each in his daily life and occupation recognizes "the established order" and, however loudly he may deprecate it with his voice, confirms its validity and invokes its advantages. The most active advocate of co-opera-tion, the bitterest denouncer of "competition" sells his labor, or its product, for what it will bring; or if he fixes an arbitrary lower price upon it thereby competes even more effectually with others of his craft, and reduces their profit. With regard to these things there is no absolute right nor absolute wrong: what is right in one age, or among the people of one race, would be wrong in another century or country. That system is wrong which is worse or better than the people among whom it obtains. He who should set up universal suffrage in Manchuria or Mashonaland[8] would be one of God's most precious fools.

Even that ancient and various device, "a republican form of govern-ment," appears to be too good for all the peoples of the earth excepting one. It is successful in Switzerland only; in France and America, where the major-ity is composed of persons having dark understandings and criminal instincts, it has broken down. In our case, as in every case, the momentum of success-ful revolution carried us too far. We rebelled against tyranny and having overthrown it, overthrew also the governmental form in which it had hap-pened to be manifest. In their anger and their triumph our good old gran'fathers acted somewhat in the spirit of the Irishman who cudgeled the dead snake until nothing was left of it, in order to make it "sinsible of its desthruction." They meant it all, too, the honest souls! For a long time after the setting up of the republic the republic meant active hatred to kings, nobles, aristocracies. It was held, and rightly held, that a noble could not breathe in America—that he left his title and his privileges on the ship that brought him over. Do we observe anything of that spirit in this generation? On the landing of a foreign king, prince or nobleman—even a miserable "knight"—do we not all execute sycophantic genuflexions?[9] Are not our newspapers full of flamboyant description and qualming adulation? Nay, does not our President himself—successor to Washington and Jefferson!—greet and entertain the "nation's guest"? Is not every American young woman crazy to mate with a male of title? Does all this represent no retrogression?—is it not the backward movement of the shadow on the dial?[10] Doubtless the republican idea has struck strong roots into the soil of the two Americas, but he who rightly considers the tendencies of things, the causes that bring them about and the consequences that flow from them, will not be hot to affirm the perpetuity of republican institutions in the Western Hemisphere. Be-tween their inception and their present stage of development there is scarcely the beat of a pendulum; and already, by almost universal corruption and lawlessness, the people of both continents, with all their diversities of race and character, have shown themselves about equally unfit. To become a nation of scoundrels all that any people needs is opportunity, and what we are pleased to call by the impossible name of "self-government" supplies it.

The capital defect of republican government is inability to repress internal forces tending to disintegration. Better, as it is, than the Anarchy which is its logical meaning and inevitable outcome, it is better only in degree; essentially, it is the same thing, for it is "self-government," and that is a contradictory term. Government means restraint by another—control by a power other than the person controlled. It does not take long for a "self-governed people" to learn that it is not really governed—that an agreement enforcible by nobody but creatures of the parties to it is not binding. We are learning this very rapidly: we set aside our laws whenever we please. The sovereign power—the tribunal of ultimate jurisdiction—is a mob. If the mob is large enough (it need not be very large), even if composed of vicious tramps, it may do as it will. It may destroy property and life. It may without proof of guilt inflict upon individuals torments unthinkable by fire and flaying mutilations that are nameless. It may call men, women and children from their beds and beat them to death with cudgels. In the light of day it may assail the very strongholds of law in the heart of a populous city, and assassinate prisoners of whose guilt it knows nothing. And these things—observe, O victims of kings—are habitually done. One would almost as lief be at the mercy of one's sovereign as of one's neighbor.

For generations we have been charming ourselves with the magic of words. When menaced by some exceptionally monstrous form of the tyranny of numbers we have closed our eyes and murmured, "Liberty." When armed Anarchists threaten to quench the fires of civilization in a sea of blood we prate of the protective power of "free speech."

If,

> girt about by friends or foes,
> A man may speak the thing he will,[11]

we fondly fancy that the thing he will speak is harmless—that immunity disarms his tongue of its poison, his thought of its infection. With a fatuity that would be incredible without the testimony of observation we hold that an Anarchist free to go about making proselytes, free to purchase arms, free to drill and parade and encourage his dupes with a demonstration of their numbers and power, is less mischievous than an Anarchist with a shut mouth, a weaponless hand and under surveillance of the police. The Anarchist is himself persuaded of the superiority of our plan of dealing with him; he likes it and comes over in quantity, impesting the political atmosphere with the "sweltered venom"[12] engendered by centuries of oppression—comes over here, where he is not oppressed, and sets up as oppressor. His preferred field of malefaction is the country that is most nearly Anarchical. He comes here, partly to better himself under our milder institutions, partly to secure immunity while conspiring to destroy them. There is thunder in Europe, but if the storm ever break it is in America that the lightning will fall.

While it is true that any Government is better than none, it is probably not true that any people has ever had the Government that it was perfectly fitted for. Certainly all modern Governments of which we have knowledge seem capable of improvement inside the limiting lines of expediency; that is to say, all could be better without being too good to be practical. Private ownership of land, which, carried to its logical conclusion (as in many European countries it very nearly has been), would enslave the landless, is not more obviously a monstrous survival of barbarism than is the devil-take-the-hindmost doctrine that it is not the business of the State to supply employment for those in need of it. Ridiculous!—to recognize our obligation to support the helpless indigent, and deny the duty of doing what can be done to prevent helpless indigence. What nearly all the cities of the Union are now doing hastily, wastefully and imperfectly by private effort under semi-official supervision, the State should do always. So unfortunate and dangerous a creature as a man willing to work, yet having no work to do, should be unknown outside of the literature of satire. Doubtless there would be enormous difficulties in devising a practicable and beneficent system, and doubtless the reform, like all permanent and salutary reforms, will have to grow. That it is already in course of evolution the private and semi-official movements referred to may be taken as evidence. The growth naturally will be delayed by the insensate opposition of the working men themselves—precisely as they oppose prison labor from the ignorance that labor makes labor. Precisely, too, as to the natural difficulties of relief generally—difficulties inhering in the fact that charity makes beggars—they add difficulties of pride. They demand, and are right in demanding, that the community care for the aged and ailing poor. The community complies and provides a home for them. And then not only do the aged and ailing poor consider it a disgrace to be supported there, but the class that was loudest in the demand is bitterest in resenting their internment. The term "Poor-House" is become so opprobrious that it is commonly supplanted by the word "Infirmary," or "Hospital." Yet most of the Poor-Houses in the country are conducted by good men and women, and the standard of comfort is as high as it can prudently be made. To the great multitude of intelligent, organized and unremitting efforts to soften the rigors of "the competitive system," the fiercest and most obdurate opposition—almost the only opposition—comes, and has always come, from those whom it is sought to help.

All working men are not stupid, all capitalists are not greedy, but in the stupidity of working men and the greed of capitalists the small minority of wise and good men and women to whose still and unselfish work are due three-fourths of all true and lasting reform find there their most dispiriting difficulties. That despite it all there is a constant and conspicuous advance, not toward the Utopia and Altrurias[13] with which writers divert themselves and delude those who know no better than to take them seriously, but toward an incomparably better life and juster distribution of life's burdens and rewards—that is indubitably true. If our civilization would last long enough some parts of the race would eventually attain to some degree of general comfort. Unhappily, there is no way to put a civilization in pickle to keep it sweet, and already signs are not wanting that ours has about run its course and that our not very remote descendants will sit upon their haunches, clad in skins of animals and gnawing raw bones.

JUDGES, LAWYERS, AND JURIES

"I Decline to Answer"

THE ANCIENT AND EFFICIENT safeguard to rascality, the right of a witness to refuse to testify when his testimony would tend to convict him of a crime, has been strengthened by a decision of the United States Supreme Court. That will probably add another century or two to its mischievous existence, and possibly prove the first act in such an extension of it that eventually a witness cannot be compelled to testify at all. In fact, it is difficult to see how he can be compelled to now if he has the hardihood to exercise his constitutional right without shame and with an intelligent consciousness of its limitless application.

The case in which the Supreme Court has made the decision was one in which a witness refused to say whether he had received from a defendant railway company a rate on grain shipments lower than the rates open to all shippers. The trial was in the United States District Court for the Northern District of Illinois, and Judge Gresham¹—who never better proved his fitness for a Presidential nomination   chucked the scoundrel into jail. He naturally applied to the Supreme Court for relief, and that high tribunal has given joy to every known or secret malefactor in the country by deciding—according to law, no doubt—that witnesses in a criminal case cannot be compelled to testify to anything that "*might tend* to criminate them *in any way,* or subject them to *possible* prosecution." We use the words of the dispatch, but the italics are our own, and seem to us to indicate, about as clearly as extended comment could, the absolutely boundless nature of the immunity that the decision confirms or confers. It is to be hoped that some public-spirited gentlemen called to the stand in some celebrated case may point the country's attention to this state of the law by refusing to tell his name, age or occupation, or answer any question whatever. And it would be a fitting *finale* to the farce if he would threaten the too curious attorney with an action for damages for compelling a disclosure of character.

If there is any reason in common sense why a witness, even a defendant, should not be compelled to criminate himself if the truth will do it, we should be pleased to hear from its proponents. The only reason that occurs to us at the moment is the probability that if a witness were not permitted to take refuge in silence he would take it in perjury, and that might "obstruct the wheels of justice." But that reason might, perhaps, be urged with a better grace, if with inferior entertainment, by a rare and radiant humorist on our side.

The Morality of Lawyers

ATTORNEY CARROLL COOK and his friends may tranquilize their perturbed spirits; the Rev. Mr. Goodwin's criticism of legal ethics does not go to the length of requiring them to violate their oaths and disobey the statutes. True the oath which it appears an attorney is expected to take to obey a law that requires him to assist known criminals in circumventing other laws, to prosecute unjust claims, and to act the scoundrel generally is an oath that no man has the moral right to bind his conscience with; but if he is bad enough to take it he ought to be bad enough to keep it. True, the law requiring him to do those things is a rascally law, but one who is capable of swearing obedience to it should be capable of thinking it decent and useful. Attorneys, like other persons, ought to observe their obligations and obey the laws; what I have to point out is that nothing compels one to be an attorney.

In all the polemical tempest blown up by the Rev. Mr. Goodwin's remarks on the badness of lying (even when done by a lawyer for hire) the point really at issue has apparently been discerned by neither side. The moral sense of the laymen is dimly conscious of something wrong in the ethics of the noble profession; the lawyers, affirming, rightly enough, a public necessity for them and their mercenary services, permit their thrift to construe it vaguely as personal justification. But nobody—not even Gen. Barnes[2] with his learned historical review of the question, which he seems to think settles it—has blown away from the matter its brumous encompassment of words and let in the light upon it. It is very simple.

Is it honorable for a lawyer to try to clear a man that he knows deserves conviction? That is not the entire question by much. Is it honorable to pretend to believe what you do not believe? Is it honorable to lie? I submit that these questions are not answered affirmatively by showing the disadvantage to the public and to civilization of a lawyer refusing to serve a known offender. The popular interest, like any other good cause, can be served by foul means. Justice itself may be promoted by acts essentially unjust. In serving a sordid ambition a powerful scoundrel may by acts in themselves wicked augment the prosperity of a whole nation. I have not the right to deceive and lie in order to advantage my fellow men, any more than I have the right to steal or murder to advantage them; nor have my fellow men the power to grant me that indulgence. It would distinctly benefit the State of California to inveigle Dan Burns and Chris. Buckley[3] into a candle factory and boil them in paraffine—have I the right to do so? Can the Legislature confer the right upon me? I do not say that I should not like to do so; that is another matter.

The question of a lawyer's right to clear a known criminal (with the several questions involved) is not answered affirmatively by showing that the law forbids him to decline a case for reasons personal to himself—not even if we admit the statute's moral authority. Preservation of conscience and character is a civic duty, as well as a personal; one's fellow men have a distinct interest in it. That, I admit, is an argument rather in the manner of an attorney; clearly enough the intent of this statute is to compel an attorney to cheat and lie for any rascal that wants him to. In that sense it may be regarded as a law softening the rigor of all laws: it does not mitigate punishments, but mitigates the chance of incurring them. The infamy of it lies in forbidding an attorney to be a gentleman. Like all laws it falls something short of its intent: many attorneys, even some who defend that law, are as honorable as is consistent with the practice of deceit to serve crime.

It will not do to say that an attorney in defending a guilty client is not compelled to cheat and lie. What kind of defense could be made by any one who did not profess belief in the innocence of his client?—did not affirm it in the most serious and impressive way?—did not lie? How would it profit the defense to be conducted by one who would not meet the prosecution's grave asseverations of belief in the prisoner's guilt by equally grave assurances of faith in his innocence? And in point of fact, when was counsel for the defense ever known to forego the advantage of that solemn falsehood? If I am asked what would become of accused persons if they had to prove their innocence to the lawyers before making a defense in court, I reply that I do not know; and in my turn I ask: What would become of Humpty-dumpty if all the king's horses and all the king's men were an isosceles triangle?

The Competence of Jurors

WE ARE HEARING a deal about "Government by injunction" and the denial of "the constitutional right of trial by jury." The constitutional right of trial by jury happens to be subject to constitutional limitations. As one of these limitations is seen in summary punishment for contempt of court in disobeying an injunction, it is rather obvious that this does not constitute the denial of a right. It is not true that every American citizen is entitled to trial by jury for every offense; it never has been true, and the assurance that it is true can be intelligently made only to deceive. "Government by injunction" can doubtless be carried to a tyrannical extreme, as can any kind of authority and power, but in so far as it supersedes trial by jury for crimes that are "popular" it subserves a good end. If our system gave us good judges; if judges were not elective, but appointive, and held office during good behavior; that is, if they were not the creatures of political bosses and newspapers, or of selfish corporations, every man of sense would wish their powers extended and those of juries curtailed more and more. Every human institution is a failure, but the jury system as a means of justice is the most lamentable failure of all. There is no way to get together twelve men of sufficient intelligence, honesty and skill in analysis of evidence to determine the simplest question of fact when the lawyers have done with it. In most jurisdictions there is not that number of such men, all told.

We have just had in San Francisco a fairly good illustration of what juries are. The "advisory jury" in the Craven[4] case stood eight to four for the validity of the "pencil will." Judge Slack discharged them with a compliment and promptly pronounced the will an obvious forgery. That it is a forgery every disinterested observer of the proceedings, having intelligence enough to distinguish a potato from an abstract proposition, has known from the beginning. Yet these eight simpletons suffered the attorneys so to sophisticate the case and tangle up their understandings that they believed, not only that black was white, but that it was shot through with gleams of rose and pearl. It is not likely that Judge Slack was for one moment misled by the ingenious nonsense of Mrs. Craven's attorneys; from the moment that the "documents in the case" were put in evidence he probably knew they were forgeries. The difference between him and the eight jurors is not wholly one of knowledge of law; it is not altogether a difference in natural intelligence or acquired worldly wisdom; he is familiar with the cheating of lawyers and the lying of coached witnesses, and skilled in the sifting of evidence and they are not. Moreover, service on the bench has given him the mental habit of impartiality; and impartiality does not come to a juror by his swearing that he will be impartial. To at least those who think that an attempt has been made to loot the Fair estate by means of counterfeited documents the jury episode of the trial is of profound significance, accentuating in a singularly emphatic way the incurable inefficiency of a "system" which exists in our modern republican life merely as a pernicious "survival." We are not likely to see it abolished in a hurry, but it is permitted to us to indulge the hope of a new golden age when all disputes will be formally submitted to the Rabelaisian arbitrament of the dice.[5]

CAPITAL PUNISHMENT

Sex in Punishment

WITH A VIEW, possibly, to promoting respect for law by making the statutes so conform to public sentiment that none will fall into disesteem and disuse, a contemporary advocates the formal recognition of sex in the penal code, by making a difference in the punishment of men and of women for the same crimes and misdemeanors. The argument is that if women were "provided" with milder punishments juries would sometimes convict them, whereas they now commonly get off altogether.

The plan is not as new as might be thought. Many of the nations of antiquity of whose laws we have knowledge, and nearly all the European nations until within a comparatively recent time, punished women differently from men for the same offenses. And as recently as the period of the Early Puritan in New England women were punished for some offenses which men might commit without fear if not without reproach. The ducking-stool, for example, was an appliance for softening the female temper only. In England women used to be burned at the stake for crimes for which men were hanged, roasting being regarded as the milder punishment. In point of fact, it was not punishment at all, the victim being carefully strangled before the fire touched her. Burning was simply a method of disposing of the body so expeditiously as to give no occasion and opportunity for the unseemly social rites commonly performed about the scaffold of the erring male by the jocular populace. As lately as 1743 a woman named Margaret Biddingfield was burned in Suffolk as an accomplice in the crime of "petty treason." She had assisted in the murder of her husband, the actual killing being done by a man; and he was hanged, as no doubt he richly deserved. For "coining," too (which was "treason"), men were hanged and women burned. This distinction between the sexes was maintained until the year of grace 1790, after which female offenders ceased to have "a stake in the country," and, like Hood's martial hero, "enlisted in the line."[1]

In still earlier days, before the advantages of fire were understood, our good grandmothers who sinned were admonished by water—they were drowned; but in the reign of Henry III a woman was hanged—without strangulation, apparently, for after a whole day of it she was cut down and pardoned. Unfaithful wives and sorceresses were smothered in mud, as also were unfaithful wives among the ancient Burgundians. The punishment of unfaithful husbands is not of record; we only know that there were no austerely virtuous editors to direct the finger of public scorn their way.

Among the Anglo Saxons women who had the bad luck to be detected in theft were drowned, while men meeting with the same mischance died a dry death by hanging. By the early Danish laws female thieves were buried alive, whether or not from motives of humanity is not now known. This seems to have been the fashion in France also, for in 1331 a woman named Duplas was scourged and buried alive at Abbeville, and in 1460 Perotte Mauger, a receiver of stolen goods, was inhumed by order of the Provost of Paris in front of the public gibbet. In Germany in the good old days certain kinds of female criminals were impaled, a punishment too horrible for description, but likely enough considered by the simple German of the period conspicuously merciful.

It is, in short, only recently that the civilized nations have placed the sexes on an equality in the matter of the death penalty for crime, and the new system is not yet by any means universal. That it is a better system than the old, or would be if enforced, is a natural presumption from human progress, out of which it is evolved. But coincidently with its evolution has evolved also a sentiment adverse to punishment of women at all, which is what our contemporary bases an argument for reversion upon. But this sentiment appears to be of independent growth and in no way a reaction against that which caused the change. To mitigate the severity of the death penalty for women to some pleasant form of euthanasia, such as smothering in rose-leaves, or in their case abolish the death penalty altogether and make their capital punishment consist of a brief internment in a jail with a softened name would probably do no good, for whatever form it might take, it would be, so far as woman is concerned, the "extreme penalty" and crowning disgrace, and the jurors would be as reluctant to inflict it as they are now to inflict hanging. In California we acquit about ninety-seven per cent of even our male murderers. It would seem that this fact points out a sufficiently broad field for those to work in who wish to inculcate respect for the law. It will be time to consider the female assassin, how she grows, when we have begun to manifest an infant sense of the undesirability of assassination.

Blathering Blavatskians

THE VOICE OF THEOSOPHY has been heard in the affair Durrant. As usual the voice is a trifle vague and—it babbles. Clear speech is the outcome of clear thought, and that is something to which Theosophists are not addicted. Considering their infirmity in that way, it would be hardly fair to take them as seriously as they take themselves, but when any considerable number of apparently earnest citizens unite in a petition to the Governor of the State to commute the death sentence of a convicted assassin without alleging a doubt of his guilt the phenomenon challenges a certain attention to what they do allege. What these amiable persons hold, it seems, is what was held by Alphonse Carr:[2] the expediency of abolishing the death penalty; but apparently they do not hold, with him, that the assassins should begin. They want the State to begin, believing that the magnanimous example will effect a change of heart in those about to murder. This, I take it, is the meaning of their assertion that "death penalties have not the deterring influence which imprisonment for life carries." In this they obviously err: death deters at least the person who suffers it—he commits no more murder; whereas the assassin who is imprisoned for life and immune from further punishment may with impunity kill his keeper or whomsoever he may be able to get at. Even as matters now are, the most incessant vigilance is required to prevent convicts in prison from murdering their attendants and one another, as Warden Hale[3] can testify from the wealth of his experience in failure. How would it be if the "life-termer" were assured against any additional inconvenience for braining a guard occasionally, or strangling a chaplain now and then? A penitentiary may be described as a place of punishment and reward; under the system proposed the difference in desirableness between a sentence and an appointment would be virtually effaced. To overcome this objection a life sentence would have to mean solitary confinement, and that means insanity. Is that what these Theosophical gentlemen propose to substitute for death?

I venture to remind these petitioners that calling the death penalty "a relic of barbarism" is neither conclusive nor true. What is required is not loose assertion and dogs-eared phrases, but evidence of futility, or, in lack of that, cogent reasoning. It is true that the most barbarous nations inflict the death penalty most frequently and for the greatest number of offenses, but that is because barbarians are more criminal in instinct and less easily controlled by gentle methods than civilized persons. That is why we call them barbarous. It is not so very long since our English ancestors punished more than forty kinds of crime with death. The fact that the hangman, the boiler-in-oil and the breaker-on-the-wheel had their hands full does not show that the laws were futile; it shows that the dear old boys from whom we are proud to derive ourselves were a bad lot—of which we have abundant corroborative evidence in their brutal pastimes and in their manners and customs generally. To have restrained that crowd by the rose-water methods of modern penology—that is unthinkable.

The death penalty, say the memorialists, "creates blood-thirstiness in the unthinking masses and defeats its own ends. It is a cause of murder, not a check." These gentlemen are themselves of "the unthinking masses"—they do not know how to think. Let them try to trace and lucidly expound the chain of motives lying between the knowledge that a murderer has been hanged and the wish to commit a murder. How, precisely, does the one beget the other? By what unearthly process of reasoning does a man turning away from the gallows persuade himself that it is expedient to incur the danger of hanging? Let us have pointed out to us the several steps in that remarkable mental progress. Obviously, the thing is absurd; one might as reasonably say that contemplation of a pitted face will make a man go and catch smallpox, or the spectacle of an amputated limb on the waste-dump of a hospital tempt him to cut off his arm.

"An eye for an eye and a tooth for a tooth," say the Theosophists, "is not justice. It is revenge and unworthy of a Christian civilization." It is exact justice: nobody can think of anything more accurately just than such punishments would be, whatever the motive behind them. Unfortunately such a system is not practicable, but he who denies its absolute justice must deny also the justice of a bushel of corn for a bushel of corn, a dollar for a dollar, service for service. We cannot undertake to do to the criminal exactly what he has done to his victim, but to demand a life for a life is simple, practicable, expedient and (therefore) right.

Here are two of these gentlemen's dicta, between which they inserted the one just considered, though properly they should go together in frank inconsistency:

> "6. It [the death penalty] punishes the innocent a thousand times more severely than the guilty. Death is merciful to the tortures which the living relatives must undergo. And they have committed no crime." ★ ★ ★
> "8. Death penalties have not the deterring influence which imprisonment for life carries [an assertion already examined]. Mere death is not dreaded. See the number of suicides. Hopeless captivity is much more severe."

Merely noting that the "living relatives" whose sorrows so sympathetically affect these soft-hearted and soft-headed persons are those of the murderer, not those of his victim, let us consider what they think they say: "Death is no very great punishment, but hopeless captivity is a very great punishment indeed. Therefore, let us spare the assassin's family the tortures they will suffer if we inflict the lighter penalty. Let us make it easier for them by inflicting the severer one."

There is sense for you!—sense of the sound old fruity Theosophical sort—the kind of sense that has lifted "The Beautiful Cult" out of the dark domain of reason into the serene altitudes of inexpressible Thrill!

As to "hopeless captivity," though, there is no such thing. In legislation, to-day cannot bind to-morrow. By an act of the Legislature—even by a constitutional prohibition, we may do away with the pardoning power; but laws can be repealed, constitutions amended.

The public has a short memory, signatures to petitions in the line of mercy are had for the asking, and tender-hearted Governors are familiar afflictions. I must remind these memorialists that we have life sentences already, and sometimes they are served to the end—if the end comes soon enough; but the average length of "life imprisonment" in this State is, I am told, a little more than seven years. Hope springs eternal in the human beast, and matters simply cannot be so arranged that in entering the penitentiary he will "leave hope behind."[4] Hopeless captivity is a dream.

I quote again:

> "9. Life imprisonment is the natural and humane check upon one who has proven his unfitness for freedom by taking life deliberately."

What! it is no longer "much more severe" than the "relic of barbarism"? In the course of a half dozen lines of petition it has become "humane"? Truly these are lightning changes of character! It would be pleasing to know just what these worthy Theosophers have the happiness to think that they think.

> "It is the only punishment which receives the consent of conscience."

That is to say, their conscience and that of the convicted assassin.

> "Taking the life of a murderer does not restore the life he took; therefore, it is a most illogical punishment. Two wrongs do not make a right."

Here's richness! Hanging an assassin is illogical because it does not restore the life of his victim; incarceration does; therefore, incarceration is logical—quod erat demonstrandum.

Two wrongs certainly do not make a right, but the veritable thing in dispute is whether taking the life of a life-taker is a wrong. So naked and unashamed an example of petitio principii[5] would disgrace a debater in a pinafore. And these wonder-mongers have the incredible effrontery to babble of "logic"! Why, if one of them were to meet a syllogism in a lonely road he would run away in a hundred and fifty directions as hard as ever he could hook it. One is almost ashamed to dispute with such intellectual cloutlings.

When the people say through their laws: "Whoever takes any of our lives shall lose his own" they perform an act of pure self-defense. Even a Theosophist will admit that one may justly kill an assassin in order to save one's own life. The fact that society cannot kill until after the mischief is done—cannot know whom to kill—cuts no figure. Society warns by pointing to the gallows, and the admonition is easy to heed. Killing the murderer does not, it is true, save the victim of the murder, but it proves to others that the threat is not an empty one. Hanging is not itself deterrent, except with reference to the person hanged; it merely puts meaning into the admonition, which otherwise would be a thing of inattention and scorn.

Whatever an individual may rightly do to protect himself society may rightly do to protect him, for he is a part of itself. If he may rightly take life in defending himself society may rightly take life in defending him. If society may rightly take life in defending him it may rightly threaten to take it. Having rightly and mercifully threatened to take it, it not only rightly may take it, but expediently must.

The law of a life for a life does not altogether prevent murder. No law can altogether prevent any form of crime, nor is it desirable that it should. Doubtless God could have so created us that our sense of right and justice could have existed without contemplation of injustice and wrong, as doubtless he could have so created us that we could have felt compassion without a knowledge of suffering, but doubtless he did not. Constituted as we are, we can know the good only by contrast with evil. Our sense of sin is what our virtues feed upon; in the thin air of universal morality the altar-fires of honor and the beacons of conscience could not be kept alight. A community without crime would be a community without warm and elevated sentiments—without the sense of justice, without generosity, without courage, without magnanimity—a community of small smug souls uninteresting to God and uncoveted by the devil. We can have too much of crime, no doubt; what the wholesome proportion is none can say. Just now we are running a good deal to murder, but he who can gravely attribute that phenomenon, or any part of it, to infliction of the death penalty, instead of to virtual immunity from any penalty at all, is justly entitled to the innocent satisfaction that comes of being a simpleton.

Some Thoughts on the Hanging

IF SYMPATHY FOR ASSASSINS is not sympathy with assassination, why is it that of all the persons who expressed so much compassion for Mrs. Rogers none expressed any at all for the man that she treacherously murdered? It is a fact that none of them did. It is a fact. It is a fact that no one ever learned from them what she was to be hanged for. Did it just happen so? Were they really as greatly shocked and pained by the death of her unoffending victim as by the prospect of death for herself, but forgot to say so? If that is so, it was a truly remarkable oversight!

Some person—a woman, I believe—took the trouble to take from Ohio ten thousand signatures to a petition for clemency, explaining that she could have obtained thirty thousand. No doubt; there are more than that number of persons in every State who will sign any petition that is put before them. Some years ago a wag in one of our great cities circulated a petition for hanging without trial all the municipal officials, from the Mayor down. He obtained hundreds of signatures in good faith from men of influence and good standing in all the walks of life. What right have the people of Ohio to suggest to the people of Vermont how they shall enforce their laws or what kind of laws they shall have? It is not merely impertinent; it is impudent.

There could be no greater error than to think all this clamor the voice of "public opinion." Men of sense, of whom there is a considerable number in this country, are not addicted to clamor, and for obvious reasons a sentiment favorable to hanging a particular murderer does not find expression in "petitions," "pleas" and letters to the press. Note carefully the intellectual status of the men (never mind the women now), who oppose generally the "legal killing," as they are pleased to phrase it, of women, and protested, particularly, against the "killing" of Mrs. Rogers. I trust they are very moral; I should not care for a sufficient intimacy with them to know.

As to the ladies—whom Heaven bless—it is difficult to understand how a woman respecting herself and claiming the respect of others can demand immunity, any degree of immunity, from punishment for crime because of her sex. To do so is to confess herself and her sex mentally incapable— irresponsible, because foolish. It is as easy for women to abstain from crime as for men; if they are better than men it is easier, and their culpability when guilty greater. Logically, therefore, their punishment should be heavier.

As a fact, we find that the women who affirm their intellectual equality with men and claim political equality because of it are those who most loudly demand this immunity. They say with insistent iteration that as they had no hand in decreeing the death penalty they should be exempt from its operation. The actual meaning of that is this: That in part compensation for their political disability they be permitted to slay whomsoever they will—not only those who imposed the disability, but those who did not. They would prefer to vote, but will accept temporarily the right to kill. This is in the true spirit of compromise.

I observe that opponents of the death penalty all unite in calling it "capital punishment," as do some folk of less unwisdom. "Capital punishment" means the gravest punishment prescribed by the statutes. That is death in some of the States; in others it is life imprisonment. "Abolition of capital punishment"—slogan so dear to the headless horsemen of reform—is impossible; so long as any penalties remain, the severest will be capital punishment. Perhaps no great accuracy of speech—which is clarity of thought—should be expected of amiables who wish to legislate for the world as it is not.[6]

The event at Windsor, Vermont, was not without its humorist. A reporter—a child of light and mercy, naturally—gravely points out that Mrs. Rogers "faced death as only a woman can." That ought to make him mighty popular with the opposing sex and get him a real good wife when he is old enough to marry.

Tariffs, Trusts, and Labor

"Protection" vs. Fair Trade

THE ORIGINAL "PROTECTIONIST" was the savage islander who persuaded his fellow-savages to go down to the beach and drive away the trading ca-noes from another island by firing arrows and throwing stones. This frank and simple form of Protection to Home Industry is still prevalent among barbarians the world over, and it is to be remarked of them that they are consistent and manly in its application: they not only drive away the traders of other countries, but keep their own traders at home, and if they want anything which they cannot themselves produce, intrust the mission of procuring it to a war-party. Every producer his own consumer is the popular motto of such peoples. They do not, as a rule, produce much, and are suspected, in some instances, of con-suming one another.

The civilized equivalent of the very patriotic savage who instigates his coun-trymen to drive away the trading-canoes, is the ingenious gentleman who in-vented the custom-house. Protective duties are a truly Christian expedient; they drive away trade without taking life. The inspector's eye is quite as effective at short range as the savage's arrow, and the prim appraiser "clothed in his right mind,"[1] is no less formidable than the naked barbarian grenadier with his arms full of rocks. The civilized Protectionist is at once less frank and less honest than his barbarous prototype. Besides accomplishing by indirection what the other achieves by force of arms, he is unwilling to "take his own medicine;" while excluding the commodities of foreign nations, he resents with bitterness and clamor any exclusion of his own products by foreigners. When Bismarck turned away the American hog from German ports, on the ground that the creature was diseased, the journals and statesmen of the "grand old (Protectionist) party" actually corruscated with indignant asseverations of his duplicity. His "unfriendly" action, they averred, was taken in the interest of German farmers who grow pork. If we rightly remember, the Hon. A. A. Sargent, then (for our sins) United States Minister at Berlin, was at the pains to adduce elaborate proofs that the German Chancellor was guilty of protection to home industry, and held him up to the scorn of the Republican party.

This is sufficiently amusing: It hardly needs to be instructive, but the lesson of it is that inter-communication and interchange of commodities among nations have become so habitual as to be unconsciously accepted as a natural and fundamental fact of modern civilization, and interference with that condition of things is tolerable only to him who supposes himself to profit by the obstruction. Free Trade is so obviously a rational and beneficent policy that it is questioned by none but those to whom it denies a dishonest advantage, or by their dupes.

But there is no principle whose practical application to the complex affairs and varying conditions of life is unattended by actual or apparent disadvantages, and Free Trade is no exception. It would be easy to show how the lifting of all protective duties would necessarily result in extinguishing some of the industries now protected, and among these might be some which, unnecessary under normal conditions, might be sadly missed in time (say) of war. A nation, for example, which from long disuse had lost the facilities for manufacturing arms and ammunition, could ill afford to go to war, particularly with a naval power which might blockade its ports or capture its purchased military supplies on the high seas. If the adoption of Free Trade would (as is falsely contended) reduce the United States to nearly the condition of a purely agricultural and pastoral community, the accretion of natural wealth from undivided pursuit of the most profitable industry, while paying less for foreign commodities than we now have to pay for domestic, would be an inadequate *solatium* for the damage we might suffer at the hands of a military nation strong in the skilled hands, versatile brains and varied resources that come of manufacture and the arts, even when some of these are promoted and fostered by an inequitable tax upon the labor engaged in them; and precisely such a tax is every protective duty upon the necessaries and comforts of life.

Absolute Free Trade is not, therefore, presently to be hoped for. Before it can be adopted there is much to be settled. A policy must be devised for preserving such industries as are necessary to military power, which it might tend to extinguish. Above all, the laboring classes must be freed from the error that Protection secures them *employment,* as distinguished from *particular kinds* of employment. All this is going to take time.

But there is one kind, or rather one degree of Free Trade which is so obviously rational that it would seem to need nothing but naming to commend it. In commercial "Reciprocity" we have nothing else than a local and partial suspension of a harsh and inelastic policy. Reciprocity required the surrender of no advantage. It is not a leap in the dark; it takes thought of where it sets its feet. It avoids the "falsehood of extremes." It is Fair Trade. If two nations, discerning in the iron application of an inelastic law certain remediable evils at points of friction, cannot devise a means of relaxing the strain and by mutual concession make all work orderly for mutual benefit, then the intelligence of man has been overrated and statesmanship is a failure. It is obvious that we need certain products (say) of Mexico, and that Mexico is equally in need of certain others of ours. What, then, can be more irrational than to say to Mexico, "You must pay us a certain sum of money for looking at your goods. You can reimburse yourself by not looking at ours until we have paid it back." If Messrs. Gilbert and Sullivan were to write a commercial *opera bouffe,* that is about the way they would probably make their traders talk and act. The method of two great nations might advantageously be distinguished by greater simplicity and common sense.

A Backslider

IN CRITICISM OF Mr. Moffett's article of the Tariff, in Monday's issue of this paper,[2] a Protectionist morning contemporary takes the intrepid stand that trusts, as we have the happiness to know them—the trusts that are made possible by shutting out foreign competition—are really very beneficent things. Mr. Moffett pointed out that foreign competition being shut out, the resulting trust immediately proceeds to shut out domestic competition also. Our contemporary is moved to ask how the trust gains the power to do so, and inspired to answer: "By reducing the cost of protection to such a figure that the single adventurer is no longer able to compete profitably." That is to say, by being able to undersell him, and of course, doing so.

It is not to be denied that this is one of the kinds of suasion by which the trust exhorts the impertinent "adventurer" not to lay up treasures on earth, where rust corrupts and moths devour and tax collectors break in and steal.[3] The trust does indubitably sometimes choose that method. But when it has been successfully employed, and the sinner converted to the religion of poverty, what occurs? Having the field to itself, the trust puts up its prices and recoups itself for its honesty. The cost of setting up a fresh opposition, added to that of conducting it to a problematical success, is in the nature of a fine for fresh adventuring by new aspirants, and under the unwritten law imposing it, the touch of the trust upon the consumers' purse is light and free.

To ruin the small competitor by underselling it is not at all necessary to produce more cheaply; it is necessary only to have a sufficiently large capital. Time is long and competition fleeting. Bread cast upon the turbulent waters of commercial combat returns to the victor an hundred fold, the increase being taken out of the mouth of the public. Trusts, however, are not insensible to the advantages of reducing the cost of production, as is abundantly attested by their habit of cutting down wages.

But the trust has more than one arrow to its bow; it has always a quiverful, and underselling, at either a loss or a profit, is only one of them. If our contemporary is familiar with the history of (say) the Standard Oil Company[4] as he is friendly to the principle it represents he must have heard something about understandings with railway and pipe lines, whereby competitors were simply unable to sell at all because not permitted to get their oil to any market. His intellectual domain must have been penetrated by advices concerning costly and harassing litigation by which the "single adventurer" was broken in fortune and spirit. Rumors must have reached his ears, or *vice versa*, of corrupted courts and legislatures working the will of the pious and philanthropic Mr. Rockefeller and his associates; of (in short) every possible kind of iniquitous advantage, within and without the law, having for object, and accomplishing it with pitiless precision, the ruin of every independent dealer. Selling low is but one of the many means to that end, has always been local in its application when employed, and without reference to cost of production, and is never continued a day longer than necessary; for the one great purpose of the combination, as of all combinations of sellers, is to sell high.

We are not much more than merely civilly solicitous for the salvation of our esteemed contemporary's soul, but having observed him for so many years living a godly life and exhorting the trusts and monopolies to mend their ways, one cannot but remark with serious concern his backsliding at the eleventh hour to serve a transient controversial need. And then to observe the need ineffectually served—that disheartens.

Commercial Retaliation

BECAUSE GERMANY PAYS a bounty on her exported sugar, America adds the amount of the bounty to the regular duty on German sugar. That prohibits America's importation of German sugar, greatly to the satisfaction of our Sugar Trust and the political philosophers whom, for advantage of that concern, Heaven has raised up to believe in Protection. But the Prussian Minister of Finance, his understanding suffused with the light of the same faith, observing that our action baffles an intelligent effort to prosper

Paul the German sugar grower at the expense of Peter the German barley grower, "retaliates" by an indirect exclusion of certain American fruits.

Retaliates on whom? Obviously, on the American fruit-grower, and no less obviously, to the same intelligence, on the German fruit-eater. (In his case "retaliation" is not quite the word, seeing that his only offense is being a German; but his interests are disastrously affected just as those of his occidental purveyor are.)

At this early stage of the merry war we find, therefore, no fewer than five unfortunates limping to cover: (1) the German non-grower of sugar, taxed to pay the export bounty, a victim of the Imperial Government; (2 and 3) the German sugar grower and the American sugar eater, victims of the American Congress; (4 and 5) the American fruit-grower and the German fruit-eater, victims of the Prussian Minister of Finance. (Of the many dealers directly, and the many more persons indirectly, hurt by this admirable fooling there is lack of space for enumeration.)

Retaliation provokes retaliation. Already some of our patriots and other statesmen are breathing fire and thunder. Already we hear the muttering of the war-storm that is to break upon the head of the German producer—but nothing of that which is to overwhelm his American customer. Already it has been suggested that on analysis Rhine wines may be found deleterious to the Yankee stomach and eminently fit for exclusion. And it has been solemnly proposed to put an export duty on the domestic horse when shipped to a German port. In other words, it is thought expedient to add four more lame ducks to the procession of wounded: the German wine grower and the American wine drinker, the German horse user and the American horse breeder. Really, it is becoming interesting, this game of flinging razors by the blades.

Of course the logical end of it all would be an entire severance of commerce between the two countries, each grimly happy in the conviction that the other suffered more than itself. We are permitted to cherish a hope that it will not come to that—that before the quarrel has reached that ultimate stage some miraculous endowment of common sense may enable our worthy statesmen to discern in commercial retaliation the mere fool's revenge that it really is. Let us at least pray—those of us who do not fear to attract the divine attention—that they may eventually be persuaded to accept the elementary truth that in a commercial transaction the advantage does not accrue to the seller only, but to the buyer as well.

The horse proposal stands a trifle apart, as a method of retaliation, and must be regarded as the dream of a genius out of touch with the principles of Protection, but all the others are clearly due to an infantile misconception of the nature

of money. It is looked upon as concentrated wealth, and always more advantageous to the owner than that which he gave for it. The man that parts with a
product of labor for money is felt to have the better end of the bargain. (That is
to say, any man but oneself; if we felt that way in our own personal affairs we
should never buy anything but the necessaries of life.) So strong is this feeling
that in the instance of a country whose imports exceed in money value its
exports—a country, that is, which buys more than it sells—the "balance of
trade" is said to be "against" it, and the situation is considered alarming. To the
person who thinks that way it is useless to point out that each individual whose
money went abroad for a foreign product preferred the product to the money—
considered himself benefited by the exchange. He may be presumed to be a
fairly good judge of his own interest. If so the funny gentleman alarmed by the
"outflow of gold" is committed to the proposition that the sum of individual
advantages makes a general adversity.

Money is not wealth. It is good for nothing but to spend or to base credits
on—which means to pledge it for expenditure later. A with one thousand dollars in his pocket and B with nothing are equally wealthy, and they so continue
until A begins to get rid of his money. When he has got rid of one hundred
dollars judiciously he is one hundred dollars wealthier than B—is wealthier by
that amount than himself was when all the money lay in his pocket.

When the "balance of trade" is "against" us the character of that phenomenon, for good or evil, depends on what we have been buying; when it
is "in our favor" the character of that depends on what we are going to do
with the money—how we are going to get rid of it. Advocates of commercial retaliation cannot understand that a commercial transaction may be
mutually advantageous. With unconscious fatuity they feel that it harms the
foreign producer worse to be prevented from selling to the domestic consumer than it does the latter to be prevented from buying.

Something of the same savage incapacity to discern the most conspicuous
truths is found in popular beliefs regarding nearly everything. For example, a
few weeks ago the whole country rang with joy because the price of wheat had
risen and the jubilations have ceased only because the subject is no longer novel.
It was called "national prosperity." It meant prosperity to a few wheat-growers,
adversity to every one else; for whereas only a few grow wheat, everybody eats
it. (The French are the only people that know how to make the stuff palatable,
but we all take it as medicine for the recurring disorder of hunger.) With the
loaves of the whole country visibly shrinking, there was no abatement of joy
over the high price of wheat; for the sale of the surplus abroad would "bring
more money into the country"—money which can benefit the country only by
going out again for something less needful than cheap wheat.

And so it occurs that all our commercial legislation is determined by the belief that money is a good thing in itself, without reference to the advantage of unloading it upon one's neighbor. To the average human understanding—that, say, of the typical American politician—it would seem advantageous in a high degree if not only all the product of our gold and silver mines could be kept at home, but that there could be an incessant influx of specie from abroad. It is easily comprehensible how to an understanding like that retaliation and other forms of protection appear to be the highest political wisdom; and if a cow could speak her mind of the matter she would indubitably take that view of it.

Concerning Trusts

"FAR-SEEING STATESMEN" addicted to circumvision of the "political horizon" have discerned the paramount "issue" of the next "Presidential campaign." It is to be, in the words of an esteemed contemporary, "destruction of criminal trusts"—for the purpose in hand all trusts, excepting newspaper trusts and labor trusts, to be regarded as criminal. As a "cry," a policy, "the destruction" and so forth has one distinct disadvantage: it is so fascinating to minds distinguished for "political sagacity" that it is pretty sure to be forced upon all the parties; so there is nothing in it for any of them, and its endorsement by success of one can be no more confidently affirmed than its repudiation by defeat of all the others. Still, it is a good "cry" and will indubitably go ringing through the land, to the unspeakable edification of the intelligent masses. Already several State legislatures have begun to "destroy" by such "drastic" and impossible laws as commonly precede the practical and moderate measures suggested by their failure. And in Ohio an energetic officer of the law, with loud asseverations of incorruptibility, is hotly prosecuting the richest and most powerful of all the "combines," with the prayers of all the Truly Good at the sturdy back of him. The battle against the trusts is conspicuously "on." I venture to predict that it will fail, and to think that it ought to fail.

That an effort ought to fail is, in this bad world, no good reason for thinking that it will fail; there is a strong numerical presumption the other way. For doubting the success of this "movement" there are many reasons having nothing to do with the righteousness of the cause. One is that the entire trend of our modern civilization is toward combination and aggression. In the larger politics this tendency is so strikingly evident that one hesitates to pronounce "the Parliament of Man, the Federation of the World,"[5] no more than a poet's dream. A generation that has seen the unification of Italy and Germany, the virtual absorption of the African native States by a few European Powers and the beginning of a similar phenomenon in Asia; that has seen even the home-keeping American cast aside his policy of seclusion and grasp distant islands of magnitude in two oceans;[6] that has witnessed the failure of such formidable schemes of disintegration as our war of secession—a generation which has seen all this can hardly shut its eyes to the fact that the day of small political holdings and petty autonomies is passing.

We have heard a good deal in the last two years of "European concert"[7]—much of it, 'tis true, from the small wits of the editorial column, to whose provincial understandings the word "concert" suggests nothing but a musical entertainment. But the "European concert" is something more than a joke. It is a new and stupendous force engaged in regulating the affairs of nations conformably to larger and more enduring interests than have ever before been considered in their control. It cannot prevent needless wars incited by ambition, greed or conceit, but it can, as in the instance of Greece and Turkey it recently did, isolate the disorder and make sure that a senseless aggressor takes nothing for his obstinacy.[8] This distinctly reduces the value of the individual initiative, and is a long step toward "the Federation of the World." And there now sits at The Hague a deliberative body that goes a deal nearer to being a "Parliament of Man" than any other assemblage that history tells us about.[9] I venture to doubt, however, if, in the Federation of the World as it will be, parliamentary representation will ever have a numerical basis; some of the most populous countries in the scheme will find themselves very meagerly supplied with accepted spokesmen.

Other striking instances of organization and aggregation are seen in the labor unions, which, as above intimated, are merely trusts to control the output and the price of labor. These unions are forming more and more into great federations—some of them even international. The same thing is observed in fraternal societies and even social clubs. "Improvement clubs," such as those for promoting good roads, follow the same law. It is not now unusual for national conventions or congresses of this or that kind of associations to be held at which thousands of local ones are represented. It is significant, too, that these vast aggregations of interests are for the most part beneficial, not only to the interests immediately concerned, but beneficial generally. Can it be that only in the commercial world organization and aggregation are malign and dangerous?

It is impossible in the limits allowed here to enumerate and explain all or many of the public advantages of combinations in production. A few may be mentioned.

Economy is one of the most obvious. A syndicate or trust requires just as many miners to dig a million tons of coal, for example, as a dozen independent companies did; but it does not require nearly as many salaried officers, nor nearly as many expensive offices. The man who is in danger of "losing his job" is not the laborer; yet it is the laborers who, like the widows of Ashur, are "loud in their wail."[10] A little reflection will suggest many other ways in which economy of production is served by combination; but deeper reflection with some knowledge of commercial phenomena are required to make it clear that economy of production benefits anybody but the producer. Well, it is of some potential advantage, at least, to the consumer that the producer is able, without bankruptcy, to lower the price of the product if heaven should put it into his heart to do so.

Stability of employment is promoted by combination of capital. A single concern employing 10,000 workmen will not hold them subject to the whims and caprices of a single mind conscious of its ability to replace them, as is the case with a man employing only a dozen. To a rich corporation carrying on a large business a strike means a great loss; to a score of small concerns it means a comparatively small loss each, and is incurred as France accepted war with Prussia—"with a light heart."[11] Labor may be very sure of having its demands attentively considered by those who employ a lot of it.

An almost certain benefit resulting from combination is improvement in the quality of the product where improvement is possible. Any one who uses kerosene oil now and used it twenty-five or thirty years ago will understand this without exposition. Even less than that long ago the annual mortality from explosions of lamps and heaters by reason of inferior oil was appalling. Now such accidents are extremely rare and due almost altogether to criminal ignorance or carelessness. Moreover, the kerosene of to-day is by no means the disgusting fluid that the late lamented generation had the unhappiness to know. All this improvement is directly due to the efforts of a company virtually without competitors. The Standard Oil Company—that type and exemplar of total depravity, that pilloried malefactor, dead-catted by public and press—has expended in mere improvement of its product hundreds of thousands of dollars. Could any of the "small dealers" whom it absorbed or effaced have afforded that expenditure, or have seen a certain profit in making it? It may properly be explained here that, as it has improved the quality of its product, the "pirate monopoly" has steadily reduced the price, until that is now, I believe, only about one-third or one-fourth what it was in the olden, golden days of competition and explosion. And that brings us to a very important advantage indeed of the commercial conditions which the trusts bring about.

A large part of the clamor against trusts is the honest expression of a belief

(promoted by many writers on political economy) that in commercial matters the only influence concerned in reduction of price is competition. Nearly
all workingmen are more or less discontented with "the competitive system" in industrial affairs, but few have learned to challenge its benignity in
trade. Competition is, in fact, only one of the several forces concerned in
cheapening commodities, and, generally speaking, not by any means the
most considerable. It requires but a brief experience in producing and selling
to convince an intelligent man that his prosperity is to be found in the large
sales that come of low prices. Having control of his market and a free hand in
the management of his business, such a man studies to reduce his selling
price to the lowest possible point. An enlightened selfishness moves him to
undersell himself wherever he can, as if he were his own competitor.

Not all men managing large commercial affairs are intelligent. Some of the
trusts are organized and conducted with a view to enhancing rather than reducing prices; but, as that most sagacious of millionaires, the late Roswell P. Flower,[12]
has pointed out, these are not dangerous, for they are bound to fail. By tempting
the small concerns to remain in or re-enter the field, the "combine" cuts its own
throat. Its primary purpose is to "crush out" the independent "small dealer," and
this it can do in only one way—lure away his customers by underselling him. If
consumers really think this is so wicked a thing to do they have the remedy in
their own hands. Let them refuse to leave the small dealer, and continue to pay
him the higher price. This course would entail a bit of a sacrifice, maybe, but it
would have the merit of freedom from cant and hypocrisy, and would give the
legislatures, the courts and the popular newspapers "a much-needed rest." I
know of nothing more ludicrous than the spectacle of these solemn consumers
appealing to the law and public opinion (their own opinion) to avenge upon the
trusts the injuries of themselves and the small dealers—they having no injuries to
avenge and the small dealer only such as themselves have inflicted by standing in
with the trusts to pluck him. The trust is condemned if it put up prices, for that
harms the consumer; it is condemned if it put them down, for that harms the
small dealer. In either case, both consumer and small dealer make common
cause against the "enemy" that can harm neither without helping the other. If
the history of human folly shows anything more absurd surely the historian must
have been Rabelais, "laughing sardonically in his easy chair."[13]

The trusts, it is feared, will become too rich and powerful to be controlled. I do not think so. The reason that some of them already defy the
power of the States is that, being so few, they have not until now attracted
the serious attention of legislatures. And even now our anti-trust legislation
is more concerned with the impossible task of abolition and prevention than
with the practicable one of regulation. When we have learned by blundering

what we cannot do we shall easily enough learn what we can do, and find it quite sufficient. Governmental ownership and Governmental control are what we are coming to by leaps and bounds; and with the industries and trade of the country in fewer hands, the task of regulating them will be greatly simplified, for it is easier to manage one man than two.

But, it will be asked, is this to become a nation of employes working for a few hundreds of taskmasters? Not at all. The spirited and provident employe can become his own employer, or the employer of others, by investing his savings in the stock of the "combine." The greater their gains are the greater will be his share of them. The "crushed out" small dealer, too, can recoup himself by becoming a part of what crushed him out. Naturally, the tendency of the trusts will be to "work with the stock market," to "put up jobs" on the small investors, and so forth. Prevention of that sort of thing is a legitimate purpose for legislation, and promises better results than "drastic" measures to prevent the trusts themselves. To do the latter the laws would have to be so drawn as to forbid any commercial enterprise requiring more capital than its manager could himself supply. That would be a monstrous law which should undertake to fix the amount of capital to be combined under one management, or limit the number of persons permitted to supply it; yet nothing less "drastic" will "down the trusts." And that would not, for it would be unconstitutional in every State of the Union. As a contribution to the literature of humor it would be slightly better than an apothegm by Josh Billings,[14] but distinctly inferior to that delicious Northwestern statute making it a felony to conduct a "department store"— every store in the country being of that felonious character.

It is not, perhaps, too late to explain that in this article the word "trust" is used in the popular sense, meaning an uncommonly large aggregation of capital by combination of several concerns under one management. It is my high privilege to know a better word for it, but in deference to those who do most of the talking on this engaging theme I assent to their kind of English.

Concerning Legislation "To Solve the Tramp Problem"

THE RIGHT TO LABOR should be legally defined.
A bill said to have been drawn by a former member of the Californian State Senate is to be introduced into every Legislature of the country. It is described as "An attempt to solve the tramp problem," but in principle it

seems to be a good deal more than that, and better worth while. It is rather an attempt to right an immemorial wrong. Briefly, it provides that any adult person without means of support and in need of the necessaries of life may obtain work from the State, with food, lodging and a low rate of wages.

The rate is to have a fixed minimum, but county authorities may in their discretion pay more. Therein lurks a peril to the plan. The workingman and the demagogue will never rest until the wage rate of relief work is equal to the current rate in private employ; and then (if, indeed, the project prosper at all) every one who is willing to work will want to work for the State. The effect on private enterprises need not be pointed out.

That, however, is a bog in which we need not mire until we step into it. The important thing is to get a definitive and legal recognition of the right to labor.

In denying that right, save as one may have the good luck to find a willing employer, society is not only unjust, but short-sighted. It says to the able-bodied poor man:

"We exact of you a certain kind of conduct. You shall not beg. You shall not steal, nor rob. You shall not sleep in shelters that you do not own. We shall not admit you to the almshouse. You may starve if you are quick about it, before we arrest you as a vagrant and send you to jail, but you must be decently clothed."

To this the gentleman in adversity might reasonably reply:

"Pardon me, but food costs money, lodgings and decent clothing cost money, and I have not the chance to earn any. If you will not assure me the employment that I am unable to persuade any one else to give me, you should let me beg for the means to meet your requirements. If you will not let me beg, you should turn your back while I steal. In brief, you have no right to demand the impossible."

There can be no question at all as to who is in the right of this; the only doubt is as to the expediency of doing right; there are persons who do not recognize in expedience the basis of morality.

The untried seems always wrong. Most of the things which society habitually does, and "sits attentive to its own applause"[15] for doing them, it would (and once did) regard with severe disfavor as innovations. If we knew nothing of public schools a proposal to make education free and compulsory would distinguish the proponent as a crank.

We all believe, or profess to believe, that popular education is necessary to the existence of good government; that ignorance is a peril to the State. Yet, an illiterate person at work is not nearly so dangerous as a cultivated one out of employment. It just happens that we supply education—such as it is—

and do not supply work. If our laws and customs were made to measure, instead of pulled down and made off with in the dark, we should have provided, many decades ago, that no man or woman willing to work should lack the opportunity. When we shall have done so, we can punish the person "without visible means of support," the sturdy beggar[16] and the rising young thief without feeling that we ought ourselves to be in jail.

The plan proposed will probably not work. One can foresee a half-dozen objections that are sure to be strenuously urged against it by the solemn theorists of conservatism and the brainless gentlemen who kindly undertake the thinking for the labor unions. In default of anything worse to be said of it, it will probably be denounced, along with the almshouse, the free clinic and other inventions of the malicious rich, as a device for humiliating the poor. But if even a bad beginning is made toward recognition of the right to work something will have been gained, and we may die in the sure and certain hope that posterity, failing to comprehend the monstrous stupidity of its ancestors, will enact practicable laws in the matter, see that they are enforced and forget that they were not in existence from the time of Adam.

The Road to Wealth Is Open to All— Get Wealthy Ye Who Can

THIS IS NOT a country of equal fortunes; outside a socialist's dream no such country exists nor can exist. But as nearly as is possible this is a country of equal opportunities for those who begin life with nothing but nature's endowments—and of such is the kingdom of success.

In nine instances in ten successful Americans—that is Americans who have succeeded in any worthy ambition or legitimate field of endeavor— have started with nothing but the skin they stood in. It may almost be said, indeed, that to begin with nothing is a main condition of success—in America.

To a young man there is no such hopeless impediment as wealth or the expectation of wealth. Here a man and there a man will rise, so abundantly endowed by nature as to overcome the handicap of artificial "advantages," but that is not the rule; usually the chap "born with a gold spoon in his mouth," puts in his time sucking that spoon and without other employment. Counting possession of the spoon success, why should he bestir himself to achieve what he already has?

The real curled darling of opportunity is the youth born with nothing in his mouth but his teeth—he who knows or is likely to know what it is to feel his belly sticking to his back. If he have brains a-plenty he will get on for he must be up and doing—the penalty of indiligence is famine. If he have not, he may up and do to the uttermost satisfaction of his mind and heart, but the end of that man is failure, with possibly socialism, that last resort of conscious incompetence.

It fatigues, this talk of the narrowing opportunities of to-day, the "closed avenues to success," and the rest of it. Doubtless it serves its purpose of making mischief for the tyrant trusts and the wicked rich generally, but in a six months' bound volume of it there is not enough of truth to float a religion.

Men of brains never had a better chance than now to accomplish all that it is desirable that they should accomplish; and men of no brains never did have much of a chance, nor under any possible conditions can have in this country or any other. They are nature's failures, God's botchwork. Let us be sorry for them, treating them justly and generously; but the socialism that would level us all down to their plane of achievement and reward is a proposal of which they are themselves the proponents.

Opportunity, indeed! Who is holding me from composing a great opera that would make me rich and famous?

What oppressive laws forbade me to work my passage up the Yukon as deckhand on a steamboat and discover the gold along Bonanza creek?

What is there in our industrial system that conceals from me the secret of making diamonds from charcoal?

Why was it not I who, entering a lawyer's office as a suitable person to sweep it out, left it as an appointed Justice of the Supreme Court?

I have had a dozen years to prove to the proprietor of this newspaper that he can afford to pay me $25,000 a year.[17]

He is just languishing, good man, to give it to me; I have only to show him that my services are worth it. What prevents me from making the proof? And what prevents you, most excellent of all possible cobblers, from beating me out of the field by writing like an angel with a reed?

The number of actual and possible sources of profit and methods of distinction is infinite. Not all the trusts in the world combined in one trust of trusts could appreciably reduce it—could condemn to permanent failure one man with the talent and the will to succeed.

They can abolish that doubtful benefactor the "small dealer" who lives by charging too much, and that very thickly disguised blessing the "drummer" whom they have to add to the price of everything they sell; but for every opportunity they close they open a new one and leave untouched a thousand actual and a million possible ones.

As to their dishonest practices, these are conspicuous and striking, because "lumped," but no worse than the silent, steady aggregate of cheating by which their constituent firms and individuals formerly consumed the consumer without his special wonder.

And when I observe the young salesman, the "wage slave" of the counter—when I mark his ways and consider him how he lies and damns his soul back without the excuse of direct personal advantage, I sometimes "thank whatever gods may be" that they have supplied his sluggish mind with a pretext for wearing the chains of servitude instead of marching out for the larger opportunity of the "small dealer."

My sympathy does not readily go out to the person (sexed malewise or otherwise) with a mouthful of falsehood always on tap for my deluding—always serviceable to the purpose of making me buy what I do not want. If by chance I am ever "waited on" by another kind of person, I am never gifted with the discernment to observe the difference.

INSURANCE

The Insurance Folly

THE LEGISLATURE HAS passed the bill authorizing the formation of mutual insurance companies. I presume it is a good bill—I don't know a word of it. If a man wants to bet that his house will burn down, or his ship sink, or a disease gather him to his fathers, and some other man wants to bet that nothing of the kind will occur, I can see no objection to affording "facilities" for making the wager. That is all there is in insurance: it is a bet in exactly the same sense that a transaction at faro is. The person who insures his life or property bets against the game of the man who keeps the table. As men commonly do not run gambling games for fun, it is obvious that when a man insures anything belonging to him he makes a bet in which the chances are against him. Whatever the company makes it gets from those who try to beat the game. The proportion of what it pays in losses to what it gets in premiums would show, if known, what its percentage of advantage is. It need hardly be stated that it does not furnish its clients with the correct figures. If it did the insurance craze would die in one decade. As things are, it will probably last for several generations, when we shall perhaps have a revival of the memorable "Tulip Mania" and a new inflation of the "South Sea Bubble."[1]

I know of nothing more laughable than insurance. It is like the dream of a humorist. By as much as the spectacle of a toper begging the boys to get him drunk and have some fun out of him transcends in absurdity the spectacle of a badgered toper who intoxicated himself for another purpose, the spectacle of a man deliberately insuring his life or property beats the spectacle of a man having his pocket picked while he is asleep. There is nothing ludicrous in the attitude of the insurer; he has an entirely clear and thrifty knowledge of the situation—which he is mighty careful not to impart to the other chap. He overwhelms him with figures; he mazes him with tabular statements; he feeds him paunch full of hopes; sophisticates and clouds the business with little ventures "on the side," which have no relevancy to insurance, tempts him with a choice of policies having captivating names, some of which even promise returns as an investment! He submits with

charming candor the tables of probabilities upon which he bases his rates—
tables constructed by his own hired actuary. Everything is open and above-
board: the intelligent client can take the tables and the reports and the exhib-
its and convince himself by his own figuring that twice two are surely five
and black is not only white but slightly scarlet. But he steers pretty wide—
this frank and voluble insurer—of the simple, basic and only essential fact, to
wit: the price at which he can afford to undertake to bear another man's
misfortune the other man cannot afford to pay.

It is admitted that the insurance folly, having become general, sometimes
"compels itself"; affairs have so adapted themselves to its prevalence that one
may have to insure his property, even his life, in order to get on. He may
wish to borrow money and be unable unless he does insure. That has nothing to do with the *principle* of insurance; necessity may compel one to endure
a smaller evil to escape a greater. Because I may have to hand my money to
a stranger to keep it out of the hands of a robber, that does not prove the
expediency and profit of intrusting money to strangers, who are merely thieves.

John Smith takes out a policy on his house, and the house burns. If the
company can study out no way to avoid payment it pays. Behold the wisdom of insuring! William Smith has no policy on his house and *it* burns.
Behold the madness of not insuring! John and William become renowned:
the underwriters blare their names abroad all over the land: you can almost
hear the roar of the flames consuming their habitations and menacing your
own. But you do not hear anything about Tom Smith, and Dick Smith, and
Harry Smith, and the nine hundred and ninety-nine other Smiths who go
on paying premiums all their lives—paying until they have paid more than
the cost of their houses, which did not burn. Another inconspicuous figure
is that hardheaded old Smith (also very comfortably housed) who, when the
insurance agents were all eager to be paid to bet him that his dwelling would
not consume, said to them: "Gentlemen, I am glad your superior knowledge
confirms my judgment: I'm betting that way myself."

There are certain wealthy and prosperous corporations, owning many
ships or other kinds of property, who "insure themselves." This phrase—an
invention of underwriters—is perfectly delicious! It marks and signalizes a
dissolution of the immemorial bond between words and things. It is language's
declaration of independence in seceding from sense. It means that they do
not insure. True, they keep up the fiction by certain convenient devices of
book-keeping, but they no more insure than a man pays when he takes a
coin from his right hand pocket and puts it into his left. "But they are so
wealthy," saith Glib the Broker, "their eggs are in so many baskets that they
can afford to stand their own losses." The dear, dear man!—what a head he

has! *Because* a man is wealthy he can afford to keep out of a "hogging" game; *ergo* a poor man should play. This is logic in her last ditch.

If the Coming Man is very long on the way he will not laugh at insurance; he will not know about it. Only on the assurance of the most credible historians will he believe that his ancestors, barbarians as they were, were addicted to so monstrous and grotesque a folly—that they were dominated by a commercial madness of so surpassing intensity. Religious heresies he will be able to understand; he will exult in some bright and beautiful ones himself. Preposterous philosophies will seem to him to have been natural and inevitable under the circumstances as they were, namely, the existence and toleration of philosophers. He will see that science must have been a hardy and intrepid liar, and the art and literature of our time will in his time have high rank as horrible examples of the unwisdom of the ancients. Of journalism—long extinct—he will have some knowledge, for its memory will be kept green (gangrene) by the everlasting infamy of the Fitches and Pickerings whereof it died.[2] But that men of business and affairs, of wealth and unweariness in well doing their neighbors; tower-builders and tamers of the seas; hard-gotten gainers who from their money were not soon or easily parted; canny old nineteenth century savages and men of prey—fellows, in short, who had sense enough to go in when it rained if they could find houses of others to go into and save roof-wear—that such persons cherished the insurance delusion with all the hopeful tenderness of an old hen for her brood of young owls will be to the Coming Man a phenomenon imperfectly assailable by the mordant fluids of his poor dyspeptic brain.

Insurance and Crime

MY ESTEEMED COLLABORATOR, Mr. Edgar Saltus,[3] is persuaded that the gentlemen who make a profession of killing girls upon whose lives they hold insurance policies are deficient in culture. That may be true—I do not know—but they are certainly lacking in that delicate consideration for the welfare of others which serves to distinguish the true Christian from the domestic hog. By the way, it is not altogether clear why society should permit its members to gamble on one another's lives. Insurance of any kind is gambling, pure and simple. The life insurance men run gaming houses, where their dupes pay for the privilege of making bets that they will die (for the advantage of certain others) before they have paid as much as the others are to get when they do die. That is, they are encouraged to play against the man who "keeps the table." By way of tempting them to try to beat his game he proves his solvency by showing how rich he has become by playing it. It is possible that the history of folly and rascality can show greater stupidity on one side of a transaction and greater effrontery on the other, but if so the historian must have eked out his facts with his imagination.

All kinds of insurance are essentially the same, and all are temptations to crime. It ought not to be a crime for the owner of insured property to destroy it; that is what the insurer should expect, and he actually does figure on the probability and charge for it in the rate. Every man who has paid a premium for fire insurance on his dwelling has bought the right to burn it down. To do so is a crime, for the law has made it so; but it is a sin for no other reason than that it may imperil the property of others or their lives.

Fire insurance, accident insurance and so forth, may reasonably enough, and consistently enough, be tolerated by a State which permits open gambling on the price of stocks, on the speed of horses, the power of business and the popularity of political candidates; but this betting on the length of human lives is a serious matter. It is a game in which "the man who keeps the table" should be translated to the penitentiary forthwith. And that would indubitably be his fate if he had not so veiled his business with sophistical deceits and complicated details and so smothered it in lying figures as to hide its real character. In Heaven lives will not be insured; not because they will be everlasting, but because the life insurance men will not be there. In the other place, by the way, there will be awkward meetings between some of the reverend fire insurance men and their premium paying parishioners.

There is another person whom you and I, dear reader, will be denied the happiness of meeting in the Bright Beyond. That is the chap who cannot be made to understand that it is not good public policy to permit A to make it to B's advantage that C shall die. He may have enough righteousness to qualify him for Heaven, but he has not enough sense. He is better fitted for Kalamazoo!

ADVANCES IN WEAPONRY

Superior Killing

T HE DREAM OF A TIME when the nations shall learn to war no more is a pleasant dream, and an ancient. Countless generations have indulged it, and to countless others, doubtless, it will prove a solace and a benefaction. Yet one may be permitted to doubt if its ultimate realization is to be accomplished by diligent and general application to the task of learning war, as so many worthy folk believe. That every notable advance in the art of destroying human life should be "hailed" by these good people as a step in the direction of universal peace must be accounted a phenomenon entirely creditable to the hearts, if not the heads, of those in whom it is manifest. It shows in them a constitution of mind opposed to bloodshed, for their belief having nothing to do with the facts—being, indeed, utterly inconsistent with them—is obviously an inspiration of the will.

"War," these excellent persons reason, "will at last become so awful that men will no longer engage in it"—happily unconscious of the fact that men's sense of their power to make it awful is precisely the thing which most encourages them to declare it. Another popular promise of peace is seen in the enormous cost of modern armaments and military methods. The shot and cartridge of a heavy gun of to-day costs hundreds of dollars, the gun itself hundreds of thousands. It is at an expense of thousands that a torpedo is discharged, which may or may not wreck a ship worth millions. To secure its safety from the machinations of its wicked neighbors while itself engaged in the arts of peace, a nation of to-day must have an almost inconceivable sum of money invested in military plant alone. It is not of the nature of man to impoverish himself by investments from which he hopes for no return except security in that condition which entails the outlay. Men do not construct expensive machinery and tax themselves poor to keep it in working order without ultimately setting it going. The more of its income a nation has to spend in preparation for war, the more certainly it will go to war. Its means of defense are means of aggression, and the stronger it feels itself to strike for its altars and its fires the more spirited becomes its desire to go across the border to do the striking by upsetting the altars and extinguishing the fires of its neighbors.

But the notion that improved weapons give modern armies and navies an increased killing ability—that the warfare of the future will be a bloodier business than that which we have the happiness to know—is an error which the observant apostle of peace is denied the satisfaction of entertaining. Compare, for example, a naval engagement of to-day with Salamis, Lepanto or Trafalgar.[1] Or, since there have been no comparatively recent sea-fights of such magnitude as those, compare the famous duel between the Monitor and the Merrimac[2] with almost any encounter between the old wooden line-of-battle ships, continued, as was the reprehensible custom, until one or both, with hundreds of dead and wounded, incarnadined the seas by going to the bottom. The thunderous affair between Farragut's fleet and the New Orleans forts, both parties armed with guns of the latest caliber and greatest precision then made—a combat during which every square yard of the principal Confederate fort was torn up by fifteen-inch shells from the mortar boats—resulted in the death of fewer men than a half company of infantry;[3] about such a loss as one of Washington's regiments, armed with flint-lock muskets, with an extreme effective range of eighty yards, might have expected to lose in a preliminary skirmish while getting into position to begin a fight.

In the stubbornest land engagements of our great rebellion, and of the later and more scientific Franco-German and Turko-Russian wars,[4] the proportionate mortality was not nearly so great as in those where "Greek met Greek" hand to hand, or where the Roman with his short sword played at give and take with the naked barbarian or the Roman of another political faith. True, we must make some allowance for exaggeration in the accounts of these ancient affairs, not forgetting Niebuhr's assurance that Roman history is nine parts lying.[5] But as European and American history run it pretty hard in that respect, something, too, may be allowed in accounts of modern battles—particularly where the historian foots up the losses of the side which had not the military advantage of his sympathies.

In actions between forts alone the case is no different. In the memorable first bombardment of Fort Sumter, lasting for more than thirty hours, where hundreds of tons of the heaviest shot and shell then known were exchanged at such short range that nearly all hit their mark, not a man on either side was killed or scratched.[6] Certainly one may discern in such facts as this something to encourage the hope that war may, indeed, eventually go out—that it may be laughed out.

A combat between two hostile forts can, in the nature of things, seldom occur, but one between the permanent works of a besieged army and the temporary ones of the besiegers is about as harmless in respect of actual mortality as those which sometimes occurred between heavily armored knights in the period immediately preceding the abolition of body armor by gunpowder. There was no danger in them unless one of the combatants happened to get himself unhorsed or to stump his toe if already on foot, when, like a turtle on its back, he was at the mercy of even a carl with a bill-hook. Oddly enough, since the absurd fight between the Monitor and the Merrimac, which "revolutionized military naval architecture," there has been no formal encounter between two great ironclads evenly matched; but one can easily conjecture the result. Either they would both withdraw "victorious," as in that instance, or several million dollars' worth of property would be captured or destroyed, along with a paltry handful of officers and mechanics. What momentous events might follow or be stayed by the action is another matter: we are considering only the immediate effect upon human life of those costly agencies which have been invented and perfected with a sole view to its destruction. It has been said that to kill a man in battle a man's weight in lead is required. But if the battle happens to be fought by modern warships or forts, or both, about a hundred tons of iron would seem to be a reasonable allowance for the making of a corpse. If the number of men who have been killed by, say, the British Navy in the last twenty years, and of those who are likely to be killed by it in the next twenty, could be known it would probably be found that the corpses came high—not less than 1,000,000 pounds sterling each. In land fighting the figures are more cheering. What it cost in our war to kill a Confederate soldier is not accurately computable: we don't know exactly how many we had the good luck to kill. But the best estimates are easily accessible, as are the very interesting figures of the national debt at the close of the war. The reader would perhaps rather make his own calculation; it is safe to promise him a surprise.

In the current number of the *Century* magazine is a paper on machine guns and dynamite guns. As might have been expected, it opens with a prediction by a distinguished General of the Union armies that so murderous have warlike weapons become, "the next war will be marked by terrific and fearful slaughter."[7] This is naturally followed by the writer's smug and comfortable assurance that "in the extreme mortality of modern war will be found the only hope that man can have of even a partial cessation of war." If this were so, let us see how it would work. The chronological sequence of events would necessarily (obviously, one would think) be something like this:

1. Murderous perfection of warlike weapons.
2. War marked by terrific and fearful slaughter.
3. Partial cessation of war and disarmament of nations.

4. Stoppage of the manufacture of military weapons, with resulting decay of industries dependent on it; that is to say, decay of the ability to produce them. Diversion of intellectual activity to arts of peace.

5. War no longer capable of being marked by terrific and fearful slaughter.

6. Revival of war.

The machine guns described by the writer in the *Century* are the Gatling, the Gardner and the Maxim. The first can fire 1,200 shots a minute; the last—which is automatic, requiring no assistance after the first discharge—about half as many; but it can fire continuously at this rate 5,000 shots, with such accuracy that the inventor is said to have written his name with bullets on a target 400 yards away, in the dark. All the armies and navies of the world are being equipped with such weapons as these. But does this insure a "terrific and fearful slaughter" in battle— a slaughter at all proportionate to the rapidity and accuracy of the firing? Assuredly not. It implies and necessitates profound modifications in tactical formations and movements—modifications similar in kind (though greater in degree) to those already brought about by the long range repeating rifle and the improved field artillery. Men are not going to march up in masses and be mown down by machinery. If the effective range of these guns is, for example, 1,000 yards tactical maneuvers in the open will be made at a greater distance. Greater use will be made of long range artillery, charged, perhaps, with dynamite shells, to smash the machine guns. But the dynamite shells will themselves (it may be urged) produce frightful slaughter among the infantry supports of the machine guns. Not at all: the troops will adopt a formation of such loose order that the explosion of a dynamite shell will kill no more of them than the explosion of an ordinary shell now does. The storming of fortifications and charges in the open ground may go out of fashion. They have, in fact, been growing more and more infrequent ever since the improvements in range and precision of firearms began. If a man who fought under John Sobieski, Marlborough or the first Napoleon[8] could be haled out of his obliterated grave and shown a battle of to-day with all our murderous weapons in full thunder, he would probably knuckle the leaf-mould out of his eyes and say: "Yes, yes, it is most inspiring!—but where is the enemy?"

It is a fact that in the battle of to-day the soldier seldom gets more than a distant and transitory glimpse of the men whom he is fighting. He is still supplied with the saber if he is "horse," with the bayonet if he is "foot," but the value of these weapons is a purely moral one. When commanded to draw the one or "fix" the other he knows he is expected to advance as far as he dares to go; but he knows, too, if he is not a very raw recruit, that he will never get within sabering or bayoneting distance of his antagonists—who will either break and run away or drop so many of his comrades that he will himself break and run away. In our civil war—and that is very ancient history to the long-range tactician of to-day—it was the writer's fortune to assist at a great number of assaults with bayonet and assaults with saber, but he has never had the gratification to see a half-dozen men, friends or enemies, who had fallen by either the one weapon or the other. Whenever the opposing lines actually met it was the rifle, the carbine, or the revolver that did the work. In these days of "arms of precision" they do not meet. There is reason, too, to suspect that, therefore, they do not "get mad" and execute all the mischief that they are capable of. It is certain that the machine guns will keep their temper under the severest provocation.

It is thus shown by various instances how the murderous effect of modern weapons so confidently relied on by the Peace Society to save human life may be neutralized in all manner of ways. Among these may be mentioned in partial recapitulation: first, the confusing effect of weapons of the same kind, to interfere with their orderly operation; second, weapons less murderous but of superior range, to "knock them out"; third, improvement of the old defenses and invention of new apparatus suggested by the weapons, such as torpedo-nettings for ships; fourth, changes in tactical formations and maneuvers; fifth, absence of the battle-frenzy which comes of personal contact between men visibly bent upon killing one another. The list might be greatly extended, but if enough has been said to pain the prophets of peace—the hailers of "the dawn of a new era"—one object of this imperfect essay may be considered to have been accomplished.

Infumiferous Tacitite

THE REPORT THAT at last an absolutely noiseless and smokeless gunpowder has been compounded by an ingenious chemist at Marseilles should make the heart of the Anarchist leap for joy under his too infrequently laundered shirt; the rest of us can contemplate this signal triumph of human ingenuity with a more subdued elation. Those of us who happen to remember things not recorded in yesterday's newspapers may possibly recall the chorus of gratulation, from scientists and laymen, that followed Nobel's great feat of "wresting from nature" the secret of nitroglycerine, parent of all the terrible "ites" known to the civil and uncivil engineer.[9] Our plaudits would have been less rapturous had we foreseen the future of nitroglycerine as an aid to the understanding in matters industrial and political. Even if we had known no more than that personal association with high explosives would beget a consuming passion for storing them in the oven of the domestic stove the advantages of their invention would have seemed less conspicuous. It is possible that silent and infumiferous gunpowder also may look less charming to the eye of retrospection than it does to that of expectation.

In the soldier's noble calling the new powder will indeed be useful. A battle in which there is no uproar—where little is heard but the curses of the combatants and the shrieks and groans of the luckless—will be vastly more enchanting than the battles which we have the pleasure of knowing now. It will engage sympathetic attention, for these are all human sounds, and the human voice has ever a lively interest for the human ear; whereas the noise of firearms is disagreeable. If the powder is not only noiseless but smokeless it will be possible, too, to get a clearer view of the dead and wounded. Indubitably the use of the new gunpowder will mark a distinct advance in the æsthetics of popular slaughter.

But the use of the Marseilles man's invention will hardly be confined to the military—and thereby hangs a tale. In the hands of gentlemen with conscientious scruples against the existence of organized society it will be less benign and wholesome. In point of power for evil the dynamite bomb of today is almost ludicrously inferior—so inferior as almost to merit attention, from physicians, sanitary engineers and boards of health, as a prophylactic. With a parlor rifle and some cartridges of the new and more discreet explosive an expounder of the principles of Philosophical Anarchy, sitting at an open window and behind a Venetian blind, can spread the light with almost absolute impunity. With a revolver suitably concealed in the side pocket of his coat and fired through the lining he will be able to advance the Cause a long way further than it can be made to go by publications setting forth the ghastly nature of the crime of wage-paying. Seated comfortably in the gallery of a theatre he can, by "the nice conduct of a clouded cane"[10] which happens to be a repeater of large calibre, remove a considerable number of despotic women and tyrannous children before the survivors will begin to suspect him of a tendency to amelioration of the lot of the poor. In short, an Anarchist having that quality and degree of intelligence sometimes designated as "knowing enough to go in when it rains"—if such Anarchists there are—need never lack safe opportunity to utilize the new compound by making the world better and less populous.

Doubtless the gory capitalist and his hirelings will make laws declaring possession of firearms a felony, and set up a regime of domiciliary visitation, but in all that they are fore-doomed to failure, for in even the most despotic countries of Europe it has been found impossible to prevent the manufacture, possession and transportation of dynamite bombs; and dynamite bombs are used for un-lawful purposes only. In the case of firearms the difficulty will be enormously enhanced by the necessity of having them in great numbers for the purpose of killing the men of other countries. Arsenals will leak, and persons skilled in making firearms for the Government will suffer themselves to be lured away, and in lonely places set up business for themselves as gunsmithing moonshiners.

The interesting outcome of all this, in so far as one may forecast it, will be a state of things in which a person will feel secure of his life in the ratio of the square of the distance between him and the nearest other man—a condition imperfectly conducive to any form of civilization with which we of this era are connusant.[11] Evidently the civilization of the future is not to be a gregari-ous one. Instead of populous cities and smiling farms heavily mortgaged, we shall have vast wooded solitudes with here and there an Anarchist stealthily skulking through the darkest thickets or roosting in a tree-top to make a prudent circumspection of his environment. But amid the wreck of his fac-ulties and accomplishments this simianescent arborean, hugging his rusty rifle, will cherish with pious assiduity the art of making noiseless and smoke-less gunpowder wherewith to spread the light and advance the Cause.

TRAVEL BY AIR

"Fly, Good Fleance, Fly!"

THE *COSMOPOLITAN* MAGAZINE has undertaken to "solve the problem" of aërial navigation—not by flying away, we are glad to know, but by encouraging various solitary "inventors" to pull together.[1] There should be no great difficulty in accomplishing the desired result; everything that is needful to practical success has already, and for long, been invented and attainable. Every one who has given intelligent attention to the matter must see clearly enough in what direction success is to be sought with a reasonable hope of attainment. Attainment is as good as assured, though the beautiful stories about dirigible airships which were lately seen hovering at great heights above the Russian frontier, and, their observation completed, sailing calmly back into Upper Germany were undoubtedly works of fiction which owed nothing to the school of realism.

The airship of the future will be an aëroplane with or without subsidiary lifting power, or rather artificial levity. With a correct adjustment of planes, horizontal with reference to the direction which is at a right angle to that of the ship's progress, and having variable "upslant" forward, nothing is needed for flight but a sufficient power to produce a sufficient speed, a plain ordinary rudder and a center-board to keep the craft from careening. The rarity of the "medium" in which the ship floats, or, more accurately, in which it is submerged, is both a disadvantage and an advantage: it affords less push to the propelling apparatus, but it interposes less resistance to propulsion.

Dr. Samuel Johnson wrote Rasselas a good many years ago, but it was from no faulty understanding of the "problem" that he explained in that charming work that the solution was a matter of renewing impulses upon the air faster than the air could escape from them.[2] The screw-propeller had not then been invented, but the screw-propellee had been, and was in action on every windmill. The air in motion renews its impulses on the wings of the windmill faster than the wings can escape them—that is how they work. Reverse the situation, turn them by power in a calm, and—tit for tat!—the air cannot escape and offers a winghold. With power enough and strength enough of material the windmill would be pushed away from the air and overturned. It is to the principle of the screw-propeller—that is to say, of the windmill, that we are to owe our success in navigating the air. Study of the wings of birds is all wasted; ship-builders might as profitably study the tails of the fishes.

It is a question of speed, which is a question of power, which is a question of expense. With every increase of speed the air becomes denser—denser under the planes, against the rudder and against the center-board: that is, it gives better support, greater steadiness and easier direction—for difficulty of deflecting the rudder means ease of deflecting the ship.

This increase of density by increase of speed has recently been aptly illustrated by the example of a man skating on thin ice. At a low rate of speed he breaks through; at a high one passes safely over, rejoicing. Let us suppose our airship, made light by a gasholder, moving at a rate of 100 feet per second, and just supported by the air. The supporting power of the air at that speed of the ship we will call 10; and in as much as it and the weight of the ship, with its machinery and crew, are equal, we will call that 10 also. But let us now suppose the engineer to "pull her wide open." The ship now travels at the rate of 500 feet a second—five times her normal speed. The effect is the same as if the 500 feet of air had been compressed into 100 feet: it is, so to speak, five times as dense—its supporting power has been multiplied by five and is now 50. But the weight of the ship, with her machinery and crew, remains the same—10. That means that at the new speed she could carry four times her own weight and load, in freight and passengers—40; or, discarding her gasholder, 40 *plus* the weight of the gasholder, *minus* the lifting power of the gas. These figures are purely arbitrary: their value is in their proportional relation; and it is thought they illustrate with simple lucidity the point that aërial navigation is merely a question of power—of speed. Given sufficient speed the weight of the ship does not matter; one made of lead would fly, precisely as a long iron chain may be dragged on the surface of the water.

But the lighter the ship, within certain limits (it must not be lighter than the air), the less power is required, for the less speed is required. With what we have learned in the manufacture of bicycles of how to combine lightness and strength and minimize friction, and with aluminum for frame and engines at one dollar a pound, it is not only possible but easily practicable to construct an airship that will go. We do not suffer ourselves to doubt that the press, represented by the *Cosmopolitan* magazine, having turned its attention to the matter, we shall soon be careering through "the illimitable inane"[3] in vessels that will look as amazingly crude to posterity as the first steamboat and railway train look now to the old chaps who as boys assisted at their performances by throwing stones at them.

The Man and the Bird

PROFESSOR LANGLEY, the distinguished scientist—all scientists are distinguished—scorns delights and lives laborious days in the study of the flight of birds. His notion is that he can steal their secret and make use of it in a flying machine. The professor has already made a flying machine which flew, but it resembled a bird mainly in not carrying passengers and freight.

There are two types of "air-ship," the flying machine and the dirigible balloon. The former is good for nothing; the latter can be made to carry a man, and will go where he wants it to if he is good. The difference is worth remarking, slight as it is, for it marks a difference in study-methods. Inventors of the flying machines study the flight of birds; those of the dirigible balloon do not. M. Santos-Dumont probably cannot tell a hawk from a handsaw.[4] That is why he can fly.

It should have been clear that nothing was to be got from a study of birds. By reasoning from analogy one should have known that. If in evolving the locomotive engine Stephenson[5] had addressed himself to the study of the movements of animals he would probably have invented some most ingenious engine running upon jointed legs with several experimental kinds of feet, but not an inch would they have budged. If only nature's crude and clumsy methods of locomotion had been studied, the automobile, the railway engine, even the primitive cart, would remain uninvented. The master genius who invented the wheel so far surpassed nature that none of her work is entitled to honorable mention in comparison. He was the founder of civilization.

Suppose the steamship had to be invented de novo—invented, not evolved. Doubtless the gentleman charged with the task would make a study of the aquatic bird, the duck. The swimming duck is partly submerged—is in the water and in the air. It is propelled by its own power, with or against the wind. These are the conditions and powers that he proposes to reproduce in his steamship. How natural that he study the duck, particularly its means of propulsion. So he did—and produced the canoe and its paddle. Now that the duck is forgotten, we have the steamship and its screw propeller.

In submarine navigation the "lessons of nature" have been profitably disregarded; the submarine boat is nothing like a fish. It does not balance itself with fins, nor move forward by wiggling its tail. It hasn't any tail. All that the flexible tail of the fish has taught us is how to scull a boat, the least effective form of propulsion.

All this ought to show Professor Langley that in studying the flight of birds he is "barking up the wrong tree." After many years of that study we have as a result the aëroplane, between whose fixed and disobedient rigidity and the infinitely delicate adjustibility and activity of the bird's wing there is a barely traceable likeness.

He is a hardy and impenitent sceptic who dares to doubt that we shall have the flying machine, as distinguished from the dirigible balloon; but in all probability the man who first successfully navigates one of his own devising will be a person who knows something of the properties of atmospheric air, a good deal of mechanics and very little about birds.

DOGS AND HORSES

The Struggle between Man and Dog

FROM THE CONGRESSIONAL RECORD of May 28 I quote the significant passage here following:

"The presiding officer laid before the Senate the amendment of the House of Representatives to the bill (S. 4792) relative to the control of dogs in the District of Columbia; which was referred to the Committee on the District of Columbia."

So it appears that both houses of Congress are pleased to entertain the conviction that the dog, as we have the distinction to know him in the District of Columbia, is vincible to the power and suasion of authority. Nothing could better illustrate the evils of "rotation in office": the continually changing personnel of Congress prevents the ordinary United States Senator or Representative from becoming really well acquainted with the District dog. If he had the advantage of knowing that unique creation as intimately as a long residence at the national capital would enable him to do, he would eschew the error that control is a feasible proposal.

The District dog is not easy to get acquainted with. He is not affable; his disposition is morose, his favor uncertain and variable as the shade by the light, quivering aspen made. He is, however, uniformly demented and consistently anthropophagous—facts which conspire to augment the sum of human apprehension, for his bite, always imminent, is of a wholesomeness inferior to that of the rattlesnake. Persons who have been bitten by both were bitten by the rattlesnake first. That sufficiently signifies their choice.

Many vain attempts have been made to "control" the bite of the District of Columbia dog by muzzling the creature, but the plan has always failed through not commending itself to the rudimentary sense of right and wrong implanted by nature in owners of dogs. These excellent persons hold that the only proper and constitutional protection from the District dog is to keep a District dog. The animal's unappeasable antipathy to his kind draws around his owner a zone of security impaired only by the guardian's occasional absence, when breaking into unguarded zones of the dogless.

The District dog is destitute of both affection and gratitude. True, he fawns upon his master, who is proud of the attention, or tolerates with studied patience the caresses of his mistress; but that is because he has the intelligence of his appetite to discern the source of his victual. His sentiments toward that useful person are those of a whale toward the scum of the sea.

In the bright lexicon of the District dog there's no such word as quail. He exults in a hardy and impenitent effrontery that serves him in place of a religion and the cardinal virtues. He knows his high place in the social hierarchy—knows that the hands which cast down the mighty Spaniard from his seat and exalted the Cuban of low degree[1] are powerless to abate his prevalence and his dominance in the nation's capital. Congress can do much. It can alter the map of the world and frame it differently. It can connect the Gulf of Mexico and the Pacific Ocean with a flow of words. It can forbid the sale of liquor in the capital and repeat the edifying performance at the close of every session. It can correct the military record of a deserter in the Civil War and honorably discharge him from an army to which he has not belonged for forty years. But it cannot cause but one District dog to grow where two grew before, nor contract their sphere of influence by so much as a hand's breadth. It cannot deprive them of life, liberty and the pursuit of the cycler. In his immemorial dispute with the moon, Congress is unable to compel the District dog to observe the decencies of debate and give the other side a chance to be heard, and cannot excise from his general conduct any particular vulgarity.

Basking in the sense of his ancestral utility and strong in modern Man's hereditary favor, this incarnate anachronism, this curled darling of the centuries, this sacrosanct survival and superfluous immune, views with a languid interest and slack attention the pigmy efforts at his "control" by legislation.

If it be urged that all this is as true of any other dog as that of the District of Columbia, I will have the candor to confess that it is open to that fatal objection.

The Future of the Horse and the Horse of the Future

CERTAIN ADMIRERS OF the useful, beautiful, dangerous and senseless beast known to many of them as the "hoss," are promising the creature a life of elegant leisure, with opportunities for mental culture which he has not heretofore enjoyed. Universal use of the automobile in all its actual and possible forms and for all practical purposes in the world's work and pleasure is to relieve the horse from his onerous service and give him a life of ease "and a perpetual feast of nectared sweets."[2]

The horse of the future is to do no work, have no cares, be immune to the whip, the saddle, the harness and the unwelcome attentions of the farrier. He is to toil not, neither spin, yet Nebuchadnezzar in all his glory was not stabled and pastured as he is to be.[3] In brief, the automobile is going to make of this bad world a horse Elysium where the tired brute can repose on beds of amaranth and moly,[4] to the eminent satisfaction of his body and his mind.

There is reason to fear that all these hopes will not come to fruitage. It is not seen just why a generation of selfish and somewhat preoccupied human beings, who know not the horse as an animal of utility, should cherish him as a creature of merit. We have already one pensioner on our bounty who does little that is useful in return for his keep, and an incalculable multitude of things which we would prefer that he should not do if he could be persuaded to forego them—the domestic dog, to wit. We are not likely to augment our burden by addition of the obsolete horse. Those of us who, through stress of necessity or the promptings of Paris, have tested our teeth upon him know that he is not very good to eat; he will hardly be cultivated for the table, like the otherwise inutile and altogether unhandsome pig. The present vogue of the horse as a comestible, a viand, is without the knowledge and assent of the consumer, but an abbatoir having its outlying corrals gorged with waiting horses would be an object of public suspicion and constabular inquiry. As a provision against human hunger the horse may be considered out of the running and off the board. Hard indeed were the heart of the father who would regale the returning prodigal with a fatted colt.

There will be no horses in our "leisure class," for there will be no horses. The species will be as effectually effaced by the automobile as if it had run over them. If the new machine fulfills all the hopes that now begin to cluster about it the man of the future will find a deal of our literature and art unintelligible. To him the equestrian statue, for example, will be an even more astonishing phenomenon than it commonly is to us.

There is a suggestion in all this to our good and great friends, the vegetarians. They do not easily tire of pointing out the brutality of slaughtering animals to get their meat, although it is not obvious that we could eat them alive. We should breed some of these edible creatures anyhow, for they serve other needs than those of appetite; but others, like the late Belgian hare, who virtually passed away as soon as the breeders and dealers failed to convince us that we were eating him, would become extinct. Many millions of meat-bearing animals owe whatever of life we grant them to the fact that we mean eventually to deprive them of it. Seeing that they are so soon to be "done for," they may not understand why they were "begun for;" but if life is a blessing, as most of us believe and themselves seem to believe, for they manifest a certain reluctance to give it up, why, even a short life is a thing to be thankful for. If we had not intended to kill them they would not have lived at all.

From this superior point of view even the royal sport of slaughtering such preserved game as the English pheasant seems a trifle less brutal than it is commonly affirmed to be by those of us who are not invited to the killing. This argument, too, has an obvious application in the instance of that worthy Russian sect that denies the right of man to enslave horses, oxen, and so forth. But for man's fell purpose of enslaving them there would be none.

And what about the American negro? Had it not been for the cruel greed of certain Southern planters and Yankee skippers, where would he be? Would he be anywhere? So we see how all things work together for the general good, and evil itself is a blessing in disguise. No African slavery, no American negro; no American negro, no Senator Hanna's picturesque bill to pension his surviving ancestors.[5] And without that we should indubitably be denied the glittering hope of a similar bill pensioning the entire race.

TEMPERANCE

Prohibition

PROHIBITION [. . .] is peculiarly unfortunate in the character, not only of some of its advocates, but in that of some of its methods. For example, in the August number of the *North American Review* are six luminations on the subject, by six of the pillars of fire directing the night march of the cause.[1] They are all "down upon" license—high or low—because it is a legal "recognition" of the liquor trade. As reasonably they might condemn fines for misdemeanor for legally "recognizing" misdemeanor. Until the liquor trade is forbidden it is legally recognized, whether licensed or not; by being made to pay a license fee, even an exceptionally high one, the dealer does not acquire, and is not thought to acquire, any additional right or privileges that he had not before. Misled by the dictionary definition of a word, these people go groping. Why cannot they accustom themselves to think, and teach their followers to think, of a license fee as a fine? They do not deny that high license abates the evils of intemperance; understood as what in fact it is, a fine, it would have to them the additional advantage of casting a public reproach upon the business. I am not loaded down with controversial weapons for the fray between liquor and water; I love neither the one fluid nor the other; but I enjoy the quarrels of others, am enamored of effective means in battle and should be miserable if I had failed to point out to any combatant in any contention how he could obtain an honest advantage.

Do I not drink water? Yes, dear, a little—when instigated by thirst. Does any one drink it under any other circumstances? Does any one drink it because he likes it?—or rather, does any one like it when not suffering from a most disagreeable disorder? We take water as medicine for the disease thirst. It is to be considered as a remedial agent—so vilely adulterated in nature's laboratory and so distasteful to the normal palate that the world in all ages has been practically united in avoiding it. Nothing has so stimulated human ingenuity and invited such heavy investments as the discovery, invention and manufacture of palatable substitutes for water; and nothing could be more unphilosophical than to attribute this universal movement to perversity or caprice. Extravagant as are some of its manifestations, deplorable as are some of its consequences, back of it all, as back of every wide and persistent trend of human activity, is some imperious and unsleeping necessity. Does Prohibition really know the character and power of its antagonist? In my poor judgment, their only hope of beating the Rum Fiend lies in letting him alone to perish of inanition when they shall have reformed the Water Fiend. Their only effective weapon is the filter. Prohibit impure water, and the distillery and the Prohibitionist can alike shut up.

Consider, if you will be so good, what "drinking-water" has the distinction to be. It is the world's sewage. It is what that dirty boy, the earth, has washed his face with. The springs and wells and river sand rills are nature's slop-buckets. It is nasty unspeakably, holding in suspension the ordure of the living, the bodies of the dead. It is the solution of abomination. It is macerated man. It is hydrate of dead dog. It is impested with germs of nameless plagues, infested with ferocious anthropophagi and loaded with poisonous minerals. Age is simply a disease caused by cumulative deposits of lime and other mineral matter in all the organs of the body; and 90 per cent of them are taken as water. If our drink were free of mineral matter and depeopled of its reptiles, we should live a thousand years and die of the minerals and reptiles in our food—if our cooks would have the forbearance to give us time enough for the charm to work.

This insufferable stuff—this liquid death—this undistilled and unfiltered "wotter," they tell us, is "the natural drink of man." We drink it from poverty, from ignorance, from hereditary habit bequeathed us by barbarian ancestors who had nothing else nor sense enough to grow the sacred vine. They ate beetles, too, and stinking fish and one another. Were these the natural food of man? Man has no natural food and drink; he takes what he can get. An infant race is like an individual: whatever it can lay its clumsy hands on goes into its dauby mouth. Water, *pure* water, has one merit—it is cheap; and one disadvantage—it is not good.

The Nations That Drink Too Much

THAT VERY SENSIBLE GENTLEMAN, Bishop Potter,[2] recently got himself into water too hot to hold him by saying a few temperate words of excuse for poor hardworking men who sometimes take too much of what is not always good for them. From the viewpoint of the sleek and well nourished Prohibitionist nothing looks easier than total abstention from liquor. Finding no difficulty in avoidance of drink himself he is pained and a bit surprised to dis-cover in his precept and example an inefficacy for which he cannot account otherwise than by the power of a habit carelessly acquired. Against this habit he naturally invokes the force of law, but with no better result.

One would think that after so many centuries of failure the worthy and well meaning proponents of total abstinence would begin to suspect the existence of an overlooked factor in the problem. At the back of the drink-ing habit is there not some constant force to which it is due—some natural necessity that created it?

Let us consider certain customs, which are habits of the people. Those which have nothing behind them but whims and caprices do not persist, fashions in dress, for example. Clothing is a necessity, so all wear clothing. But any particular fashion in clothing is not a necessity; so nothing is more variable than fashion. Our women will wear wide sleeves one year and nar-row the next, for there is no reason why sleeves should be either wide or narrow; but all wear sleeves to keep their arms warm.

Recreation is necessary to health; we all play games. But as it does not greatly matter what kind of a game we play, so that it exercises the body and the mind, we run to baseball in one decade, to cycling in another; golf succeeds lawn tennis and from golf many turn to ping-pong. Twenty years ago billiards was far more popular than now. In the next century the favorite sports of to-day may be forgotten. If any persist they will be those which in a special and particular way minister to some constant and natural need.

All peoples in all ages have used intoxicants, even those whose religions forbade. Probably there is no one thing upon which so much human inge-nuity has been expended as invention of alcoholic substitutes for water, which we are told is our "natural" drink. We never drink water because we like it, as we do wine, coffee and half a score of other beverages. We take it only as a handy medicine for the recurrent disorder known as thirst. When thirsty we like it, as we like almost anything that is wet; and it is cheap, accessible and abundant.

Have these large facts no meaning? It is most unscientific to think so. I venture to believe that they have a profound and important one, to the discovery and understanding of which the friends and proponents of tem-perance might more advantageously address themselves than to reclamation that does not reclaim and prohibition that does not prohibit. If it is true that in the human system is a natural *demand* for alcohol it is none the less, but all the more, true that alcohol is a dangerous food, and all the current, imme-morial dissuasions from excessive use remain in full force and effect. To recognize the real character and power of an enemy is not a disadvantage, but an advantage. Convinced of his invincibility to heroic measures for his destruction we shall the more intelligently devise some homely, practical means to control him.

I know not what value and significance there may be in the fact that the dominant races and nations are hard drinkers, but it is indubitably true. The abstemious Mahometan goes down like grass before the scythe when pitted against the gluttonous Christian. A hundred thousand beef-eating and brandy-drinking Englishmen hold in subjection three hundred million vegetarian abstainers of the same Aryan race in India. With what an easy grace the whisky-loving American pushed the temperate Spaniard out of Cuba. The vodka-sodden Tartar who calls himself a Russian has a "picnic" in Manchuria, which drinks tea.

Everywhere it may be observed that the nations which drink too much fight rather well and not always righteously. Possibly their hard drinking and hard fighting have nothing to do with each other. One would wish to know that they have no other than an accidental coexistence. Even if their relation were seen to be that of cause and effect the estimable ladies of both sexes who abolished the army canteen in the interest of abstract temperance will hardly call themselves to repentance for crippling the military strength of their country. Some observers will think that they have conspicuously augmented it.

REFLECTIONS ON THE FUTURE

Will the Coming Man Sleep?

IT IS HARDLY a "burning question"; it is not even a "problem that presses for solution." Nevertheless, to minds not incurious as to the future it has a mild, pleasing interest, like that of the faintly heard beating of the bells of distant cows, that will come in and demand attention later.

It by no means appears that sleep is a natural function, the necessity of which inheres in animal life and the constitution of things; there is much reason to regard it as a phenomenon due rather to stress of circumstances—a kind of intermittent disorder incurred by exposure to conditions that are being slowly but surely removed. Precisely as sanitary and medical science and improved methods of living are gradually extending the average length of human life in every civilized country and threatening the king of shadows himself with death ere, in the poet's sense, "Time shall throw a dart"[1] at him, so we may observe already the initial stages of a successful campaign against "his brother Sleep."[2] Civilized people sleep fewer hours than savage ones, and the dwellers in cities fewer than the country folk. The reason is not far to seek: it is a matter of light.

Primitive Man, like the savages of to-day, had at night no other light than that of the moon and that of wood fires. For countless ages our ancestors lived without candles, and when they had learned the trick of burning rushes soaked in the fat of neighboring tribesmen their condition was not greatly better. Beyond Primitive Man we may venture to survey *his* ancestors—unmentionable to ears un-Darwinized—who lived for ages even more hopelessly countless with no artificial light at all. In the darkness of the night (and, in the case of the remoter progenitors, always that of the forest) what could these ancient worthies do. They had little enough to do at any time, but even their rudest occupations could not be pursued in darkness. They simply did nothing, and naturally assumed the most comfortable posture in which to accomplish it, the earlier sort suspending themselves by their tails, the later lying down as we do at present, having no tails. It is a law of nature that the moment any organ or member of the body is at rest a kind of torpor ensues. The blood circulates with a more feeble flow, molecular changes take place with less activity—in short, it begins to die, and can be restored to full life only by a renewal of use. With continued inaction it dies altogether. In the case of the brain this torpor means unconsciousness—that is to say, sleep. To put the matter briefly, darkness compelled inaction, inaction begot sleep.

Another law of nature—a rather comical one, by the way—is that acts which we do regularly, from necessity or choice, set up a tendency in us to do them involuntarily when we don't care to and when the original necessity has been replaced by this new and equally imperative one to which, in both its mental and its physical aspect, we give the name of habit. And by still another law of nature (the term is used here only to denote a universally recurrent phenomenon) habit in both its aspects is hereditary. Because for millions of generations our "rude forefathers,"[3] unable by reason of darkness to indulge during the whole twenty-four hours in the one-sided pleasures of the chase and the mutual delight of braining one another in tribal wars, had to go to sleep, *we* have to go to sleep, although we have (by paying roundly for it) plenty of light to make ourselves objectionable in an infinite variety of ways, both entertaining and profitable.

But little by little we are overcoming the sleep habit without loss of health, if not with positive sanitary advantage. As above mentioned, the people of our lighted cities sleep less than the rural population, and this less than it did before the improvement in lamps. And nothing is more certain, despite popular opinion to the contrary, than that the men of cities are superior in strength and endurance to those of the country, as is abundantly attested by army life, in camp and field. That this is wholly or even greatly due to their nocturnal activity is not affirmed; only that their addiction to the joys of insomnia has not appreciably counteracted the sanitary advantages of city life—amongst which we are tempted by the casting of the physicians to give an honorable prominence to defective drainage, sewer gas and drinking-water that is largely solution of dog and hydrate of wronged husband.

The electric light has apparently come to stay, but more likely it will in good time be replaced by something that so far exceeds it as it beats the hallowed tallow candle of our grandmothers. Not only will the streets and shops and dwellings of our cities be illuminated all night with a splendor of which we can have hardly a conception, but the country districts as well; for it is now known that plants (which apparently are not creatures of habit) do not need sleep, and that by continuous light the profits of agriculture could be enormously increased. The farmers will no longer retire with the lark, but will work night shifts, as is already done in factories and mines, and eventually work all the time, as most of them would be glad to do now in order to support the rest of us in the style to which we have been accustomed.

On the whole, we think it not unreasonable to look forward with pleasant anticipation to a time, some millions of years hence, when the literature of sleep will be no longer intelligible and the people of even this country be sufficiently wide awake to prevent the ten per cent of their number devoted to patriotic pursuits from plundering the other ninety per cent and to make the Judges obey the laws.

The Decay of the Nose

A GERMAN PHYSICIAN of some note has given it out as his solemn conviction that civilized man is gradually but surely losing the sense of smell through disuse. It is a well-known fact that savages have keener noses than we; which is well for them, for we have a dozen "well-defined and several" bad odors to their one—and this is not written figuratively, with reference to methods of political thrift. It is possible, indeed, that it is to the alarming prevalence of bad odors that our olfactory inferiority is in some degree due: civilized man's habit of holding his nose has begotten in that organ an obedient habit of holding itself. This, by the way, leaves both his hands free to hold his tongue, but as a rule he prefers to make another and less pleasing use of them. Having a nose dowered with primitive activity, civilized man would find it difficult to retain his supremacy over the forces of nature; the assassinating odors evolved from the industries and conditions accompanying, and in part constituting, it would engage him in a new "struggle for existence," incomparably more arduous than any of which he has present experience. And herein we get an intimation of a hitherto unsuspected cause of the rapid decadence of savage peoples when brought into contact with civilization. Various causes, doubtless, are concerned, but the slaughter house, the glue factory, the gas main, the sewer, the person of the silurian and the other sources of exhalations which "rise like the steam of rich-distilled perfumes"[4] (which in no other respect they resemble) are the actual culprits. Unprepared with a means of defense at the point where he is most accessible to assault, the reclaimed savage falls into a decline and, accepting the Christian religion for what he conceives it to be worth, turns his nose to the wall and dies in the secret hope of an inodorous eternity.

With the effacement of the sense of smell we shall doubtless lose the feature which serves as intake to what it feeds upon; and that will in many ways be an advantage. It will, for example, put a new difficulty in the way of that disagree-able person, the caricaturist—rather it will shear him of much of his present power. The fellow never tires of furnishing the rest of us forth incredibly snouted in an infinite variety of wicked ways. When noses are no more, caricature will have stilled some of its thunder, and we can all venture to be eminent.

To art, the effacement of the nose—the wiping it out, so to say—will be of inestimable benefit. In statuary, for example, we shall be able to hurl a qualified defiance of Time, the iconoclast, who now hastens to assail our carven cherished images in that most vulnerable part, the nose, tweaking it off and throwing it away almost before the sculptor's nose of flesh is blue and cold beneath the daisies. In the statue of the future there will be no nose, consequently no damage to it; and although the statue may when new and perfect differ but little from the mutilated antiques that we now have, there will be a certain satisfaction in knowing that it has not been "retouched." In the case of portrait statues and busts the advantage is obvious. When the nose goes the likeness goes with it, but where there has never been a nose its absence is not likely to be felt as a calamity.

Perhaps the best effect of all will be felt in literature. To the scribbling physi-ognomist—that capital bore of letters—the nose is almost as necessary as to the caricaturist. He is never done finding strength of mind and spirit in large noses, though the small ones of Gibbon and Gortschakoff[5] "shrieked against his creed,"[6] and intellectual feebleness in "snubs," though Cicero's was the snubbiest of all antiquity. Socrates had a nose—a veritable snout it was—which a famous physi-ognomist of his day pronounced the outward and visible sign of a bestial parent-age and denoting all the cardinal vices. When there are no noses the physiogno-mist can base no theories on them. It would be worth something to live long enough to be rid of even a part of his gabble.

But is it true that the sense of smell, and with it the nose, is doomed to extinction? As to that we are not prepared to say; the evidence is not all in. Moreover, the conditions under which we live may so alter that the sense of smell may be again advantageous in the "struggle for existence," and by the survival of those in whom it is keenest regain its pristine place in our meager equipment of powers and capacities. But philosophers to whom millstones are translucent will deem it significant that the sense in question and the facial feature devoted to its service have fallen into something of the disre-pute that foretokens deposal. It is now hardly polite to speak of smells and smelling, without the use of softened language, and the nose is frequently subjected to contumelious and jocose remark unwarranted by anything in its personal appearance or the nature of its pursuits. It is as if man had with-drawn his lip service from the nasal setting sun.

The Head of the Future

THAT THE HUMAN RACE will some day lack noses and the sense of smell is a scientific deduction which it was our privilege to discuss in these columns a few weeks ago with such earnestness as its gravity seemed to demand. Now comes a celebrated German physician named Muller (the German who is not named Muller has had a narrow escape) and signifies his conviction that the Coming Man will be not only noseless but hairless as well. Dr. Muller points out the increasing prevalence of baldness and declares it hereditary. That many human beings are born partly bald is not, we take it, what he means, but that the tendency to lose the hair early in life is transmitted from father to son. It is understood that the ladies have nothing to do with the matter; they are never bald, but the hair of none of them, we understand, is as long and thick as it once was.

It is easily seen that in our modern civilization the human hair is not an advantage in the "struggle for existence." It is not now, as in the time of Samson, a reservoir of strength; so the man addicted to arduous employment has but scant need of it. In some of the industries and professions the man who is somewhat profanely said to part his hair with a towel has a better chance than the man who has more hair than can be conveniently so parted. Gentlemen who keep intelligence offices affirm the superior attractions of the bald to those wishing to engage bank presidents; and in the vocation of presiding at public meetings a nude head is a precious possession, enabling the person wearing it to "distance all competitors" not similarly gifted. As a qualification for the Bench (with which, singularly enough, it never comes into contact) it is of the first importance. No church congregation clothed and in its right mind would hesitate a moment in passing upon the rival claims of two applicants for the pastorate, one bald and the other not, but in all other things equal: it would "call" the bald one forthwith, consoling the dissentient ewes of the flock by conceding them a curled darling to "preside" at the organ. It would be easy, in short, to mention a hundred employments in which gentlemen having the gift of little hair are distinctly the fittest to survive. Snugly entrenched in profitable place, they naturally outlive their hirsute competitors, leaving more progeny than they; and the progeny born to baldness as a heritage will eventually overrun the land.

It is difficult to offset these facts with facts of an opposite sort. Cowboys and artists—sometimes poets—are found with long hair, but long hair is not thought to be an advantage to them, if, indeed, any hair at all is. For wiping the bowie knife, the paint-brush or the pen, hair, no doubt, is useful, but hardly more so than the coat-sleeve, and for wiping the nose obviously inferior. Even in these instances, then, where at first thought there might seem to be a relation of cause and effect between length of hair and length of life, the appearance is fallacious. A bald-headed cowboy would, indeed, be less liable to scalping by the Red Man.

It appears, then, that Dr. Muller's cheerful prediction regarding the heads of Posterity rests upon a foundation of facts. Those herein given are not adduced by him but presented to him, to go with those of his own invention which we forbear to name, as they are mostly of German origin and import and it is not with the head of the Coming German that we are mainly concerned. Moreover, some of the doctor's arguments seem to us erroneous. For example, he thinks the masculine fashion of cutting off the hair an evidence that men instinctively know hair to be injurious—that is to say, a disadvantage in "the struggle for existence." This we cannot admit—it does not follow, for testators have a fashion of cutting off heirs-expectant; yet heirs-expectant are not injurious—until known to be cut off, and then the testator's struggle for existence is commonly finished. Capitalists have a fashion of cutting off coupons; it hardly needs to be pointed out that coupons are not amongst the malign influences tending to the shortening of life. We have tried (with some success we hope) to show that hair is a disadvantage, but this view derives no support from the scissors. If the hair of men were obviously, conspicuously beneficial; if it made them healthy, wealthy and as wise as they care to be; if they needed it in their business; if they could not at all get on without it—they would doubtless cut it a little oftener than they do now. Men are that way.

Dr. Muller, we observe with joy, adds to those already on file a fresh conjecture as to the cause of baldness in men—aside from heredity. It is not important what his conjecture is; the truth of the matter is plain enough. Men become bald because they keep cutting their hair. Every man has a certain amount of capillary energy, so to say. He can produce such a length of hair and no more, as the spider can spin only so much web and then must cease to be a spinster. By cutting the hair it is kept exhausting its allowance of energy by growth; when all is gone growth stops and the roots, having no longer a function, decay. By letting their hair alone women retain it. The difference is that between two coils of rope, equal in length, one of which is constantly "payed out," the other not. If this explanation does not compose the immemorial quarrel about the cause of men's baldness the prospect of its composure by that phenomenon's universality will be hailed with delight by all who love a quiet life. The first generation to forget that men ever had hair will be the first to know the happiness of peace; the succeeding one will begin a dispute about the cause of hair in woman.

Some Trivial Privations of the Coming Man

IT IS NOW well understood, even outside of "scientific circles," that the in-compatibility of civilization and the human nose is more than a golden dream of the optimist. Indubitably that once indispensable organ is falling into the sere and yellow leaf of disuse and in the course of a few thousand generations will have been wiped off the face of the earth. Its utility as an organ of sense decreases year by year—except as a support for the kind of eyeglasses bearing its name; not a sufficiently important service to warrant nature in preserving it. The final effacement of the nose has been foreseen from the earliest dawn of art. The ancient Grecian sculptors, for example, who were great trimmers and ever so-licitous to know which way the physiognomical cat would jump, tried to repre-sent the human face of the future rather than that of their period; and it is noticeable that most of their statues and busts are distinguished by a striking lack of nose. That is justly regarded as a most significant circumstance—a prophecy of the conclusion now reached by modern science working along other lines. The Coming Man is to be noseless—that is settled; and there are not wanting those who support with enthusiasm the hypothesis that he is to be hairless as well.

It is to be observed that these two effects, effacement of the human nose and obliteration of the human hair, are to be brought about differently—at least the main agency in the one case is different from that in the other. The nose is departing from among us because of its high sense of duty. Most of the odors of civilization being distinctly disagreeable, and in the selection of our food chemical analysis having taken the place of olfactory investigation, there is little for the modern nose to do that the modern nose-owner is willing to have done. One of the most useful of all our natural endowments is what we may venture to call the conscience of the organs. None of the bodily organs is willing to be maintained in a state of idleness and depen-dence—to eat the bread of charity, so to speak. Whenever for any cause one of them is put upon the retired list and deprived of its functions and just influence in the physical economy it begins to withdraw from the scheme of things by atrophy. It withers away, and the place that knew it knows it no more forever. That is what is occurring in the instance of the human nose. We make very little use of it in testing our food—it has, in truth, lost its cunning in that way—in tracking our game, or in taking note of a windward enemy; albeit to most of the enemies of the race the nose is almost as good an annunciator as the organ which they more consciously address. So the idle nose is leaving us more in sorrow than anger, let us hope.

With the hair the case is different. It goes, not merely because its mandate is exhausted, but because it is really detrimental to us in the struggle for existence. Its departure is an instance, pure and simple, of the survival of the fittest. But little reflection is required to show the superior fitness of the man who is bald. Baldness is respectability, baldness is piety, rectitude and general worth. Persons holding responsible and well-salaried positions are commonly bald—bank cashiers especially. The prosperous merchant is usually of shiny pate; the head of most of the great corporations are thinly haired. Of two otherwise equal applicants for a position of trust and profit who would not instinctively choose the bald one, or, both being bald, the balder? Having, therefore, a considerable advantage in the struggle for existence, the bald person naturally lives longer than his less gifted competitor (any one can observe that he is usually the older) and leaves a more numerous progeny, inheriting the paternal endowment of precarious hair. In a few generations more those varieties of our species known as the Mophead and the Curled Darling will doubtless have become extinct, and the barber *(Homo loquax)*[7] will have followed them into oblivion.

An important discovery recently made and stated with confidence is that to the human tooth, also, civilization is hateful and insupportable. Dr. Dennison Pedley, whose name carries great weight (and would to whomsoever it might happen to belong) has examined the teeth of no fewer than 3,114 children, and only 707 had full sets of sound ones. That was in England; what would be shown by "a look in" at the mouths of the young of a more highly civilized race—say the Missourians—one shudders to conjecture. That nearly all the savages whom one meets have good enough teeth is a matter of common observation; and missionaries in some of the remoter South Sea Islands attest this fact with much feeling. Yet in all enlightened countries the prosperous dentist abounds in quantity.

But perhaps the most significant testimony is that of another English gentleman with another English name—J. K. Mummery, who has examined every skull that he could lay his eyes on during the past twenty years. He affirms an almost total absence of *caries*[8] among the oldest specimens, those belonging to the Stone Age. Among the Celts, who succeeded these, and who knew enough to use metal weapons, the decayed tooth was an incident of more frequent occurrence; and the Roman conquest introduced it in great profusion. When the Romans were driven out they took their back teeth along with them, but the flawless incisor, the hale bicuspid and the sane molar are again rarely encountered. Craniologists affirm a similar

state of things wherever there have been successive or overlapping civilizations: the skulls all tell the same story. If the alarming progress of enlighten-
ment be not stayed by such beneficent agencies as Chinese immigration,
General Stephen Maybell[9] and the *Morning Call* the hairless and noseless man
of the future will undoubtedly subsist, not as we, upon his neighbor and
other solid food, but upon spoon-victuals and the memory of the past. In the
matter of language he will pass, by painful stages, through an era of
Stumpspeech to a permanent régime of Gum Arabic.

APPENDIX

A Screed of the Future Historian

THE YEAR 1903, as the ancient Americans reckoned time, was a memorable one in the annals of that strange and unfortunate people. In the latter part of that year Señor Tomas Lupton, a famous Spanish pirate, inspired partly by revenge for the wrongs of his country and partly by greed of gain, sailed into the port of New York with a fleet of warships and attacked the American vessels lying at anchor there, each held by a sand hook of such enormous dimensions that the resulting engagement took its name from them. That inaccurate historian, Dumbleshaw, endeavors to show that he had made a previous attack of the same kind at the same place, but the evidence adduced is unworthy of attention. The result of the battle was disastrous to the Americans, and Señor Tomas sailed away with immense booty, including what was known as "America's Cup," an enormous flagon of pure gold, having a capacity of 907 smackims of Bourbon wine and supposed to symbolize the national supremacy in the matter of drink.

The calamity seems to have driven the losers wild. In the recriminations that ensued the army and navy, both severely blamed by the people, became involved, each accusing the other of delinquent courage and imperfect vigilance. The Secretary of War was compelled to retire from office and Admiral Langley, commanding a fleet on the lower Potomac, a confluent of the Mississoppy, drowned himself in the most spectacular manner while flying from his accusers.[1]

In an astonishingly brief time the dissension reached the dimensions of actual warfare between the army on one side and the navy on the other. The Democratic party, an organization of patriotic civilians, took up arms against both, while the Republicans and Sinners, an association of persons in authority, k[nowing that they were] outnumbered, retired to [. . .] fortified them with cann[. . . de]clare themselves favorable [. . .] and the spoils.

During the dark of the h[. . .] Atlantic squadron, consisting [. . .] of the line, commanded by [. . .] sailed out of Hohokus h[arbor] and moved upon Sportland [. . .] on the coast of the Stat[. . .] land. As soon as the mo[. . .]tected all the land forces [. . . Gen]eral Corbin[2] being ill, were [. . .] toward the same place. T[. . . Com]mander-in-Chief, General M[iles, whom the] President had cast into p[rison . . .] with chains, was released [. . . and re]stored to power. Comma[nd . . . of re]serves was conferred upon [. . .] Smith (retired) and orders [. . .] if Admiral Schley, a well-k[nown pirate of] the Spanish main, acting [. . .] should be taken no quarter [should be] given him. All these prep[arations were] made by the President, who [. . . dis]tinguished solder, naturally [. . .] army. Unfortunately his na[. . .]scended to us.

The fighting was terrible! [. . . bar]barous times human life [. . .] cheap that historians of the [. . .] no record of the number s[lain . . .] an ancient manuscript attr[ibuted to an] Ordnance Officer of the la[. . .] learn that the consumption [. . .]tion was no less than 7,000 [. . .] gunpowder, and that the co[. . .] and shell expended on bor[. . .] 6,439 "orphannuals." (The [orphannual] as a unit of value appears to [belong to a] later date. It was the cost [of feeding] one orphan one year.) Th[e entire A]tlantic Squadron was totally [destroyed, and] the rest of the navy soon [surren]dered, excepting a fleet on [. . .] commanded by Rear-Admiral [. . .] illustrious warrior attempted [. . .] the island of Guam, but b[. . .] by the village schoolmaster, [. . .] vessels on the high seas, an[. . . en]deavor to reach Japan afoot [. . . un]fortunately drowned.

Introduction

1. Another item, "In the Year 2002" (*W,* Sept. 20, 1884), is possibly by Bierce; but as the editors are less certain of AB's authorship of this sketch, it is not included here.

2. AB to Stone & Kimball, Jan. 12, 1896, MS, Univ. of Pennsylvania.

3. AB to Myles Walsh, Dec. 23, 1897, MS, Univ. of Cincinnati.

4. AB to Myles Walsh, May 19, 1898, MS, Univ. of Cincinnati.

5. AB to Robert Mackay, Mar. 1, 1905, MS, Yale Univ.

6. AB to Robert Mackay, Sept. 28, 1905, MS, NP.

7. AB to Robert H. Davis, June 20, 1906, MS, NP. The book was published as *The Cynic's Word Book.*

8. AB to John O'Hara Cosgrave, Nov. 8, 1906, MS, VA.

9. AB to Herman Scheffauer, Aug. 17, 1907, MS, BL.

10. AB to Herman Scheffauer, Sept. 30, 1907, MS, BL.

11. AB to Walter Neale, Apr. 17, 1908, MS, HL.

12. AB to Walter Neale, June 3, 1908, MS, HL.

13. The typesetting copy of this volume does exist at HL, but it is difficult to conjecture from it what the putative *Fall of the Republic* might have been. All that is evident is that at one time the order of "Ashes of the Beacon" and "The Land Beyond the Blow" were reversed.

14. AB to Walter Neale, Dec. 2, 1910, MS, HL.

15. Carey McWilliams, *Ambrose Bierce: A Biography* (New York: A. & C. Boni, 1929), 84.

16. AB to Walter Neale, Nov. 20, 1908, MS, HL.

17. *Lucian,* with an English translation by A. M. Harmon (Cambridge, Mass.: Harvard Univ. Press, 1913), 1:251.

18. *Lucian's Works,* with "Life" by Ferrand Spence (London, 1864).

19. AB to Blanche Partington, Aug. 17, 1892, MS, BL.

20. See "Ambrose Bierce's Concern with Mind and Man" (Ph.D. diss., Univ. of Pennsylvania, 1962).

21. First published in the *Oakland Tribune,* July 26, 1890; rpt. in *Fantastic Fables* (*CW* 6.359).

22. "Prattle" (*E,* Oct. 21, 1894, 6). Lawrence I. Berkove addresses this issue in detail in "Two Impossible Dreams: Ambrose Bierce on Utopia and America,"

Huntington Library Quarterly 44 (1981): 283–92. Berkove's perspicacious article is one of the few devoted to Bierce's political satires.

23. Cited in William Dean Howells, *The Altrurian Romances* (Bloomington: Indiana Univ. Press, 1968), xxx.

24. H. P. Lovecraft to Robert E. Howard, Nov. 7, 1932, *Selected Letters 1932–1934,* ed. August Derleth and James Turner (Sauk City, Wis.: Arkham House, 1976), 106–7.

25. "Prattle," *A,* Dec. 21, 1878, 17.

26. "Prattle," *A,* May 24, 1879; rpt. *SS* 150–51.

27. "The Passing Show," *NJ,* Aug. 5, 1900, 26; *E,* Aug. 5, 1900, 24.

28. See the Little Johnny sketch "The Nan Patterson Case," *NA,* May 21, 1905, 22; *E,* May 28, 1905, 48, and "Views of One," *NA,* June 14, 1905, 14; *E,* June 21, 1905, 16.

29. See the extracts cited in *SS* 96–97, 227–39.

30. "Prattle," *E,* July 8, 1888; in *SS* 219.

31. "Prattle," *E,* July 24, 1892, 6.

32. AB to George Sterling, Mar. 15, 1902, in *The Letters of Ambrose Bierce* (San Francisco: Book Club of California, 1922), 53.

Ashes of the Beacon

This story was published in rudimentary form as "The Fall of the Republic" (*E,* Mar. 25, 1888), then revised under its present title (with the subtitle "Written in 3940: An Historical Monograph") for publication on an entire page of *NA* (Feb. 19, 1905) and *E* (Feb. 26, 1905). When included in the first volume of AB's *Collected Works* (1909), it was further revised by the insertion of two separate items, "The Jury in Ancient America" (*Co,* Aug. 1905) and "Insurance in Ancient America" (*Co,* Sept. 1906).

1. See *DD:* "Republic, *n.* A nation in which, the thing governing and the thing governed being the same, there is only a permitted authority to enforce an optional obedience. In a republic the foundation of public order is the ever lessening habit of submission inherited from ancestors who, being truly governed, submitted because they had to. There are as many kinds of republics as there are gradations between the despotism whence they came and the anarchy whither they lead."

2. Alexander Pope, *The Dunciad* (rev. ed. 1742–43), bk. 4, ll. 655–56. In the earlier version of *The Dunciad* (1728), bk. 3, ll. 355–56, Pope has written "covers" for "buries."

3. This paragraph and the following were inserted from "The Jury in Ancient America" (*Co,* Aug. 1905). The opening paragraph of that sketch reads:

"Of all the nations of antiquity the one that has been most studied in our day by those desiring to profit by the lessons of experience and avoid the errors of an imperfect civilization is the great American republic known as the Connected States. In the study of some others we are aided by a greater and more varied literature (for the ancient Americans were not, even according to the standards of the time, a literary people), but of none are the writings that have come down to us so rich in warning significance."

4. AB mockingly alludes to the concluding words of Abraham Lincoln's Gettysburg Address. See also note 41 below.

5. In reference to an "Altrurian" colony near Santa Rosa, California (i.e., a colony inspired by W. D. Howells's *A Traveler in Altruria* [1894]; see Introduction, p. xviii), AB speaks scornfully of "the Ancient and Honorable Order of the Dupes of Hope" ("Prattle," *E,* Dec. 13, 1896, 6).

6. In "The Jury in Ancient America" the phrase here reads: "as lately as the year 3157, as the Americans, for some reason not now known, reckoned time." The suggestion of that last remark (found in many other satires in this book) is that the chronology of the Christian era, and therefore Christianity itself, has fallen out of use.

7. Perhaps meant to echo the "Year of the Four Emperors" in Roman history, when the emperors Pertinax, Didius Julianus, Pescennius Niger, and Septimius Severus all vied for supremacy in 193 C.E.

8. AB frequently quotes from the writings of his (fictitious) contemporary, Jamrach Holobom, in his later writings.

9. Ireland did not officially become a republic until 1948, but it had been virtually independent since 1921, with the establishment of the Irish Free State. AB's prescient remark points to his belief that Home Rule for Ireland (involving the establishment of an independent parliament but still entailing recognition of the British Crown), widely discussed in the later nineteenth century, would lead eventually to actual independence.

10. The census of 1900 recorded the U.S. population at 75,994,575.

11. Dumbleshaw is first mentioned in "John Smith: An Editorial Article from a Journal of May 3rd, A.D. 3873" (*Fu,* May 10, 1873). AB removed the reference to him from the revised version of the tale (see "John Smith, Liberator"). AB himself wrote a brief memoir entitled "A Sole Survivor" (1890; *SS* 298–306).

12. In *DD,* AB defined liberty as "one of Imagination's most precious possessions."

13. See "Prattle" (*E,* Aug. 6, 1893, 6): "The essential principle in this rule of the majority . . . is the right of might. The majority governs, not for it ought, but for it can. Majorities are no more likely to hold correct views than minorities, and there is only one valid reason why Tom's and Dick's views should prevail over Harry's, namely, that it is the only practical way to get on. In the last analysis a balloting is only a counting of noses to ascertain the relative military strength of the parties balloting. Commonly the weaker submits rather than risk a war for

principles or interest not deemed vital to the national welfare. But when the principles at stake are embedded in the consciences and sentiments of the voters, and when those 'defeated at the polls' think themselves sufficiently strong in other ways to make up for their numerical weakness, they do not submit: they rebel and deliver such battle as they can. If beaten in the field the rising remains a rebellion; by success it becomes a revolution, and has, usually, the approval of the world and of posterity."

14. Richard Anthony Proctor (1837–1888), British writer on mathematics, astronomy, and other scientific subjects. AB probably refers to Proctor's book, *Chance and Luck: A Discussion of the Laws of Luck, Coincidences, Wagers, Lotteries, and the Fallacies of Gambling* (1887).

15. AB apparently refers to a charlatan named John Ernst Worrell Keely (1827–1898). In the 1870s Keely proposed to build a motor powered "from intermolecular vibrations of ether," and sold many shares of stock to fund the Keely Motor Company; but investigations after his death proved the venture to be a fraud. AB refers to Keely in some of his columns, spelling his name correctly there; the misspelling here is presumably deliberate.

16. See "The Curmudgeon Philosopher" (*E*, June 19, 1902, 14): "'Fetish is the adoration of a material object, which the worshiper conceives to have a certain sanctity or peculiar power. It is one of the most marked characteristics of barbarism—and civilization.'"

17. The U.S. presidents up to 1901 who died in office were William Henry Harrison (1841), Abraham Lincoln (1865), James A. Garfield (1881), and William McKinley (1901). Harrison died of illness, and the other three were assassinated. Only McKinley died at the hands of a professed anarchist.

18. AB's defense of Chinese immigrants in California was of long standing: "Put a principle into the ear of a fool, and it will reappear at his mouth as a prejudice. Of ten men who write or speak against Chinese immigration, eight do the cause incalculable harm, for the unwisdom of their method makes it obvious to the observant that they are merely echoing local mobgabble, or voicing the reasonless antipathies of race" (*A*, Mar. 9, 1878; cited in *SS* 147).

19. In 1896, when AB was in Washington attacking the efforts of railroad magnate C. P. Huntington to persuade Congress to pass legislation granting him a long extension in repaying government debts, Huntington maintained that *E*'s opposition to him was a result of his cutting off payment of $12,000 a year to the paper. In a letter published as "Bierce to Huntington," AB stated: "if he makes his accusation good I will take him by the hand, which recently I have twice refused when he offered it—once in presence of three members of the press in the corridor of the Capitol, and again in the room of the Senate Committee on Pacific Railroads in the presence of the committee and many gentlemen attending one of its meetings. As to this latter promise I exact but one condition: Mr. Huntington is not to object to my glove" (*E*, Mar. 21, 1896, 14).

20. The quotation is from T[homas] V[incent] Cator (1851–1920), *Millionaires*

or Morals: Which Shall Rule? (San Francisco: W. M. Langton & Co., 1890), a lecture delivered by Cator at the Metropolitan Temple in San Francisco on July 4, 1890. AB quotes the passage in "Prattle" (*E,* July 6, 1890, 6).

21. AB himself is probably the author of these lines.

22. Beginning with this sentence, most of "The Jury in Ancient America" is inserted into the narrative, beginning with the fourth paragraph. (For the first three paragraphs see note 3 above.)

23. "A jury of [one's] peers."

24. Magna Carta was a charter of liberties that King John was pressured into proclaiming in 1215 following a rebellion of barons who objected to his exploitation of royal power. AB probably derived his interpretation of the early jury system from a landmark work by Sir Frederick Pollock and Frederic William Maitland, *The History of English Law before the Time of Edward I* (Cambridge: Cambridge Univ. Press, 1895; rev. ed., 1898), but his reading of this work appears to be highly selective. AB was no doubt thinking of such statements in Pollock and Maitland as the following: "The essence of the jury . . . seems to be this: a body of neighbours is summoned by some public officer to give upon oath a true answer to some question" (1.138); and "it is now generally admitted that the phrase *iudicium parium* [in Magna Carta] does not point to trial by jury" (1.173n). But AB has ignored the following remark, made in reference to court procedures in the early Middle Ages: "No less deep is the gulf which separates them [the jurors] from witnesses adduced by a litigant" (1.140).

25. Edward William Bok (1863–1930), editor and essayist. In 1899 he took over editorship of the *Ladies' Home Journal.*

26. Compensation for injured feelings (as distinct from financial loss or physical suffering).

27. The source of this quotation appears to be AB himself.

28. Actually Ho-Ho-Kus, a town in northeastern New Jersey. AB apparently found the name humorous, for he uses it so from time to time in his writings.

29. Beginning with this paragraph, the bulk of the sketch "Insurance in Ancient America" (*Co,* Sept. 1906) is inserted into the narrative.

30. A *tout* is one who obtains information on racehorses and their prospects and sells it to bettors; a *capper* is one who acts as a decoy in a confidence game.

31. See *DD:* "Insurance, *n.* An ingenious modern game of chance in which the player is permitted to enjoy the comfortable conviction that he is beating the man who keeps the table."

32. In the San Francisco earthquake and fire of April 18, 1906, 452 people were officially reported killed (although the actual number was probably higher, perhaps being as high as two or three thousand), and damage was estimated at $350 million.

33. The Chicago fire of October 8–11, 1871, was reputed to have been started when a cow belonging to a Mrs. O'Leary kicked over a lantern. In fact, the fire was started in the barn of a laborer, Patrick O'Leary.

34. The Chicago fire resulted in damage estimated at \$196 million, of which only \$96.5 million was covered by insurance. Nevertheless, fifty-eight insurance companies across the country went out of business as a result of claims. In fact, most insurance companies fulfilled their contractual obligations following the fire.

35. Most insurance companies in San Francisco did not insure against earth-quake, only fire. Some companies claimed that they were not liable for fires caused directly by the earthquake; however, most of the fire damage was deter-mined not to be a direct result of the earthquake. In the ensuing months, twenty-seven insurance companies paid claims in full or close to full; nineteen paid 90¢ and up on the dollar; four companies settled for 80¢ and up; twenty-eight paid 75¢ and up; twenty-six paid less than 75¢; and four European companies denied liability because of the earthquake and paid nothing. Many of the companies that eventually paid spent months or years in litigation to avoid meeting their commit-ments. AB commented on the matter in a letter written two months after the earthquake: "Yes, I've observed the . . . determination to 'beat' the insurance companies. Insurance is a hog game, and if they (the companies) can be beaten out of their dishonest gains by superior dishonesty I have no objection; but in my judgment they are neither legally nor morally liable for the half that is claimed of them. Those of them that took no earthquake risks don't owe a cent." (AB to George Sterling, June 11, 1911, MS, NP.)

36. At this point "Insurance in Ancient America" reads: "But it seems to have been a just claim to the second place in the scale of crime indicated in an epigram of the period: 'The next worse thing to an insurance business dishonestly con-ducted is an insurance business conducted honestly.' So far as we of to-day have knowledge of the matter, life insurance was conducted as honest gambling, as both payment of bets and distribution of winnings. If accusations to the contrary were made they have not come down to us; the ink in which they were written has faded from the scroll of history. The only writer of antiquity who is known to have mentioned them at any considerable length is Tomlawson, nicknamed, for some unknown reason, 'the Bostonian,' an author of great repute in that age, according to Ginkler. From certain fragments of the Bostonian's work that were extant in Ginkler's day, that acute historian inferred that life insurance was free from the base practices characterizing kindred forms of gambling, and that the care and investment of its profits were a trust honorably administered by those having them in custody—whom the elder author names. It is no small distinction to have been chosen by one's country's gods to instate in the seats of honor the philanthropists and benefactors worthy to sit in what the greatest and most original of our contemporary poets has called,

"'The fierce light that beats upon a throne.'"

The above line is from Tennyson's *Idylls of the King* (1869–85), Dedication, l. 24 ("which" for "that" in Tennyson).

37. In "Insurance in Ancient America" there is an additional paragraph:

"Students of the history of those troublous times need not be told what other and bloodier events logically followed that awful reprisal, until the whole stupendous of popular government, temple and citadel of all fallacies and abuses, crashed to ruin, and among its fallen columns and scattered stones gave shelter to a diminishing population of skulking anarchists, who finally vanished from history into a darkness impenetrable to conjecture."

38. In "The Passing Show" (*NA*, Jan. 17, 1904, 24; *E*, Jan. 31, 1904, 52), AB wrote: "Montesquieu says: 'The foundation of political stability is the people's respect for their rulers.'"

39. In the appearance of this story in *NA* (Feb. 19, 1905) and *E* (Feb. 26, 1905), the text reads "Muliolatry." See AB to George Sterling (Apr. 17, 1905; MS, NP): "The compound 'Mulolatry,' [*sic*] which I made in 'Ashes of the Beacon', would not, of course, be allowable in composition altogether serious. I used it because I could not at the moment think of the right word, 'gyneolatry', or 'gynecolatry', according as you make use of the nominative or the accusative. I once made 'caniolatry' [p. 56, as "Cynolatry"] for a similar reason—just laziness. It's not nice to do things o' that kind, even in newspapers." AB refers to the erroneous creation of a compound word from both Latin (*mulier,* woman) and Greek (*latreia,* servitude) rather than from one language only (in this case, the Greek *gyne* and *latreia*).

40. At the battle of Gettysburg (July 1–3, 1863), the combined Federal and Confederate casualties are officially estimated as 7,053 killed, 33,264 wounded, and 10,790 missing. Other estimates yield substantially lower casualties for the Confederates and slightly lower ones for the Federals.

41. From Lincoln's Gettysburg Address (Nov. 19, 1863): "that government of the people, by the people, for the people, shall not perish from the earth."

42. Cf. *DD:* "Multitude, *n.* A crowd; the source of political wisdom and virtue. In a republic, the object of the statesman's adoration. 'In a multitude of consellors there is wisdom,' saith the proverb. If many men of equal individual wisdom are wiser than any one of them, it must be that they acquire the excess of wisdom by the mere act of getting together. Whence comes it? Obviously from nowhere—as well say that a range of mountains is higher than the single mountains composing it. A multitude is as wise as its wisest member if it obey him; if not, it is no wiser than its most foolish."

43. *Vox populi vox Dei.* The earliest recorded expression of the utterance occurs in Alcuin's letter to Charlemagne (c. 800 C.E.). AB uses the Latin expression in the earlier appearance of this story as "The Fall of the Republic" (see p. 106).

44. The Grand Army of the Republic was formed in 1866 by veterans of the Federal army. By the 1880s, with a membership of more than 400,000, it was a formidable political force. In 1887 Congress passed legislation granting pensions to all veterans suffering from any type of disability; President Cleveland's veto of the bill was a significant factor in his defeat in the presidential election the next year.

In 1890 Congress passed a similar bill, and it was signed by President Benjamin Harrison. By 1949 the pensions had totaled $8 billion.

45. The reference is to the American War of Independence (1775–83), the War of 1812 (1812–14), and the Civil War (1861–65).

46. The statement actually derives from a line by the German poet and dramatist Johann Christoph von Schiller (1759–1805), in his verse drama *Die Jungfrau von Orleans* (1801), act 3, scene 6: "Mit der Dummheit kämpfen Götter selbst vergebens" (Against stupidity the gods themselves battle in vain). In "Aphorisms of a Late Spring" (*NA*, Apr. 24, 1904, 25), AB wrote: "Against stupidity the gods are said to be powerless; against intelligence they do not contend."

47. "I stood in Venice, on the Bridge of Sighs; / A palace and a prison on each hand: / I saw from out the waves her structures rise / As from the stroke of the enchanter's wand . . ." Byron, *Childe Harold's Pilgrimage* (1812–18), canto 4, ll. 1–4. AB quotes the line also in "Mr. Masthead, Journalist" (1874; *CW* 8.191) and "Prattle" (*E*, Nov. 18, 1894, 6).

48. "Therefore all things whatsoever ye would that men should do to you, do ye even so to them: for this is the Law and the Prophets" (Matt. 7:12). Commonly known as the Golden Rule.

The Land Beyond the Blow

This story was assembled from eleven different stories, all published separately in *E, NA,* or *Co,* between 1888 and 1907. The very brief opening and closing chapters, "Thither" and "Hither," are largely original, although parts of even these were taken from some of the separately published items.

"Sons of the Fair Star" (*E,* June 10, 1888) is chiefly a satire on the accumulation of wealth: unlike the "ancient" Americans satirized in "Ashes of the Beacon," with their single-minded devotion to money, the Golampis seek to free themselves of their wealth as much as possible. AB, however, was by no means opposed to securing wealth: see the essay "The Road to Wealth Is Open to All" (p. 179).

"An Interview with Gnarmag-Zote" (first published as "The Golampians," *E,* Nov. 24, 1889) is devoted to the expounding of a variety of philosophical doctrines, chiefly relating to death, the soul, and the afterlife, derived from Epicurus and Schopenhauer.

"The Tamtonians" (*E,* Nov. 11, 1888) lampoons many of the features of republican government as practiced in America. The words from the Tamtonian language are of course reversed forms of English political terms, particularly as they relate to presidential elections, party politics, and office seeking in general. For AB's views on the subject see the essays in the section "Government vs. Anarchy."

"Marooned on Ug" is a fusion of two stories, "Marooned on Ug" (*E,* Feb. 20,

1898) and "The War with Wug" (*E*, Sept. 11, 1898). The former story is chiefly concerned with bribery in politics, and the latter presents a veiled account of the Spanish-American War. AB wrote extensively on the war and its aftermath in 1898–1901; many of his articles have now been collected in *Skepticism and Dissent: Selected Journalism, 1898–1901*, ed. Lawrence I. Berkove (1980; rev. ed., Ann Arbor: UMI Research Press, 1986).

"The Dog in Ganegwag" (*NA*, May 12, 1904) is a satire on human beings' fondness for dogs. This was a topic that long exercised AB: see the essays in the section "Dogs and Horses."

"A Conflagration in Ghargaroo" (*Co*, Feb. 1906) is another send-up of the notion of accumulating wealth, stressing the paradox of a Christian doing so when Christ taught the virtues of poverty.

"An Execution in Batrugia" is made up of two items, "A Letter from a Btrugumian" (*NA*, Apr. 30, 1903) and "An Execution in Batrugia" (*Co*, May 1907). The former concerns the wondrous architecture of New York, something AB must have noted on his frequent trips to New York during his years in Washington (1900–13). In a letter written about a month prior to the publication of the article, AB notes that New York is a "city of giants" and adds: "Really it is amazing; everything on so colossal a scale. . . . The architecture may not please you; it doesn't please me. It only stuns me. In calling it a city of giants I unintentionally expressed the feeling it gives me. But where are the giants? Alas! it is infested by pigmies, or at least the giants remaining are seen only away up in the sky rearing new structures for their masters, the pigmies. They look like ants, these titans up there, but of course one knows they are a hundred feet in stature. Even so I think the gods must come down from Olympus to take a hand in the work, especially in that of bridge-building" (AB to Herman Scheffauer, Mar. 27, 1903; MS [transcript], BL). "An Execution in Batrugia" deals with capital punishment, a frequent topic in AB's columns. See the essays in the section "Capital Punishment."

"The Jumjum of Gokeetle-guk," first published as "Trustland: A Tale of a Traveler" (*E*, Nov. 19, 1899), deals with the economic efficiency of "trusts," or monopolies. For AB's position on this subject see "Concerning Trusts" (p. 173).

"The Kingdom of Tortirra" is in fact the earliest of the stories, published in *E*, April 22, 1888. Its chief objects of satire are "protection" (i.e., tariffs) and the judicial system.

1. AB's original coinage here was Doosno-Zwair, but he amended it probably because he had used the name Doosnoswair in several fables in *Fantastic Fables* (1899), including "The Reform School Board" (*CW* 6.189).

2. AB may be imitating *Gulliver* here: "But I shall not anticipate the reader with farther descriptions of this kind, because I reserve them for a greater work, which is now almost ready for the press, containing a general description of this empire . . . : their plants and animals, their peculiar manners and customs, with other matters very curious and useful" (*GT* 51).

3. In the original version of this story, they were known as Golampians.

4. See "Prattle" (*E,* July 14, 1895, 6): "In nations that cover the body for another purpose than decoration and protection from the weather, disputes as to how much of it, and under what circumstances, should be covered are inevitable and uncompassable. Alike in nature and in art, the question of the nude will be always demanding adjustment and be never adjusted. This eternal wrangle we have always with us as a penalty for the prudery of concealment, creating and suggesting the prurience of exposure.

> Offended Nature hides her lash
> In the purple-black of a dyed mustache,

and the lash lurks in every fold of the clothing wherewith Man has insulted her. In ancient Greece the disgraceful squabble was unknown: it did not occur to the great-hearted, broad-brained and wholesome people of that blessed land that any of the handiwork of the gods was ignoble. Nor are the modern Japanese vexed with 'the question of the nude'; save where their admirable civilization has suffered the polluting touch of ours they have not learned the infamy of sex. Among the blessings in store for them are their conversion to decorous lubricity and instruction in the nice conduct of a clouded mind."

5. Cf. AB's comment when he learned that Doubleday, Page & Co. wished to publish *The Devil's Dictionary* as *The Cynic's Word Book:* "Here in the East the Devil is a sacred personage (the Fourth Person of the Trinity, as an Irishman might say) and his name must not be taken in vain" (AB to George Sterling, May 6, 1906; quoted in *SS* 315).

6. See "Prattle" (*E,* Aug. 4, 1895, 6): "nothing is so practical and logical as religious persecution. If carried to the point of extermination—and despite the hoary platitudes about the blood of the martyrs being the seed of the church, and so forth, it is easily capable of that extension—it is from the view point of religion the most wisest and most rational of religious methods. That it is acceptable to God—to his God—every religionist is bound to believe, and in his heart does believe. If I can exterminate a heresy that is peopling Hell I am a rascal not to do so—an unfaithful servant of the Lord. If by putting to the sword one generation of the irreclaimable and already damned I can save many generations from damnation, that, clearly, is mercy—that, clearly, is duty. Women being both religious and practical will favor the remarriage of Church and State—will set up a Theocracy and the Devil will do the rest."

7. In "Sons of the Fair Star" AB supplies two poetic extracts, the first of which reads:

> Truth when flattened out will become again vertical:
> She owns God's everlasting years:
> But a hurt mistake twists in discomfort,
> And its adorers see it breathe its last.

The second corresponds with the one here printed, and is prefaced by the remark: "Another, whom their critics esteem the greatest poet who ever lived, writes: . . ."

8. Cf., in *Gulliver,* the King of Brobdingnag's comment after Gulliver has recounted the political, legal, and social customs of the English: "by what I have gathered from your own relation, and the answers I have with much pains wringed and extorted from you, I cannot but conclude the bulk of your natives to be the most pernicious race of little odious vermin that nature ever suffered to crawl upon the surface of the earth" (*GT* 154).

9. "Now it is impossible to conceive the incorporeal as a separate existence, except the void: and the void can neither act nor be acted upon, but only provides opportunity of motion through itself to bodies. So that those who say that the soul is incorporeal are talking idly." Epicurus, *Letter to Herodotus,* in Cyril Bailey, *Epicurus: The Extant Fragments* (Oxford: Clarendon Press, 1926), 41, 43.

10. Cf. Arthur Schopenhauer (1788–1860): "The pleasure in this world, it has been said, outweighs the pain; or, at any rate, there is an even balance between the two. If the reader wishes to see shortly whether this statement is true, let him compare the respective feelings of two animals, one of which is engaged in eating the other." *Studies in Pessimism,* trans. T. Bailey Saunders (London: Swan Sonnenschein, 1893), 12.

11. "[D]eath is nothing to us. For all good and evil consists in sensation, but death is deprivation of sensation." Epicurus, *Letter to Menoeceus,* in Bailey, *Epicurus: The Extent Fragments,* 85.

12. "So death, the most terrifying of ills, is nothing to us, since so long as we exist, death is not with us; but when death comes, then we do not exist." Epicurus, *Letter to Menoeceus;* in Bailey, *Epicurus: The Extent Fragments,* 85.

13. Cf. Schopenhauer, *Studies in Pessimism:* "A man finds himself, to his great astonishment, suddenly existing, after thousands and thousands of years of non-existence: he lives for a little while; and then, again, comes an equally long period when he must exist no more." Bailey, *Studies in Pessimism,* 33–34.

14. Cf. Schopenhauer: "If children were brought into the world by an act of pure reason alone, would the human race continue to exist? Would not a man rather have so much sympathy with the coming generation as to spare it the burden of existence? . . . Human life must be some kind of mistake." Bailey, *Studies in Pessimism,* 15, 37.

15. *Note in original:* The Tamtonian language forms its plurals most irregularly, but usually by an initial inflection. It has a certain crude and primitive grammar, but in point of orthoepy is extremely difficult. With our letters I can hardly hope to give an accurate conception of its pronunciation. As nearly as possible I write its words as they sounded to my ear when carefully spoken for my instruction by intelligent natives. It is a harsh tongue.

16. See "The Passing Show" (*E,* Apr. 22, 1900, 26; *NA,* Apr. 22, 1900, 26): "If I rightly understand [the slogan 'Principles, not men'] it means that so long as the party platform is all right, the characters of the party candidates are of little or

no importance. If it does mean that, or anything like that, it is a reasonless and pernicious thing which one should be ashamed to say. There is no political principle or set of political principles of which the profession and possession by men in power can give us good government. That can be assured only by personal character. . . . 'Principles, not men,' when not the motto of a dupe is the motto of a duper. It is a pickpocket's claim to inattention." AB also treats of this matter in the fable "Party Manager and Gentleman" (*CW* 6.246–47).

17. Cf. AB's comment to his readers during the presidential campaign of 1888: "Every man Jack of the lot of you honestly and calmly believes that the election is going his way. He is incapable of the conception of so worthy a man as he in a minority; he could as soon think of an archangel caught in a quail trap; and when the ugly fact is borne in upon the consciousness of him he feels as if he had fallen out of a clear sky and struck astride of his own neck" ("Prattle," *E,* July 8, 1888, 4; cited in *SS* 218).

18. An allusion to the six consecutive defeats suffered by the Democrats in the presidential elections of 1860 (J. C. Breckinridge lost to Abraham Lincoln), 1864 (George B. McClellan lost to Lincoln), 1868 (Horatio Seymour lost to U. S. Grant), 1872 (Horace Greeley lost to Grant), 1876 (Samuel J. Tilden lost to Rutherford B. Hayes), and 1880 (Winfield S. Hancock lost to James A. Garfield).

19. Cf. AB's pungent comment, addressed to the wife of President Benjamin Harrison, who declared, "I do not wish my husband to be President again": "Wishes, madam, do not appear to count for much in this matter. With a single exception, your husband is the only man in the United States of whom it is certainly known that several millions of his fellow citizens did not wish him to be President this time" ("Prattle," *E,* Nov. 3, 1889, 6).

20. Richard Neville, Earl of Warwick (1428–1471) was called the "Kingmaker" because he was largely responsible for establishing Edward IV as king of England in 1461; Warwick actually ruled England for the next three years. In 1470 he helped to place Henry VI to the throne. Otto von Bismarck (1815–1898) helped to free Prussia from Austrian control, unified the German states, and then became chancellor of Germany (1871–90). Throughout his term he was a stronger political and military force than the German emperors of the period.

21. AB presumably witnessed such actions when Andrew Johnson succeeded Lincoln in 1865 and Chester Alan Arthur succeeded Garfield in 1881.

22. Cf. AB's comment following the presidential campaign of 1884, then regarded as one of the most vicious in American history: "Thank Heaven, it is over, and may we never have any more of it! . . . If ever, O good Satan, this faithful people celebrated thy praise, served thine altars and walked with humility along the line of thy desires; if ever it dedicated to thy service its hearts and brains and blood and bones; if ever it lied and cheated with incessant iteration and the heat of a noble zeal; if ever, in short, it was wholly overgiven to the love and lust of a folly that is barbarous, an ignorance that is brutal and a wickedness that is

savage, mean and unspeakable, may it please thee now to reward the service and waive its repetition." "Prattle," *W* no. 432 (Nov. 8, 1884): 5.

23. In the presidential election of 1884, candidate James G. Blaine violated Republican precedent by going on the stump himself, while Democratic candidate Grover Cleveland delivered two speeches and attended a large celebration at his hometown, Buffalo.

24. At this point in "The Tamtonians" AB writes: "As one of the most celebrated of Tamtonian poets sarcastically says:

> "Ill fares the land, to hastening ills a prey,
> Where statesmen rise by throwing shame away."

The first line is from Oliver Goldsmith's *The Deserted Village* (1770), l. 51; the second is AB's. See also p. 109.

25. AB had spent most of the summer of 1896 (one and a half years before writing this segment) in Englewood, New Jersey, recovering from the grueling four months (February–May) spent in Washington writing more than sixty articles against C. P. Huntington (see "Ashes of the Beacon," n. 19).

26. In "Marooned on Ug" the text here reads: "upon which I was marooned in the year 1872, and from which I escaped only last summer."

27. Probably an allusion to C. P. Huntington's scheme to convince Congress to appropriate funds for a harbor at Santa Monica (near property owned by him), which would have resulted in a virtual private harbor, as opposed to a harbor at San Pedro, which several Congressional investigations had deemed a superior harbor for the Los Angeles area. The specific target of AB's attack may have been Stephen Benton Elkins (1841–1911), who as Secretary of War in the Harrison administration (1891–93) had opposed the Santa Monica harbor but as U.S. Senator from West Virginia (1895–1911) favored it. In "Another Thieves' Scheme on the Pacific Coast" (*NJ,* May 4, 1896, 4) AB casts doubt on the sincerity of Elkins's about-face.

28. *Ben-Hur: A Tale of the Christ* (1880), by General Lew Wallace (1827–1905), sold two million copies and was widely translated.

29. The name Scamadumclitchclitch resembles the name of Gulliver's "little nurse" in Brobdingnag, Glumdalclitch.

30. A parodic description of the Spanish-American War. The Spaniards (Wuggards) refused to countenance the independence of their colony, Cuba (Scamadumclitchclitch). Two months after the explosion of the U.S. battleship *Maine* in Havana harbor on February 15, 1898, the United States (Uggards) declared war on Spain, and on April 22 President McKinley ordered the blockading of all Cuban ports. The war was over by August.

31. In the Spanish-American War, only 379 U.S. soldiers died in combat, but more than 5,000 died of disease.

32. This scene appears to be an imitation of the opening chapter of book 4 ("A Voyage to the Houyhnhnms") of *Gulliver,* when Gulliver, encountering a hideous monster (who later turns out to be a Yahoo), attacks him: "I drew my

hanger [sword], and gave him a good blow with the flat side of it, for I durst not strike him with the edge, fearing the inhabitants might be provoked against me, if they should come to know that I had killed or maimed any of their cattle. When the beast felt the smart, he drew back, and roared so loud that a herd of at least forty came flocking about me from the next field, howling and making odious faces" (*GT* 266–67). Gulliver is finally saved by a horse (Houyhnhnm).

33. In fact, the Egyptians worshipped a god, Anubis, who was conceived as having the head of a dog or jackal.

34. See "Ashes of the Beacon," n. 39.

35. Perhaps an imitation of the bizarre language of Luggnagg in *Gulliver:* "I pronounced the following words, as they had been taught me the night before, *Ickpling gloffthrobb squutserumm blhiop mlashnalt zwin tnodbalkguffh slhiophad gurdlubh asht.* This is the compliment established by the laws of the land for all persons admitted to the King's presence. It may be rendered into English thus: *May your Celestial Majesty outlive the sun, eleven moons and a half* " (*GT* 244).

36. AB refers to such utterances by Jesus as: "Blessed are the poor in spirit: for theirs is the kingdom of heaven" (Matt. 5:3) and "Verily I say unto you, that a rich man shall hardly enter into the kingdom of heaven. And again I say unto you, It is easier for a camel to go through the eye of a needle, than for a rich man to enter into the kingdom of God" (Matt. 19:23–24).

37. Cf. Eccles. 1:2–4: "Vanity of vanities, saith the Preacher, all is vanity. What profit hath a man of all his labour which he taketh under the sun? One generation passeth away, and another generation cometh: but the earth abideth for ever."

38. Cf. *DD:* "Pardon, *v.* To remit a penalty and restore to a life of crime. To add to the lure of crime the temptation of ingratitude."

39. In the original sketch, "An Execution in Batrugia," instead of the first four paragraphs here printed, the text reads: "In the year 1892 (said the Returned Traveler), while on a voyage to Polati, I had the misfortune to disagree with the crew as to the expediency of killing the captain and his officers, taking possession of the ship, and setting up as pirates. As a result of this inharmony I was marooned on the island of Batrugia, whose capital, Ogamwee, is the most ancient city in the world."

40. At this point AB inserts the sketch entitled "A Letter from a Btrugumian."

41. See "Prattle" (*E,* Feb. 26, 1888, 4): "The argument against capital punishment may start how it will, but at the last it commonly rests itself upon the postulate that it is better that ninety-nine guilty men escape than that one innocent man should be punished. This obviously has no more to do with hanging than with any other punishment. Whether it *is* better depends on what is meant by it. It is better for the ninety-nine escapers; it is worse for everybody else. The loss that the State, community, society sustains in the death of an innocent man is insignificant—particularly the kind of innocent man that is likely to be accused and convicted of murder. We lose such men by death every day and hour. But the escape of ninety-nine murderers is a very serious matter indeed. The frosty truth of it is that, so far as the public interest is

concerned, it would pay to hang every actual murderer, even if we had to hang an innocent man alongside of him. If ever we have to do that we can lighten our loss by taking the County Assessor."

42. In "Trustland" the text here reads: ". . . an exceedingly grave and dignified person about three hundred years old, as I afterward learned, . . ."

43. In "Trustland" the text reads: "a term of one hundred and fifty years . . ."

44. In "Trustland" the text reads: ". . . saluted me by taking his right foot in his left hand and carrying it to his lips, . . ."

45. The Populist is associated with Kansas because this political party had been organized in the late 1880s by farmers in the Midwest and Far West. Cf. *DD:* "Populist, *n.* A fossil patriot of the early agricultural period, found in the old red soapstone underlying Kansas; characterized by an uncommon spread of ear, which some naturalists contend gave him the power of flight, though Professors Morse and Whitney, pursuing independent lines of thought, have ingeniously pointed out that had he possessed it he would have gone elsewhere. In the picturesque speech of his period, some fragments of which have come down to us, he was known as 'The Matter with Kansas.'"

46. AB wrote often about this phenomenon. Cf. "The Town Crier," *Fi* no. 408 (June 28, 1873, 5), listing some of things that AB admits not knowing: "I don't know why a jackass raises his tail when he brays."

47. The original sketch "The Kingdom of Tortirra" opens with a prefatory account as follows:

> By the arrival of the schooner Jabez Jones, Capt. Taylor, we are put in possession of further knowledge concerning the recently discovered Tortirra Islands, some account of which appeared in this journal last October. The information then obtained from the trading vessel Ecuador, which, driven from her course, had touched at one of the smaller islands of the group, was imperfect and fragmentary, the vessel having been compelled by the natives to go to sea again within twenty-four hour after dropping anchor in their port. They discerned her true character of merchantmen, despite the clever ruse by which her master and crew endeavored to give her the appearance of a pirate, and sent her to the right about in short order.
>
> Our present advices are less meager, being derived from one James Donelson, who lived on Tanga, the largest of the group, for more than three years, the first European, and, excepting the crew of the Ecuador, the only one who is known to have seen these islands. Donelson was an able seaman on board the British barque Arethusa, which on the 5th of November, 1884, was wrecked on an uninhabited island some three hundred miles to the northeast of Tanga. As the island upon which the vessel went ashore afforded neither food nor water, the seven survivors, including the Captain, left it in an open boat with such provisions as they

had been able to save, choosing a course almost at random in the faint
hope of finding a more hospitable Land. After incredible sufferings,
Donelson, now the sole survivor, unconscious in the bottom of his boat,
drifted ashore on Tanga, and was restored to strength and health by the
natives. He remained among them until November last, when finding the
situation intolerable he embarked in a small boat which he had secretly
provisioned, and set sail, trusting to the remote chance of being picked up
by some ship, if spared by the winds and waves. In case of failure and the
exhaustion of his food and water, he resolved to die by his own hand. By
good fortune the Jabez Jones, hence from Teluga, which, like the Ecuador, had been blown many leagues out of her course, found and rescued
him and brought him to this port.

To an EXAMINER reporter, who visited Mr. Donelson on Wednesday
last, that gentleman appeared somewhat reluctant to say much concerning
the hitherto almost unknown people among whom he had lived so long.
He even refused to say what had been the character of his treatment by
them; but from the desperate chances of escape which he took it may
safely enough be considered to have been not altogether friendly. "I must
decline to answer all your questions," said Mr. Donelson. "While on
board the Jones I began, at the suggestion of her Captain, a narrative of
my adventures and an account of the extraordinary people among whom I
was thrown, of whom and of whose no less extraordinary country the
world will be first fully apprised by my book. Naturally I do not wish to
publish in advance any particulars which would add interest to the
volume. I appreciate the enterprise of the EXAMINER in trying to obtain
them, all the same," he added with a smile. Mr. Donelson, by the way, is
an educated and singularly intelligent man—a very able seaman indeed.
How he came to ship as a sailor before the mast he declines to say.

At a later interview he said: "On reflection, and influenced, I confess,
by the handsome offer that your paper has made me, I am disposed to
surrender to you such parts of my manuscript as I think can best be spared
from my book. I must tell you frankly that my choice has been determined by considerations purely selfish: I offer to you that part of my
narrative which I conceive to be the least credible—that which deals with
certain monstrous and astounding follies of that strange people. Their
ceremony of marriage by decapitation; their custom of facing to the rear
when riding on horseback; their reversal of the law of hereditary succession to the throne—the father succeeding the son; their practice of
walking on their hands in all ceremonial processions; their selection of the
blind for military command; their pig-worship—these and many other
interesting particulars of their religious, political, intellectual and social life
I reserve; but if you think that without risking its reputation for veracity
the EXAMINER can publish the extraordinary statements contained in the

manuscripts which I now hand you, they are at your service. I am convinced that they would seriously impair the reader's faith in the general credibility of my book."

Assuring Mr. Donelson that the EXAMINER would publish them for what they are worth, the reporter accepted the manuscripts, and they are here printed without material alteration.

In "The Kingdom of Tortirra" the first paragraph following the prefatory account reads:

> The politics of Tortirra are no less remarkable than the laws. Something has been already said of the political system—a limited monarchy, with a commonly vacant throne (the sovereign's functions *in interregno* being performed by a designated Minister), a supreme and many subordinate legislatures and an executive head of each island. The system is good enough, but in its practical working the prodigious folly and dark ignorance of the people deprive it of all beneficent effectiveness and make it an instrument of evil. To most of the multitude of offices men are chosen for a brief incumbency by what is called a popular election; that is to say, on certain stated days every adult male not legally disqualified is supposed to designate for any certain office the 'man of his choice,' and actually believes himself exercising the largest liberty of preference. But by the previous action of a few men whose political existence is unknown to the Constitution, whose meetings are secret and whose methods wicked, his choice is limited to one of two or three men. It is so arranged that he must vote for the man of another man's choice or his vote is wasted. Yet he is no less zealous and enthusiastic in assertion of this worthless right than if he were really recording an intelligent preference. So great is the earnestness of these voters that they sometimes engage in the most acrimonious disputes, and even in bloody fights, very few important elections taking place without men justifying with their hearts' blood to the worth of candidates, about whom they know nothing except what they have been told by interested persons, and to whom they are not only themselves unknown but objects of profound indifference.

48. In the original sketch "The Kingdom of Tortirra" there is the following additional text:

> Sometimes they push their power to so bold an extreme, by nomination of a man so notoriously unfit, that an important group of his own party refuse to support him. Upon these conscientious dissenters the great body of the party, taking the cue from the discomfited leaders, heaps the vilest and most opprobrious abuse and fastens some abominable nickname to serve in place of argument. To the civilized observer this is inexpressibly shocking, and he can but wonder that Heaven permits this abominable race to exist.

To show how thoroughly, to the mind of the typical Tortirran, loyalty
to party is identical with loyalty to country, and with the service of reason,
I may relate that at a public dining-table I once heard a political conversation among five natives, each of whom, with a single exception, boasted
that he had never voted anything but the "straight ticket" of his party. If
these men had been told that in ignoring such small reason as God had
given them for their guidance, and submitting with sheeplike docility to
the direction of a long succession of scheming men whom they did not
even know by name, they had, within the limits of their narrow capacity,
done the worst possible disservice to their country, they would not have
known what was meant, or knowing, they would have resented it. The
resentment of the ignorant is not a thing to be courted, nor could it be
expected that I, a foreigner, should rebuke a savage in his own land, and I
was silent, as became me; but I could not help thinking how appropriate
to each of these men would be "the Fool's Prayer" of one of our minor
poets:

> Earth bears no balsam for mistakes:
>> Men crown the knave and scourge the tool
> That did his will; but thou, O Lord,
>> Be merciful to me, a fool.

The fifth native of this group of statesmen—he who had not always
"voted the straight ticket of his party"—was too young to vote, but I
suppose he lived in the comforting hope of always voting it when
qualified by age and a ripe judgment.

The quatrain is from Edward Rowland Sill (1841–1887), "The Fool's
Prayer" (1879).

49. The object of attack appears to be William McKinley (1843–1901), who
during his years as a U.S. Representative from Ohio (1877–91) was the leading
proponent of high tariffs. AB's words are prophetic, as McKinley's name was
attached to the tariff act of 1890 and he continued to pursue the policy during his
presidency (1897–1901).

50. In the original sketch the text here reads: "by smallpox; and some go so far
as to argue that every instance of a broken leg is clearly traceable to the importation of foreign goods."

51. The references are to a variety of judicial and legislative branches of the
government: "Supreme Legislature" = U.S. Congress; "Subordinate Council" =
state legislatures; "Great Court" = Supreme Court; "Minor Great Court" = state
supreme courts.

52. "[O]ur entire system of laws . . . [is] so complicated and contradictory that a
judge simply does as he pleases, subject only to the custom of giving for his action
reasons that at his option may or may not be derived from the statute. He may
sternly affirm that he sits there to interpret the law as he finds it, not to make it

accord with his personal notions of right and justice. Or he may declare that it could never have been the Legislature's intention to do wrong, and so, shielded by the useful phrase *contra bonos mores* [contrary to good morals], pronounce that illegal which he chooses to consider inexpedient. Or he may be guided by either of any two inconsistent precedents, as best suits his purpose. Or he may throw aside both statute and precedent, disregard good morals, and justify the judgment that he wishes to deliver by what other lawyers have written in books, and still others, without anybody's authority, have chosen to accept as a part of the law." AB, [Editorial], *W* no. 397 (Mar. 8, 1884, 4); rpt. *The Shadow on the Dial,* ed. S. O. Howes (San Francisco: A. M. Robertson, 1909), 65.

53. AB frequently alludes in his writings to the notion of deciding legal cases (or making any important decision) by a throw of the dice, in the manner of the corrupt judge Bridoye (Bridlegoose) in François Rabelais's *Gargantua et Pantagruel.* Cf. *DD:* "Appeal, *v t.* In law, to put the dice into the box for another throw"; and "Recount, *n.* In American politics, another throw of the dice, accorded to the player against whom they are loaded."

54. "As long as there exists the right of appeal there is a chance of acquittal. Otherwise the right of appeal would be a sham and an insult. . . . So long as acquittal may ensue guilt is not established. Why, then, are men sentenced before they are proved guilty? Why are they punished in the middle of proceedings against them?" AB, [Editorial], *W* no. 397 (Mar. 8, 1884, 4); rpt. *The Shadow on the Dial,* 64.

55. *Note in original:* Klikat um Delu Ovwi.

Letters from a Hdkhoite

These four letters were published in *NL* on April 4, April 11, April 18, and April 25, 1868. They appeared anonymously and have been assigned to AB on internal evidence. Assuming them to be AB's, they are the first instances of his use of a visit by an inhabitant of an imaginary realm to our civilization, although the topics here addressed are not as wide-ranging as in AB's later work: the first letter is chiefly a satire on the press, the second and third on religious disputes, and the fourth on the building of a church. The second article was published as "Letters from a Kdhoite," and that version of the proper name was used throughout the article; but we have amended it to match the spelling found in the other articles.

1. Cf. *DD:* "Absolute, *adj.* . . . An absolute monarchy is one in which the sovereign does as he pleases so long as he pleases the assassins."

2. See "Prattle" (*E,* May 30, 1897, 6): "However it may be customary for English newspapers to designate the English sovereign . . . they are at least not addicted to sycophancy in designating the rulers of other countries than their own.

They would not say 'his Abracadabral Humptidumptiness Emperor William,' nor 'his Raw-gust Pestilency Speaker Reed.' They would not think of calling even the most ornately self-bemedaled American sovereign elector 'his Badgesty.'"

　　3.　*Cotemporary* was at this time an acceptable variant spelling of *contemporary*.

　　4.　The Central Pacific Railroad was requesting permission to purchase 6,620 acres of waterfront and tidelands south of San Francisco and had a bill introduced in the state legislature on March 5, 1868. Public opposition to the selling of such an immense quantity of land caused the legislature to reject the bill and, on March 30, to donate only thirty acres each to the Western Pacific and Southern Pacific Railroad.

　　5.　The references are to some of the leading newspapers in San Francisco at the time: the *Bulletin* (founded 1855), the *Alta California* (founded 1849), the *Morning Call* (founded 1856), and the *Times* (founded 1854 as *Town Talk*). At the time, the impeachment trial of Andrew Johnson (1808–1875), seventeenth president of the United States, was in progress, the key votes occurring on May 16 and 26.

　　6.　The references are to the following:

　　　　Henry Huntly Haight (1825–1878), governor of California (1867–71).

　　　　Hugh Patrick Gallagher (1815–1882), Catholic priest who came to California in the mid-1850s and helped build churches in Benicia, San Francisco, and Oakland. In 1861 he established St. Joseph's parish in San Francisco.

　　　　Horatio Stebbins (1821–1902), minister at the First Unitarian Church in San Francisco, who performed AB's marriage service on December 25, 1871.

　　　　Henry Martyn Scudder (1822–1895), at this time pastor of the Howard Presbyterian church in San Francisco.

　　　　Oscar Penn Fitzgerald (1829–1911), Methodist bishop who remained in California from 1855 to 1878 and edited the *Pacific Methodist,* the *Christian Spectator,* and other papers.

　　　　Charles Wadsworth (1814–1882), Presbyterian minister whose departure from Philadelphia to the Calvary Church in San Francisco in 1861 was a blow to Emily Dickinson, who was apparently in love with him.

　　　　"The rev. B. T. Martin, late Assayer of the Branch Mint" (see "The Town Crier," *NL,* Sept. 4, 1869, 11). AB was employed at the U.S. Branch Mint in 1867–68.

　　　　Jacob Knapp (1799–1874), a local cleric. AB repeatedly twitted him in *NL,* especially in "Confessions of a Weak-Minded Man" (Mar. 7, 1868, 9; Mar. 14, 1868, 9; and Mar. 21, 1868, 2), all signed "Gwinnett." Knapp's *Autobiography* was published in 1868.

　　　　Peter Job, a restaurateur (see "The Town Crier," *NL,* Nov. 12, 1870, 9).

　　　　Michael Reese, a wealthy San Francisco businessman involved in a number of unsavory financial transactions as well as a breach of promise suit in 1866–67.

　　　　Joshua A. Norton (1819–1880) came to California in 1849, made and lost a fortune, and after several years of seclusion reemerged and declared himself emperor of the United States and protector of Mexico. He remained a well-known and colorful figure in San Francisco until his death.

Eels and Jobson are unidentified.

7. John 21:16, 17. Sheep, when used in reference to human beings, are persons who are weak, timid, or submissive; persons who are easily swayed or led. In the gospel of John, Jesus refers to himself as the Good Shepherd—someone to lead those who need someone to lead them.

8. Cf. Luke 20:17: "And he beheld them, and said, What is this then that is written, The stone which the builders rejected, the same is become the head of the corner?"

9. AB refers to the term *superstition,* derived from two Latin words, *super* ("above") and *stare* ("to stand"), meaning "to stand over a thing in amazement or awe."

10. Matt. 16:18. The word *Peter* (= Greek *Cephas*) means "rock."

11. Josiah Dwight Whitney (1819–1896), the state geologist of California and author of numerous treatises on the geology of the state.

12. Cf. *DD:* "Trinity, *n.* In the multiplex theism of certain Christian churches, three entirely distinct deities consistent with only one. Subordinate deities of the polytheistic faith, such as devils and angels, are not dowered with the power of combination, and must urge individually their claims to adoration and propitiation. The Trinity is one of the most sublime mysteries of our holy religion. In rejecting it because it is incomprehensible, Unitarians betray their inadequate sense of theological fundamentals. In religion we believe only what we do not understand, except in the instance of an intelligible doctrine that contradicts an incomprehensible one. In that case we believe the former as a part of the latter."

The Aborigines of Oakland

This whimsy appeared anonymously in *NL* (Nov. 7, 1868) and has been assigned to AB on internal evidence. It reflects AB's frequent condescension toward the less glamorous sister city of San Francisco (see, e.g., the poem originally titled "The Restaurants of Oakland: By Their Victim," *W,* Apr. 3, 1886; rpt. as "Famine's Realm"). Almost twenty years after writing this squib, AB actually lived in Oakland for at least a few months in the late summer of 1887; it was here that the young William Randolph Hearst came to AB and asked him to write for *E* (see "A Thumb-Nail Sketch," *CW* 12.305).

1. The name is a play on *fustian* or bombastic language.

2. The "coolies" were Chinese immigrants who came to California and worked in a variety of menial or low-paying occupations, notably the construction of the railroad. They were the victims of serious resentment and violence on

the part of the Anglo-Saxon population. AB resolutely defended the coolies throughout his career; see *SS* 145–48.

3. Victoria, the capital of British Columbia, was founded in 1843 by the Hudson's Bay Company. The Chinese and other nonwhite ethnic groups in the city in fact suffered discrimination and harassment in the later nineteenth century. The Chinooks are a tribe of Native Americans living mainly along the north side of the Columbia River in what is now Washington state.

4. The Megatherium was a large ground sloth flourishing in the Pleistocene epoch (two million to eleven thousand years ago), and growing up to twenty feet in length. *Behemoth* (the word is plural) means "great sea-monsters"; they are mentioned in the Bible (Gen. 1:21) as being created on the fifth day of creation. A Castilian is an inhabitant of Castile, the historical name for a region in central and northern Spain.

5. Stockton is a city in San Joaquin County, about fifty miles east of Oakland. The Diablo range is now called the Contra Costa Hills, about thirty miles east of Oakland; its highest point, Mt. Diablo, is 3,800 feet above sea level. San Leandro is a city directly south of Oakland, on the east shore of San Francisco Bay. Vallejo is a city in Solano county, on the north shore of San Pablo Bay. The Carquinez Strait lies directly south of Vallejo and connects San Pablo Bay and Grizzly Bay. Goat Island is now called Yerba Buena Island, and is the land mass on the southern end of Treasure Island in San Francisco Bay.

6. The deformed creatures (analogous to human beings) dwelling in the land of the Houyhnhnms in *GT*. See also "The Land Beyond the Blow," n. 32.

7. The College of California was founded in 1860 in Oakland, but moved to Berkeley in 1864 and later became the University of California. Other branches were founded after AB wrote the present sketch.

8. An Aramaic phrase found in 1 Cor. 16:22 ("If any man love not the Lord Jesus Christ, let him be Anathema Maranatha"), formerly thought to be an imprecation.

A Scientific Dream

This story also appeared anonymously in *NL* (Nov. 14, 1868) and has been assigned to AB on internal evidence. It is simultaneously a satire on Darwin's theory of evolution and on the frequency of earthquakes in San Francisco. It was published a few weeks after a major earthquake in San Francisco on October 21, 1868.

1. Charles Darwin (1809–1882), *On the Origin of Species by Means of Natural Selection* (1859).

2. AB discussed the earthquake in "Earthquake Items" (*NL* 18, no. 34 [Oct. 24, 1868]: 5) and "A Tale of the Great Quake" (*FD* 36–37).

Across the Continent

This story, published under the pseudonym "Samboles" in *NL,* May 15, 1869, has been assigned to AB on internal evidence. Assuming the work to be AB's, it is his first "futuristic" story, set in the year 3973, and begins the pattern of citing erroneous or fragmentary accounts of "ancient" history (including, in this case, the Mormons and the Transcontinental Railroad). This obvious fiction appeared in a department called "White Pine News" with the following "Notice": "It is our intention to make summary of White Pine News as complete and comprehensive a collection of matter as is possible. Valuable facts from the mining districts will be contributed by our correspondents in Nevada and other places in addition to the news supplied us on the same subject from reliable sources in San Francisco, so that we may fairly anticipate being in a position to afford the most authentic information to our readers. Should any deviation from the most accurate statement occur in our columns, we shall at all times be willing to correct it."

1. The Mormon sect was founded in 1830 by Joseph Smith in Fayette, New York. Vicious persecution by other religious groups, largely over the practice of polygamy, forced the Mormons to relocate successively to Ohio, Missouri, and Illinois. There, in the town of Nauvoo, Smith was murdered by a mob in 1844, and more than 20,000 homes of Mormons were burned. Under the leadership of Brigham Young, the Mormons moved to Utah and established themselves at Salt Lake City. AB frequently defended the Mormons against those who would persecute them. See "Prattle" (*A,* May 31, 1879, 9; rpt. *W,* Mar. 26, 1881, 196): "This by way of illustration; it is right to explain that I have a sincere respect for the Mormons. Surviving one of the most hateful and sneaking aggressions that ever disgraced the generally straightforward and forthright course of religious persecution—an aggression that lacked alike the sanction of authority and the lustre of success—they dragged the feeble remnant of their dispirited body into the horrible wilderness, where, a thousand miles beyond the reach of cupidity's most extravagant claim, they made a garden of abundance. There they reared the edible beast and the succulent vegetable, and to the feast came Famine from over the seas to line his ribs with leaves of firm white tallow, box-plaited and scalloped. Following his dusty toes thither, Nakedness was fearfully and wonderfully clad, yet warmly withal. There the stomach of intemperance paled its ineffectual fires, and Immorality was fain to hide his diminished head. In short, Mormonism proved the greatest practical benefaction of the century. If it ruined any souls it had the right, for the starving carcasses of its converts had none until souls were created under their skeleton ribs by Mormon meats and herbs. And now we want to rout out the Mormons again, rapacity arming itself for the purpose with

religion's exhausted mandates copied from the archives of Nauvoo and telegraphed out to Ogden."

2. In fact, the name Nevada derives from the Spanish word *nevada* ("snow-capped"), referring to the Sierra Nevada mountain range in the western part of the state.

3. AB refers to the completion of the Transcontinental Railroad, which was celebrated by the driving of a golden spike at a ceremony at Promontory Point, Utah, on May 10, 1869.

4. Just prior to the completion of the Transcontinental Railroad, an unsigned article (probably not by AB) appeared in *NL* commemorating the event. Accompanying the article was an illustration of a railroad spike upon which was inscribed the following: "With this Spike the 'San Francisco News Letter' offers its homage to the great work which has joined the Atlantic and Pacific Oceans this Month May 1869." See "Finis," *NL* 9 [*sic*], no. 14 (May 8, 1869): 1.

John Smith, Liberator

This story first appeared as "John Smith" in the British humor magazine *Fun* for May 10, 1873, and was reprinted with revisions under its present title in *CW* 1. It is simultaneously a literary satire (in its suggestion that some mediocre writers of AB's day would be the only ones whose work would survive in the future) and a political satire (in that the "Smithocratic form of government" is in fact never defined).

1. Shakespeare, *Julius Caesar,* 5.5.68. Said of Brutus by Mark Antony.

2. Napoleon, then emperor of France, was defeated by the British, led by the duke of Wellington, at the battle of Waterloo on June 18, 1815. He subsequently abdicated and was exiled to the island of St. Helena, in the South Atlantic. "Chickenhurst" alludes to Chislehurst, a town near London where Napoleon III and his family remained after France's defeat in the Franco-Prussian War of 1870–71.

3. Martin Farquhar Tupper (1810–1889), a widely published British poet of the day whom Bierce disdained. See "Prattle" (*A,* July 14, 1877, 5): "Mr. Martin Farquhar Tupper, the author of *Philosophomic Proverbiage,* has written a drama in five acts, called 'Washington.' And now it is said that strange, unearthly noises are heard at night in the vicinity of Mt. Vernon—something like the subdued swearing of a cat under a floor!" See further n. 7.

4. A reference to the seven Greek cities that claimed to be the birthplace of Homer.

5. In the eighteenth century biographers of Shakespeare claimed that he had been arrested for deer-stealing, but the veracity of this incident is now regarded as highly suspect.

6. Claudius Salmasius (1588–1653) was a minister against whom John

Milton's two polemical works, *Pro Populo Anglicano Defensio* (1650, 1654), were directed. Milton's eyesight began to fail in the mid-1640s, and by 1651 he was totally blind.

7. Tupper's *Proverbial Philosophy,* published in four series (1838–71), was a series of poetic aphorisms and was widely reprinted throughout the nineteenth century.

8. A reference to Ella Wheeler Wilcox (1850–1919), a popular writer and poet whose later work often appeared adjacent to AB's in the Hearst papers.

9. In "Little Johnny, the Nature Faker" (MS, BL), Bungoot is a town in India.

"The Bubble Reputation"

This squib, appearing in the *Wasp* for May 8, 1886, and reprinted in the eighth volume of *CW,* is chiefly a satire on newspapers. It suggests that unscrupulous editors and reporters deliberately write biased and misleading stories in order to secure a "bubble reputation" (i.e., short-lived celebrity).

1. A parody of the Knights of Labor, a union initially organized by garment workers in Philadelphia. Growing rapidly in membership in the later 1870s and attracting workers from many occupations, it achieved a membership of 500,000 by 1886. AB's story was published only a few days after the Haymarket riots in Chicago (see "Prevention vs. No Cure"), for which the Knights of Labor were later unjustly blamed, leading to their rapid decline.

2. A play on Laurel Hill Cemetery at Bush Street and Presidio Avenue in San Francisco, one of the city's oldest cemeteries, with interments dating to 1854.

3. AB knew full well that *inhumation* derives from the Latin *inhumare* (to bury in the ground). He is suggesting that the newspaper editor thinks the act of burial is inhuman. Cf. "What Civilization Does" in the symposium, "Does Civilization Civilize?" (*E,* Dec. 25, 1891, 7): "every custom of our barbarian ancestors in historic times survives in some form to-day. . . . We bury our dead instead of burning them, yet every cemetery is set thick with urns for their ashes. As there are no ashes for the urns we do not trouble ourselves to make them hollow, and we say their use is 'emblematic.' When, following the best of our savage instincts, we go on, age after age, in the performance of some senseless act which once had a meaning we excuse ourselves by calling it symbolism."

For the Ahkoond

This story first appeared in *E,* Mar. 18, 1888, and was reprinted with revisions in the first volume of *CW.* It purports to depict the journey of an explorer from California (now labeled Citrusia, and the only inhabited part of the continent) to the deserted areas east of the "Ultimate Hills" (Rocky Mountains). The title "Ahkoond" became popular when in 1878 American poet George Thomas Lanigan (1845–1886) wrote a comic poem, "A Threnody" (1878), on the "Akhoond of Swat"—i.e., Abdul Ghafur (1794–1877), the Akhund (or Akhond) of Swat, a region in northwestern India.

1. See "Prattle" (*E,* Apr. 30, 1893, 6): "When I am Minister of the Fine Arts to his Majesty the Ahkoond of Citrusia every picture made will be submitted to the untutored eye of a South Sea islander freshly imported. If he sees in it a resemblance to any thing on the earth, in the heavens above the earth, or in waters beneath the earth, it will be destroyed and its maker put to death." The name is a play on *citrus,* referring to the abundant cultivation of citrus fruits in the state.

2. A play on the Central Pacific Railroad. AB is making a pun on the root meaning of the word *Pacific* (peaceful).

3. Tennyson, *In Memoriam: A. H. H.* (1850), stanza 56, ll. 22–23.

4. Pike's Peak (14,109 ft.) is in central Colorado, about sixty miles south of Denver.

5. *Galoot* was a slang term of humorous contempt, used largely in the western states, in reference to a man, frequently suggesting awkwardness or weakness.

6. *Note in original:* This satire was published in the *San Francisco Examiner* many years before the invention of wireless telegraphy; so I retain my own name for the instrument.—A. B.

7. *Puke* was a slang term for a disgusting person, and also a vulgar nickname for a native of Missouri.

8. A play on *mugwump.* The term was coined in the 1830s from an Algonquin word, *mugquomp,* meaning "great man, chief, captain, leader." In U.S. slang it came to be used derisively for a man who thought too highly of himself. In 1884 it was a term of abuse directed against Republicans who refused to support their presidential candidate, James G. Blaine. In 1888 AB declared himself a mugwump (see *SS* 219). AB uses the word *smugwump* on occasion in letters, once in reference to Andrew Carnegie (AB to John H. E. Partington, Oct. 7, 1892; MS, BL) and twice in apparent reference to easterners (AB to S. O. Howes, Apr. 5, 1906 [MS, HL]; AB to George Sterling, Apr. 5, 1906 [MS, NP]). AB's meaning in these instances is unclear, nor is it clear whether he actually coined this term or whether it was a slang term in general use. See also "The Extinction of the Smugwumps" (p. 127).

9. *Note in original:* At one time it was foolishly believed that the disease had been eradicated by slapping the mosquitoes which were thought to produce it;

but a few years later it broke out with greater violence than ever before, although the mosquitoes had left the country.

The Fall of the Republic

Published in *E,* Mar. 25, 1888, this story is an early version of "Ashes of the Beacon," but is significantly different in many particulars. Although many of the same issues are treated—the fallacy of republican government, the bane of high tariffs, the danger of anarchists, troubles between capital and labor—the material has been arranged differently and a considerable body of text was not reprinted in the later work.

1. Pescadero is a small town near the coast of northern California, about twenty miles west of San Jose.
2. Pope, *An Essay on Man* (1733–34), Epistle 3, ll. 303–4.
3. A reference to the Republican politician John James Ingalls (1833–1900), U.S. senator from Kansas (1873–91) and a vigorous supporter of the Grand Army of the Republic.
4. This couplet was later used in the original version of "The Tamtonians." See "The Land Beyond the Blow," n. 24.

The Wizard of Bumbassa

First published as "Rabid Transit," an unsigned editorial in *E,* Aug. 28, 1892, and later reprinted in *CW* 12, this sketch pokes fun at George Westinghouse (1846–1914), American inventor of the air brake, which made high-speed rail travel possible, and founder of the Westinghouse Electric Corporation in 1884. The Railroad Safety Appliance Act of 1893 made air brakes compulsory on all American trains. Since at least the 1870s AB had spoken of the dangers of railway travel and the inadequate safety measures instituted by the leading railroad companies, as in the following extract:

> A grand jury in Kern county has investigated the causes of the recent railroad slaughter at Tchachapi Pass, and in its report attributes the disaster, not to the employees of the lost train, who acted under instructions and are still in the service of the company, but to "the general management of the road." The report affirms that the road at Tchachapi is illegally constructed and dangerous, and that rains are run over it with the same reckless disregard of precautions as before the accident. The Southern Pacific Railroad Company is therefore "strongly censured," and the public assured that it is

"entitled to such immediate changes as may effectually place beyond possibility the recurrence of such a calamity" as the comminution and combustion of passengers. In case Messrs. Stanford, Crocker and Huntington should have their attention directed to this report, and should impenitently refuse to fall sick about it, we have the honor to recommend that another and more terrible grand jury be convened, and that it do not confine itself to so mild a measure as "strong censure," but go to the length of "sharp rebuke." It may perhaps be urged that having been proved culpable they might properly have been indicted; but this inhuman course might have resulted in an injury to their finest feelings; for even if sent to the State Prison their characters are so bad that the Warden would undoubtedly turn them into the street. As for the public, now that it knows what it is entitled to, it would apparently be legally justified in wishing that it may get it. ([Editorial], *W,* May 19, 1883, 4)

The name Bumbassa is presumably a play on Mombasa, an island off the coast of Kenya.

Modern Penology

This selection, from "Prattle," *E,* Feb. 10, 1895, reflects AB's contention that society is not dealing harshly enough with criminals. The title has been supplied by the editors. The extract served as the final segment of the essay "The Death Penalty" in S. O. Howes's assemblage of AB's journalism, *The Shadow on the Dial* (1909), later reprinted in *CW* 11.

1. William Wordsworth, *The Excursion* (1814), 8.461 (also 9.725).
2. Percy Bysshe Shelley, "Ozymandias" (1817), l. 14 ("stretch" in Shelley).

The Great Strike of 1895

First published as "The Strike of 1899" in *E,* May 5, 1895, this story was reprinted under its present title in volume 12 of *CW,* although there it was dated 1894 to suggest that it was written in advance of the events it purports to record. A lighthearted satire on authors who unionize for protection against rapacious publishers, the story allowed AB to poke fun at several leading authors of the day as well as some of his own literary colleagues. The inspiration for the story appears to have been AB's election to a group called the American Authors' Guild in 1894 (see AB to Charles Burr Todd, May 15, 1894; MS, BL). Little is known of this group; but as one scholar on authors' unions notes, "Several rival writers' groups formed in the 1890s, successors to the groups that had promoted the cause of international copyright, but the rivalries and factionalism that resulted from so many competing organizations guaranteed their failure, especially since all faced the unanimous hostility of publishers, magazine editors, and the press" (Richard Fine, *James M. Cain and the American Authors' Authority* [Austin: Univ. of Texas Press, 1992], 62). The first significant authors' society in the United States was the Authors League of America, founded in 1912; in 1920 it established the Authors Guild as a subsidiary. In Great Britain, the Society of Authors was founded in 1883. AB was indeed generally on the side of authors as opposed to publishers, who he felt did not reward authors sufficiently for their work.

1. William Dean Howells (1837–1920) was one of the most respected authors and critics of his day, but AB did not think much of him or his work: "Men of letters manufacture one another. The two finest products of the mill are [Henry] James and Howells. Neither can think and the latter cannot write. He can not write at all. The other day . . . I took a random page of this man's work and in twenty minutes had marked forty solecisms—instances of the use of words without a sense of their importance or a knowledge of their meaning—the substitution of a word that he did not want for a word that he did not think of" ("Prattle," *W*, Feb. 17, 1883, 5). Howells's chief publisher was Harper & Brothers.

2. A deliberate confusion of two authors, the American poet and editor Richard Henry Stoddard (1825–1903) and the British poet Richard Henry (or Hengist) Horne (1803–1884).

3. Brander Matthews (1852–1929), a leading American critic and editor of the period. In late 1892 AB had written to Matthews thanking him for his favorable notice of *Tales of Soldiers and Civilians* in his article "More American Stories," *Cosmopolitan* 13, no. 5 (Sept. 1892): 629–30. See AB to Brander Matthews, Nov. 28, 1892; MS, Columbia Univ.

4. Thomas Wentworth Higginson (1823–1911), American essayist and first editor of the poems of Emily Dickinson. He commanded a regiment of African Americans during the Civil War, attaining the rank of colonel.

5. The first free library in New York, founded in 1854 and located at 425 Lafayette Street. In 1911 its holdings were merged with two other collections to form the New York Public Library.

6. The American author Julia Ward Howe (1819–1910) composed "The Battle Hymn of the Republic" in 1861; it was published the next year. Bellevue Hospital, the oldest general hospital in North America, was dedicated in 1816. It is located on the East River between 26th and 30th Streets.

7. The Pinkertons, a private detective agency founded in 1850, were frequently used in the later nineteenth century by owners of factories and other businesses to protect property and, in some cases, to intimidate striking workers. In a notorious incident in July 1892, a battle between Pinkertons and strikers at the steel plant in Homestead, Pennsylvania, owned by Andrew Carnegie, resulted in the deaths of ten strikers and three Pinkertons.

8. Cincinnatus Hiner Miller (1837–1913), who adopted the pseudonym Joaquin Miller, was born in Indiana but moved to California and achieved celebrity both for his poetry and for his flamboyant personality. For a time he lived with a tribe of Digger Indians. He was a longtime friend of AB.

9. The mayor of Chicago in 1893–95 was John Hopkins (1858–1918), the city's first Irish Catholic mayor. "The Beautiful Snow" was a popular sentimental poem written by John Whittaker Watson (1824–1890) and included in *Beautiful Snow and Other Poems* (1869). Its authorship was claimed by several poets.

10. Percival Pollard (1869–1911), critic, playwright, and friend of AB. Hamlin Garland (1860–1940), novelist and memoirist.

11. Opie Read (1852–1939), novelist, journalist, and editor. AB's misspelling of his last name is probably inadvertent.

12. AB submitted several works to the Chicago firm of Stone & Kimball in the period 1893–96, including *The Fall of the Republic and Other Satires*. See Introduction (p. xi).

13. The Cooper Union for the Advancement of Science and Art, at Astor Place and East 7th Street, was founded by Peter Cooper in 1859 as an institution offering free education to the sons and daughters of working-class families. It is now associated with New York University.

14. Edward W. Townsend (1855–1942) was a friend of AB and author of *"Chimmie Fadden"; Major Max; and Other Stories* (1895).

15. Richard Harding Davis (1864–1916), novelist and journalist.

16. Thomas Bailey Aldrich (1836–1907), once-celebrated poet, novelist, and dramatist.

17. Walter Blackburn Harte (1867–1898), essayist, editor of the *New England Magazine,* and friend of AB. His book *Meditations in Motley* (1894) was published by the Arena Publishing Co.

18. Louise Chandler Moulton (1835–1908), poet, journalist, and children's writer.

19. Pseudonym of Samuel Langhorne Clemens (1835–1910). He and AB had been sporadically acquainted since the 1870s.

20. John Vance Cheney (1848–1922), California poet and friend of AB.

21. For Lew Wallace see "The Land Beyond the Blow," n. 28.

Annals of the Future Historian

"The Fall of Christian Civilization" from "The Passing Show" (*NJ,* Feb. 18, 1900; *E,* Feb. 18, 1900) discusses the invention of a smokeless and noiseless gunpowder. The title has been supplied by the editors. For further reflections on this theme see "The Dispersal" and the section "On Advances in Weaponry."

"On the Canal"—extracted from "The Passing Show" (*NJ,* Apr. 15, 1900; *E,* Apr. 16, 1900; title supplied by the editors)—is a satire on the long and seemingly fruitless discussions in Congress, extending back at least to the 1870s, over the viability of an isthmian canal linking the Atlantic and Pacific Oceans. AB supported the construction of a canal in Nicaragua (see "Ambrose Bierce Says: The Nicaragua Canal Is Not Yet Assured," *NJ*, Jan. 17, 1900, 8). France had attempted in the 1880s to construct a canal in Panama, but the effort collapsed through bad planning and lack of funds. AB's remarks here were probably inspired by President William McKinley's appointment in 1899 of an Isthmian Canal Commission. U.S. work on the Panama Canal did not begin in earnest until 1904. See further "The Republic of Panama" below.

"The Minister's Death," from "The Passing Show" (*NJ*, July 1, 1900; *E*, July 1, 1900; title supplied by the editors), deals with Wu Ting Fang, Chinese minister to the United States, who in late June 1900 had asked the United States for an armistice during the Boxer Rebellion. (U.S. troops had been sent to China to protect American missionaries and other foreigners from attacks by the Chinese.) AB had recommended that Wu himself be held hostage until the Americans' safety was assured. See "Ambrose Bierce Says: We Should Hold Wu Ting Fang as a Hostage," *NJ*, June 21, 1900, 8; *E*, June 23, 1900, 6 (as "We Should Hold Minister Wu Ting-Fang as a Hostage").

A pungent satire on Carry Nation, the temperance advocate (published in *NJ*, Mar. 10, 1901, and *E*, Mar. 19, 1901), "The Maid of Podunk" is only to have been expected from a man who violently opposed any attempts at the prohibition of alcohol; see the essays reprinted in the section "Temperance." The title is meant as a parody of "the maid of Orleans," the customary designation of Joan of Arc. AB may have been following the example of Voltaire's mock-epic poem *La Pucelle d'Orleans* (1755, 1762), a risqué burlesque in which Joan of Arc is depicted as a hapless maiden whose virginity is frequently in danger of being violated. The work was frequently translated as *The Maid of Orleans*. AB may also have had Mark Twain's *Personal Recollections of Joan of Arc* (1896) in mind, although that work is a largely factual and respectful historical account of Joan. Note that Twain is actually mentioned in the sketch.

"The Extinction of the Smugwumps" (published in *NJ*, July 19, 1901, and *E*, Aug. 12, 1901) is chiefly a satire on the extremes of heat found in the eastern United States—something that AB, a Californian transplanted to Washington in 1900, perhaps found disconcerting. AB treats the issue tangentially in "The Domestic Heat Escape" (*NA*, June 25, 1903, 16), in which he advocates the use of gardens in public and private dwellings: "In this climate the domestic roof garden, as a place to escape from the insupportable heat and pass in hammocks a comfortable night, would be indispensable for only three or four months of the year." For the name Smugwump see "For the Ahkoond" (p. 98, and also n. 8).

"Industrial Discontent in Ancient America" (published in *NJ*, Aug. 14, 1901) treats an issue that AB had discussed frequently in both stories and essays—the bane of unionism.

"The Future Historian and His Fatigue" (published in *NA*, July 8, 1903, and *E*, Sept. 5, 1903) concerns the yacht race between the United States and Great Britain whose winner would receive "America's Cup." Sir Thomas Lipton (1850–1931), the British merchant who in 1890 began vigorous marketing of the tea that bears his name, was an ardent yachtsman who tried on five occasions to win America's Cup (1899, 1901, 1903, 1920, and 1930), but lost every time. On each occasion his ship was called the *Shamrock*. In 1903, the race, in which the contestants were to sail ten to fifteen nautical miles from the Sandy Hook Lightship (stationed eight nautical miles southeast of Sandy Hook, New Jersey) and return, was to have been run in late August, but bad weather prevented it until September 3, when the U.S. yacht *Reliance* easily beat Lipton's *Shamrock*.

"A Chronicle of the Time to Be," published in *NA* (May 6, 1904), deals with the Russo-Japanese War (1904–5), triggered by Japan's concern over Russia's increasing influence in Manchuria. When Russia acquired a lease on Port Arthur, on the Liaotung Peninsula in China, the Japanese invaded on February 8, 1904. In the resulting war, which ended with a treaty signed on September 6, 1905, Russia was driven out of Korea and Manchuria. AB wrote frequently on the course of the war in columns of 1904 and 1905, and in "Small Contributions" (*Co*, Aug. 1908) gave brief notice to *The Truth about Port Arthur* by E. K. Nojine, translated and abridged by A. B. Lindsay; edited by E. D. Swinton (London: John Murray, 1908).

"The Republic of Panama," extracted from "The Passing Show" (*NJ*, Feb. 7, 1904; *E*, Feb. 21, 1904; title supplied by the editors), deals—as does "On the Canal" (see p. 123)—with the Panama Canal, although the situation surrounding the canal was now very different. As a result of Colombia's rejection of the Hay-Pauncefote Treaty, in which Great Britain yielded its interests in a Panama canal to the United States, revolutionaries in Panama (then a Colombian colony) rose in rebellion, declaring independence on November 3, 1903. The rebellion was covertly aided by the United States, which recognized the new state on November 6. On November 18 the Hay-Bunau-Varilla Treaty was negotiated, giving the United States full control of a ten-mile canal zone. The treaty was formally ratified on February 26, 1904.

"The Second American Invasion of China" is an extract from a column, "The Views of One" (*NA*, Mar. 12, 1906; *E*, Mar. 17, 1906; title supplied by the editors), dealing with the possibility of a conflict between the United States and China. In mid-February 1906, the War Department was contemplating sending troops to the Philippines as part of a plan to invade the Chinese mainland during the summer in order to forestall an uprising of Chinese natives against the many Americans and other foreigners in the country. The plan was vigorously opposed by Eugene Hale (1836–1918), U.S. senator from Maine (1881–1911), who, although a Republican, had repeatedly condemned the military actions of the McKinley and Roosevelt administrations, including the Spanish-American War and the Philippine War. AB's reference to a "second" invasion of China alludes to the Boxer Rebellion of 1900, in which the United States and several European nations sent troops to quell a nationalist uprising in China.

"Rise and Fall of the Aëroplane," originally published as "The Rise and Fall of the Aeroplane" (*Co*, Oct. 1908), is a reflection of AB's skepticism regarding the feasibility of flight by air; a skepticism that was expressed both before and after the successful flight by the Wright brothers in 1903 (see the section "Travel by Air").

"The Dispersal," originally published as "The Reversion to Barbarism" (*Co,* Mar. 1909), is an elaboration of a "Future Historian" extract from "The Passing Show" of 1900 (see p. 122) dealing with the invention of the "silent firearm." AB paid frequent attention to advances in weaponry, at the same time expressing skepticism regarding certain startling claims made by inventors of new weapons. See the essays reprinted in the section "Advances in Weaponry."

"An Ancient Hunter," originally published as "The Advance Agent" (*Co,* Apr. 1909), deals with Theodore Roosevelt's hunting trip to Africa following the end of his presidency. He sailed to Africa from Hoboken, New Jersey, on March 23, 1909. Over the next year he sent frequent accounts of his travels, published as articles in *Scribner's Magazine* and later as a two-volume book, *African Game Trails* (1910). By March 1910 he had reached Khartoum, where the party disbanded. The expedition killed three thousand animals during the journey. AB mingles Roosevelt's exploits with those of Heracles as a means of deflating Roosevelt's bombast.

"A Leaf Blown In from Days To Be"—one of the relatively few works AB published following his resignation from William Randolph Hearst's employ in the spring of 1909—was published in the New York society magazine *Town Talk* (Mar. 17, 1910). It again deals with Theodore Roosevelt, incorporating historical tidbits from ancient and modern history, and even ancient myth, to poke fun at Roosevelt's political, military, and other achievements. Roosevelt broke from the Republican party in 1912 and ran for president on the Bull Moose ticket; as a result, both he and the Republican incumbent William Howard Taft were defeated and the Democrat Woodrow Wilson was elected. After the election AB remarked in a letter: "The defeat of Teddy fills my soul with a great white peace" (AB to Walter Neale, Nov. 6, 1912; MS, HL).

1. This geographical distinction corresponds roughly to that outlined in "For the Ahkoond" (pp. 96–99).

2. A pun on *Washing*ton.

3. A reference to Gen. Nelson Appleton Miles (1839–1925), who since 1895 had been commander in chief of the U.S. Army. In July 1900 (after AB wrote this story), Miles requested permission to lead a large force of troops to China to raise the Boxers' siege of Peking, but Secretary of War Elihu Root sent a smaller force as part of the International Relief Force, which lifted the siege in August.

4. *Podunk* is a slang term used to designate any small, isolated town, place, or region regarded as unimportant.

5. Carry (frequently but erroneously spelled Carrie) Nation was born Carry Amelia Moore on November 25, 1846, in Girard County, Kentucky. She died on June 9, 1911.

6. Cf. "The Town Crier" (*NL,* Apr. 1, 1871, 9; rpt. *FD* 102–3 under "Current Journalings"): "Some raging iconoclast, after having overthrown religion by history, upset history by science, and then toppled over science, has now laid his impious hands upon babies' nursing bottles. 'The tubes of these

infernal machines,' says this beast, 'are composed of India-rubber dissolved in bisulphide of carbon, and thickened with lead, resin, and sometimes oxysulphuret of antimony, from which, when it comes in contact with the milk, sulphuretted hydrogen is evolved, and lactate of lead formed in the stomach.' This logic is irresistible. Granting only that the tubes are made in that simple and intelligible manner (and anybody can see for himself that they are), the sulpheretted hydrogen and the lactate of lead follow (down the œsophagus) as a logical sequence. But the scientific idiot seems to be profoundly unaware that these substances are not only harmless to the child but actually nutritious and essential to its growth. Not only so, but nature has implanted in its breast an instinctive craving for these very viands. Often have we seen some wee thing turn disgusted from the breast and lift up its voice: 'Not for Joseph; give me the bottle with the oxysulphuret of antimony tube. I take sulphuretted hydrogen and lactate of lead in mine every time!' And we have said: 'Nature is working in that darling. What God hath joined together let no man put asunder!' And we have thought of the wicked iconoclast."

7. Nation divorced her first husband, Dr. Charles Gloyd (an alcoholic), shortly after their marriage in 1867. In 1877 she married David Nation and by the 1890s had settled in Medicine Lodge, Kansas. She began entering saloons in various Kansas towns and destroying their liquor supplies. In January 1901 she elicited great notoriety when she destroyed one such saloon in Wichita with a hatchet, which henceforth became her defining symbol. AB's deliberate error "Mormont" is meant to refer to the Mormons, who are teetotalers.

8. Nation in fact admitted to hearing voices and having other mystical experiences. See her autobiography, *The Use and Need of the Life of Carry A. Nation* (1904).

9. AB railed tirelessly against such constructions. See "Prattle" (*E*, Feb. 19, 1888, 4): "*Roomer,* for *lodger.* This is one of the most abominable words in the language of illiteracy. How it came I cannot imagine. I have myself, by way of experiment, and perhaps revenge, tried to give it company, having 'invented and gone round advising' the words *bedder* and *mealer,* constructed on the same lines, but they lack some mysterious vital quality and will not 'stick.'"

10. Cf. Worgum Slupsky, the "author" of some verses in the *DD* entry "Portable."

11. Jules Bastien-Lepage (1848–1884), French painter. AB has misspelled the name, whether deliberately or not. For Twain see "The Great Strike of 1895," n. 19.

12. Domrémy-la-Pucelle, a small village in eastern France, is the birthplace of Joan of Arc.

13. For another example of false philology, see "Prattle" (*A,* Apr. 27, 1878, 9): "Advices from Japan state that Iwakuru is arranging to celebrate the 2538th anniversary of the death of Jimmu Tenno. Jim was the founder of the present dynasty, which is therefore officially known—to distinguish it from its immediate predecessors and prevent confusion in the State archives—as the Jim dynasty, a

designation contracted, in popular speech, to Jimnasty. Hence our word gymnastics (which inferior philologists have professed to derive from the Greek), gymnastics being a sort of thing in which the Japs can beat a circus. From gymnastic we get the word gum-eleastic, an indiarubber man, or contortionist, being an indispensable attraction at every show."

14. See *DD*: "Ablative, *adj*. A certain case of Latin nouns. The ablative absolute is an ancient form of grammatical error much admired by modern scholars."

15. Edwin Markham (1852–1940) was a California poet and once a friend of AB; but the latter severed relations with him shortly after publication of his celebrated poem, "The Man with the Hoe" (1899), in which AB felt Markham had subordinated his artistic feeling to propaganda. Markham was actually born in Oregon City, Oregon.

16. A parody of the story of George Washington's chopping down the cherry tree, fabricated by Mason Locke (Parson) Weems (1759–1825), American clergyman and itinerant book agent. The fiction was inserted into the fifth edition (1806) of his book *The Life and Memorable Actions of George Washington* (1800).

17. The verb *galumph* means to move with a clumsy, heavy tread.

18. See "Nature as a Reformer," *Cosmopolitan* 45, no. 1 (June 1908): [1]: "As a habitation for man as he is, this world—the material spheroid upon which he lives as long as he can—is a singularly inhospitable dwelling-place. Upon only about one-eighth part of its surface can he live at all, and for only a little time, in an unequal struggle with the malign forces of nature."

19. Samuel Gompers (1850–1924), labor leader who founded the American Federation of Labor in 1886.

20. AB preferred this original spelling of the city to the later spelling, Pittsburgh. See "Prattle" (*E,* Aug. 31, 1890, 6): "I should like to know, for an unlawful purpose, who set the irritating fashion of writing Pittsburg with a final h. 'Burg' means a town, and is pronounced as it looks, but 'burgh' is pronounced like 'burro,' a donkey, being a contracted form of 'borough,' of which another contraction is 'boro.' The name of the Cinder City at the fork of the Ohio is not Pittsburgh but Pittsburg, and the man who first tacked on the final h is a person of high unworth whom it were Christian toleration to hang."

21. First cited in "For the Ahkoond" (see n. 1).

22. See n. 19 above.

23. Eugene V. Debs (1855–1926), Socialist leader. While president of the American Railway Union he led a bitter strike against the Great Northern Railroad and the Pullman Company in 1895. AB remarked on the strike with considerable heat, so much so that William Randolph Hearst urged AB to take a "vacation" until the strike was over.

24. John Pierpont Morgan (1837–1913), railroad magnate, founder of the U.S. Steel Corporation (1901) and accumulator of an immense personal fortune.

25. In his Little Johnny sketches, AB used Kibosh as the name of an Indian native and also as the name of a fictitious country.

26. Matthew Quay (1833–1904), U.S. representative (1865–67) and U.S. senator (1887–89, 1901–4) from Pennsylvania.

27. The original "dark horse" was James Knox Polk (1795–1849), who unexpectedly defeated Martin Van Buren as Democratic presidential candidate in 1844 and went on to become the eleventh president of the United States (1845–49). The term was coined by Andrew Jackson.

28. Second largest city of northeastern China and capital of Heilungkiang Province, on the Sungari River. A small fishing village before 1896, it thereafter became the construction center for the Chinese Eastern Railway, which by 1904 linked the Trans-Siberian Railroad with the Russian port of Vladivostok on the Sea of Japan. Harbin was a base for Russian military operations in Manchuria during the Russo-Japanese War.

29. France had sold its interest in the Panama Canal to the U.S. in February 1904. See further below (p. 134).

30. Peter Alekseyevich Kropotkin (1842–1921), Russian scientist, revolutionary, and proponent of "anarchist communism," was imprisoned in 1874 but escaped two years later, spending the next thirty-one years in England before returning to Russia in 1917.

31. AB refers to the defeat of the ancient Huns, led by Attila, in 451 at the hands of the Romans, led by the general Aetius, at the battle of the Catalaunian Plains near the present-day town of Châlons-sur-Marne, France.

32. AB opposed the partition of China by Western nations, largely because of the impracticability of the task, not out of any respect for Chinese sovereignty. See "Ambrose Bierce Says: We Should Beware of Mixing in Partition of China," *NJ,* July 10, 1900, 8; *E,* July 11, 1900, 6 (as "The 'Partition' of China").

33. George Frisbie Hoar (1826–1904), senator (Republican) from Massachusetts (1877–1904); John Tyler Morgan (1824–1907), senator (Democrat) from Alabama (1877–1907); Arthur Pue Gorman (1837–1906), senator (Democrat) from Maryland (1881–99, 1903–6).

34. The poem is by AB himself. The last line derives from an editorial in *W* (Aug. 21, 1886).

35. Deriving from the word *cyclic,* meaning of, relating to, or being a cycle.

36. See n. 40 below.

37. AB later gave the title "The Scrap-Heap" to a selection of minor verse in his book *Shapes of Clay* (rev. ed. 1910 [*CW* 4]).

38. AB makes this same joke ("Wyo Ming" regarded as a Chinese province) in the fable "The Massacre" (*E,* Aug. 6, 1893, 12; rpt. in the first edition of *Fantastic Fables* [1899]).

39. The political organization known as Tammany Hall, associated with the Democratic party, began in 1789 and largely controlled New York City politics up to the 1930s, when it was finally weakened by the joint efforts of Mayor Fiorello La Guardia (1934–45) and Franklin Delano Roosevelt. Theodore Roosevelt was in fact instrumental in limiting Tammany Hall's control of New

York City politics, working in 1884 as an assemblyman with Gov. Grover Cleveland on a variety of municipal reforms.

40. A reference to Theodore Roosevelt's leading the Rough Riders into battle on San Juan Hill in Cuba in July 1898, during the Spanish-American War.

41. For the imaginary realm of Bumbassa, see "The Wizard of Bumbassa" (p. 114).

42. Antrolius was first cited in "The Fall of the Republic" (p. 112).

43. A parodic reference to Ella Wheeler Wilcox (see "John Smith, Liberator," n. 8) and to Homer's catalogue of ships in book 2 of the *Iliad*.

44. AB's mock Latin means "hairy erect ape-man." Ernst Heinrich Haeckel (1834–1919), German philosopher and naturalist, coined the term *Pithecanthropos* to denote the putative link between apes and human beings.

45. From Lewis Carroll's "Jabberwocky," in *Through the Looking-Glass* (1871).

46. AB's mock Latin means "Ananias the flabbergaster." Ananias is the name given to three different individuals in the Bible. AB frequently alluded to the one cited in Acts 2:24–27 and 4:32–37, whom God punished for deceit.

47. AB's mock Latin means "skinned cat."

48. For "jeewhillikins" see "Little Johnny" (*E,* Jan. 15, 1888, 4), in which there is an *Ovis geewhillikins* ("Common Doe-headed Sheep of California"), and the Little Johnny sketch "The Snowty Geewhillikins and Other Animals" (*NA,* Oct. 14, 1904, 16), in which the characteristics of the beast are not specified other than that it is "snowty" and a foe of the whale.

49. The adjective derives from Stymphalos, a city and mountain in Arcadia. AB alludes to one of the labors of Heracles, in which he subdued the Stymphalian Birds.

50. AB's mock Latin means "unlocated one-footed mole."

51. The Hydra of Lerna, near Argos, was destroyed by Heracles.

52. AB's mock Latin means "undesirable citizen."

53. For Gompers see n. 19 above.

54. AB appears to allude to Joel Chandler Harris (1848–1908), whose *Uncle Remus: His Songs and His Sayings* (1880) is an American classic of dialect literature. AB also alludes to the tale of Little Black Sambo (referred to below as "Bueno Gumbo"), who tricked the tigers that pursued him into chasing themselves, thereby turning themselves into butter, which he and his family then ate. The book *Little Black Sambo* (1899) was written by Helen Bannerman, a Scottish woman, and takes place in India. Sambo, an Indian boy, appears African in the book's illustrations.

55. In AB's Little Johnny sketches, the rhinoceros is always called the "rhi nosey rose."

56. In AB's Little Johnny sketches, AB frequently referred to the hippopotamus as "hi potamus."

57. *Riparian* means of or relating to the banks of a natural course of a river.

58. AB's mock Latin means "docile wood-carrier."

59. AB's mock Latin means "circumspect thief." In his "Little Johnny" sketches, AB sometimes calls the giraffe the "giraft."

60. The teddy bear was in fact named after Theodore Roosevelt.

61. AB's mock Latin means "flabbergasting curiosity." AB used the name *Flashawful flabbergastor* in *DD*.

62. AB's mock Latin means "lion who uses a plow."

63. The Smithsonian Institution had partly funded Roosevelt's African expedition. He later sent 23,000 specimens to the Smithsonian.

64. A play on Nairobe, the capital of Kenya, and Niobe of Greek mythology, daughter of Tantalus. According to the *Iliad,* as punishment for her pride, Apollo killed all her sons and Artemis killed all her daughters.

65. AB alludes to Roosevelt's son Kermit (1889–1943).

66. Sir Henry Morton Stanley (1841–1904), Anglo-American explorer, located the lost explorer David Livingstone in Africa in November 1871. The Greek troops led by Xenophon cried "Thalassa, thalassa!" (The sea, the sea!) as they retreated from Persia in 399 B.C.E. and reached the shore of the Aegean Sea in Asia Minor. See Xenophon's *Anabasis* 4.7. The Rubicon is the small river outside Rome that Julius Caesar crossed with his army on January 10, 49 B.C.E., thereby initiating the civil war that eventually ended the Roman republic.

67. Elba is the island off the west coast of Italy where Napoleon was exiled from May 3, 1814, to February 26, 1815. Gifford Pinchot (1865–1946) headed the U.S. Forest Service from 1898 to 1910. He was a close friend of Roosevelt. Mark Antony is reported to have attempted several times to place a diadem, or crown, on Julius Caesar's head during a festival of the Lupercalia on February 15, 44 B.C.E. See Suetonius, *Divus Julius,* 79.2. Suetonius does not specify the number of times Antony made the gesture, writing only *saepius* (frequently); but it became customary in antiquity to claim that the gesture was made three times (cf. Plutarch, *Caesar,* 61.3–4). Shakespeare follows this tradition in *Julius Caesar,* 1.2.250f.

68. An allusion to William Howard Taft (1857–1930), twenty-seventh president of the United States (1909–13) who, at three hundred pounds, was the country's heaviest president.

69. For Ananias see n. 46 above.

70. AB refers to "nature fakers" in "Small Contributions" (*Co,* Jan. 1908), "Little Johnny on the Dog" (*Co,* Apr. 1909), and "Little Johnny, the Nature Faker" (MS, BL). AB appears to use the term to designate someone who falsely claims a great familiarity with wild nature or knowledge of natural science.

71. This legend in the life of the Titan Prometheus can be found, *inter alia,* in Aeschylus' *Prometheus Bound* (c. 460 B.C.E.). AB equates the vultures who pecked at Prometheus' liver with epicures, who would delight in such a delicacy as a liver pâté.

Government vs. Anarchy

The first two items in this section are unsigned editorials; the third, a signed column. "Prevention vs. No Cure" (*E*, July 11, 1887) is a rumination on the Haymarket riots of May 4, 1886, when police broke up a workers' meeting at Haymarket Square in Chicago; in the resulting riot, seven policemen and two civilians were killed, and many injured. In the ensuing trial eight alleged anarchists were convicted of various charges. Several of the workers' leaders were indeed professed anarchists, but the trial was widely seen as unfair. After several appeals failed, four of the prisoners were hanged on November 11, 1887, and another committed suicide. On June 26, 1893, Illinois Gov. John Altgeld pardoned the remaining three prisoners, creating an uproar. AB himself commented on this event in "Prattle" (*E*, July 13, 1893, 6): "Although I forgive, as Peter Robertson jokes, 'with difficulty,' I might have been taught by time to overlook in Governor Altgeld's nature the primal savage whose upthrust compelled him to the brutality of pardoning the Chicagoan anarchists; but his explanation and defense of his motives in a pamphlet of seventeen thousand words!—that is a grave matter. I observe that the Oakland *Times* avers more in sorrow than in anger that Governor Altgeld is 'the leading ass of the country.'" There is also a denuciation in verse with the definition of "respite" in *DD*.

"The Failure of 'Rotation'" (*E*, Feb. 24, 1889) is a satirical lament on the shortage of offices in the American republic. AB's "Prattle" column (*E*, Dec. 31, 1893), here titled "Republican Government," is a follow-up to a column published two weeks earlier, in which he had expressed severe criticism of anarchists.

1. Sir James Fitzjames Stephen (1829–1894), British judge and prolific author on criminal law.

2. Slight misquotation of Tennyson's "You ask me, why, though ill at ease" (1833), ll. 7–8: "The land, where girt with friends or foes / A man may speak the thing he will."

3. Warner Miller (1838–1918), paper manufacturer and Republican politician. He served as U.S. representative from New York (1878–81) and U.S. senator (1881–87), but was defeated in his reelection bid in 1886 and also lost the gubernatorial election in New York in 1888. Miller supported Benjamin Harrison in the presidential campaign, but after Harrison's election he wrote a letter to him declaring that he did not wish to be in his cabinet.

4. Samuel Taylor Coleridge, *The Rime of the Ancient Mariner* (1798), l. 518.

5. Pope, *An Essay on Man*, Epistle 1, l. 294.

6. Herbert Spencer (1820–1903), British philosopher. In *The Proper Sphere of Government* (1843) and other works, Spencer had defended private ownership of property, but in *Social Statics* (1851) he argued that exclusive ownership of land infringed upon the freedom of the landless to exercise their faculties.

7. Henry George (1839–1897), American economist and author of *Progress*

and Poverty (1879). Appalled by the increasing disparity of wealth in the U.S. and attributing it chiefly to the rapacious snatching up of land by wealthy capitalists, which deprived others of their "natural" right to labor on the land, George recommended that taxes should be laid upon land values only. This notion of the "single tax" was widely popular in radical politics of the later nineteenth century.

8. Mashonaland is the traditional region in northeastern Zimbabwe, bordering Zambia to the north and Mozambique to the northeast and east.

9. See "Prattle" (*E*, May 30, 1897, 6): "At the very foundation of our political system lies the denial of hereditary and artificial rank. Our fathers created this Government as a protest against all that and all that it implies. They virtually declared that kings and noblemen could not breathe here, and no American loyal to the principles of the Revolution which made him one will ever say in his own country 'your Majesty' or 'your lordship'—the words would choke him, and they ought. Yet when a foreign nobleman's prow puts in to shore the American shin is pickled in brine to welcome him; and if he come not in adequate quantity those of us who can afford the expense go swarming over the sea to struggle for front places in his attention."

10. *The Shadow on the Dial* was the name of a collection of AB's essays published in 1909. The text here was part of the title essay.

11. See n. 2 above.

12. Shakespeare, *Macbeth*, 4.1.8.

13. A reference to W. D. Howells's *A Traveler from Altruria* (1894). See the introduction, pp. xvii–xviii.

Judges, Lawyers, and Juries

Throughout his life AB commented on abuses and paradoxes in the judicial system. The following three articles probe some of these issues. "'I Decline to Answer'" (*E*, Jan. 15, 1892) is an unsigned editorial that was later incorporated into the essay "Some Features of the Law" (*CW* 11). In it AB expresses opposition to a Supreme Court decision that interpreted in its broadest sense a defendant's right against self-incrimination as stipulated in the Fifth Amendment. The case (*Counselman v. Hitchcock*) focused on alleged violations of the Inter-State Commerce Act by officers and agents of the Rock Island, the Burlington, and the Chicago, St. Paul and Kansas City Railway Companies. The Supreme Court opinion read in part: "It is impossible that the meaning of the constitutional provision [against self-incrimination] can only be that a person shall not be compelled to be a witness in a criminal prosecution against himself. The object was to insure that a person should not be compelled, when acting as a witness in any investigation, to give testimony which might tend to show that he himself had committed a crime. The privilege is limited to criminal matters, but it is as broad as the mischief against which it seeks to guard." See "The Rights of Witnesses," *New York Times,* Jan. 12, 1892, 10.

In "The Morality of Lawyers" (an extract from "Prattle," *E,* Nov. 24, 1895, also incorporated into "Some Features of the Law"; title supplied by the editors), AB addresses the dilemma of lawyers who choose to defend individuals whom they know to be guilty of crimes. "The Competence of Jurors" (an extract from "Prattle," *E,* Sept. 19, 1897; title supplied by the editors) focuses on an instance of judicial incompetence and suggests that juries are by nature unfit to decide upon complex legal issues.

1. Walter Quintin Gresham (1832–1895), circuit judge of the 7th judicial district. In 1883 President Chester Alan Arthur briefly contemplated Gresham as a running mate, and in the Republican national convention of 1888 he received 107 votes from delegates for the presidential nomination. Gresham later became a Democrat and served as Grover Cleveland's secretary of state (1893–95).

2. General W. H. L. Barnes (1836–1902), army officer and lawyer, and frequent object of AB's attacks, of which the following is typical: "On Monday last . . . W. H. L. Barnes was safely delivered of a masterly address and is now doing well. An Oakland newspaper explains that it was the future of which he spoke, not of the battles of thirty years ago. Well, Comrade Barnes has seen just as much of the future as he saw of the battles, and it is a good deal more to his liking. The gallant comrade is a man of peace and recoils with horror from memories of the dreadful thirty days when he was a serried rank and a charging squadron. Yet the somber picture has a touch of light. When the war broke out he happened to be in negotiation for a policy of life insurance: his enlistment as a member of the New York Seventh secured a reduced rate" ("Prattle," *E,* Apr. 29, 1894, 6). The source of his remarks on lawyers has not been located.

3. Col. Dan Burns was a Republican politician frequently attacked by AB. At this time he was secretary of state of California. Chris Buckley was an unscrupulous Democratic political "boss" in late nineteenth-century San Francisco who was finally driven out of town by state Senator Jeremiah Lynch.

4. Margaret Craven had claimed that documents signed by James G. Fair had bestowed upon her his property, valued at $1.5 million. On September 13, 1897, the jury ruled eight to four in favor of Craven; but as nine jurors had to agree for a proper verdict, Judge Charles William Slack (1858–1945), superior court judge in San Francisco (1890–98), dismissed them. The next day Judge Slack deemed the documents a forgery.

5. See "The Land Beyond the Blow," n. 53.

Capital Punishment

The following items concern disparities in the infliction of capital punishment based on gender and a general attack on arguments put forward by theosophists against the death penalty. "Blathering Blavatskians" (*E,* Nov. 28, 1897) takes issue with the theosophists—individuals following the quasi-religious mystical theories of Madame Helena P. Blavatasky (1831–1891), who had formed the Theosophical Society in 1875—opposed to the death sentence of Theodore Durrant, who was convicted of murdering Blanche Lamont in San Francisco on April 3, 1895. After numerous appeals going up to the Supreme Court, based largely on contentions that Durrant had been deprived his right of habeas corpus, Durrant was executed at San Quentin on January 7, 1898.

"Sex in Punishment" (*E,* May 1, 1892) and "Some Thoughts on the Hanging" (*NA,* Dec. 12, 1905; *E,* Dec. 19, 1905) address the issue of applying the death penalty to women. The latter deals with the case of Mrs. Mary Mabel Rogers, convicted of murdering her husband, Marcus Rogers, on Aug. 13, 1902. She was hanged on December 8, 1905—the first woman in Vermont to be executed. Gov. Charles J. Bell refused to grant a reprieve, even though he had been vociferously lobbied by many groups and individuals to do so, including a petition by thirty thousand women in Ohio. The murder of Marcus Rogers was clearly premeditated, as the *New York Times* reports: "At the time the crime was committed in Bennington . . . Mrs. Rogers was only 19 years old. She had been separated from her husband some time, and desired to marry Maurice Knapp. She arranged to meet Rogers, pretending to desire reconciliation, in the woods near the Wallomsac River. While caressing him she induced him to allow her to bind his hands, and while he was powerless she chloroformed him. In this she was aided by Leon Pernam, a half-witted boy. Another woman, Estella Bates, was present. After chloroforming Rogers, Pernam and Mrs. Rogers rolled the body into the river, where it was found the next day, with a note giving the impression that he had committed suicide." ("Mrs. Rogers Hanged, Bell Upholding Law," *New York Times,* Dec. 9, 1905, 7.)

Much of "Blathering Blavatskians" was reprinted by S. O. Howes in his compilation of Bierce's journalism, *The Shadow on the Dial* (1909), in the article "The Death Penalty." For another segment from that article, see "Modern Penology" above.

1. See Thomas Hood (1799–1845), "The Epping Hunt" (1829):

> His antler'd head shone blue and red,
> Bedeck'd with ribbons fine;
> Like other bucks that come to 'list
> The hawbucks in the line. (ll. 209–12)

2. Alphonse Carr: unidentified.

3. W. E. Hale, Warden of the California State Prison at San Quentin.

4. "Cease, every joy, to glimmer on my mind, / But leave, oh! leave the light of Hope behind!" Thomas Campbell, *Pleasures of Hope* (1799), pt. 2, ll. 375–76. There may also be an echo of Dante's "All hope abandon, ye who enter here" (*Inferno,* 3.9), referring to Hell.

5. *Petitio principii:* "Begging the question," the philosophical error of fashioning a syllogism in which the conclusion is assumed in the premise.

6. AB is in error. The term *capital punishment* derives from the loss of the *caput* (head), hence any punishment that results in death.

Tariffs, Trusts, and Labor

Throughout the late 1880s and 1890s AB repeatedly addressed the issues of tariff regulation, "trusts" (or monopolies), disputes between management and labor, and other economic issues. In an unsigned editorial, "'Protection' vs. Fair Trade" (*E,* June 20, 1887), AB declares himself staunchly in the camp of free traders; a later signed article, "Commercial Retaliation" (*E,* Feb. 12, 1898), emphasizes the dangers of punitive tariffs. "A Backslider" (*E,* Mar. 4, 1892) is rare among AB's works in criticizing a trust's stifling of competition; more representative is "Concerning Trusts" (*San Francisco Evening Post Magazine,* June 3, 1899), which argues that trusts are beneficial in that it is to their own benefit to sell products as cheaply as possible. In "Concerning Legislation 'To Solve the Tramp Problem'" (*E,* June 19, 1900; first published as "Ambrose Bierce Says: The Right to Labor Should Be Legally Defined," *NJ,* June 15, 1900), AB argues that government should ensure that all persons willing to work should be guaranteed a livelihood. "The Road to Wealth Is Open to All—Get Wealthy Ye Who Can" (*E,* Aug. 26, 1900) claims that economic prosperity is available to all who have the intelligence and desire to achieve it.

1. Cf. Luke 8:35: "Then they went out to see what was done; and came to Jesus, and found the man, out of whom the devils were departed, sitting at the feet of Jesus, clothed, and in his right mind: and they were afraid."

2. Samuel Erasmus Moffett (1860–1908), writer on politics and economics and correspondent of AB. His articles in *E* were collected as *The Tariff: What It Is and What It Does* (1892).

3. Cf. Matt. 6:19–20: "Lay not up for yourselves treasures upon earth, where moth and rust doth corrupt, and where thieves break through and steal: But lay up for yourselves treasures in heaven, where neither moth nor rust doth corrupt, and where thieves do not break through nor steal."

4. The Standard Oil Company of Ohio was founded in 1870 by John D. Rockefeller (1839–1937). Within ten years it had a near monopoly of the American oil industry; by 1881 it had become the first "trust" by establishing a board of

trustees who took over all the stock and issued certificates of interest in the trust estates.

5. Tennyson, "Locksley Hall" (1837–38), l. 128 ("man" not capitalized in Tennyson).

6. The reference is to Guam and the Philippines, which the United States won from Spain during the Spanish-American War. In the Philippines, however, the United States was compelled to quell a local independence movement (1898–1901).

7. The European Concert (or the Concert of Europe) was a loose federation of the leading European nations in the later nineteenth century designed to quell revolutionary insurrections. It played a central role in the Boxer Rebellion in China (1900).

8. The Turko-Grecian war of 1896–97 was initiated by Christians in Crete who sought independence from the Ottoman Empire. Although the Cretans were suppressed by the Turks, the European powers stepped in and made Crete a self-governing nation separate from Turkish control. AB wrote several columns on the conflict, some of them gathered in the essay "The Turko-Grecian War" (*CW* 9).

9. At The Hague Conference of 1899 a Permanent Court of Arbitration was established for the purpose of resolving disputes between nations before they resulted in warfare.

10. The phrases "The widows of Ashur" and "loud in their wail" derive from l. 21 of Byron's poem "The Destruction of Sennecherib" (1815).

11 Shakespeare, *Measure for Measure*, 4.3.147.

12. Roswell P. Flower (1835–1899), American financier, U.S. representative from New York (1881–83, 1889–91), and governor of New York (1892–95).

13. A paraphrase of Pope's *The Dunciad* (1728), bk. 1, l. 20: "Or laugh and shake in Rab'lais' easy Chair" (= rev. ed. [1742–43], bk. 1, l. 22).

14. Josh Billings was the pseudonym of the prolific American humorist Henry Wheeler Shaw (1818–1885).

15. Pope, "An Epistle from Mr. Pope, to Dr. Arbuthnot" (1735), l. 210 ("sit" in Pope).

16. See "Prattle" (*E*, Jan. 15, 1899, 12; *NJ*, Jan. 22, 1899, 28): "In England a man able but unwilling to work is called a 'sturdy beggar.'"

17. AB's salary at this time was $100 a week, or $5,200 a year.

Insurance

AB's relentless opposition to insurance in all forms—especially life and property insurance—is exhibited in extracts from "Prattle" (*E*, Feb. 17, 1889) and "The Passing Show" (*NJ* and *E*, Oct. 28, 1900), here titled "The Insurance Folly" and "Insurance and Crime," respectively. In both pieces AB likens insurance to gambling in which the insurer is the "one who keeps the table," thereby making it impossible for the customer to prevail against him.

1. The "tulip mania" occurred in Europe in the years 1634–37, when the tulip (introduced from Turkey in the sixteenth century) was the subject of wild financial speculation, enormous prices being paid for individual bulbs. The South Sea Bubble was a financial boondoggle in England in 1720 involving the South Sea Company and resulting in the bankruptcy of many individuals and the fall of the government led by Charles Spencer and James Stanhope.

2. George K. Fitch (1826–1906), deacon and also editor of the *San Francisco Bulletin,* was often attacked by AB, as in the poem "A Vision of Resurrection" (1889; *CW* 5.116). AB incessantly poked fun at Loring Pickering, "the famous tombstone poet" of San Francisco and co-owner of the *San Francisco Morning Call.*

3. Edgar Saltus (1855–1921), American essayist, novelist, and journalist who once enjoyed great popularity. His newspaper work began to be syndicated in *E* around 1900.

Advances in Weaponry

Having been a soldier who fought in some of the most vicious battles of the Civil War, AB retained a lifelong interest in military matters and frequently looked with wry amusement upon the claims of those who maintained that advances in the destructive power of modern weapons would make war so devastating that it would be abolished. "Superior Killing" (*E,* Oct. 7, 1888) is AB's most exhaustive treatment of the subject. The unsigned editorial "Infumiferous Tacitite" (*E,* Feb. 11, 1894) deals with the supposed invention of a noiseless and smokeless gunpowder. Both words in the title are AB's coinages, *infumiferous* meaning "smokeless" and *tacitite* a neologism (based upon analogous terms coined by Alfred Nobel for his various explosives [see n. 9 below]) referring to a putative "silent" explosive (from the Latin *tacere,* to be silent).

1. AB refers to three significant naval battles. The battle of Salamis (an island in the Aegean Sea) was fought between the Greeks and the Persians in 480 B.C.E., resulting in the collapse of the Persian military power. The battle of Lepanto (now the town of Návpaktos, Greece) was fought between Christians and Turkish Muslims on October 17, 1751; the resulting victory by the Christians curbed the Turks' westward expansion. The battle of Trafalgar, off Cape Trafalgar, Spain, was fought between the British and a Franco-Spanish fleet on October 21, 1805, resulting in a decisive British victory and the collapse of French naval power.

2. The ironclads *Monitor* and *Merrimack* (not *Merrimac*) fought to a draw on March 9, 1862. AB wrote a wry fable (in "The Fables of Zambri, the Parsee," *Cobwebs from an Empty Skull* [1874], no. 129) on the battle, depicting a conflict between a tortoise and an armadillo.

3. The Federal admiral David Glasgow Farragut (1801–1870) began the bombardment of New Orleans on April 18, 1862, attacking Forts Jackson and St.

Philip relentlessly for a week with mortar shells. Farragut then proceeded upriver to New Orleans, losing only one ship while destroying the Confederate river fleet. He captured the city on the 25th, which surrendered on the 29th. In all, only thirty-six Federals and fifty Confederates were killed in the entire engagement.

4. The Franco-Prussian War occurred in 1870–71. The Russians and Turks engaged in a succession of wars between the seventeenth and nineteenth centuries, most notably in the Crimean War of 1853–56.

5. Barthold Georg Niebuhr (1776–1831), author of the landmark *Romische Geschichte* (1811–12), the first work to deal with Roman history in a critical and scientific spirit.

6. The Federal troops in Fort Sumter, South Carolina, were bombarded by the Confederates on April 12–14, 1861, commencing the Civil War. The fort was evacuated on April 14. One man, Pvt. Daniel Hough, was killed, but not as a result of the bombardment; another died of his wounds, and a third was seriously injured. These were the only casualties.

7. William R. Hamilton, "American Machine Cannon and Dynamite Guns," *Century Magazine* 36, no. 6 (Oct. 1888): 885–93. The Federal general quoted in the article was not identified by name.

8. Jan Sobieski (1629–1696), Polish commander who defeated the Turks at the battle of Khotin (1674) and was elected King John (III) Sobieski (r. 1674–96). John Churchill, first duke of Marlborough (1650–1722), British general who routed the French-Bavarian army at Blenheim in 1704. Napoleon Bonaparte (1769–1821), French general and emperor.

9. Alfred Nobel (1833–1896), Swedish inventor, exploded nitroglycerine in 1862 and used it in his new invention, dynamite, in 1867. He later developed ballistite, a smokeless powder produced from nitroglycerine.

10. Pope, *The Rape of the Lock* (1712–14), canto 4, l. 124.

11. *Connusant:* obsolete form of *cognizant.*

Travel by Air

The following two articles show AB expressing some skepticism about the possibility or practicability of travel by air. "'Fly, Good Fleance, Fly!'" is an unsigned editorial (*E*, May 22, 1892) that examines in detail the engineering problems of heavier-than-air vehicles. The title derives from *Macbeth*, 3.3.17. "The Man and the Bird" is chiefly devoted to the work of Samuel Pierpont Langley (1834–1906), scientist and pioneer in aviation research. Langley, secretary of the Smithsonian Institution (1887–1906), had begun investigating the possibility of flight using heavier-than-air machines in the 1880s. In 1896 he flew two aircraft weighing about twenty-five pounds. But attempts to build a larger vehicle, launched by a catapult, failed on two occasions in late 1903—almost exactly the time when the Wright brothers successfully flew their biplane on December 17, 1903. AB took no notice in print of the Wright brothers' achievement.

1. AB appears to be referring to two articles, S. P. Langley, "Mechanical Flight," *Cosmopolitan* 13, no. 1 (May 1892): 55–58, and Hiram S. Maxim, "The Aeroplane," *Cosmopolitan* 13, no. 2 (June 1892): 202–8.

2. Chapter 6 ("A Dissertation on the Art of Flying") of Samuel Johnson's *The History of Rasselas, Prince of Abyssinia* (1759) deals with the attempt of a "man eminent for his knowledge of the mechanick powers" to build a "sailing machine" (actually, a pair of large wings). But when the man leaps off a promontory with the wings, he "in an instant dropped into the lake."

3. Tennyson, "Lucretius" (1868), l. 40. An imitation of Lucretius's frequent use, in *De Rerum Natura*, of *inane* ("empty") as a noun, referring to empty space.

4. Alberto Santos-Dumont (1873–1932), Brazilian pioneer in aviation who experimented for many years with air flight. On October 19, 1901, using a lighter-than-air craft, he flew an airship from St. Cloud to the Eiffel Tower and back, a distance of about seven miles. He successfully flew a heavier-than-air craft on October 12, 1906.

5. George Stephenson (1781–1848), British engineer who invented the steam locomotive (1814–30).

Dogs and Horses

Throughout his life AB was relentlessly hostile to dogs. In 1903, responding to an article on dogs sent to him by a colleague, AB remarked: "Pretty nearly all the anti-dog literature gets to me, as I seem to be recognized as the captain of the cult. I sometimes fancy that even the dogs know me and assume the attitude toward me that is dictated by their feeling and interest" (AB to S. O. Howes, June 16, 1903; MS, HL). "The Struggle between Man and Dog" (*NA*, June 7, 1902) is one of many treatments of the subject. (For further passages from AB's journalism, see *SS* 195–98.) In "The Future of the Horse and the Horse of the Future" (*NA*, Feb. 17, 1903; *E*, Apr. 5, 1903) AB ponders whether the prevalence of the automobile will render the horse extinct.

1. A parody of Luke 1:52: "He hath put down the mighty from their seats, and exalted them of low degree."

2. Milton, *Comus* (1634), l. 479.

3. "Consider the lilies of the field, how they grow: they toil not, neither do they spin. And yet I say unto you, That even Solomon in all his glory was not arrayed like one of these." Matt. 6:28–29.

4. Amaranth is an imaginary flower, said never to fade, frequently cited by

poets. It is also the name for various annuals of the genus *Amaranthus* having dense green or reddish clusters of tiny flowers, and including several weeds, ornamentals, and food plants. Moly is an herb said by Homer to have been given to Odysseus by Hermes as a charm against Circe (see *Odyssey*, 10.305).

5. Marcus Alonzo Hanna (1837–1904), leading Republican politician and U.S. senator from Ohio (1897–1904). In early 1903 Hanna proposed a bill granting pensions to ex-slaves, but it did not pass.

Temperance

As one who took moderate pleasure in alcohol, AB found himself a frequent opponent of measures to prohibit or limit the consumption of alcoholic beverages. In "Prohibition" (an extract from "Prattle," *E*, Oct. 14, 1888), AB claims that a desire for spirits is inspired by the simple fact that water tastes bad. "The Nations That Drink Too Much" (*E*, Nov. 6, 1902; *NA*, Nov. 13, 1902) claims that those nations that excel in warfare have all been vigorous imbibers.

1. Actually, the item referred to—"Prohibitory Law and Personal Liberty," *North American Review* 381 (Aug. 1888): 121–49—consisted of brief statements by seven writers: Julius H. Seelye, I. K. Funk, Henry W. Blair, Neal Dow, John Bascom, G. F. Stewart, and Charles F. Deems.

2. Henry Codman Potter (1834–1908), sixth Episcopal bishop of New York.

Reflections on the Future

In a succession of editorials, mostly unsigned, AB whimsically and satirically addressed possible future developments of the human race. In "Will the Coming Man Sleep?" (*E*, Jan. 14, 1892), later reprinted as "Sleep" (*CW* 9), AB wonders whether sleep is slowly being abolished in civilized society. "The Decay of the Nose" (*E*, Apr. 24, 1892) ruminates on the possibility that the nose is headed toward extinction. "The Head of the Future" (*E*, June 5, 1892) discusses the possibility that baldness is an advantage in the "struggle for existence." In "Some Trivial Privations of the Coming Man" (*E*, Nov. 3, 1893) AB again ruminates on the coming loss of nose and hair. The last three articles were incorporated, in truncated form, in the essay "Some Privations of the Coming Man" (*CW* 9).

1. William Browne (1591–1643), "Epitaph on the Countess of Pembroke" (1621), l. 6.

2. Several poets, including Homer, Hesiod, and Tennyson, referred to Sleep as the brother of Death.

3. Thomas Gray, *Elegy Written in a Country Churchyard* (1751), l. 16.

4. Milton, *Comus,* l. 556 ("Rose" in Milton).

5. Edward Gibbon (1737–1794), British historian. Aleksandr Mikhailovich Gorchakov (1798–1883), Russian foreign minister in the reign of Emperor Alexander II (r. 1855–81).

6. Tennyson, *In Memoriam: A. H. H.,* stanza 56, l. 16.

7. AB's mock Latin means "talkative man."

8. *Caries:* decay of the bones or teeth.

9. Stephen Maybell was the author of *Civilization Civilized; or The Process of Nationalization* (1889), *Science of the Millennium* (1897), and *The Mystery of Civilization* (1899).

Appendix: A Screed of the Future Historian

This sketch is another treatment of the America's Cup yacht race (see "The Future Historian and His Fatigue"), but with a further elaboration on its supposed political and military ramifications. Its sole appearance was in *NA,* September 3, 1903, but the microfilm of the newspaper presents the item in fragmentary form, with a large portion of the second column mutilated. We have conjecturally restored as much of the text as possible.

1. The secretary of war under McKinley and Theodore Roosevelt was Elihu Root (1899–1903); he resigned in August 1903 because of failing health and his wife's wishes. He was not well liked by AB, as evidenced by the quatrain "Elihu Root" (*CW* 4.361):

> Stoop to a dirty trick or low misdeed?
> What, bend him from his moral skies to it?
> No, no, not he! To serve his nature's need
> He may upon occasion rise to it.

"Admiral Langley" likely refers to Samuel Pierpont Langley (1834–1906), American aeronautics pioneer who built the first heavier-than-air flying machine to achieve sustained flight. AB wrote on several occasions about Langley's failed experiments. See the essay "The Man and the Bird" (p. 195).

2. Gen. Henry Clark Corbin (1842–1909), adjutant-general of the U.S. Amy during the Spanish-American War.

SOURCES

Fiction

"The Ashes of the Beacon." *New York American,* Feb. 19, 1905, 22. *San Francisco Examiner,* Feb. 26, 1905, 44. In *CW* I: [15]–86. Incorporates the following:

"The Jury in Ancient America: An Historical Sketch Written in the Year of Grace 3687: Translated by Ambrose Bierce." *Cosmopolitan* 39, no. 4 (Aug. 1905): 384–88.

"Insurance in Ancient America: Translated from the Work of the Future Historian." *Cosmopolitan* 41, no. 5 (Sept. 1906): 555–57.

"The Land Beyond the Blow." In *CW* I: [87]–196. "Thither" and "Hither" were first published in *CW.* Original appearances of the other chapters are as follows:

"Sons of the Fair Star." *San Francisco Examiner,* June 10, 1888, 11.

"An Interview with Gnarmag-Zote." *San Francisco Examiner,* Nov. 24, 1889, 11 (as "The Golampians").

"The Tamtonians: Some Account of Politics in the Uncanny Islands." *San Francisco Examiner,* Nov. 11, 1888, 9.

"Marooned on Ug." *San Francisco Examiner,* Feb. 20, 1898, 18.

"The War with Wug." *San Francisco Examiner,* Sept. 11, 1898, 20.

"The Dog in Ganegwag." *New York American,* May 12, 1904, 14.

"The Conflagration in Ghargaroo." *Cosmopolitan* 40, no. 4 (Feb. 1906), 457–58.

"An Execution in Batrugia." In "Small Contributions," *Cosmopolitan* 43, no. 1 (May 1907): 96–97.

"A Letter from Btrugumian." *New York American,* Apr. 30, 1903, 16.

"The Jumjum of Gokeetle-Guk." *San Francisco Examiner,* Nov. 19, 1899, 15 (as "Trustland: A Tale of a Traveler").

"The Kingdom of Tortirra." *San Francisco Examiner,* Apr. 22, 1888, 12.

"Letters from a Hdkhoite—No. 1." *San Francisco News Letter and California Advertiser* 18, no. 6 (Apr. 4, 1868): 4 (unsigned).

"Letters from a Kdhoite [*sic*]—No. 2." *San Francisco News Letter and California Advertiser* 18, no. 7 (Apr. 11, 1868): 4 (unsigned).

"Letters from a Hdkhoite—No. 3." *San Francisco News Letter and California Advertiser* 18, no. 8 (Apr. 18, 1868): 14 (unsigned).

"Letters from a Hdkhoite—No. 4." *San Francisco News Letter and California Advertiser* 18, no. 9 (Apr. 25, 1868): 2 (unsigned).

"The Aborigines of Oakland." *San Francisco News Letter and California Advertiser* 18, no. 36 (Nov. 7, 1868): 2 (unsigned).

"A Scientific Dream." *San Francisco News Letter and California Advertiser* 18, no. 37 (Nov. 14, 1868): 8 (unsigned).

"Across the Continent." *San Francisco News Letter and California Advertiser* 9 [*sic*], no. 15 (May 15, 1869): 4 (as by "Samboles").

"John Smith." *Fun* 17 (May 10, 1873): 199 (unsigned). In *CW* 1: [215]–22 (as "John Smith, Liberator").

"'The Bubble Reputation.'" *Wasp* no. 510 (May 8, 1886): 3 (unsigned). In *CW* 8.211–16.

"For the Ahkoond." *San Francisco Examiner*, Mar. 18, 1888, 13 (as by "A. B."). In *CW* 1: [197]–214.

"The Fall of the Republic: An Article from a 'Court Journal' of the Thirty-first Century." *San Francisco Examiner*, Mar. 25, 1888: 12. Early version of "The Ashes of the Beacon."

"The Wizard of Bumbassa." *San Francisco Examiner*, Aug. 28, 1892, 6 (unsigned; as "Rabid Transit"). In *CW* 12.338–42.

["Modern Penology."] Extract from "Prattle," *San Francisco Examiner*, Feb. 10, 1895, 6. Rpt. as the final segment of "The Death Penalty." In *The Shadow on the Dial*, ed. S. O. Howes (San Francisco: A. M. Robertson, 1909), 138–39; rpt. *CW* 11.222–24.

"The Great Strike of 1895." *San Francisco Examiner*, May 5, 1895, 26 (as "The Strike of 1899"). In *CW* 12.297–304.

["The Fall of Christian Civilization."] Extract from "The Passing Show," *New York Journal*, Feb. 18, 1900, 26. *San Francisco Examiner*, Feb. 18, 1900, 26.

["On the Canal."] Extract from "The Passing Show," *San Francisco Examiner*, Apr. 15, 1900, 27. *New York Journal*, Apr. 16, 1900, 8 (as "Ambrose Bierce Says").

["The Minister's Death."] Extract from "The Passing Show," *New York Journal*, July 1, 1900, 34. *San Francisco Examiner*, July 1, 1900, 14.

"The Maid of Podunk." *New York Journal*, Mar. 10, 1901, 26. *San Francisco Examiner*, Mar. 19, 1901, 14 (as "Ambrose Bierce's History of the Maid of Podunk").

"The Extinction of the Smugwumps." *New York Journal*, July 19, 1901, 14. *San Francisco Examiner*, Aug. 12, 1901: 12.

"Industrial Discontent in Ancient America." *New York Journal*, Aug. 14, 1901, 14.

"The Future Historian and His Fatigue." *New York American*, July 8, 1903, 14. *San Francisco Examiner*, Sept. 5, 1903, 14.

["The Republic of Panama."] Extract from "The Passing Show," *New York American*, Feb. 7, 1904, 24. *San Francisco Examiner*, Feb. 21, 1904, 44.

"A Chronicle of the Time to Be." *New York American*, May 6, 1904, 16.

["The Second American Invasion of China."] Extract from "The Views of One,"

New York American, Mar. 12 1906, 16. *San Francisco Examiner,* Mar. 17, 1906, 20.

"Rise and Fall of the Aëroplane." In "Small Contributions," *Cosmopolitan* 45, no. 5 (Oct. 1908): 565–66 (as "The Rise and Fall of the Aeroplane"). Incorporated into "The Future Historian." *CW* 12.346–49.

"The Dispersal." In "Small Contributions," *Cosmopolitan* 46, no. 4 (Mar. 1909): 472–73 (as "The Reversion to Barbarism"). Incorporated into "The Future Historian." *CW* 12.343–46.

"An Ancient Hunter." In "Small Contributions," *Cosmopolitan* 46, no. 5 (Apr. 1909): 597–98 (as "The Advance Agent"). Incorporated into "The Future Historian." *CW* 12.349–55.

"A Leaf Blown In from Days To Be." *Town Talk* 63, no. 11 (Mar. 17, 1910): 21.

Essays

Government vs. Anarchy

"Prevention vs. No Cure." *San Francisco Examiner,* July 11, 1887, 4 (unsigned).
"The Failure of 'Rotation.'" *San Francisco Examiner,* Feb. 24, 1889, 4 (unsigned).
["Republican Government."] Extract from "Prattle," *San Francisco Examiner,* Dec. 31, 1893: 6. Rpt. (in part) in "The Shadow on the Dial," *The Shadow on the Dial,* 20–23; *CW* 11.43–46 (revised).

Judges, Lawyers, and Juries

"'I Decline to Answer.'" *San Francisco Examiner,* Jan. 15, 1892, 6 (unsigned). Rpt. (in part) in "Some Features of the Law," *The Shadow on the Dial,* 67–68; *CW* 11.110–13 (revised).
["The Morality of Lawyers."] Extract from "Prattle," *San Francisco Examiner,* Nov. 24, 1895, 6. Rpt. (in part) in "Some Features of the Law," *The Shadow on the Dial,* 70–72; *CW* 11.110–13 (revised).
["The Competence of Jurors."] Extract from "Prattle," *San Francisco Examiner,* Sept. 19, 1897, 18.

Capital Punishment

"Sex in Punishment." *San Francisco Examiner,* May 1, 1892, 6 (unsigned). Rpt. (in part) in "Some Features of the Law," *The Shadow on the Dial,* 76–79; *CW* 11.117–21 (revised).
"Blathering Blavatskians." *San Francisco Examiner,* Nov. 28, 1897, 18. Rpt. (in part) in "The Death Penalty," *The Shadow on the Dial,* 129–34; *CW* 11.213–15 (revised).

"Some Thoughts on the Hanging." *New York American*, Dec. 12, 1905, 16; *San Francisco Examiner*, Dec. 19, 1905, 20 (as "The Views of One").

Tariffs, Trusts, and Labor

"'Protection' vs. Fair Trade." *San Francisco Examiner*, June 20, 1887, 4 (unsigned).
"A Backslider." *San Francisco Examiner*, Mar. 4, 1892, 6 (unsigned).
"Commercial Retaliation." *San Francisco Examiner*, Feb. 12, 1898, 6.
"Concerning Trusts." *San Francisco Evening Post Magazine*, June 3, 1899. Rpt. (in part) as "In the Infancy of 'Trusts.'" *CW* 9.91–100.
"Ambrose Bierce Says: The Right to Labor Should Be Legally Defined." *New York American*, June 15, 1900, 8; *San Francisco Examiner*, June 19, 1900, 6 (as "Concerning Legislation 'To Solve the Tramp Problem'").
"The Road to Wealth Is Open to All—Get Wealthy Ye Who Can." *San Francisco Examiner*, Aug. 26, 1900, 30. Rpt. as "Opportunity," *The Shadow on the Dial*, 169–71.

Insurance

["The Insurance Folly."] Extract from "Prattle." *San Francisco Examiner*, Feb. 17, 1889, 4.
["Insurance and Crime."] Extract from "The Passing Show." *New York Journal*, Oct. 28, 1900, 26; *San Francisco Examiner*, Oct. 28, 1900, 26.

Advances in Weaponry

"Superior Killing." *San Francisco Examiner*, Oct. 7, 1888, 9. Rpt. (in part) in "Modern Warfare." *CW* 9.216–18, 220–25.
"Infumiferous Tacitite." *San Francisco Examiner*, Feb. 11, 1894, 6 (unsigned).

Travel by Air

"'Fly, Good Fleance, Fly!'" *San Francisco Examiner*, May 22, 1892, 6 (unsigned).
"The Man and the Bird." *New York American*, Dec. 11, 1902, 14; *San Francisco Examiner*, Dec. 27, 1902, 12.

Dogs and Horses

"The Struggle between Man and Dog." *New York American*, June 7, 1902, 8.
"The Future of the Horse and the Horse of the Future." *New York American*, Feb. 17, 1903, 16; *San Francisco Examiner*, Apr. 5, 1903, 48. Rpt. as "The Passing of the Horse." *CW* 9.147–50.

Temperance

["Prohibition."] Extract from "Prattle," *San Francisco Examiner,* Oct. 14, 1888, 4
"The Nations That Drink Too Much." *San Francisco Examiner,* Nov. 6, 1902: 16;
    New York American, Nov. 13, 1902, 16.

Reflections on the Future

"Will the Coming Man Sleep?" *San Francisco Examiner,* Jan. 14, 1892, 6 (un-
    signed). Rpt. as "Sleep." *CW* 9.203–7.
"The Decay of the Nose." *San Francisco Examiner,* Apr. 24, 1892, 6 (unsigned).
    Rpt. (in part) in "Some Privations of the Coming Man." *CW* 9.17–19, 22–23.
"The Head of the Future." *San Francisco Examiner,* June 5, 1892, 6 (unsigned).
    Rpt. (in part) in "Some Privations of the Coming Man." *CW* 9.27–30.
"Some Trivial Privations of the Coming Man." *San Francisco Examiner,* Nov. 3,
    1893, 6 (unsigned). Rpt. (in part) in "Some Privations of the Coming Man."
    CW 9.24–27, 30–31.

Appendix

"A Screed of the Future Historian." *New York American,* Sept. 3, 1903, 16.

The Fall of the Republic and Other Political Satires was designed and typeset on a Macintosh computer system using PageMaker software. The text is set in Bembo Old and the chapter openings are set in Benguiat. This book was designed by Ellen Beeler, typeset by Kimberly Scarbrough, and manufactured by Thomson-Shore, Inc. The paper used in this book is designed for an effective life of at least three hundred years.